Beyond
Labor's Veil

Robert E. Weir

Beyond
Labor's Veil

The Culture of the
Knights of Labor

The Pennsylvania State University Press
University Park, Pennsylvania

Library of Congress Cataloging-in-Publication Data

Weir, Robert E., 1952–
    Beyond labor's veil : the culture of the knights of labor /
Robert E. Weir.
        p.   cm.
    Includes bibliographical references and index.
    ISBN 0-271-01498-9 (cloth)
    ISBN 0-271-01499-7 (paper)
    1. Knights of Labor—History.   2. Knights of Labor (Canada)—
History.   3. Labor movement—North America—History—19th century.
4. Social conflict—North America—History—19th century.
5. Popular culture—North America—History—19th century.
6. Working class—Religious life—North America—History—19th
century.   7. Working class writings, American—History and
criticism.   8. Working class writings, Canadian—History and
criticism.   9. Working class—North America—Songs and music—
History and criticism.   I. Title.
HD8055.K7W45   1996
331.88'33'097—dc20   95-13166
                                                                     CIP

Copyright © 1996 The Pennsylvania State University
All rights reserved
Printed in the United States of America
Published by The Pennsylvania State University Press,
University Park, PA 16802-1003

It is the policy of The Pennsylvania State University Press to use acid-free paper
for the first printing of all clothbound books. Publications on uncoated stock
satisfy the minimum requirements of American National Standard for Information Sciences—Permanence of Paper for Printed Library Materials, ANSI
Z39.48-1992.

Contents

01/21/97 22.50

List of Abbreviations

AFL	American Federation of Labor
AK	*Adelphon Kruptos*
BLE	Brotherhood of Locomotive Engineers
CAIL	Church Association in the Interests of Labor
CIO	Congress of Industrial Organizations
CLU	Central Labor Union
CMIU	Cigar Makers International Union
CMPU	Cigarmakers' Progressive Union of North America
DA	District Assembly
FOTLU	Federation of Trade and Labor Unions
GA	General Assembly
GEB	General Executive Board
GMW	General Master Workman
ITU	International Typographical Union
IWW	Industrial Workers of the World
JKL	*Journal of the Knights of Labor*
JUL	*Journal of United Labor*
KOL	Knights of Labor
LA	Local Assembly
NLU	National Labor Union
PP	The Papers of Terence Powderly
PPHP	Porter-Phelps-Huntington Papers
S.O.M.A.	"Secrecy, obedience, and mutual assistance"
UMWJ	*United Mine Workers Journal*
WCTU	Women's Christian Temperance Union

List of Illustrations

Acknowledgments

In the course of this study I have racked up more debts of gratitude than I can ever hope to repay. This study began life as a doctoral dissertation at the University of Massachusetts at Amherst. George Carey, David Glassberg, and Ron Story offered useful advice and commentary at that stage, and the University's interlibrary loan department helped me track down materials.

The dissertation was directed by Bruce Laurie, my advisor, mentor, and friend. Bruce's scholarly excellence, wit, criticisms, and suggestions were invaluable on the dissertation level, and again as this work evolved into a manuscript. He spent many patient hours discussing ideas with me and listening to half-baked ramblings that he carefully dissected and reformulated. His gift of cutting to the chase inspires me, though I have yet to master the art.

I have also enjoyed the privilege of exchanging ideas with spirited and intelligent colleagues at both Smith College and Bay Path College. I would like to thank R. Jackson Wilson who, as much as any person, opened my eyes to how careful historians think. I am especially grateful to Daniel Horowitz. Dan's warmth, humor, and basic humanity sustained me during moments when I wondered if this book would ever get done, and my conversations with him yielded numerous ideas and pearls of wisdom that are more the products of his insightful mind than my own musings.

Thanks also to the interlibrary loan department of Smith's Neilson Library, the National Endowment for the Humanities for a travel grant that helped locate materials for the study, and the archives and special collections staff at The Catholic University, the Museum of Our National Heritage, the Schlesinger Library at Vassar, the University of Michigan, the Wisconsin State Historical Society, the Smithsonian Institution, and the Ohio Historical Society. Thanks also to Bay Path College for supporting me financially and intellectually in the final phases of this book.

I could not have asked for a more helpful editor than Peter Potter at The Pennsylvania State University Press. Peter delivered on all of his promises, returned all my phone calls, graciously laughed at my quips, and offered useful comments and suggestions throughout the process. Patricia Mitchell meticulously copyedited the manuscript. Any eloquence contained herein is probably the result of her labors, not my mastery of English prose. Thanks also to Bryan Palmer, who read an earlier draft of the manuscript. Finally, thanks to Shelton Stromquist, who offered invaluable suggestions on organization, content, and style. Thanks to Shel, the book finally came together.

This work is dedicated to my wife, Emily, whose love, friendship, editing skills, and patience made the work possible. She believed in me when I stopped believing in myself, sustained me during my dark moments, and roped me in when my enthusiasms got the better of me. I credit whatever quality I have as a scholar and as a human being to her guidance, and I lovingly dedicate this book to her.

Preface

Scholars following the lead of Clifford Geertz use the concept of "thick description" in order to assemble as many details as possible about a group of people. Such an approach pays as much attention to the everyday and ordinary as to proscribed and ceremonial behaviors. The key to formulating thick description is to resist temptations to analyze a subject before a requisite number of details are revealed and clear patterns can be discerned. Sometimes such a construction requires the realization that some behaviors have no discernible logic, some meanings are ambiguous, and a few cultural productions can be appreciated but not fully understood. Often thick description tends to reveal cultural secrets in a deeper, if less determinate, way.[1]

It is with the goal of providing thick description that I turn to a historical look at the Noble and Holy Order of the Knights of Labor (KOL), the largest and most powerful labor organization of late-nineteenth-century North America. This study will not deal with the institutional history of the Knights so much as it will wrestle with the practices and behaviors of those men and women who identified with the Order. Political and organization studies show clearly why labor in general, and the Knights in particular, fared poorly during the nineteenth century. But such a focus tells us little about the men and women who took part in the struggle. What was it like to be part of the Knights of Labor? What were the Order's values and how did members respond to them? How did values and practices change over time? Why did organized capital react so viciously to the KOL? What, if anything, remained when the KOL passed?

For answers to these questions I turn to KOL cultural production. My use of the term "culture" is a broad one gleaned from those of anthropologists Clyde Kluckhohn and E. B. Tylor. By "culture" I refer to a set of group practices that are learned, shared, and socially influenced.[2] To

---

1. For more on "thick description," see Clifford Geertz, *The Interpretation of Cultures* (New York: Basic Books, 1973).

2. Cf. Clyde Kluckhohn, *Mirror for Man: The Relation of Anthropology to Modern Life* (New York: McGraw-Hill, 1949); E. B. Tylor, *Primitive Culture* (Gloucester, Mass.: Peter Smith, 1970; reprint of 1871 edition).

put it in the parlance of more recent cultural analysis, I assume that culture is received, but that it is also constructed and reconstructed. As such, my view of culture as dynamic and shifting forms the rationale behind my heuristic device of following certain cultural practices from inception to passing before I take up the next item.

I also view cultural production as dialogic and dialectical processes from which new combinations are continually formed and broken apart. As Lawrence Levine argues, the boundaries between what has been dubbed "elite," "folk," and "popular" cultures, if they exist at all, are razor-thin and porous.[3] The constant interplay among cultural sensibilities is complicated by power relationships and the emergence of commercialism. From the former come struggles that reshape cultural expression; from the latter, subversions of ideology into faddishness, heterosociality, and market preferences. Most individuals end up consuming culture as so many choices from an á la carte menu. At any given moment, certain inter- and intra-group practices can be said to be hegemonic, but many of them are transitory, which is another reason why I trace cultural phenomena across a time continuum. The only constant I see is change.

I do not, however, believe that shifting practices rob us of the ability to make meaningful analytical statements, though I counsel caution about how we label them. I have chosen culture as my focus for studying the Knights of Labor precisely because I think it reveals what other approaches obscure. First, a cultural approach corrects a historiographical imbalance by giving us a new way to reconcile ambiguities inherent in the examination of the Knights of Labor. Despite several superb community studies of the KOL, and a few equally insightful probes into specific aspects of the Order, there has been no comprehensive overview of the Knights since that of Norman Ware in 1929.[4] Contrast the lack of work

3. See Lawrence Levine, "The Folklore of Industrial Society: Popular Culture and Its Audiences," *American Historical Review* 97, no. 5 (December 1992): 1369–99.

4. This remark is in no way meant to denigrate the fine work that has been done on the Knights of Labor. To survey KOL historiography, one should begin with Norman J. Ware, *The Labor Movement in the United States, 1860–1895: A Study in Democracy* (New York: D. Appleton, 1929). I have also found the following studies particularly useful, though this list is not exhaustive and other useful studies will be cited later: Paul Buhle, "The Knights of Labor in Rhode Island," *Radical History Review* 17 (Spring 1978): 39–73; Leon Fink, *Workingmen's Democracy: The Knights of Labor and American Politics* (Urbana: University of Illinois Press, 1983); Judith L. Goldberg, "Strikes, Organizing and Change: The Knights of Labor in Philadelphia, 1869–1890," (Ph.D. diss., New York University, 1985); Gregory S. Kealey and Bryan D. Palmer, *Dreaming of What Might Be: The Knights of Labor in Ontario, 1880–1890* (Cambridge: Cambridge University Press, 1982), especially the Preface; Melton A. McLaurin, *The Knights of Labor in the South* (Westport, Conn.: Greenwood Press, 1978);

done on the KOL with the number of volumes written on the Industrial Workers of the World (IWW), an organization of far fewer members, a shorter period of vital existence, and fewer accomplishments than the Knights of Labor.

All organizations and time periods are complex in their own way, but they are not equally so. The Knights of Labor had both the fortune and misfortune to rise, thrive, and decline in an exceptionally fluid time, one whose appearance failed to match its realities so often that Mark Twain and Charles Dudley Warren dubbed it the "Gilded Age." Survival in a period of such rapid change required the KOL to be adaptive. It was broadly based and inclusive in its membership, and general, nondogmatic, and visionary in its worldview. It was not, however, clear, consistent, logical, or predictable. Friedrich Engels was among those who couldn't make up his mind about the KOL. He called it

> an immense association spread over an immense extent of the country in innumerable "assemblies," representing all shades of individual and local opinion within the working class; the whole of them sheltered under a platform of corresponding indistinctness and held together much less by their impracticable constitution than by the instinctive feeling that the very fact of clubbing together for their common cause makes them a very great power in the country; a truly American paradox clothing the most democratic and even rebellious spirit behind an apparent, but really powerless, despotism. . . . Whatever their shortcomings and little absurdities, whatever their platform and constitution, here they are, the work of practically the whole class of American wageworkers, the only national bond that holds them together, that makes their strength felt to themselves not less than their enemies, and fills them with the proud hope of future victories.[5]

The attract-repulse instinct roused in Engels has doubtless deterred some would-be historians of the Knights. Cultural analysis may afford a way out of the bind that Engels identified and that less charitable observ-

---

Richard Oestreicher, *Solidarity and Fragmentation: Working People and Class Consciousness in Detroit, 1875–1900* (Urbana: University of Illinois Press, 1986); Peter J. Rachleff, *Black Labor in the South: Richmond, Virginia, 1865–1890* (Philadelphia: Temple University Press, 1984); Charles Scontras, *Organized Labor and Labor Politics in Maine, 1880–1890* (Orono: University of Maine Press, 1966); Shelton Stromquist, *A Generation of Boomers: The Pattern of Railroad Labor Conflict in Nineteenth-Century America* (Urbana: University of Illinois Press, 1987).

5. Engels is quoted in Kenneth Lapides, ed., *Marx and Engels on the Trade Unions* (New York: International Publishers, 1987), 141–42.

ers used to dismiss the Order. Samuel Gompers called the Order a "hodgepodge with no basis for solidarity"; a later historian suggested the KOL was reactionary in its refusal to accept the permanence of the wage system.[6] Much of this sort of criticism dissolves if one separates organizational structure from members, and rhetoric from practice. As Herbert Spencer warned us, "How often misused words generate misleading thoughts."[7]

The behavior of individuals is often a better indication of the nature of their organizations than the resolutions and position papers those structures generate. Nineteenth-century Americans were so imprecise about the labels they used that it is easy to be led astray by their rhetoric and ideology. The term "anarchist" is an example. Who was an anarchist in the 1880s? Both Victor Drury and Joseph R. Buchanan claimed the mantle. Both men were Knights, yet they hated one another and disagreed over tactics. Drury helped draft the 1883 Pittsburgh Manifesto,[8] which recommended overthrow of existing social structures by force, while Buchanan was a devoted trade unionist who counseled against violence. The KOL was made up of many individuals who called themselves "anarchists," and a leadership that constantly denounced them. We would do well to take these individuals and their leaders with a grain of salt. Looking beyond rhetoric allows us to observe the nuances of the KOL, and avoid typecasting its actors.

Second, cultural practices usually reflect changing perspectives long before official positions are articulated or institutional adaptations occur. From culture, one often gets a better sense of the evolution of ideas, situations, and local responses. Historians of the past thirty years, affected by what is now incongruously called the "new labor history," have emphasized a "bottom up" history in which masses become actors,

6. Samuel Gompers, *Seventy Years of Life and Labor: An Autobiography of Samuel Gompers*, ed. Nick Salvatore (Ithaca, N.Y.: Industrial and Labor Relations Press, 1984), 76; Gerald Grob, *Workers and Utopia: A Study of Ideological Conflict in the American Labor Movement, 1865–1900* (Evanston, Ill.: Northwestern University Press, 1961). Others who have viewed the KOL as outmoded or inappropriate to Gilded Age realities include Robert Hoxie, *Trade Unionism in the United States* (New York: D. Appleton, 1936); John R. Commons et al., *History of Labour in the United States*, Volume One (New York: Augustus M. Kelley, 1966). See also Philip Foner, *History of the Labor Movement in the United States*, vol. 2: *From the Founding of the American Federation of Labor to the Emergence of American Imperialism* (New York: International Publishers, 1955); Frederich Sorge, *Labor Movements in the United States: A History of the American Working Class from Colonial Times to 1890*, ed. Philip Foner and Brewster Chamberlin (Westport, Conn.: Greenwood Press, 1977).

7. The Spencer quote comes from his *Principles of Ethics* (New York: D. Appleton, 1892–93) and is cross-referenced in *The Concise Oxford Dictionary of Quotations* (New York: Oxford University Press, 1981), 244.

8. See Richard Ely, *The Labor Movement in America* (New York: T. Y. Crowell, 1886).

not mere receivers.[9] A look at cultural production allows us to contrast the "official" history of the Knights of Labor with how Knights actually behaved. Such an examination is then beneficial because, as Engels noted above, nearly every "official" pronouncement, platform principle, or executive board decision the KOL put to paper spawned defiance, exception, and nonimplementation.

Third, culture was an arena of struggle for Gilded Age men and women. As Herbert Gutman reminds us, power relationships are embedded in cultural production.[10] Late Victorian culture was an interplay between those who produced culture and those who consumed it. No one social class monopolized cultural production, and none could manipulate intended meanings to match exactly audience readings of the cultural text. The KOL drew from a deep reservoir of working-class experience, and hoped to merge its various streams into one torrent. Such a vision inevitably involved class conflict. Thus even the price charged to view a baseball game could become part of the effort to transform society (see Chapter 7).

Because cultural production and reception are dialogic, a fourth reason emerges to study KOL details: they reveal much about the nature of a larger American cultural history. Late Victorian culture was a pastiche of various groups and classes who sought to dominate the cultural agenda, but largely failed to do so. If some Knights sought to transform society by marching in parades or attending KOL picnics, others were simply caught up in the excitement, and still others routinely read newspapers and smoked cigars the Order sought to boycott. Likewise, bourgeois publishers found it necessary to print fiction in which labor heroes appeared, hardly their ideological preference. Acknowledging the malleable nature of Gilded Age culture and society leads me to distrust hard and fast categories—so much so, in fact, that I use the term "working class" more out of convention than conviction. As Gutman demonstrates, the American labor force of the nineteenth and early twentieth centuries was continually reconstituted through new ethnic, ideological, gender, and racial infusions.[11] Class consciousness was the Holy Grail for which many crusaded, but the Gilded Age "working class" remains, at best, a term that describes work and power relationships only in isolated moments.

9. A good general overview on the "new" labor and social history is David Brody's essay, "The Old Labor History and the New: In Search of the American Working Class," *Labor History* 20 (Winter 1979): 111–26.

10. See Herbert Gutman, *Power & Culture: Essays on the American Working Class* (New York: Pantheon Books, 1987).

11. See Herbert Gutman's eponymous essay in *Work, Culture & Society in Industrializing America* (New York: Alfred A. Knopf, 1976).

All of this leaves us with the problem of trying to make sense out of chaos. If every general statement is violated by particulars, how can one hope to understand anything about the Knights of Labor, class relationships, or Gilded Age culture and society? A starting point would be to give up notions that history is objective, ordered, or neat. One can begin to comprehend history's nuances more deeply without first apprehending them in total. In truth, this method puts us closer to the way history actually unfolds. The Gilded Age was a whirl of activity, change, and imagination that no one understood very well. We often see more clearly when we look back at a period than when we view events unfolding before us, but neither vantage point affords perfect vision. It was hard for Knights to understand their own experiences: one of the reasons for the KOL's creativity and experimentation.

We can also organize our knowledge if we accept that categories are spongy, and that social science is not hard science. Given that codicil, I see a paradigm of two periods and five overlapping phases that characterize the developmental path of KOL cultural expression. Pre-1882 culture was a period of labor fraternalism marked by secret ritualistic behavior, the mysteries of which circulated orally. Such activity produced a fraternal, unified, secret, exclusive, and mostly male culture. During the post-1882 period, culture was rooted in solidarity and was more diffuse, open, public, and literary than its predecessor. But 1882 is not a cut-off date for fully realized cultural systems. Roughly, 1869 to 1879 marked a phase of the evolution of labor fraternalism. The years 1878 to 1884 formed a transitional phase in which Knights debated, reshaped, and began to abandon fraternalism. This frequently produced an intense backlash that retarded cultural transformation.

The third phase ran from 1882 to about 1889. Here the Order forged a public, literary culture with universalist pretensions in the hope that solidarity would effect social transformation. It was a time of experimentation, excitement, and polarity, one in which the KOL borrowed and modified older working-class cultural forms, and evolved new ones. But it was also the roller-coaster period of political and institutional success and failure. Capital's assault began to weaken the Order just as it looked like it might be a countervailing power with which to reckon.

A fourth transitional phase, 1887 through 1895, was a time of national decline in which local cultures paradoxically grew richer and more dense. As the central organization began to crumble, KOL locals were left to their own devices and briefly thrived. By the 1890s, however, local cultures fell increasingly to the blandishments of commercialized mass culture. By 1895, most urban KOL culture was dead. The fifth phase involved an attempt to turn back the clock. After 1895, the few remaining Knights returned to the oath-bound ritual secrecy of the first phase.

Like all models, mine is an abstraction for which concrete exceptions abound. Many KOL locals were not formed until the third phase was under way, and only a few lasted through all five. Several locals—most notably Local Assembly (LA) 1562 of Brooklyn—were rooted in labor fraternalism for their entire existence, while others—like Scranton Local 222—abandoned it long before the KOL as an organization relaxed its ritual. Likewise, some assemblies peaked in 1886, others much later. How a given local assembly experienced KOL culture was a function of its time, place, and circumstance, and none of the phases passed without leaving something behind. For example, long after labor fraternalism faded as actual practice, it continued to shape KOL debates, policy, and values.

This study has no ideological or historiographical axes to grind, beyond a single admission: I reject the idea that the Knights of Labor was ill-adapted to Gilded Age realities and that it left little of substance in its passing. The KOL was not a "bread and butter" union. The Order addressed Gilded Age fragmentation and tried to rebuild community by constructing an entire KOL universe that embraced not only work and ideology, but also badges, parades, picnics, music, poetry, literature, and religion. If the Order failed—a claim of which I am dubious—it is because it tried to do so much.

The Knights of Labor peaked at a time when America was on the cusp of becoming a rationalized, corporatized entity, and the triumph of mass consumer culture was nearly complete. As the transformations matured, the Knights faded. The Order was riddled with conflict and contradiction, yet managed to attract masses of workers and frighten most capitalists. In the end, the KOL was crushed by organized capital, not by outmoded ideas or contradictions. Apparently there was something about the organization that resonated with the rhythms of Gilded Age culture.

The Knights are a vital link in the chain of labor history. The KOL drew on earlier labor reform movements, just as there is continuity between the Knights and subsequent groups like the Industrial Workers of the World (IWW) and the Congress of Industrial Organizations (CIO). American labor history is not the story of discrete organizations with self-contained histories, but rather of stacked building blocks. The KOL borrowed from the past, just as groups like the IWW and the CIO borrowed from it. The KOL bequeathed a rich treasury of ideas, tactics, and cultural artifacts that other groups used to good advantage.

A word of explanation on the organization of this study: it is neither topical nor chronological in the conventional sense, rather it is constructed around broad cultural categories. Each chapter opens with a cultural "moment" that frames the overall analysis, and then uses thick description to penetrate more deeply. I trace the evolution of various cultural expressions through time, often moving from 1869 through 1893 several times in the same chapter. The Introduction provides a general overview of Gilded Age and KOL history and establishes a context and structure for undergraduates, general readers, and those unfamiliar with the broader outlines of labor or late-nineteenth-century North American history. The first three chapters deal with ritual, religion, and music, cultural expressions perceived to be private ones shared among initiates. The next four chapters—those on poetry, fiction, material culture, and leisure—deal primarily with public cultural products.

What follows is a look at the Knights of Labor's efforts to transform Gilded Age culture and society between the years 1869 and 1893. I have chosen 1893 as my cut-off point as it is the year Terence V. Powderly was ousted as the KOL's leader and it marks the end of the KOL's most active, most public history. Exposing the inequities of the Gilded Age is easy; one has only to scratch its surface for the glitter to fall away. Penetrating the Knights is a bit more difficult. Even after going public, many of the Order's inner workings were shielded from view. Official records are often spotty, some have been ravaged by time, and still others show disturbing signs of tampering. Journals, memoirs, and personal papers contain editorial bias, and few accounts of any sort have surfaced for thousands of local assemblies. Nonetheless, the Knights of Labor left behind scores of local papers, its official records and journal, much of its material culture, and the musings of former leaders. It is to these sources that I turn in an attempt to cross beyond the veils of secrecy, ideology, and culture, and thickly describe the Noble and Holy Order of the Knights of Labor.

Introduction

The year was 1875, and a young man stood among hooded figures. After a long evening of questions, quasi-religious lectures, and mysterious hand signals exchanged to knowing nods, the hoods were lifted. An officer calling himself a "Master Workman" spoke:

> On behalf of the toiling millions of earth, I welcome you to this Sanctuary, dedicated to the service of God, by serving humanity. Open and public associations having failed, after a struggle of centuries, to protect or advance the interests of labor, we have lawfully constituted this Assembly. Hid from public view, covered by an impenetrable veil of secrecy, not to promote or shield wrong doing but to shield ourselves and you, from persecution and wrong by men in our own sphere and calling as well as out of it, by endeavoring to secure the just reward of our toil. . . . We mean to uphold the dignity of labor, to affirm the nobility of all who live in accordance with God, "in the sweat of thy brow shalt thou eat bread."

The speech continued for another five minutes, and there were handshakes all around. An officer called the "Venerable Sage" appeared and, by the evening's end, the young man could decode the hand signs that had baffled him earlier in the evening. He was now a full-fledged member of the Noble and Holy Order of the Knights of Labor.[1]

Ten years later, shopmen laboring on Jay Gould's Wabash Railroad were fed up. They endured three wage cuts in just two and one-half years, only to find that the parsimonious Gould planned to close many shops altogether. Along with thousands of others along Gould's Southwestern conglomerate, they reluctantly engaged in a desperate strike. In less than two months Gould capitulated.[2] Like hundreds of thousands

1. Terence V. Powderly, *The Path I Trod: The Autobiography of Terence V. Powderly*, ed. Harry Carman, Henry David, and Paul Guthrie (New York: AMS, 1968), 47–53.

2. For more on the Southwestern strikes, see Shelton Stromquist, *A Generation of Boomers: The Pattern of Railroad Labor Conflict in Nineteenth-Century America* (Urbana: University of Illinois Press, 1987); see also Norman J. Ware, *The Labor Movement in the United States, 1860–1895: A Study in Democracy* (New York: D. Appleton, 1929).

across North America, Southwestern workers filled out applications and begged entry into the organization that directed the strike: the Knights of Labor. By mid-1886, there were as many as one million workers who called themselves Knights. Within two years, most of them quit the Order, and by 1893, there were fewer than 75,000 members left in the organization that forced Jay Gould to the bargaining table.[3]

These anonymous dramas are at once distant and familiar to us, reminders of how far yet near we are to the experiences of late-nineteenth-century working people. Labor rituals seem quaint, archaic, and alien, a bit of costumed theater still played out by Freemasons and Shriners, but not to be taken seriously by others. The strike scenario, however, is as familiar to Americans as the evening paper, though union victory is more rare these days (although gains won, and then lost, is a disturbingly common feature of late-twentieth-century capital/labor relations). Yet both scenes involved the same organization—the Knights of Labor— and embodied actions and thoughts common to late-nineteenth-century workers. The Knights of Labor was an odd organization by modern standards, but then, the late nineteenth century was an unusual time. These events remind us that a fuller understanding of those men and women requires appreciation of their world and logic on their own terms, not on preconceived notions of how a working-class movement *ought* to look.

In 1873, Mark Twain and Charles Dudley Warren penned *The Gilded Age*, a novel destined to lend its title to a period of American history stretching roughly from the end of the Civil War to 1900. In this fictional narrative, the simple, virtuous Hawkins family from rural Tennessee is cheated, corrupted, and torn apart by various rogues, including corrupt newspaper editors, land speculators, mashers, silver-tongued politicians, social climbers, and venture capitalists. Although the novel's upbeat resolution lacks the sarcastic undertones of subsequent Twain offerings, it leaves little doubt that the age was "gilded," one whose superficial gloss barely disguised festering problems lying beneath the surface.[4]

Four years before *The Gilded Age* appeared, nine veterans of antebellum labor reform movements reached the same conclusion. They convened in an upstairs room of the American Hose Company on Jayne Street in Philadelphia. On December 9, 1869, they dissolved their ineffective national union—the Garment Cutters' Association—and, on De-

3. Ware, *The Labor Movement in the United States*, 66.
4. Mark Twain and Charles Dudley Warren, *The Gilded Age: A Tale of Today* (Garden City: Doubleday, 1969).

cember 28, launched a new organization: the Noble and Holy Order of the Knights of Labor.[5]

Before 1869 closed, the small band of Knights was buoyed by the addition of six new members. Uriah Stephens was the leading spirit of the new organization, and his impassioned rhetoric foretold great things. Still, a dispassionate observer would have been skeptical about the future of an order whose name was nearly as long as its membership roll. For the next ten years, the Knights of Labor remained small in number and operated in near-total secrecy. For all of that, the KOL was destined to lead the fight to strip away the real gilding that Twain and Warren parodied in fiction.

There was little denying the inequities besotting North American society in the closing decades of the nineteenth century, problems exacerbated by real-life counterparts to Twain and Warren's fictional villains. These problems led many working-class men and women to turn inward and put their faith in organic institutions. As Terence V. Powderly, the future leader of the Knights of Labor recalled, "The great bulk of the [Civil War] army was made up of *workingmen*," but Congress was made up of

> *bankers* who enacted such legislation as was beneficial to themselves. . . . Those who returned to the walks of peace after the war flocked to the cities and towns in search of employment, where they were forced to the conclusion that while the war for the preservation of the Union was over, the battle for the preservation of life itself was still being waged with unrelenting fury.[6]

The injustices to which Powderly alluded took place in the midst of an industrial expansion that was both undeniable and deceptive. The production of coal, pig iron, steel, and refined oil soared between the years 1870 and 1900, and railroads expanded at a rate of nearly 4,000 miles per year. Likewise, production of consumer goods and food skyrocketed. Coupled with low inflation and rising wages, the closing three decades of the nineteenth century should have been good ones for North American working people.[7] They were not.

5. Terence V. Powderly, *Thirty Years of Labor, 1859–1889* (reprinted, New York: Augustus M. Kelley, 1967), 73–76.

6. Powderly, *Thirty Years of Labor*, 35–36.

7. Gilded Age production increases were indeed dramatic. The amount of coal mined in the United States increased from 45 million tons in 1870, to more than 120 million tons in 1885. Pig iron production jumped from 631,000 tons in 1850 to 15.4 million tons in 1900, while steel mills, virtually nonexistent in 1850, churned out more than 10 million tons

Changes in large-scale industrial production led to new modes of production, with workers caught in the middle of changing labor systems. Thousands of workers lost control over tools, materials, knowledge, and wage-bargaining. Labor movements were weakened by new technologies and management techniques that de-skilled and homogenized the work routine of large numbers of laborers. But the transformation of labor was not linear, and the very unevenness of development added to the social and economic turmoil experienced by Gilded Age workers. The years 1873, 1877 to 1878, 1884, and 1893 to 1894 were depression years, and smaller recessions were even more commonplace.[8]

Sporadic employment, long hours, and inadequate wages were the norm for Gilded Age workers. Even those who embraced industrial progress longed for a larger share of the wealth they produced. In 1880, Robert Ingersoll wrote to the *Journal of United Labor (JUL)*, the Knights of Labor's official newspaper, and asserted:

> Reasonable labor is the source of joy. To work for wife or child, to toil for those you love is happiness, provided you can make them happy. . . . With the vast and wonderful improvements of the 19th century there should be not only the necessities of life for those who toil, but comforts and luxuries as well.[9]

Ingersoll's letter encapsulates both the promise and the problem of the age. Few workers could expect comfort, luxury, or leisure when they

annually by 1900. Only 9,000 miles of railroad crossed the countryside in 1850, but by the time the Civil War ended that figure stood at 36,000, with 4,000 new miles being added each year. Domestic consumer and agricultural production were equally dramatic. By 1881, the United States had supplanted Great Britain in manufacturing production, and stood as the world's leader. For more on production during the Gilded Age, see Sidney Ratner, James Soltow, and Richard Sylla, *The Evolution of the American Economy: Growth, Welfare, and Decision Making* (New York: Basic Books, 1979).

8. Susan E. Hirsch describes this process in one American city; see her *Roots of the American Working Class: The Industrialization of Crafts in Newark, 1800–1860* (Philadelphia: University of Pennsylvania Press, 1978), 15. Hirsch overstates her case, perhaps, by calling industrialization the "graveyard of the artisan class." In Philadelphia, for example, only 57 percent of the city's workers worked in large, automated factories as late as 1880. See also the synopsis of the work of Bruce Laurie and Mark Schmitz contained in David M. Gordon, Richard Edwards, and Michael Reich, *Segmented Work, Divided Workers: The Historical Transformation of Labor in the United States* (Cambridge: Cambridge University Press, 1982), 87–89. For the complete study, see Bruce Laurie and Mark Schmitz, "Manufacture and Productivity: The Making of an Industrial Base," in *Philadelphia: Work, Space, Family, and Group Experience in the 19th Century*, ed. Theodore Hershberg (Oxford: Oxford University Press, 1981), 43–92. For more on the uneven development of capitalist expansion, see Gordon, Edwards, and Reich, *Segmented Work, Divided Workers*; Ratner, Soltow, and Sylla, *The Evolution of the American Economy*.

9. *Journal of United Labor* [hereafter cited as *JUL*], August 1880.

toiled ten to twelve hours daily and averaged a meager $558.68 per year in 1883, a year in which an average family needed $754.42 to survive. Few men could manage unless wives and children also worked, and even then prolonged unemployment could force the most frugal family into destitution. The work day was not only long and arduous, it was also dangerous. By 1890, the railroad industry averaged one death per 306 employees and one serious injury for every thirty workers.[10]

The deferment of working-class dreams contrasted vividly with the glittering opulence of monopolists, entrepreneurs, and assorted robber barons. Despite the preaching of persuasive clergymen like Henry Ward Beecher and the pseudoscientific justifications of wealth by Social Darwinists like William Graham Sumner, few workers accepted an ideology of greed masquerading as progress. Cornelius Vanderbilt was worth over $100 million in 1877, a year in which federal troops and state militia were called out against striking railroad workers whose brakemen averaged less than $400 per year. And although Andrew Carnegie announced his support of unions and spoke wistfully of his impoverished immigrant past, he mused from the luxury of a Scottish castle, collected $20 million per year in untaxed profits, and employed one of the most brutal managers of the era, Henry Clay Frick. The extremes of wealth and poverty were obvious to anyone who cared to look. Small wonder that the labor press attacked Social Darwinism as unsound, labeled Carnegie a hypocrite, called for an end to the wage system, and made Henry Ward Beecher a hated figure among workers.

The backdrop for many of the age's challenges took place in a relatively new setting, the industrial city. The population of the United States nearly tripled from 1865 to 1917. In 1860, a scant 20 percent of Americans resided in clusters of 2,500 or larger; by 1890, 33 percent did. A substantial number of urban dwellers were immigrants, and more than a third of the total population increase came from that source. Immigrants were suspect and the xenophobic diatribes of Anglo-Saxon supremacists like Josiah Strong reigned as conventional wisdom.[11] With the lamentable exception of the Chinese, the Knights offered protection for many immigrant urban workers.

10. Powderly, *Thirty Years of Labor;* Gordon, Edwards, and Reich, *Segmented Work, Divided Workers;* Bruce Laurie, *Artisans into Workers: Labor in Nineteenth-Century America* (New York: Noonday, 1989); David Montgomery, *The Fall of the House of Labor* (Cambridge: Cambridge University Pres, 1989). Nearly 2,500 railroad workers died in 1890.

11. Cf. Josiah Strong, *Our Country,* ed. Jurgen Herbst (Cambridge, Mass.: Harvard University Press, 1963), 134–62. Strong estimated that the nation's fifty largest cities contained 39.3 percent of all German immigrants and 45.8 percent of all the Irish. In several cities, immigrants dramatically outnumbered native-born Americans. Cincinnati was 62 percent nonnative-born, Cleveland 83 percent, Boston 63 percent, and Chicago 91 percent.

Cities were often far removed from the promises of progress. Population growth outpaced that of institutions and infrastructures. Urban areas lacked adequate housing or transport, and very few had zoning laws. By 1880, New Yorkers inhaled the fumes of over 125 refineries and tanneries. Garbage and untreated sewage flowed into the rivers that formed the city's supply of "fresh" water. The urban poor crowded into tenements that lacked basics like cross ventilation, which exacerbated epidemics of influenza, typhus, and yellow fever. In Memphis, three yellow fever outbreaks between 1853 and 1878 led to over 16,000 deaths. The 1868 scourge carried off the husband and four children of Mary "Mother" Jones, who scarcely got out of Memphis to start a new life when a new urban tragedy befell her: the loss of all she had in the Great Chicago Fire of 1871. Like subsequent champions of the working class, Mary Jones questioned the nature of her society. In the same Chicago that claimed her worldly goods, Jones encountered the Knights of Labor, an experience she credited with her decision to dedicate her life to the struggle for working-class justice.[12]

The Gilded Age held special challenges for farmers, women, and people of color. Despite the prevalent myth of frontier independence, by the 1880s nearly 40 percent of all farmers were tenants. In many counties of the deep South over 80 percent of black farmers were sharecroppers.[13] Everywhere, farmers experienced rising costs and railroad rates, expensive credit, and falling commodity prices. Rural Americans often felt threatened by emergent cities and urban culture, though few could resist the lure of industrial employment when farming failed. Those who stayed on the land began to organize for mutual protection. The KOL took in agricultural workers as early as 1880, and it lingered in rural America into the late 1890s, long after its urban following faded.

Post–Civil War America was a time of upheaval for women as well. Women made tentative breaks with the private sphere through antebellum movements such as moral reform, the temperance movement, suffrage, and abolitionism, and resisted Victorian attempts to confine them. For some, the Emancipation Proclamation and subsequent Thirteenth, Fourteenth, and Fifteenth Amendments represented a window of op-

12. Mary Jones, *The Autobiography of Mother Jones* (Chicago: Charles H. Kerr, [1925] 1980), chap. 1.

13. For a more thorough discussion, see Roger L. Ransom and Richard Sutch, *One Kind of Freedom: The Economic Consequences of Emancipation* (Cambridge: Cambridge University Press, 1977).

portunity. If the rights of black men were constitutionally guaranteed, then what of the rights of women? After 1880, women activists found the Knights of Labor a receptive forum for their views; Frances Willard, Susan B. Anthony, and Elizabeth Cady Stanton all held membership cards in the KOL.

Changing economics eroded the borders between private and public spheres. By 1880, over 2.6 million women were nonfarm laborers, a 30 percent increase in ten years that made women 15.2 percent of the total work force. Ten years later, the number of working women swelled to more than 4 million, or 17.2 percent of the total labor force. For black women the figures were more dramatic. Whereas a scant 7.3 percent of married white women worked in 1880, 35.4 percent of married black women toiled. For single black women the figure stood at 73.3 percent (23.8 percent for whites).[14] White middle-class women had the luxury of contemplating Victorian notions of true womanhood, but for the millions of women who worked, such stereotypes were an unaffordable luxury. Thus more than 60,000 working women joined the Knights of Labor in the 1800s.

There was precious little luster to the Gilded Age for people of color. The promises of emancipation dissolved with the collapse of Radical Reconstruction and the emergence of Jim Crow laws and customs. Soon many African Americans found themselves as politically and economically disenfranchised as they were before the Civil War. In addition, debt peonage reduced many black sharecroppers to positions of semiserfdom scarcely distinguishable from their former slave status. Those who went North found Jim Crow waiting for them. Few skilled positions were open for black men, and many trade unions excluded them. African-American women fared even worse, carrying the double burden of racism and sexism. Of those thousands of black women who worked for wages, nearly all were employed as domestic servants.[15] African Ameri-

14. Philip S. Foner, *Women and the American Labor Movement* (New York: Free Press, 1979), 70, 71; William H. Harris, *The Harder We Run: Black Workers Since the Civil War* (New York: Oxford University Press, 1982), 23, 24.

15. See Ransom and Sutch, *One Kind of Freedom;* also, Harris, *The Harder We Run,* 52. Harris provides data showing that the percentage of blacks living north of the Mason-Dixon line only increased from 8.4 percent in 1870 to 10 percent in 1900. See also Herman Bloch, "Labor and the Negro," *Journal of Negro History* 50 (July 1965): 163–84. Useful studies on the ensuing tragedy left with the collapse of Radical Reconstruction include David Montgomery, *Beyond Equality: Labor and the Radical Republicans 1862–1872* (Urbana: University of Illinois Press, 1981), and Eric Foner, *Reconstruction: America's Unfinished Revolution 1863–1877* (New York: Harper & Row, 1988).

cans did not passively or stoically accept their fates; by 1887, more than 90,000 had joined the Knights of Labor.

The problems of Gilded Age America were obvious, but solutions were elusive. The dilemma facing Uriah Stephens and his compatriots in 1869 was personal and immediate. They had seen Philadelphia workers thrown into poverty and insecurity as a result of ruthless exploitation and unsound business speculation. But mere resolve to organize for mutual benefit and protection could not mask the fact that their own garment cutters' union had just collapsed, and few alternatives loomed within the contemporary labor movement.

The garment cutters were emblematic of organized labor's record up to 1869, a saga of false starts and shattered hopes devoid of long-lasting gains. As a boy growing up in Cape May, New Jersey, Stephens probably heard stories of Working Men's parties, but they were a fading memory by 1846, when the twenty-five-year-old Stephens went to Philadelphia to work as a tailor.[16] By 1858, little was left of the city's labor movement. The Panic of 1857 had decimated Philadelphia's organizations, as well as trade unions nationwide.[17]

The Civil War and early Reconstruction provided a brief opportunity for laborers who wished to organize. Several future Knights of Labor helped revitalize trade unionism, and Stephens himself co-founded the Garment Cutters' Association in 1862. In addition, labor reform conventions abounded, eight-hour leagues formed in eastern cities, and the National Labor Union (NLU) appeared in 1866, announcing its intention to unite workers from all trades into a single organization. Yet by 1869, little organization remained; even the NLU was only three years from total collapse. Of the trades, only the shoemakers, in the highly-secretive Knights of St. Crispin, showed much vitality. Its 50,000 members easily made it the largest trade union in the United States.[18] Most unions suffered the same fate as Stephens' garment cutters, and disbanded.

On December 9, 1869, a discouraged Stephens met with James L. Wright, William Phillips, Robert McCauley, William Cook, James Hilsea, Joseph Kennedy, Robert Keen, and David Westcott to mull over future options. From this meeting came "The Noble and Holy Order of the

16. For a thorough description of Philadelphia's antebellum workers, see Bruce Laurie, *Working People of Philadelphia 1800–1850* (Philadelphia: Temple University Press, 1980).

17. By 1858, only the printers, shoemakers, stone cutters, and hat finishers still had strong national unions. On the Panic of 1857, see Philip Foner, *History of the Labor Movement in the United States*, vol. 1: *From Colonial Times to the Founding of the American Federation of Labor* (New York: International, 1982), chap. 12.

18. Ware, *The Labor Movement in the United States*, chap. 1.

Knights of Labor."[19] All that was decided then was that the Knights would not be a conventional trade union and that ritual would be used to initiate and bind members. The KOL was hardly ready to tangle with the monied interests that controlled Gilded Age society.

The Committee on Ritual's initial report of January 6, 1870, largely defined the new organization by pointing out the flaws of its predecessors, a negation as much as a construction. As the small band secretly gathered as the Tea Pot Society (so called because an officer, called a "purveyor," carried tea fixings to meetings), it turned increasingly to a more successful model, the fraternal brotherhood. The founders dreamed of moving beyond the limits of "bread-and-butter" unionism by creating an oppositional culture based on the brotherhood of all toilers. Stephens envisioned a "City of Refuge, over which is inscribed, in letters of living light, 'Organization' [sparkling] with the unutterable truth, 'Brotherhood' . . . a beloved fraternity upon which God's seal of approval has been set."[20] In that vein, Stephens—his de facto leadership conferred by the title Grand Master Workman—fashioned an elaborate ritual based on Freemasonry.

If the KOL began life as a different kind of labor organization, it was not immediately apparent that it would survive infancy. Not until 1872 was a second local assembly (LA) formed, and another year passed before enough LAs existed to justify creating a district assembly (DA) to coordinate the efforts of all locals. The Order remained confined to the greater Philadelphia area until New York City gold beaters formed LA 28 in early 1874. The KOL did not live up to its universalist pretensions, however. Women were excluded because Stephens doubted they could keep secrets, and so the exclusively white, male membership was largely confined to skilled craftsmen.

Westward and northward expansion altered this exclusionary policy. By mid-1875, the Knights had reached Pittsburgh and took hold in a locale where socialism, greenbackism, and ballot box politics were hotly debated in the city's mills and mines. By 1876, the KOL's strength was

19. Powderly, *Thirty Years of Labor*, 72–78. There is some confusion about who the founders were. Though nine men met on December 9, 1869, two of them—William Phillips and David Westcott—were absent from the December 23, 1869, meeting in which the name "The Noble and Holy Order of the Knights of Labor" was chosen. As a result, neither Phillips nor Westcott is usually included among the founders. The seven usually credited are Uriah Stephens, James L. Wright, R. W. Keen, James M. Hilsea, Joseph Kennedy, William Cook, and Robert McCauley.

20. Ibid., 88–89. The Committee on Ritual was placed in the hands of James Wright at the December 9, 1869, meeting, but it was Stephens and H. L. Sinexon—one of the Order's earliest initiates—who assumed most of the responsibility for its development.

split among its Philadelphia birthplace, the coal fields around Pittsburgh, and northeastern Pennsylvania, where seed work was done by John Siney of the Miner's National Association. Scranton, Pennsylvania, was transformed by coal, politics, and the KOL. The Knights arrived there in 1875, and in 1876, its LA 222 elected Terence V. Powderly, a twenty-seven-year-old machinist, to be its Master Workman. Two years later, he became Scranton's mayor.

The Philadelphia craftsmen who founded the Knights tended to be more conservative, less ethnic, and more suspicious of politics than miners and mill workers. Several conferences were held to air differences before dramatic labor unrest spurred the Knights to call a convention. Few Knights participated in the 1877 railway strikes, but the KOL was affected nonetheless. The collapse of the strikes and the brutality with which they were suppressed led workers to scramble for options. Few trade unions survived the assault. Only the KOL emerged from 1877 stronger than it went in. It added eleven new district assemblies in 1877, bringing the total to fourteen, when representatives gathered in Reading, Pennsylvania, on January 1, 1878, for the KOL's first Grand Assembly.[21]

Until the 1878 Grand Assembly, the KOL had no preamble or constitution. The convention fashioned them from documents gleaned from the defunct Industrial Brotherhood. It also corrected confusion over proper ritual procedures, which resulted from the oral circulation of ritual. After 1878, more printed copies of the Order's ritual book, the *Adelphon Kruptos,* became available. Also discussed was the wisdom of maintaining secrecy, but proposals for a public order were swept aside by the older members who controlled whatever official machinery existed.[22]

The impressive work of the Reading convention aside, the Knights of Labor remained a humble body with big ideas. Its 1879 membership stood at a mere 9,287.[23] But 1879 was a fateful year. Founder Uriah Stephens resigned to run for U.S. Congress, and the Grand Assembly chose Terence Powderly to replace him as Grand Master Workman of the Order. Powderly represented different values and experiences than Stephens. The machine and locomotive shops in which Powderly labored in his youth held industrial solidarity in higher regard than the artisanal

21. The best general history of the Knights of Labor remains Ware, *The Labor Movement in the United States.* Also helpful are Powderly's two autobiographies, *Thirty Years of Labor,* and *The Path I Trod.* A recent work that deals nicely with the early KOL in Philadelphia is Judith L. Goldberg, "Strikes, Organizing and Change: The Knights of Labor in Philadelphia, 1869–1890" (Ph.D. diss., New York University, 1985).
22. 1878 *Proceedings of the Knights of Labor Grand Assembly* (Reading, Pa.).
23. Ware, *The Labor Movement in the United States,* 66.

fraternalism of Stephens' garment cutters. In addition, Powderly was bothered by the Order's secrecy; he was an Irish Catholic and subject to the Church's condemnation of ritualistic secret societies, which it assumed were atheistic, Molly Maguire clones.

Powderly lobbied for an open order and, though total secrecy was not abandoned until 1882, the KOL became increasingly public under his tutelage before then. Growth was slow, however, and the KOL actually contracted between 1880 and 1881. When KOL membership grew to 42,517 in 1882, it was due as much to Joseph Buchanan's organizing among Western railroad men and miners as the KOL's public posture that year.[24] Perhaps the only tangible immediate effect of the decision to become a public order was the disappearance of the term "grand" in official KOL titles; it was thought to smack of aristocratic pretension and was replaced with the more modest adjective "general."

As a public order, the KOL became embroiled in its first major strike in 1883, that of the telegraphers versus Jay Gould and Western Union. It, like most other strikes in 1883 and 1884, ended in defeat for the workers. Also lost were miner strikes in Pennsylvania, Ohio, and Indiana; as well as actions by Philadelphia carpet weavers, Troy iron molders, and Fall River textile spinners. Only Philadelphia shoemakers, Pittsburgh glassworkers, and Union Pacific shopmen led by Joseph Buchanan won strikes. Nonetheless, the KOL grew to over 74,000 members in 1884, and to more than 111,000 in 1885, on the eve of its successful strike against Gould's South West railway conglomerate.[25]

One reason for its growth, despite meager results, is that the Order sought to bring fringe groups to its center and into accord with the rhetoric of its constitution. In theory, only bankers, lawyers, gamblers, speculators, and liquor tradesmen were banned from KOL membership. By the early 1880s, the KOL was already a diverse assortment of Marxists and Lassallean socialists in New York City, anarchists in Chicago and Denver, Germans in Cincinnati, French Canadians in New England mill

24. For more on KOL growth, see Ware, *The Labor Movement in the United States*. For more on Joseph Buchanan and early expansion, see Joseph R. Buchanan, *The Story of a Labor Agitator* (Freeport, N.Y.: Books For Libraries, 1971). Part of the reason the KOL declined between 1880 and 1881 was because of Grand Treasurer Charles Litchman's mismanagement of the Defense Fund, which left it short of money to support strikers and boycotters. In fact, Litchman's crippling of the fund may have been in part responsible for the Order's strident antistrike posture. For more, see Ware, *The Labor Movement in the United States*, 122–23; Robert Weir, "When Friends Fall Out," in *Labor in Massachusetts: Selected Essays*, ed. Martin Kaufman and Kenneth Fones-Wolf (Westfield, Mass.: Institute of Massachusetts Studies, 1990).

25. For more on the KOL and strikes, see Ware, *The Labor Movement in the United States*, 117–54.

towns, and scores of reformers, temperance advocates, socially conscious ministers, ritualists, small employers, and trade unionists. (The presence of trade unionists led the 1884 General Assembly to authorize the chartering of National Trade Assemblies.) In addition, the Order took in women and African Americans.

The first women Knights were organized into an all-female local in 1881 when Mary Stirling and Harry Skeffington organized Philadelphia shoe operatives into LA 1684. Soon both mixed-gender and single-sex locals emerged, and by 1885 a permanent women's department was formed. In 1886, Leonora Barry was chosen as General Investigator of Women's Work.

African Americans, spurned by the rest of the labor movement, approached the KOL with caution, then enthusiasm. Although there were rumors of all-black locals as early as 1880, the first confirmed black assembly was of coal miners in Ottumwa, Iowa (LA 1637). Organization spread to industrial cities like New York, where Frank Ferrell represented DA 49 at the 1886 General Assembly, and to the South. Richmond's DA 92 was all-black, and scores of all-black locals dotted the South. (When the KOL membership declined in the late 1880s and 1890s, it actually increased its black membership in several Southern states.)

By any reckoning, however, the event that catapulted the KOL to world attention was the 1885 strike against Jay Gould's Southwest Railway Conglomerate. Gould's defeat caused a stampede to the Knights that can be likened to the faithful embracing a savior. Officially, the Order swelled from 111,395 to 729,677 members in a single year.[26] Actually, over 1 million individuals probably called themselves Knights. Locals formed so quickly that the General Executive Board (GEB) declared a moratorium against chartering new LAs, which did little to deter enthusiastic individuals who met without benefit of charters, or the burden of dues-paying.

In 1886 the Knights of Labor continued to grow, while trade unions met in Columbus, Ohio, to form the American Federation of Labor (AFL). Despite fizzled efforts to call a general strike for an eight-hour work day, culminating in the Haymarket riot in Chicago, eight-hour advocates remained organized and strong. In November elections, KOL candidates, independent labor parties, and socialist groups not only increased their vote tallies, but often won local and state offices.[27]

26. Ibid., 66.
27. For more on the elections of 1886, see Leon Fink, *Workingmen's Democracy: The Knights of Labor and American Politics* (Urbana: University of Illinois Press, 1983); Richard Oestreicher, *Solidarity and Fragmentation: Working People and Class Consciousness in Detroit, 1875–1900* (Urbana: University of Illinois Press, 1986).

For the Knights of Labor, however, its moment of triumph was ephemeral; seeds of future decline simmered beneath the surface. The Order was plagued by intense ideological debates and fierce factionalism, the most troublesome of which was led by New York City–based Lassalleans, anarchists, and ritualists calling themselves the Home Club.[28] One result of internal discord was a loosened sense of solidarity with the rest of the labor movement that spilled over into jurisdictional fights with trade unions. Likewise, Powderly's pig-headed refusal to add his voice to those pleading for clemency for the Haymarket anarchists further isolated the Knights.

New issues highlighted a larger problem for the Order. After 1884, the KOL comprised a mostly reconstituted membership that frequently misunderstood the Order's history, workings, and principles. Those who rallied to the Knights after the first Gould strike failed to note that the Order was officially against strikes, just as those who cast votes in the 1886 elections ignored pronouncements that the KOL was a nonpartisan organization. Religious issues emerged as well. The new rank and file was increasingly Protestant; many members resented the Order's mostly Catholic leadership and thought overtures to win papal sanction of the Order were a waste of time.

Rank-and-file discipline was difficult to maintain given the KOL's cumbersome and vague bureaucratic structure. In theory, power flowed from the top down, though not exclusively so. Local assemblies combined to send representatives to district, state, and national trade assemblies. These local assembly members, in turn, elected representatives for annual General Assemblies from which a GEB and a slate of officers were chosen. Those individuals made policy that pertained to the entire organization and issued directives to coordinate efforts between districts. The GEB also had the authority to call, suspend, or abandon strikes and to grant, suspend, and revoke local and district charters.

On paper, the KOL seemed a nascent modern bureaucracy with a flow chart of power and authority. In truth, the structure was ripe for subversion by democrats and tyrants alike. Local assemblies needed sanction only for those actions for which they expected support, and often bitterly resented GEB intervention into what they perceived as

28. The Home Club actually gained control of the Knights of Labor at a June 1886 Special Assembly after plotting to do so since the early 1880s. Its hold on power was brief and began to wane by 1887. By the 1888 General Assembly Powderly forces were back in control, but over a weakened order in which Home Club dissidents, their clones, with anti–Home Club factions continuing to cause trouble. For more information on the Home Club, see Robert Weir, "Tilting at Windmills: Powderly and the Home Club," *Labor History* 34, no. 1 (Winter 1993): 84–113.

local matters. Further, the dynamics of local operations usually revolved around personality as much as procedure, a practice that encouraged local leaders to set agendas that might or might not be in accord with official directives. As often as not, rank-and-file members applauded such independence.

If local power was a mix of personality and bureaucracy, it was nonetheless more democratic than the larger structures. Big districts tended to dominate conventions and their agendas, with national leaders coming from their ranks because the number of General Assembly (GA) representatives was determined by district membership size. Thus, candidates preferred by large DAs came to the GA with ready-made voting blocs. The same pattern was repeated in district and state assemblies.

But the diffusion of power mitigated against anyone being able to control the Order in total. Each level of authority had its own officers and institutions through which policy was made. Some local and district assemblies were strong enough to ignore directives from the top, even if their charters were revoked. This phenomenon, coupled with ideological differences between Knights, served to fragment the Order even as it grew. As national authority eroded, LAs grew more experimental and independent.[29]

None of these problems should have been fatal, and given time the KOL might have sorted out many of its glitches through indoctrination of members, leadership changes, nonraiding pacts with other organizations, selective expulsions, and structural evolution. But the KOL never got the breathing space necessary to transform itself from an organization whose focus was ritual fraternalism to one grounded in class solidarity, grassroots organizing, and pragmatic unionism. In many respects, victory over Gould was the most disastrous fate to befall the KOL. New Knights brought with them raised expectations, but little patience. In keeping with Stephens's original vision, Powderly continued to stress the need to "educate" workers, employers, and the public, while much of the new membership—encouraged by the Order's left wing—clamored for strike leadership and support. The left wing dominated from 1886 on, but at a colossal cost to the Order. The KOL suffered a disastrous loss during the second Gould strike of 1886, which was followed by setbacks in the Chicago meat-packing industry, on the Reading Railroad, and in New England shoes and textiles. While Powderly counseled caution, members saw betrayal and left the KOL in droves.

---

29. For more on KOL structure, see William Birdsall, "The Problem of Structure in the Knights of Labor," *Industrial and Labor Relations Review* 6 (July 1953): 532–46. See also Weir, "When Friends Fall Out."

It was capital's attitude that sealed the KOL's fate. The victory over Gould created a false impression of KOL strength. The business community closed ranks and offered no quarter in its confrontations with the KOL. During the Philadelphia and Reading Railroad strike of 1887, the company made little attempt to disguise the contempt that it held for the KOL. Similarly, in 1890 New York Central discharged individuals merely for being Knights, precipitating a strike the purpose of which was to rid the line of the Order. The company then rebuffed all offers of arbitration—including one from the Governor of New York—and rode out the strike to the applause of the business community.[30]

Financial woes also plagued the Knights. After the first Gould strike, the KOL constructed bureaucratic structures that were designed to serve a mass organization. By 1888, the KOL had an administrative machine that spent more money than it took in. Across the country, KOL locals took out mortgages to construct new assembly halls, raised cooperative stores, and sponsored public rallies, but had no mechanism to compel members to pay assessments. An elaborate headquarters was built in Philadelphia to house KOL central offices and *The Journal of United Labor* (*JUL*), but as members quit the KOL, revenues declined and the Order was left without funds to support lecturers, office staff, and organizers. Worst of all, the strike assistance fund was depleted.

In 1890, the New York Central strike decimated the Order in the industrial Northeast and Midwest. After the strike, the KOL became an increasingly rural organization. Eighty-two Knights took part in the 1892 Omaha convention that led to the founding of the Populist party, and by the mid-1890s, rural Knighthood was often indistinguishable from Populist and the Farmers Alliance groups. In 1893, KOL agrarians cooperated with remaining urban radicals, spearheaded by Daniel DeLeon, to topple Powderly as General Master Workman, and replace him with Iowa's James Sovereign.

But Sovereign proved to be a less capable leader than Powderly. In 1895, the KOL came full circle, returning to the oath-bound secrecy of 1869. Fragmentary evidence suggests the Order enjoyed a brief revival, but it was not to last. By century's end, the KOL was an eviscerated organization with few hopes of recovery. Knights drifted from the Order until 1917, when the last official General Master Workman, John Hayes, closed the KOL's national headquarters and moved its records to a leaky shed behind a Washington, D.C., insurance agency. Even then, a few Knights lingered. In the 1930s, Boston's Thomas Canning, calling him-

---

30. See Powderly, *The Path I Trod*, 163–74; *Albany Evening Journal, New York Times,* and *New York Tribune,* August 9–September 28, 1890; Ware, *The Labor Movement,* 117–54.

self General Master Workman, convened a KOL "convention" in 1932. The last KOL assembly, a group of fifty Boston motion picture operators (LA 5030), did not abandon its charter until 1949 when it merged with a larger AFL local.[31]

This study does not seek to explain in full the reasons for the KOL's collapse, rather it highlights the culture and expressions of the organization while it thrived. Knighthood's central tenets came to be understood under the rubric of S.O.M.A.—secrecy, obedience, and mutual assistance—a noble, but vague set of ideals. Many of the Order's mottos—such as "An Injury to One is the Concern of All"—were specific enough to suggest the need for solidarity, but flexible enough to attract men and women of various ideological stripes. "Knighthood" came to embody an array of visions for a better society, and what allowed contradictory viewpoints to coexist was the mutability of KOL culture.

The KOL abandoned attempts at a monocultural Order after 1882, but there was enough commonality to give common identity. By 1886, the KOL existed in virtually every large industrial city in the United States and Canada. It was also present in smaller industrial towns, one-industry villages, the Deep South, West Coast port cities, rural backwaters across the continent, and in several foreign nations. All told, as many as 2 and one-half million individuals passed through KOL ranks at some point in the Gilded Age; at the Order's peak, as many as one of five workers was a Knight.[32] Irrespective of the KOL's ultimate fate, if we are to make sense of Gilded Age working-class experience, we must consider what made the Knights of Labor attractive.

The exploits and expressions of Knights also reveal much about Amer-

31. Fred Landon, "The Knights of Labor: Predecessors of the C.I.O.," *Quarterly Review of Commerce* 20 (Summer–Autumn 1937), 133–39; Foner, *History of the Labor Movement*, vol. 2.

32. My figure of 2 and one-half million is admittedly speculative, based partly on figures collected by Ware and partly on my own projections, which are based on the fact that the KOL founded more than 15,000 locals by 1900. Ten members were required for a charter; one must assume that many contained far more. Even if we revise downward to 2 million members, the KOL still comprised between 6 and 8 percent of all workers, based on National Bureau of Economic Research estimates of a work force of 23,320,000 in 1890, and of 29,070,000 in 1900. The American Federation of Labor had over one million members by 1905; thus many historians and labor analysts have assumed it supplanted the Knights. Perhaps it did, but the highwater mark for the AFL-CIO is 15.5 million in 1956. Based on a work force of over 70 million, the AFL-CIO represented only three times as many workers by percentage, not 700 percent more as suggested by raw numbers. Today, the AFL-CIO represents a smaller percentage of all American workers than the KOL did during 1886, when as many as 20 percent of all workers claimed at least brief KOL affiliation.

ican culture. Few Gilded Age concerns were beyond the KOL's purview, and it took positions on issues as broad and diverse as the abolition of the wage system, convict labor, cooperative production, currency reform, equal rights for women, immigration restriction, land redistribution, race relations, religious hypocrisy, temperance, and government ownership of transportation and communications systems. It also took stands on issues far less weighty, like the opposition to the production of oleo margarine and the campaign to have stockyard workers refrain from swearing. To further muddy the labor waters, the Knights allowed interested employers to join the Order.

The KOL emerged in a world in which notions of bureaucratic unionism were inchoate, when the wages, hours, and conditions troika of the "pure and simple" unionism later embraced by the AFL was viewed by contemporaries as indicating a hopelessly narrow perspective. The utopian goal of making "industrial and moral worth—not wealth—the true standard of individual and national greatness"[33] did not sound naive to Gilded Age workers.

Such high-sounding rhetoric reminds us that the Gilded Age imagination was perhaps broader than our own. The KOL envisioned a different sort of society than that which was, or that came to be. If some workers grew skeptical of edenic rhetoric, hundreds of thousands of others devoured utopian novels like Edward Bellamy's *Looking Backward*.[34] The KOL's most vital period was the 1880s, an understudied but crucial decade in the creation of American culture. There was, up to that time, no unified national culture, and though mingling took place at venues like baseball parks and city theaters, sharp class distinctions generally marked the types of culture one consumed, the sites where one consumed it, and the values inherent in cultural objects.

Even if we make allowances for substantial amounts of trait borrowing and large numbers of individuals moving in either elite or working-class cultural circles, the barriers between classes were much sharper than in the age of commercial, mass-produced, nationally disseminated culture that loomed on the horizon. The Knights of Labor represent a superb case study of an organization caught between three cultural systems: its own system, hegemonic bourgeois culture, and emergent mass commercial culture. The KOL labored to shape and adapt to cultural change in an age of rapid but ambiguous transformation. Its cultural losses, victories, compromises, and adaptations foreshadowed and mirrored larger changes in American society.

33. From the Preamble to the KOL Platform and Principles, printed in most issues of the *JUL*.

34. Edward Bellamy, *Looking Backward, 2000–1887*, ed. John L. Thomas (Cambridge, Mass.: Belknap Press of Harvard University Press, 1967).

1 The Knights in Ritual

A Culture of Fraternalism

In 1874, a twenty-five-year-old machinist attended an antimonopoly convention in Philadelphia. He took comfort in the presence of like-minded men and was honored when William Fennimore invited him to his room for what he assumed would be a social evening. Thus he was surprised when Fennimore locked the door and asked him to kneel. He did so in anticipation of prayer, but was instead queried on a variety of subjects concerning capital and labor relations. Fennimore then asked him to join the Noble and Holy Order of the Knights of Labor (KOL). He agreed, took an oath, and was told never to utter or write the name of the Order in public.

The young man returned to his home and job in Scranton, Pennsylvania, and heard little of the KOL until September 6, 1876. On that night, a shopmate invited him to attend a labor lecture. The two met at the designated time and place, only to confront a masked figure in a black gown. They were questioned and taken into a room with other robed men. An elaborate ceremony filled with symbolic allusions to death and rebirth ensued. After seemingly endless questions, lectures, oaths, and mystical allegories, the young man was officially welcomed into the Knights of Labor and was given over to the Venerable Sage in order to learn the secret handshakes, signs, and rituals necessary to be a fully functioning Knight.[1]

The machinist's name was Terence Vincent Powderly, and in less than three years after that meeting he headed the KOL. His wistful ex post facto recollections of his initiation seem odd, given that he used his power to erode KOL ritual. Powderly explained:

> Traveling slowly, building carefully, and working silently, it would take many years to build an organization of sufficient strength or importance, numerically or otherwise, to command attention on the part of workers or employers. When you reflect

1. Powderly, *The Path I Trod*, chap. 5.

that each man had to be sought out, questioned, or sounded as to his views, and then balloted for separately before being admitted to membership, you will realize that the battlements of the fortress of organized greed were in no immediate danger of crumbling before the assaults of organized labor.[2]

At the 1881 KOL convention, Powderly prevailed, and on January 1, 1882, the Knights of Labor became a public organization.

By modern standards, Powderly's assessment of ritual sounds correct, just as the spectacle of robed men, secret handshakes, and mystical signs appears arcane, even silly. Most historians have sided with Powderly on this issue, if on little else.[3] Few scholars pay much attention to the KOL's secret phase because the Order remained small and relatively powerless. Indeed, if we measure importance by surging membership rolls, won strikes, and influence over social policy, there is little about the early KOL that warrants attention. Nonetheless, to dismiss ritual as psychic babble is to ignore the concrete connections between it and the character and history of the Knights of Labor. Many of the later successes the Order achieved, as well as problems with which it wrestled, came from an organizational style and identity partially forged in its formative years.

If the KOL had a dominant feature, it was its inclusiveness. All manner of races, creeds, and ethnic backgrounds passed through the veils of KOL assembly halls. Alone in this respect among American labor organizations until the twentieth century, the KOL even entertained the idea that unskilled African Americans and women were equals to white craftsmen. Such notions cannot be divorced from the idea of Universal Brotherhood that infused the Order's rituals. Those same rituals shaped the Order's rhetorical style, peppering it with terms such as "honor," "manhood," and "nobility."

2. Powderly, *The Path I Trod*, 48.
3. Historians who have down-played the importance of KOL ritual, or have seen it as detrimental to the Order's development, include Philip Foner, *History of the Labor Movement in the United States*, volume 2: *From the Founding of the American Federation of Labor to the Emergence of American Imperialism* (New York: International Publishers, 1955); Gerald Grob, *Workers and Utopia: A Study of Ideological Conflict in the American Labor Movement 1865–1900* (New York: Quadrangle, 1961); Frederick Sorge, *Labor Movement in the United States: A History of the American Working Class From Colonial Times to 1890*, ed. Philip Foner and Brewster Chamberlin (Westport, Conn.: Greenwood Press, 1977). In fact, few historians give more than passing reference to KOL fraternalism. Notable exceptions include Judith Goldberg, "Strikes, Organizing, and Change"; and Gregory Kealey and Bryan Palmer, *Dreaming of What Might Be: The Knights of Labor in Ontario, 1880–1890* (Toronto: New Hogtown Press, 1987).

Ritual was a key element in what the KOL called "education," as well as in its effort to communicate an understanding of the political economy to members and form the basis by which novices were socialized. Likewise, ritual was connected to many of the KOL's organizational values, as well as to its idiosyncracies. The antipartisan political stance with which members often quarreled was rooted in ritual. So too was a quasi-religiosity that simultaneously gave Knights a sense of righteous superiority and guaranteed repeated clashes with Gilded Age clerics. Ritual defined "Knighthood" as an exalted model of personal behavior that dictated how members related to each other, and how they encountered the outside world. Put directly, ritual behavior was important to Gilded Age workers, fraternal experience bonded diffuse interests, and its mysteries had profound meaning for those who practiced it.

Much of the KOL's organizational history involved ritualism and secrecy. A secret, fraternal model made sense when the KOL was founded; indeed, it may have been the most logical of all choices for organizing. From 1869 through 1878, such a model offered protection for members at a time in which most labor organizations withered, and provided ideals and practices that sustained hope and allowed for modest growth. As the Order expanded, some members began to debate the wisdom of secrecy. That discussion—one that began in earnest in 1877—culminated in the decision in 1881 to make the KOL a public order in 1882.

Once secrecy and ritual were no longer inextricably linked, modification of the ritual became inevitable but not easily accomplished. The period between 1881 and 1890 saw numerous changes to the ritual, many that exacerbated tensions and factionalism among Knights. "Traditionalists," thoroughly inculcated with both the form and ideals of ritual, arose to defend ritual against "modernizers," while a host of malcontents found it a useful tool in building oppositional power coalitions. In the KOL's crucial period of growth, activity, and decline, it was an open question as to whether ritual would serve to unify or divide the Knights; in the end, it did both. Many African Americans, for example, were drawn to the ritual, while it probably hampered the effort to organize women.

The ritual was simplified from 1886 through 1893, timing that coincided with the KOL's apex, steady contraction, and efforts at revitalization. In retrospect, simplification was a spectacular failure that served mainly to rob the ritual of its symbolic power and reduce it to the hollow triteness claimed by its harshest critics. That phase gave way to another beginning around 1893, when the hemorrhaging Order tried to staunch its wounds by returning to the prelapsarian days of the 1870s. In 1895, the Knights of Labor returned to complete secrecy with a complex ritual that it retained for the rest of its days.

In the pages that follow, I intend to take ritual fraternalism and early KOL history seriously, and to demonstrate the connections between ideals and practice. I will also highlight the way in which the KOL never resolved the tensions between private and public cultural pursuits, or those between rhetoric and behavior. Above all, though, I wish to demonstrate that ritual was at the core of KOL identity. It was not some quaint quirk that passed when the leadership torch passed to a Scranton machinist.

Joiners All: The Lure of Ritual

Uriah Stephens (Fig. 1) was a moral man who once longed to be a Baptist minister. Although family poverty led him to the garment trade, Stephens retained a fondness for middle-class refinement. This was much in evidence in his passion for joining. He was a Freemason, an Odd Fellow, and a Knight of Pythias, despite the fact that only the Pythians contained large numbers of working-class men in their ranks.[4]

Many of the KOL's early leaders were similarly disposed to be joiners. Cofounders Robert Keen and Robert Macauley belonged to the Grand Army of the Republic and the Knights of Pythias, respectively. Charles Litchman, who served as Grand/General Secretary from 1878 to 1881, and from 1886 to 1887 belonged to the Pythians, the Masons, the Odd Fellows, the Improved Order of Red Men, the Royal Arcanum, and the Order of the Golden Cross. Powderly himself took membership in the Workingmen's Benevolent Association, the Ancient Order of Hibernians, and the Irish Land League.

The class ambiguities and idiosyncrasies of early KOL leaders are often cited as reasons why the organization was infused with a laborist version of fraternalism. A less discussed, but more important reason, is

---

4. For more on the types of individuals who joined fraternal organizations, see Mark Carnes, *Secret Ritual and Manhood in Victorian America* (New Haven: Yale University Press, 1989); Mary Ann Clawson, *Constructing Brotherhood: Class, Gender, and Fraternalism* (Princeton: Princeton University Press, 1989); Lynn Dumneil, *Freemasonry and American Culture* (Princeton: Princeton University Press, 1984); Barbara Franco, *Fraternally Yours: A Decade of Collecting* (Lexington, Mass.: Museum of Our National Heritage, 1986); Noel P. Gist, "Secret Societies: A Cultural Study of Fraternalism in the United States," *University of Missouri Studies* 15 (1940); Dorothy Ann Lipson, *Freemasonry in Federalist Connecticut* (Princeton: Princeton University Press, 1977).

Fig. 1. Uriah Stephens, founder of the Knights of Labor. Stephens gave the Order its early emphasis on fraternalism. When he resigned as Grand Master Workman in 1879, he was succeeded by Terence V. Powderly, who sought to modernize the Order. Stephens was largely estranged from the Knights when he died in 1882. Powderly Papers, The Catholic University of America.

that Gilded Age fraternal organizations were far more viable than labor unions, especially in 1869 when Stephens sought a way to bind members of the numerically superior working class. In the wake of a nationwide collapse of trade unionism, the ineffectiveness of third-party political activity, and the dominance of free-labor ideology in American society, where was one to turn?[5]

With the exception of the churches, the Gilded Age's most successful voluntary associations were fraternal orders. Deeply rooted in American culture, fraternal orders successfully weathered anti-Masonic attacks in the early nineteenth century and were gaining members precisely when union movements were shrinking.[6] By 1901, there were more than six hundred societies in existence and the Masons had six million members, far outstripping the number of unionized workers. Community studies reveal that cities like Albany, Newark, Philadelphia, and Fall River and Lynn, Massachusetts, were crisscrossed by fraternal networks, as was the entire state of Missouri.[7] Skilled artisans were uncomfortable with

5. For more on conditions in the 1860s and 1870s, see Montgomery, *Beyond Equality*; and Ware, *The Labor Movement in the United States*. The classic study on free labor ideology is Eric Foner, *Free Soil, Free Labor, Free Men: The Ideology of the Republican Party Before the Civil War* (New York: Oxford University Press, 1970).

6. Fraternal organizations were part of the cultural practices that were inherited from Britain and survived the American Revolution. Many of the Founders were Freemasons, and several belonged to other orders as well. Freemasonry came under attack in the early nineteenth century. Much of the controversy centered on the 1826 disappearance of William Morgan, a Masonic apostate who announced his intention to publish an exposé of Masonic rituals. He was widely assumed to have been murdered, and anti-Masonic hysteria—akin to twentieth-century Red scares—swept across North America. Anti-Masonic political parties did well in the 1830s, but by the late 1840s they were a spent force. By the 1850s, fraternal lodges were again proliferating and orders began to recover lost prestige. Die-hard antiritualists survived into the twentieth century. They were vocal and troublesome, but did little to retard the advance of fraternalism. For more on early fraternalism in the United States, see Dumneil, *Freemasonry and American Culture*; Gist, "Secret Societies"; Lipson, *Freemasonry in Federalist Connecticut*; Bobby J. Demott, *Freemasonry in American Culture and Society* (Lanham, Md.: University Press of America, 1986). Most rituals have long since been published. In the nineteenth century, organizations like the National Christian Association published rituals in order to expose fraternal secrets and warn Christians from them. It is now possible to find printed rituals in retail bookshops. For example, see Malcolm Duncan, *Duncan's Ritual of Freemasonry* (New York: Donald McKay, n.d.).

7. See Goldberg, "Strikes, Organizing, and Change"; John T. Cumbler, *Working Class Community in Industrial America: Work, Leisure and Struggle in Two Industrial Cities, 1880–1930* (Westport, Conn.: Greenwood Press, 1979); Hirsch, *Roots of the American Working Class*; David Thelen, *Paths of Resistance: Tradition and Dignity in Industrializing Missouri* (New York: Oxford University Press, 1986); Michael Cassity, "Modernization and Social Crisis: The Knights of Labor in a Midwest Community, 1885–1886," *Journal of American History* 66, no. 2 (February 1979): 41–61.

middle-class Masonry, but began to join the Independent Order of Odd Fellows. By the late 1880s there were 2,253 Odd Fellows lodges.[8]

One reason for the popularity of fraternal orders was a desire to echo trends in England, where chivalric ideals abounded. Most ritualists shared a commitment to perceived chivalric values such as bravery, loyalty, truthfulness, deference, fair play, and consideration for women and social inferiors. Medievalism and antimodernism held powerful sway in America, particularly among those most suspicious of emergent industrial society. Mark Twain snidely noted "an American fondness for absurd chivalry," a trend he lampooned in *A Connecticut Yankee at King Arthur's Court*.[9]

But Twain's criticism underestimates American adaptations, and ignores the conditions that made fraternalism popular in the first place. English Odd Fellows and Masons were quick to note that American rituals were more complex and grandiose than their own.[10] Gilded Age Americans faced changes and challenges they poorly understood. Many spoke of a perceived loss of community and yearned for a romanticized past that they described as a lapsed *gemeinschaft* society. As fraternalism harkened back in time, it did so as a conscious reaction to disturbing modern trends. No class was excluded: Andrew Carnegie had his Scottish castle, the middle class had Freemasonry and workers had the Knights of Labor.

Fraternal orders went to great lengths to construct ritual practices that separated the initiated from the outside world. Lodges were havens

8. Membership figures for fraternal orders are available in standard works such as Arthur Preuss, *A Dictionary of Secret and Other Societies* (St. Louis: B. Herder Book Co., 1924); Albert C. Stevens, *The Cyclopedia of Fraternities* (New York: E. B. Treat, 1907); William J. Whalen, *Handbook of Secret Organizations* (Milwaukee: Bruce Publishing, 1966).

Brian Greenberg's study of seven Albany, N.Y., Odd Fellows lodges reveals typical sentiments held by Gilded Age artisans whose social and economic pretensions are middle class, but whose self-identification is working class. See Brian Greenberg, *Worker and Community: Response to Industrialization in a Nineteenth Century City, Albany, New York, 1850–1884* (Albany: State University of New York Press, 1985). Mary Ann Clawson's work reveals high working-class participation in the Odd Fellows and the Knights of Pythias in four communities: Belleville, Ill.; Buffalo, N.Y.; Lynn, Mass.; and Providence, R.I.; see Clawson, *Constructing Brotherhood*.

9. Mark Girouard, *The Return to Camelot: Chivalry and the English Gentleman* (New Haven: Yale University Press, 1981); T. J. Jackson Lears, *No Place of Grace: Antimodernism and the Transformation of American Culture, 1880–1920* (New York: Pantheon, 1981); John Fraser, *America and the Patterns of Chivalry* (Cambridge: Cambridge University Press, 1982). Mark Twain is quoted in Fraser, *America and the Patterns of Chivalry*, 8.

10. For more on the difference between English and American practices, see Carnes, *Secret Ritual and Manhood*.

where members abandoned worldly competition in the name of Universal Brotherhood. Once inside the lodge, members experienced feelings of fellowship, protection, mutualism, prestige, and self-worth. To safeguard members from external contaminants, fraternal orders typically insisted on secrecy and rigid membership criteria.[11]

Ritual was essential in building psychic community. As one writer put it, "Fellowship was well and good, but men needed something to whet their appetites, to tease their imagination, and to retain their interest. Thus the mysteries were incorporated to hold the attention of all and create a plane of commonality."[12] Ritual created a symbolic social order that embodied utopian notions of the perfect society. The immutability of rituals offered further appeal; they were "never-changing, highly sacred, and infused the order with a sense of formality and stability."[13]

But fraternalism was more than mere antimodernism. It was deeply rooted in Western work cultures. The French custom of *compagnonnage* drew upon an unbroken tradition of ritualized solidarity among journeymen that originated in the medieval guilds. Initiations were secular conversion ceremonies involving birth, life, death, and rebirth metaphors similar to those Powderly experienced. The same practices were widespread in England, and were a colonial import to America.[14] Long before the Knights of Labor, trade unions such as the Knights of St. Crispin (shoemakers), the Knights of St. Joseph (carpenters), the Patriarchal Order of Adam (tailors), and the Grand Accepted Order of Bakers experimented with ritual secrecy. Several KOL cofounders acknowledged the role of the Industrial Brotherhood in shaping KOL ritual, and Stephens probably knew of George Lippard's Brotherhood of the Union, a Philadelphia-based fraternal order that blended Christian socialism, self-improvement, Masonic ritual, and labor reform.[15]

Like Lippard, Stephens put a laborist twist on practices borrowed from the Pythians, the Odd Fellows, and speculative Freemasonry, the latter being the major inspiration. The earliest extant version of ritual is a hand-written document marked "Something to be Done in Secret."

11. Franco, *Fraternally Yours*, 33.

12. Demott, *Freemasonry in American Culture and Society*, 10.

13. Dumneil, *Freemasonry and American Culture*, 24.

14. Cynthia M. Truant, "Solidarity and Symbolism Among Journeymen Artisans: The Case of Compagnonnage," *Comparative Studies in Society and History* 21 (April 1979): 214–26; Clawson, *Constructing Brotherhood*.

15. Sean Wilentz, *Chants Democratic: New York City and the Rise of the American Working Class, 1788–1850* (New York: Oxford University Press, 1984), 368–69. George Lippard was a novelist who specialized in Victorian romances. My speculation that he may have influenced early conceptions of Knighthood is strengthened by the fact that his stories and poems were occasionally reprinted in KOL journals.

All officer titles and ritual elements are recorded in Masonic language with new terms written above them. What was later called the esquire veil, or entrance to the assembly anteroom, was first called the Outer Phylon, and the Esquire himself was a Phylaz. Even incidentals such as raps with one's right hand were coded with terms like "dockamon" and "cheirostones." A local assembly was called an "archeon."[16] Knights, like Masons, referred to their assembly hall as a "temple," placed an open Bible on an "altar," and used an elaborate array of passwords, grips, and signs. Some Masonic lodges were headed by a Grand Master who presided over "noble brothers," while Knights' assemblies were headed by a Master Workman who likewise guided "noble brothers."[17]

The Knights of Labor also borrowed ideological tenets from the Masons. Similarities can be seen most clearly in the Knights' attitudes toward politics and religion, both of which were banned, in theory, from assembly room debate.[18] According to Powderly, Stephens wrote, "Creed, party, and nationality are but the outward garments and present no obstacle to the fusion of the hearts of worshippers of God, the Universal Father, and the workers for men, the Universal Brother."[19]

Though Stephens's faith in the ability of "workers for men" to get beyond politics was more sanguine than the Masonic point of view, in practice, KOL ritual tended to create an antipartisan bias in the Order manifested in the ever-present suspicion that politics diverted one from the true goal of Universal Brotherhood. Although individual Knights—including Stephens and Powderly—ran for political office and campaigned vigorously for other politicans, there was a reluctance to identify the organization with any party, a point of contention for Lassalleans and labor party advocates who later entered the Order. Apoliticism later became an issue that divided local members and national leaders.[20]

16. Document is located in *The Papers of Terence V. Powderly* (Microfilm collection owned by the University of Massachusetts at Amherst; originals housed at Catholic University, Washington, D.C.) [hereafter cited as *PP*].

17. The Knights of Malta called the head of their order "Grand Master Workman." That order was affiliated with Freemasonry.

18. Dumneil, *Freemasonry and American Culture*, 92.

19. Stephens quote in Powderly, *Thirty Years of Labor*, 88.

20. See Foner, *History of the Labor Movement*, vol. 2. The KOL's disdain for politics was not merely a Masonic import. Several historians have located a profound distrust of politics within the American working class that dates from the days of the early republic (see Wilentz, *Chants Democratic*). Within the KOL, the antipolitics bias even extended through the Great Upheaval, during which time independent labor parties and KOL campaign slates won elections. See Fink, *Workingmen's Democracy*. It was not until the 1890s that the Order—largely due to pressures from its left wing—endorsed political action and third parties such as the New York state People's Party and, later, the Populists.

These facts should remind us to be careful before denouncing the KOL's stance on

The KOL was infused with moralism and religiosity, which were likewise borrowed from Freemasonry and enshrined in ritual. Both the Freemasons and the Knights made overt use of generic, yet high-toned, religious language. Uriah Stephens's invocation of the Universal Father watching over Universal Brothers is reminiscent of the Masonic slogan of "no creed but the fatherhood of God and the brotherhood of man."[21] Each group used courts to expel members whose behavior was found to be "unmasonic" or "unknightly." The KOL demanded a code of personal behavior that often seemed far removed from a practical labor agenda, but such expectations were in accord with a "noble and holy" fraternal order.

Ideals abounded for Knights who waded through the cumbersome ritual found in a booklet known as the *Adelphon Kruptos (AK)*, or Secret Brotherhood. The *AK* was not printed for internal use until sometime after 1872, and only a few copies circulated until 1879. Barring written instructions, a member from the original branch, Local Assembly 1 (Philadelphia), was dispatched to organize assemblies, or a prospective assembly was attached to an existing one with the status of "sojourner" until officers memorized the ritual. Since leaders insisted on strict adherence to the ritual, organization was laborious until the *AK* was printed. Such attention to secrecy and form led some observers to see the KOL as a fraternal order first and a labor organization second.[22]

Contemporary observers agreed on the importance of early KOL fra-

---

politics as hypocritical. It is true that its platform contained goals that could only be achieved through political action. Here one must distinguish between nonpartisanship and apoliticism. Most KOL leaders were careful to separate their political activities from the Order, even when they felt strongly about a candidate or cause. Stephens resigned as Master Workman when he ran for U.S. Congress; Charles Litchman quit as General Secretary when he went to work on Benjamin Harrison's campaign staff. That aside, leaders saw no contradiction in participating in the democratic process. In fact, they felt that the exercise of one's vote was the hallmark of a true patriot. The Knights of Labor frequently endorsed candidates and policies, but tried to avoid party affiliation. In many ways, the KOL's policies mirrored the AFL's strategy of rewarding one's friends and punishing one's enemies.

As in all things, one should also separate national policy from local and district practices. Stephens and Powderly might insist on nonpartisanship, but local Knights often disagreed. As Leon Fink, Richard Oestreicher, and others have shown, Knights were very active in state and local politics. Many of them ignored nonpartisan policies and immersed themselves with enthusiasm in partisan battles. Of all those elements of Freemasonry borrowed by the KOL, the rhetoric of being above politics may have been the most naive. Gilded Age political participation was one of the most active in American history and was as much a cultural as a political expression.

21. Dumneil, *Freemasonry and American Culture*, 49; Powderly, *Thirty Years of Labor*, 88.

22. Stevens, *Cyclopedia of Fraternities*; Preuss, *A Dictionary of Secret and Other Societies*. Neither Stevens nor Preuss pays much attention to the KOL's political and social agita-

ternalism. Carroll Wright noted that the Knights drew on Masonic and Odd Fellow rituals in order to broaden the movement and "to harmonize all individual and separate interests in the interest of the whole."[23] In George McNeill's *The Labor Movement: The Problem of Today* (1887), Uriah Stephens is liberally quoted and his ideal of a "brotherhood of toil" is an organizing theme of the book.[24]

Secrecy and ritual clearly attracted some workers to the Knights. An 1875 *National Labor Tribune* enthusiastically observed the movement of the veiled Order into Pittsburgh and trumpeted:

> We have noticed from time to time the growth of one of the most powerful of these [secret] orders. . . . Its numbers and the harmony and unity produced entitle it to our attention. . . . In it all are heard, respected, and benefited. . . . If there is a spark of manhood in a man this order will kindle it into a flame of general warmth for all who toil. . . . Its objects are *noble* and *holy*. The Order is moving Westward. . . . To such we say enter the *holy of holies* and know all.[25]

The words "noble" and "holy" were emphasized and the flavor of the entire piece is one of mysticism and high drama. Several weeks later the same paper noted:

> The name of the order is not divulged, nor is anyone allowed to tell the name of anyone belonging to it. The obligation is strong and binding. . . . It brings men together as brothers, and requires no laws to make them observe their vows. . . . It is labor's coming

---

tions. Although this is understandable, given the nature of their collections, it is also a measure of the pervasiveness of the KOL's ritual practices.

23. Carroll Wright, "An Historical Sketch of the Knights of Labor," *Quarterly Journal of Economics* 1 (January 1887): 137–38.

24. George McNeill, *The Labor Movement: The Problem of Today* (New York: Augustus M. Kelley, 1887). Stephens figures more prominently than Powderly in much of McNeill's book. McNeill was something of a romantic and clearly attracted to the KOL's ritual. He and Powderly soon parted company over trade unionism, but before that they clashed over the release of McNeill's book, which McNeill claimed was endorsed by the KOL and that Powderly insisted was not. Powderly's motives for this were petty: his own book, *Thirty Years of Labor*, was delayed and thus McNeill beat him to the press. Given Powderly's legendary egoism, it is certainly feasible that he was also upset by the positive interpretation of Stephens and ritualism that appeared in McNeill's book. Powderly had long repudiated Stephens-style ritualism, and he was likely vain enough to interpret McNeill's slant as back-handed criticism.

25. *National Labor Tribune* (Pittsburgh, Pa.), April 24, 1875.

salvation . . . the door is open to all good men, and they are welcomed as brothers of toilers, who are making the elevation of Labor their religion.[26]

Here *Tribune* editor John M. Davis evokes the language of evangelical Protestantism. Davis was an early Knights' convert, having been initiated into a Philadelphia cigarmakers' local in 1874. He returned to Pittsburgh in 1875 to organize the city's iron molders into a KOL local. By 1879, the *Tribune* was an official organ for the Order, referred to in print as the *****.[27] Although Davis lost his zeal for the Knights through personal disputes with Powderly and anger over the establishment of a competing journal, he remained true to his perceptions of Knightly brotherhood; he did not mention the KOL by name or criticize it until well into the 1880s. Such was the power of KOL ritual.

The Psychic Universe of Knighthood

Before the KOL became an open order in 1882, Knighthood was as much psychic as material, and the Order's identity was shaped in the mind as much as the workplace. Ritual integrated once liminal individuals into a body knit together by character, honor, and mutuality. The lodge was a place where one could hobnob with like-minded men and learn from them, fusing socializing and socialization functions. It was a safe harbor shielded from one's enemies, one in which mutualism and cooperation could flourish. Further, although roles were collectively acted out, personal identity was strengthened. Steadfast men like John Davis felt the power of the fraternal ideal developed by the Knights, one in which knighthood, brotherhood, secrecy, and manhood converged.

Every aspect of KOL ritual was imbued with meaning, including the very choice of the Order's name. The KOL summoned forth a golden past embodied by the valiant medieval knight of legend. But the image underwent updating that cast off much of the association with caste and military service in favor of merit, honor, and reputation. A Brooklyn Knight explained that the term "knight" derived from the Celtic *gnoacht*, meaning "hand-worker." He waxed philosophic about the significance

---

26. *Ibid.*, June 19, 1875.

27. Since it was forbidden to use the name of the Order in public, written references used five stars or asterisks. Each one stands for an upper-case word in the title, Noble and Holy Order of the Knights of Labor.

of the "hand," a symbol of work as well as fighting.[28] The KOL shared the term "knight" with sixty-six other organizations; countless others conferred degrees of knighthood.[29]

W. L. Tisdale's *The Knights' Book* (1886) linked the Knights of Labor to the historical sweep of knighthood (Fig. 2). A biographical sketch of Powderly, an overview of KOL history, and reflections on social questions were juxtaposed with the poetry of Thomas Hood and Sir Thomas More. In a burst of dubious historical accuracy, Tisdale traced an "unbroken" chivalric tradition from Hugh Capet (998) through the Knights of Labor. He stressed that all orders of knights were "champions of

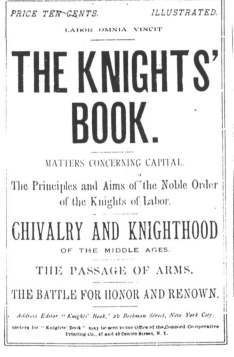

Fig. 2.   Cover page of *The Knight's Book*. In the early days of the KOL, meetings involved pageantry worthy of a medieval knight. This book attempted to place the KOL within an unbroken chivalric tradition.

28. *JUL*, June 1880; Carnes, *Secret Ritual and Manhood*, 22.

29. Frances Gies, *The Knight in History* (New York: Harper & Row, 1984). See also Girouard, *The Return to Camelot*; Lears, *No Place of Grace*; Fraser, *America and the Patterns of Chivalry*.

Christianity," and compared the persecution of Powderly to that of Christ![30]

In the early days, meetings involved pageantry worthy of a medieval knight. The meeting hall was divided into two rooms, an anteroom whose outside door was called the Outer Veil and an inner Sanctuary that lay beyond a second door, the Inner Veil. Members knew a meeting was about to commence when a globe was placed outside the Outer Veil and a closed copy of Scripture appeared on a triangular altar that was flanked by a red basket filled with blank cards. When the assembly was in session, a lance was placed outside the Inner Veil. In addition to its obvious association with medieval knighthood, the lance had several commonly understood folkloric meanings, including the ability to distinguish right from wrong, and as a symbol of honor and martial readiness. It also reminded Christian Knights of Christ's crucifixion.

Before the session began, officers delivered a series of symbolic raps. A Knight entered the Sanctuary after writing his full name on a card and passing it through the Inner Veil to the "Worthy Inspector." He entered to a precise arrangement of officers bearing exotic titles and wearing specialized insignia, answered a prescribed set of questions, and exchanged the correct passwords, hand grips, and signals. The Master Workman opened the meeting by announcing:

> In the beginning the great Architect founded the Universe;
> The governing principle of which is Immutable Justice.
> In its Beautiful proportions is displayed Omniscient Wisdom;
> And sealed His work with the signet of Everlasting Truth;
> Teaching that everything of value, or merit, is the result of
>   creative Industry;
> And the cooperation of its harmonious parts evermore
>   inculcates perfect Economy.[31]

The officers formed an arch—in time, a circle—and listened to mystical discourses, eyes diverted to a square altar where an opened copy of Scripture lay. After music, a series of raps preceded various pledges and

---

30. W. L. Tisdale, *The Knights' Book*, 37–38, in *PP.*

31. Handwritten work located in *PP;* undated *Adelphon Kruptos* (circa 1874), in *PP.* After 1872, some of the more obvious Masonic references were dropped. Instead of appeals to a deistic "great Architect," a more specific Judeo-Christian God appears and the Master Workman's shorter speech exhorted, "Behold how good and how pleasant it is for brethren to dwell together in unity. It is like precious ointment upon the head, as the dew of Mt. Hermon, and as the dew that descended upon the mountains of Zion, for there the Lord commanded the blessing, even life forevermore." *AK* in *PP.*

statements of duties for officers and members. Then came a final appeal to the "Supreme Master of the Universe." All of this took place before any business was transacted. If there were to be initiations, another set of elaborate ceremonies ensued. Ending an evening entailed ceremony as well. After the Worthy Inspector secreted away all books and assembly property, and the Master Workman gave "a few well-chosen remarks," three raps were given and everyone formed a circle around the altar to "assume the attitude of devotion" while a designate addressed "the Deity."[32]

As Samuel Gompers discovered, the recruitment and initiation of new members was an act of high drama. He entered the Knights in 1873, when he was working at David Hirsch and Company in New York City.[33] A shoemaker from an adjoining factory took Gompers to a darkened room where he was questioned and swore several oaths. He was then taken to an assembly meeting for the initiation ceremony. (He was not allowed to witness the opening ceremony because he was not yet a member.) After more questions, he listened to several speeches on the nobility of labor, the evils of wage slavery, monopoly, and accumulation.[34] Several more oaths were sworn before Gompers retired to the anteroom while a vote was taken. Once accepted, the Venerable Sage taught Gompers the secret signs, grips, passwords, and ritual answers he needed to function as a Knight. He was also given his Knights of Labor number, which was written into the roll book by the Worthy Inspector.[35]

For any candidate who weathered the test, KOL initiation was a mysti-

32. Handwritten work, in *PP.*

33. Samuel Gompers, *Seventy Years of Life and Labor: An Autobiography*, ed. Nick Salvatore (Ithaca, N.Y.: ILR Press, 1984), 27.

34. Candidates were asked three questions. The first was whether or not they believed in God, "the Universal Father of all"; the second, whether or not they would "obey the Universal Ordinance of God in gaining your bread by the sweat of your brow"; and the third, whether or not they were willing "to take a solemn vow binding you to secrecy, obedience and mutual assistance." It should be noted that the initiation speeches were not the same as those given during a regular meeting. Initiation speeches consisted largely of sermonlike overviews of capital/labor relations whereas those of the regular meeting were more fraternal.

35. Experience extrapolated from Powderly, *The Path I Trod*, and the *AK.* True to form, there was a formula for assigning membership numbers. The following numbers were added: the month of the year in which initiation took place, the day of the month, the year of the initiation, the initiate's age at his next birthday, and the year in which he was born. That total was divided by the number of the DA in which his local was located. The number was rounded, and then entered. Apparently not all Worthy Inspectors were adroit at math, since one *AK* advises that once entered on the rolls the number "stands whether right or wrong."

cal experience of symbolic death and rebirth. The "resurrected" candidate came to see the sanctuary veils as psychic barriers between noble toilers and greedy monopolists, the dividing line between a sacred realm and a profane one. Pledges of assistance, honesty, and personal integrity taught initiates that brotherhood transcended goal-directed expediency. They were exhorted to "glorify God" in the execution of their work as they had "been selected from among [their] fellows for that exalted purpose." The ceremony let the initiate know "that something more was expected of him than to allow others to do his future thinking for him."[36]

The candidate also learned that his lodge was literally a "sanctuary," a place of shelter, refuge, and protection. The KOL saw the world as the arena in which the forces of light battled those of darkness; its sanctuaries offered safe harbors from the oppression that raged outside. Because the Sanctuary had to be guarded from that outside world, the portals were not mere doors, but "veils" that concealed the mysteries of their "noble and holy" Order from undeserving eyes.[37]

Knights outside the Sanctuary required passwords and signs to identify brothers from potential enemies. If one placed the two index fingers of the left hand on the inside of the right sleeve with the thumb on the outside and received the Sign of Recognition (the right hand drawn across the forehead from left to right), one was in the safe presence of a brother. Should one need to alert a brother of distress, one needed only to draw the right index and forefinger across the brow from left to right. If these did not suffice, one could always rely on an elaborate series of passwords developed by local, district, and general executive boards.[38]

36. Powderly, *The Path I Trod*, 50, 56. Victor Turner describes another dimension of the death to resurrection and rebirth ritual. In his paradigm, individuals move through three phases—separation, liminality, and aggregation—in which a person is divorced from his culture, social group, or normative system to such a degree that he perceives himself a radical outsider. At that juncture he is brought into a new normative group through the process of aggregation. See Victor Turner, *The Ritual Process: Structure and Anti-Structure* (Ithaca: Cornell University Press, 1969).

37. Powderly, *The Path I Trod*, 431.

38. Passwords were used throughout the life of the Order and were often passed on in cipher code if communicated through the mail. In *PP*, see Powderly to Charles Litchman, November 22, 1880, for an example of a typical annual password; Powderly to Frederick Turner, December 6, 1883, for the password for local assemblies under the General Assembly; and Powderly to Turner, June 17, 1884, for a typical General Assembly password. It is interesting to note that in 1892–93, when Powderly was not on speaking terms with Secretary-Treasurer John Hayes, the two did correspond cordially on matters concerning passwords. See also Powderly, *The Path I Trod*, 65. These signs were taken quite seriously. Several of Powderly's opponents tried to challenge his authority at the 1884 General Assembly by asserting that he did not know the ritual or the signs of the Order. In secret session he was quizzed, and Powderly so "dumbfounded" his inquisitors with his "mas-

For the most part, the KOL did not confer degrees like other fraternal orders; its one flirtation with degrees came back to trouble the Order.[39] Central to much of the KOL's imagery was the "philosopher's stone," the legendary rock that turned dross to gold, but which was interpreted by the KOL to mean the ability of labor to create wealth.[40] In 1878, Uriah Stephens created the Philosopher's Stone degree to honor Knights with long or distinguished service to the Order. He conferred it upon Powderly and eleven others. The Knights abandoned the conferring of degrees before 1880, but the Philosopher's Stone degree remained in the minds of many. Periodic clamors to reinstitute degrees were heard, especially after the Order began to decline. Powderly claimed to have little use for such flights into ritual symbolism, but he fought bitterly with John Hayes to retain the instructions for the degree and was eventually expelled for refusing to turn them over.

Why did men construct such elaborate rituals to reinforce common bonds that ought to have been obvious? Why did John Davis and Samuel Gompers remain steadfast to their vows long after they broke with the KOL? For Gompers, his devotion to secrecy was a point of pride: "I am unwilling to give the nature of the obligation . . . for since I assumed [it] . . . I have never violated it."[41] And why would Terence Powderly, the architect of KOL modernization, fight to hang on to archaic degree order secrets? More was afoot than the desire for costumed drama, the sacredness of one's word, or the pettiness of one man seeking to make life difficult for his enemies. Ritual content was serious—even sacred—to those who experienced it. In short, KOL ritual taught values.

A central value was that of brotherhood. Many nineteenth-century fraternal orders glorified preindustrial values and celebrated collectivism over individualism.[42] Most Knights of Labor were not deeply antimodernist, but they did question the practices and values associated with industrial capitalism. In a speech on the "ideal organization," Stephens demonstrated how brotherly ties could purge modernization of its more pernicious elements:

---

tery of the mysteries" that a motion ensued to canonize Powderly's revelations. The subsequent issuance of a secret circular, "Explanation of the Signs and Symbols of the Order," led to a brief resurgence of ritualism.

39. Gist, "Secret Societies." Stratification is common to fraternities. Freemasons offer thirty-three degrees, the Odd Fellows and the Grange seven each, the Owls and the Knights of Columbus four each, and the Knights of Pythias three.

40. The symbolism of the Philosopher's Stone emblem is explained by Powderly in an appendix to his *The Path I Trod*.

41. Gompers, *Seventy Years of Life and Labor*, 27.

42. For more on the question of whether or not nineteenth-century fraternalism challenged capitalism, see Carnes, *Secret Ritual and Manhood*, 31–33.

> This fraternity [has the job] of knitting up into a compact and homogeneous amalgamation all the workers in one universal brotherhood, guided by the same rules, working by the same methods, practising [*sic*] the same forms for accomplishing the same ends. It builds upon the immutable basis of the Fatherhood of God and the logical principle of the Brotherhood of man. . . . it calls for an end to wage slavery and the elimination of the great anti-Christ of civilization manifest in the idolatry of wealth and the consequent degradation and social ostracism of all else not possessing it.[43]

Brotherhood, as Stephens understood it, had a universal component: all one's fellows were linked. But it also retained more circumscribed meanings such as comraderie, fellowship, and shared social status.

Closely linked to brotherhood and Knighthood was the idea of "manhood." In the Gilded Age, the concept was understood broadly. Patriarchy remained the social ideal for men of all classes, but manhood also implied certain gender-neutral qualities no longer associated with the term. It was a close synonym for "reputation" or "character," and allied to the chivalric ideal of the sacredness of one's word.[44] When Davis and Gompers took a secrecy vow when initiated into the Order, they put their manhood on the line. They further promised to obey the dictates of the Order, to aid one another, and to assist the less fortunate. All of this is a logical outgrowth of the chivalric ideal, but it also steeped in mutual responsibility and personal accountability. A manly Knight upheld and renewed his community. A correspondent to the *Journal of United Labor* declared that one who neglected to do so was "not living up to his pledge of Knighthood."[45]

In a world where a man's word was his bond, Knights took promises seriously. Joseph R. Buchanan related an incident that occurred during a railway strike. During a meeting with Denver business leaders, Phillip Trainstine charged that no deals could be struck since Buchanan was untrustworthy. An indignant Buchanan roared, "Did you ever know me to commit a dishonest or unmanly act?" To which Trainstine humbly confessed, "I never did."[46]

---

43. *JUL*, June, 1880.

44. For more on the overt masculinity embedded within nineteenth-century fraternalism, see Carnes, *Secret Ritual and Manhood;* and Clawson, *Constructing Brotherhood.* For a superb discussion of the concept of nineteenth-century manhood, see Nick Salvatore, *Eugene V. Debs: Citizen and Socialist* (Urbana: University of Illinois Press, 1982).

45. *JUL*, April 14, 1888.

46. Joseph R. Buchanan, *The Story of a Labor Agitator* (Freeport, N.Y.: Books for Libraries, 1971), 209.

Knights showed little tolerance for those who violated notions of manhood. In 1883, coal magnate William Wyatt complained to Grand Secretary Robert D. Layton that his 250 "men" were being bombarded with KOL pamphlets, but wanted no part of the organization. In a withering reply, Layton charged:

> Your claim to employ two hundred and fifty *men* is a bald lie. They are not men, only like yourself, THINGS, as no *man*, in the sense of a man, would permit another to dictate to him whether or not he would or would not join, or refuse to join any organization or society, and nothing but a *brute* void of the commonest instincts of a man would think of interfering in the equal rights of others. Your invitation to visit you is hereby declined. I refuse to associate with a hog.[47]

Layton's ringing indictment sums up the Order's view of manhood: men should be a moral free agents who put individual talents to work for the common good.[48]

KOL ritual reinforced values like freedom of conscience, friendship, harmony, independence, and manliness. Secrecy, obedience, and mutual assistance (S.O.M.A.) constituted the discipline necessary to bring free men into a just society and were codified in the shorthand "rule of S.O.M.A.," with which each member was familiar. The cement of the code was religion, and the entire quest of the "noble and holy order" was enveloped in sacredness.

Uriah Stephens understood brotherhood as a religious ideal, one consonant with his ministerial ambitions. The Brotherhood of Man extended logically from the Fatherhood of God, and the Antichrist took the form of "the idolatry of wealth." When one took an oath of Knighthood, it was sworn before God, as well as to one's future comrades. KOL religious practice was distinct by design from that of middle-class America. Some have argued that fraternal religious practices were patriarchal in reaction to a perceived feminization of Gilded Age religion.[49] Though there is truth in this, class also played an important role in the way the KOL used religious imagery.

47. Layton's letter reprinted in *JUL*, March 15, 1883. Emphasis in original.

48. The KOL did not invent the concept of moral free agency. Such ideas flooded America during the Second Great Awakening and remained part of the social discourse. Once appropriated, however, the KOL applied it with impunity against its "unmanly" enemies.

49. For more on the process by which Gilded Age fraternal orders created male religious practices in reaction to feminized mainstream religion, see Carnes, *Secret Ritual and Manhood*, 59.

The oppositional nature of ritual metaphors led to clashes with Gilded Age churches, especially the Roman Catholic Church. For some clerics, the swearing of oaths stamped the KOL as a quasi-religious body designed to compete for the hearts and souls of the working class.[50] In the original oath, members swore a "covenant" with God.[51] The language changed after 1874, and later initiates took a "pledge" to obey "laws, regulations, and solemn injunctions" of the Order, promised to help brothers in distress, and vowed never to reveal "by word, act, art, or implication" any of the "signs, mysteries, arts, privileges, or benefits . . . except in a legal, and authorized manner." Later, Thomas Crowne and Terence Powderly convinced the Order to add the codicil phrase "except to my Religious Confessor at the Confessional" to the pledge in an attempt to blunt Catholic Church criticism of the Knights.[52]

Codicils notwithstanding, the free mix of Masonic and Christian images in KOL ritual imbued both early Knighthood and its quest with sacredness. The piety of Uriah Stephens dominated the language of the Order until Powderly toned it down. Even then, few moments passed without reference to the Deity; the work of the Order was seen as "holy," and the Sanctuary was referred to as "the holy of holies." Any attempt at secularization raised hackles. In 1882, Robert Lind complained that the removal of religious language "work[ed] injury to our N. & H.O. [Noble and Holy Order]." He argued that the "N. & H.O. is more than a mere protective labor society. Its founders had a social, industrial, and moral mission . . . which is lost sight of in some of the changes made." Lind lamented "shutting out of sight man's responsibility to a Supreme Being and Creator. And oh how much sweeter and ennobling was the old phrase 'Universal Brotherhood' to even that of 'Universal Organization.' "[53]

The ritual Lind lamented still had plenty of religious references. Even after streamlining the ritual, Knights continued to call their assembly halls "sanctuaries" rather than "lodges," and to view articles such as the symbols of the Order, the local assembly charter, and the *AK* as so many sacred relics. No amount of tampering on Powderly's behalf could erase the fervor with which some Knights held those symbols, or the religiosity with which they embraced the mysteries that unfolded inside the "holiest of holies."

50. For more on the Catholic Church's opposition to KOL ritual, see Henry Browne, "The Catholic Church and the Knights of Labor" (Ph.D. diss., Catholic University, Washington, D.C., 1949).
51. Handwritten work, in *PP.*
52. *AK* (circa 1873), in *PP*; Powderly, *The Path I Trod.*
53. *JUL*, April 1882.

The Knights Bury Their Founder

Aside from minor adjustments in terms used in the *Adelphon Kruptos,* and the proviso allowing members to confide with religious confessors, the 1870s saw few changes to Stephens's original handwritten ritual. Discussions to abandon secrecy were even more rare. It was assumed that the current state of capital/labor relations made it unwise for union members to reveal themselves. All of this began to change after Knights gathered for their first Grand (later General) Assembly in 1878, and the pace accelerated when Powderly succeeded Stephens as Grand Master Workman in 1879. By 1882, Uriah Stephens was dead; in his final days he was estranged from the organization he helped create.

But Stephens's vision was not buried with his corpse. Even as Powderly sought to modernize the Order, many Knights castigated him as the subverter of Stephens's ideals. When Powderly assumed control of the KOL, he was the sitting mayor of Scranton, Pennsylvania, an area on the fringe of Molly Maguire agitations. As a Catholic, Powderly took heat from local clerics and was anxious to disassociate the Knights from the Mollies.[54] He admitted, "Everything in the shape of a society, which was at all secret or new, was supposed to be the outcome of Molly Maguireism."[55]

Unfortunately for Powderly, few aspects of KOL ritual were taken as seriously as the secrecy vow. When he raised the issue at the 1878 Reading convention he gained only a small victory: district and local assemblies were allowed to consider public operations. Efforts to do more were thwarted when delegate John Langdon of Ohio was seen "in suspicious intimacy" with a reporter from the Reading *Daily Eagle.* It was feared "that the object of the convention, as well as the name of the Order, had been divulged and made public." Though it turned out that Langdon was too drunk to reveal anything of consequence, he was expelled from the Order and the GA dropped the secrecy debate.[56]

By the 1879 St. Louis convention, only Schuylkill County, Pennsylvania, coal miners had voted to abandon secrecy, and General Secretary

54. For more on Powderly and the Catholic Church, see Browne, "The Catholic Church and the Knights of Labor"; Powderly, *The Path I Trod,* chap. 27.

55. Powderly, *The Path I Trod,* 133. To be fair to Powderly, several locals breached the issue of becoming public before he raised the issue. These assemblies included LA 82 in Brooklyn, and a splinter group within Stephens's own LA 1 in Philadelphia.

56. 1878 *Proceedings of the Knights of Labor Grand Assembly* (Reading, Pa.), in *PP; Daily Eagle* (Reading, Pa.), January 4, 1878, in *PP.* The article that finally surfaced in the *Daily Eagle* was harmless. There was one unattributed quote about how the men assembled in Reading were not Molly Maguires, although they did operate in secrecy.

Charles Litchman opined that most members opposed a public Order. When Powderly and Dominick Hammer (DA 7, Akron) renewed proposals for a public order, the debate degenerated into arguments over whether Scripture references should be expunged from the *AK*. The delegates decided to retain the Order's secrecy except "in private consultations with the clergy for the good of the Order," a practice already in place. Powderly's only sop was the GAs agreement to abandon degree work.[57]

Powderly's own DA 16 (Scranton/Wilkes-Barre) went public, but subsequent conventions continued to dodge the issue.[58] Nonetheless, the die was cast at the Chicago session (September 2–6, 1879) when Stephens resigned as Grand Master Workman and Powderly succeeded him. As more locals went public, hot debate raged in Knight ranks. Cofounder James L. Wright complained, "the good old way . . . worked well and in my opinion should never be changed."[59] More troubling was a note to Powderly from Stephens: "I have many misgivings in relation to their having taken an open and public stand. . . . They will have a hard road to travel on account of this and the enormous dead weight of ignorance they will have to carry so publicly."[60]

Stephens's misgivings guaranteed passionate debate over the issue of secrecy, with the *JUL* serving as a sounding board for both sides. On June 15, 1880, an editorial headlined "Name of the Order" warned that

> in districts where the name has been made public, the leaders have been singled out, blacklisted, and victimized, and the Order consequently made to suffer. But the worst feature has been that new Locals, hardly within the Order, have rushed with unseemly haste, even before they comprehend . . . its objects or principles, to vote to make the name public. We cannot but feel this is a great mistake.[61]

Exactly one year later, readers were informed that Detroit Grand Assembly would rule on secrecy. Seven arguments for going public were juxta-

57. 1879 *Proceedings of the Knights of Labor Grand Assembly* (St. Louis, Mo.), in *PP.* The reason that those Schuylkill County coal miners affiliated with District 20 were the first Knights to go public can be explained by the fact that their county was the center of alleged Molly Maguire activity. All secret societies were under tremendous pressure there, including that exerted by the Catholic Church. Many of the Irish miners of the district were Catholics.

58. *Proceedings of District Assembly 16* (Scranton, Pa.), March 28, 1879, in *PP.*

59. James L. Wright to Powderly, September 19, 1879, in *PP.* Powderly furiously scrawled "BAH" atop Wright's letter and filed it without dictating an answer.

60. Uriah Stephens to Powderly, May 10, 1880, in *PP.*

61. *JUL*, June 1880. The *Journal of United Labor* began publication in 1880.

posed to three against.[62] Attempts to stack the debate failed to blunt opposition. A writer calling himself "Cyclops" challenged the Order to guarantee "that I will not be thrown out of employ, as soon as the sneak thief who now steals my labor finds out I am engaged in assisting to destroy the present system of robbery and starvation upon which he thrives."[63]

Powderly prevailed when delegates voted 28 to 6 to make the Order public beginning January 1, 1882. After the appointment of a committee to revise the *AK*, Theodore Cuno of LA 1562 (Brooklyn) introduced an unsuccessful resolution to cut off the Grand Master Workman's salary. Local Assembly 1562 unilaterally ignored the secrecy decision, remaining a secret, oath-bound local for most of its life, and a constant thorn in Powderly's side.[64]

Cuno's legal brief against Powderly was grounded more in political differences than love for ritual, but his rebellion energized those who opposed the changes on principle. Leading the way was Uriah Stephens, his shabby treatment at the hands of the Order's new leaders casting him as a martyr for others to exploit. Stephens voiced displeasure at the decision by demanding that his own name be removed from the Executive Board before the proceedings were published. To Powderly he wrote:

> The Order has drifted so far away from the primary landmarks, has so completely changed from the original that a strong feeling begins to manifest itself in my L.A. to sever its connection with the organization. In this feeling I also coincide.[65]

In response, Stephens became an object of ridicule for Powderly and Grand Secretary Robert Layton. Layton sneered that the old work "is about as foolish as though we were all ministers and wanted to start a little camp meeting." He sarcastically remarked, "Brother Stephens *is* perfection, *was* perfection, and *always* will *continue* to be perfection through all time." Several weeks later he complained, "I don't think it is fair [that] for years I have stood by the organization as faithfully as he, and yet I was opposed to the oath. Now that it has changed he should do the same until it has had a fair test. . . . I don't think it is manly for Brother Stephens to try to create a revolt."[66]

62. Ibid., June 1881.
63. Ibid., August 1881.
64. 1881 Proceedings of the Knights of Labor Grand Assembly (Detroit), in *PP.*
65. Stephens to Powderly, October 22, 1881, in *PP.*
66. Robert Layton to Powderly, October 28, 1881, in *PP*; Layton to Powderly, November 18, 1881 and November 24, 1881, in *PP.*

It was left to Powderly to spill the darkest bile. In letters to Layton and Worthy Foreman Richard Griffiths, he wrote:

> Bah, the old man is in his dotage. We'll get him a slice of the catacombs, one of the pyramids of Egypt, one of the Cyclops famous in mythology, the bones of Zephna Penoneah. . . . If we could thus revel in the mysterious and marvelous, to say nothing of the *spiritualistic* and still more *individualistic* . . . we would introduce a form of ceremony that would come up to the old man's conception of the proper thing. But the real question is "Shall labor have its rights?" That and not the tomfoolery of the past is what we must consider and while I respect Brother Stephens, if he insists on making a fool of himself he'll do it outside the Order for I won't trifle with him much longer.[67]

At the end of 1881, Layton was still grumbling over the founder's views: "As I understand Stephens . . . religion consists of parading your views and thrusting them down the throat of every man he [sic] meets at the outer vail [sic]. . . . It will never occur to him that his *name* is not in the A.K."[68] Stephens's role in the debate ended with his death on February 13, 1882. By then, his estrangement from the KOL was complete. Powderly only learned about the founder's passing two days after the funeral; no KOL officer attended the rites.[69]

In death, Uriah Stephens became a symbol for schemes and ambitions by both Powderly and his opponents. He was invoked in reverential terms, and while votes were taken to build a monument to his honor, none was ever built. Years later, the last trace of Stephens was expunged when John Hayes unceremoniously fired Stephens's daughter Mary from her post at general headquarters. But many Knights remembered Stephens and held Powderly responsible for his mistreatment. One was cofounder James L. Wright, who became a harsh Powderly critic. Revenge was exacted in 1893 when Wright stood at the fore of the group that removed Powderly from office.

Ritual and New Knights

On January 1, 1882, the Knights of Labor became a public organization. In theory, debates over ritual secrecy were a thing of the past; reality was

---

67. Powderly to Richard Griffiths, November 24, 1881, in *PP*; Powderly to Layton, November 24, 1881, in *PP*. Emphasis in original. In another letter he added that James L. Wright was similarly disposed to make the assembly a "spiritualistic medium," though it was more "ridicualistic" than spiritualistic.
68. Layton to Powderly, December 6, 1881, in *PP*.
69. Gilbert Rockwood to Powderly, February 16, 1882, in *PP*.

quite a different matter. Modernization generated little passion, though nonfraternal bickering ran rampant. In his zeal to reform, Powderly soon learned that the ritual that once united Knights could be divisive in the hands of those administration opponents who were willing to evoke Stephens's memory. Compounding the tension was a larger, more diverse membership infused once the veils were lifted. Most troublesome was what to do with political radicals, African Americans, and women, whose position on ritual could be characterized variously as utilitarian, enthusiastic, and indifferent. Far from being resolved in 1882, the issue of ritual came to solidify or fragment the Order, depending on whose hands were on the *AK*.

There was little ideological unity among the Order's assorted Marxists, Lassalleans, anarchists, syndicalists, and free thinkers, who frequently found common cause in their opposition to Powderly. Most troublesome of all was the unlikely alliance of Marxists, Lassalleans, anarchists, and ritualists, who led New York City's powerful DA 49. In their fight against Powderly, they found ritual to be a useful tool.

District Assembly 49 was organized on July 1, 1882. By then, New York City and Brooklyn were awash with Powderly opponents. Local Assembly 1562 continued to operate under the old *AK* and was led by William Horan, a Stephens fundamentalist who thought the founder's works sacrosanct. Others using the old ritual included John Caville, the Knights' auditor, and Theodore Cuno, its statistician. Their refusal to abide by GA mandates constituted a direct and visible challenge to constituted authority.

More serious was Cuno's involvement in an ill-fated boycott of the Duryea Starch Company of Glen Cove, New York. Even though the KOL's own investigation exonerated Duryea, the ideologues of newly founded DA 49 — who viewed the boycott as a blow against capitalism — backed Cuno.[70] Cuno was suspended, but matters lay unresolved going into the 1882 convention. Before Cuno's fate could even be discussed, Horan, James Quinn of DA 49, and John Eliot of Baltimore each introduced resolutions to readopt the old *AK*, and to rescind the order making the KOL public. These challenges were swept aside, while Caville, Cuno, Horan, and three others were expelled over the Duryea boycott.[71]

Angry DA 49 officials began to hatch schemes to take control of the Knights. Plots coalesced around Victor Drury, a French anarchist, whose "Spread the Light" clubs taught revolutionary ideology to New York

70. For a full account of the Duryea investigation, see *JUL*, December 1882; 1882 *Proceedings of the Knights of Labor Grand Assembly* (New York), in *PP*; 1883 *Proceedings of the Knights of Labor Grand Assembly* (Cincinnati), in *PP*.

71. 1882 *Proceedings*.

City Knights. Drury formed "concentric circles" to expand his message, while Horan traveled to Hamilton, Ontario, on a similar mission after his explusion from the KOL. Drury's efforts created the Home Club, an oath-bound secret conspiracy that seized control of the Knights in 1886, and held the Order and Powderly in its clutches until after 1888.

The Home Club grew by appealing to ritual. Theodore Cuno provided that opportunity though he was not a Home Club member. (Anarchists and Lassalleans distrusted Cuno, a doctrinaire Marxist.) Before the 1882 Grand Assembly, Cuno made his disputes with Powderly public by quoting KOL ritual in a *New York Herald* article, charging that the openness of the revamped KOL had led to "the persecution of members." In a eulogistic evocation of fraternalism, Cuno wrote:

> The "working" of an assembly combines the mysticism of the Masonic lodge with the beneficiary element of a mutual aid society and the protective and defensive phases of a trade union after the old English pattern. . . . All the symbols are important object lessons and have their teachings applied to the labor movement. The surroundings in the meeting hall are made inspiring and elevating. . . . The opening service is calculated to remind members of their duties as fighters and defenders of labor's rights, and the forming of an unbroken circle of harmony and friendship is intended to remind them that they should not relax in the fight until the battle is won!![72]

Cuno's remarks masked his own distaste for ritual, but greatly inspired opponents of modernization. Cuno kept up his assault on Powderly through a series of vitriolic letters, and DA 49 flaunted its defiance by electing all six of the expelled men as delegates to the 1883 Grand Assembly. Powderly revoked the district charter, but Drury-led dissidents continued to operate as usual. By the time the GA met, secrecy advocates were gathering steam. Powderly tried to derail them and told delegates:

> I do not advocate a return to the oath-bound secrecy formerly in vogue in the Order, but I do not advocate the adoption of everything which was formerly a safeguard, except the oath. Our affairs have been made public property by men who are not members, and who did not sympathize with us or our aspirations. Too much indiscriminate interviewing has wrought a great deal

72. *New York Herald,* April 23, 1882.

of injury to certain localities, and this convention should define the boundary which no member can further venture without incurring a penalty.[73]

Nonetheless, delegates reinstated DA 49, LA 1562, and the six expelled Knights. Even this did not prevent the bolt of an oath-bound secrecy group, the Independent Order of the Knights of Labor based in Binghamton, New York.

By late 1883, the KOL's future direction was so confused that Robert Layton told a U.S. Senate committee that the KOL was a secret organization, and Reginald Nuthall contributed "Why Secrecy is Necessary" to the *JUL*. In New York City, *John Swinton's Paper* advised that Knights there "maintain a degree of secrecy unknown to the Order in any other part of the country. Outsiders are kept in the dark as to their places of meeting, their active questions and other things which in other cities are freely published through the press."[74]

At the 1884 General Assembly, the Home Club tried to subvert Powderly by exposing his ignorance of *AK* procedures. At the last moment Powderly was tipped off by John McClelland, who warned him to "brush up on your mummery old boy." Powderly staved off a return to secrecy, but gained a Pyrrhic victory when he so impressed delegates that they clamored for more details, and Powderly was forced to issue a secret circular on ritual.[75]

Home Club conspirators continued to ride the secrecy bandwagon. Their moment of opportunity came after the 1885 Gould strike. The influx of new members led to the calling of a Special Assembly in June 1886, which the Club packed in order to secure nine of the top thirteen posts on the GEB. For the next two years Powderly was forced to cooperate with the Home Club to stay in office. Once in power, however, the Club's embrace of ritual and secrecy was broken. In truth, most Club members cared little for mystical rambling; appeal to ritual was merely a power ploy. The conspirators did little to reinstate the old work, and the fragile coalition between radicals and fundamentalists unraveled.[76]

73. 1883 *Proceedings.*

74. Layton's testimony can be found in John Garraty, ed., *Labor and Capital in the Gilded Age: Testimony Taken by the Senate Committee Upon Relations Between Labor and Capital, 1883* (Boston: Little, Brown & Co., 1968). Nuthall's article is in *JUL*, March 1882, but was referred to in correspondence long afterward. For comments on secrecy in New York City, see *John Swinton's Paper*, January 27, 1884.

75. John McClelland to Powderly, July 7, 1884, in *PP*; secret circular entitled "Secret Work and Instructions" is found in the *PP*, reprinted in 1892.

76. For more on the Home Club, see Weir, "Tilting at Windmills."

The Home Club knew that the ritualists were a minority among the thousands of new members who flooded the KOL after 1885, and quickly moved on to other things. William Horan died in 1889 as disillusioned as his hero, Uriah Stephens. Nonetheless, the Home Club's ability to exploit ritual secrecy shows that old practices retained great power long after 1882.

If ritual, in the hands of radicals, was divisive and calculating, it was not so with African Americans. The KOL attracted some 95,000 blacks to the Order, and fraternalism, with its lofty ideals of Universal Brotherhood, was one of the reasons. Ritual fraternalism was rooted deeply in the African-American experience, especially in the South.[77] In Missouri, one in six black males was a Freemason, while in Richmond, Virginia, over four hundred secret societies crisscrossed the black community, and the city's KOL District Assembly 92 was all-black.[78] One scholar has written that

> Well-versed in secrecy and ritual, [African Americans] were attuned to symbolism and to the "inner workings" of the Order. They expanded their experience with self-organization, self-education, and self-government and integrated these new experiences into their own social and intellectual frame of reference.[79]

From the beginning, the KOL upheld racial solidarity as a natural part of Universal Brotherhood. Uriah Stephens—the offspring of an abolitionist household—announced, "I can see ahead of me an organization that will include men and women of every craft, creed, and color"[80] (Fig. 3). Terence V. Powderly's actions at the 1886 General Assembly in Richmond demonstrated that he was equally committed. Powderly was outraged when black delegate Frank Ferrell (Fig. 4) ran afoul of city Jim Crow ordinances and had to stay in a different hotel than white Knights. When informed that Ferrell could not introduce Virginia's governor to the GA, Ferrell instead introduced Powderly. Governor Fitzhugh Lee squirmed in embarrassment as Powderly delivered an impassioned speech on the KOL's commitment to racial equality. Later, eighty of

77. Loretta J. Williams, *Black Freemasonry and Middle-Class Realities* (Columbia: University of Missouri Press, 1980).
78. Thelen, *Paths of Resistance*; Peter J. Rachleff, *Black Labor in the South: Richmond, Virginia, 1865–1890* (Philadelphia: Temple University Press, 1984).
79. Rachleff, *Black Labor in the South,* 157.
80. Quoted in Bloch, "Labor and the Negro," 174.

LEADERS OF THE KNIGHTS OF LABOR.

Fig. 3.   Terence Powderly and the leaders of the Knights of Labor in 1886, four years after the Order became a public organization. Courtesy, Smithsonian Institution.

Fig. 4.   Terence Powderly and Frank Ferrell at the 1886 General Assembly in Richmond. When Ferrell was prohibited from introducing Governor Lee of Virginia, Ferrell instead introduced Powderly. For many blacks, ritual eased their integration into the order. Courtesy, Neilson Library, Smith College.

Ferrell's white New York brothers helped him to integrate a Richmond theater.[81]

The public drama of Richmond notwithstanding, many African Americans found KOL ritual attractive, and secrecy necessary. Evidence suggests that black membership was far greater than official figures indicated. Where local conditions were too dangerous for open work, KOL locals were masked as fraternal orders under names such as "Franklin," "Washington," "Protective," and "Progressive." This is corroborated by the gap between official and local assembly reports. *John Swinton's Paper* contains news briefs from African-American assemblies in places such as Kansas City, Kansas; Whistler, Alabama; San Antonio, Texas; Dayton, Ohio; Carroll, Maryland; Clover Hill, Virginia; Raleigh and Durham, North Carolina; Terre Haute, Indiana; and Brooklyn, New York, which do not appear on official assembly lists of the Order.[82]

Knights of Labor ritual eased the integration of African Americans into the Order because it so closely paralleled their own fraternal experiences. By 1886, Powderly routinely approved black organizers to go into the field. Whether mixed or segregated, new assemblies used the *AK* as the basis for local assembly practices. Black members seized upon *AK* references to Universal Brotherhood. They were likewise impressed by the willingness of KOL leaders to put their own lives on the line for black workers. In 1887, white organizer H. F. Hoover was lynched for trying to unite black South Carolina plantation workers. In the deep South, repression was so brutal that the *Labor Leaf* demanded federal protection for KOL organizers.[83]

Most African-American ministers were also less disturbed by KOL ritualism than their white Christian counterparts. Some, like the Rev. W. H. Johnson of Albany, New York, joined the Order and rose as high as District Worthy Foreman. Knights of Labor ritualism was reinforced by black religious experience, itself ritualistic and highly expressive.[84] One historian claims that some African Americans "saw the Knights as some-

81. *Montgomery Advertiser* (Alabama), October 6, 1886; Philip S. Foner, *American Socialism and Black Americans: From the Age of Jackson to World War II* (Westport, Conn.: Greenwood Press, 1977), 62–69.

82. *John Swinton's Paper*, November 8, 1885; December 13, 1885; December 27, 1885; March 7, 1886; June 16, 1886; July 4, 1886; October 24, 1886; December 26, 1886; January 9, 1887; February 13, 1887. I cross-referenced these local assembly notes with Jonathan Garlock, *Guide to Local Assemblies of the Knights of Labor* (Westport, Conn.: Greenwood Press, 1982).

83. Sidney Kessler, "The Organization of Negroes in the Knights of Labor," *Journal of Negro History* 37 (1952): 248–76.

84. Kessler, "The Organization of Negroes."

thing of a religious organization and Powderly as a high priest who possessed powers approaching the supernatural."[85]

Though hyperbolic, this assertion underscores the ways that the African-American community fused religion and ritual. The KOL's ability to attract black ministers—who served as role models and community leaders far more often than white clerics—aided recruitment of black workers. The Knights' black assembly in Mattoon, Illinois, counted two ministers as charter members, and numerous others wrote positively of the Order. The Rev. Henry L. Phillips of the Protestant Episcopal Church of the Crucifixion in Philadelphia wrote to the *JUL* to say that if the Knights of Labor could "truly aid the Negro . . . [it] will forever deserve to be called the saviour . . . not only of a race, but of the whole country, and will receive the unstinted praise of unborn millions."[86]

Other black leaders were willing to take KOL rhetoric at face value. Editors D. A. Straker, T. McCants Stewart, and T. Thomas Fortune saw the KOL as a positive force. Fortune filled his *New York Age* with KOL tidbits, especially those involving black/white cooperation. In 1886, Fortune printed positive quotes from black communities across the nation. Typical was a comment from North Carolina: "Whatever may be said in criticism . . . of the Knights of Labor, the fact remains that they are doing more to blot out color prejudice and recognize the equality of manhood in all the races than any other organization in existence." Predictably, Fortune interviewed Frank Ferrell after the 1886 General Assembly.[87]

Certainly, the KOL faced opposition from both black leaders, like William Councill, and rank-and-file racists. One Knight who did not think that Universal Brotherhood included African Americans complained, "Nigger and Knight have become synonymous terms," while organizer Victor St. Cloud claimed his efforts in the South were being thwarted because, "I have been trying to organize the Colored Race. I claim that they should all be brought under our shield, while my opponents work to keep them out and I say an effort will be made . . . to entirely exclude them."[88] And while Powderly sympathized with African Americans, fel-

85. Melton A. McLaurin, *The Knights of Labor in the South* (Westport, Conn.: Greenwood Press, 1978), 577.

86. *Labor Leaf and Vindicator* (Detroit), May 26, 1886; *JUL*, June 30, 1887.

87. For examples of positive reporting on the Knights of Labor in papers edited by T. Thomas Fortune, see his *The New York Freeman*, March 6, 1886; April 10, 1886; July 17, 1886; October 16, 1886. The report on Frank Ferrell appears November 20, 1886. Fortune took over a failing newspaper and made it profitable. In the transition period it operated under different names, including the *New York Globe* and the *New York Freeman*, before settling on the *New York Age*.

88. *JUL*, June 11, 1887, quoted in McLaurin, *The Knights of Labor in the South*, 580; Victor St. Cloud to Powderly, September 24, 1889, in *PP*. For diversity of opinion regarding labor

low Board member and Secretary-Treasurer John Hayes did not. Sent by the GEB to make arrangements for the 1889 General Assembly, he acidly remarked that Atlanta "is a h___ of a place and the nigor [sic] is in the majority from the looks of the town." In 1894, new General Master Workman James Sovereign horrified older Knights by calling for blacks to return to Africa.[89]

Still, those whose minds were broader found that African Americans made good fraternal brothers. The *Journal of United Labor* abounds with complaints of women violating secrecy; not even racist Knights made this claim of African Americans. In places where ritual was strong—DA 49, for example—Knights were capable of extraordinary brotherhood. The eighty Knights who rallied to Frank Ferrell's aid in 1886 made a quantum leap in Gilded Age logic when they accepted him as a fraternal equal. That condition abounded in New York, where there were some three thousand black Knights, but only one segregated assembly.

Whatever the KOL's limitations, African Americans found the Order attractive. At least twenty-six new African-American assemblies were formed after 1887, with no fewer than thirty-four still active in 1889— thirty-one in the deep South. African-American carpet mill operatives in New York City maintained a KOL local until 1913. In 1891, whites in North Carolina complained that the State Assembly was three-quarters black.[90] In the 1890s, like the rest of the Order, black assemblies declined in the urban centers and grew in the rural backwaters. There, both black and white assemblies attained a dubious equality: both slowly faded away.

The same rituals that attracted African Americans generated little enthusiasm among women who joined the Order. Most fraternal orders constructed a distinctly male world designed to be a haven from feminized homes and churches.[91] Uriah Stephens believed that women could not be trusted with secrets and excluded them from KOL membership. It was not until 1881 that a women's assembly was chartered—and then only after a heated debate over whether women should adopt the *AK*. It took an impassioned plea from Powderly to stave off those who de-

---

movements in the black community, see August Meier, *Negro Thought in America, 1880– 1915, Radical Ideologies in the Age of Booker T. Washington* (Ann Arbor: University of Michigan Press, 1963), 45.

89. John W. Hayes to Powderly, October 26, 1889, in *PP*. For more examples of how race-baiting disrupted the Knights of Labor, see Fink, *Workingmen's Democracy*, esp. chaps. 5–7.

90. Fink, *Workingmen's Democracy*, chap. 6; Melton McLaurin, "The Radical Policies of the Knights of Labor and the Organization of Southern Black Workers," *Labor History* 17 (Fall 1976): 568–85; Montgomery, *The Fall of the House of Labor*, 200–203.

91. Carnes, *Secret Ritual and Manhood*; Clawson, *Constructing Brotherhood*.

manded a separate ritual.[92] The Committee on Ritual finally decided to allow women to use the existing *AK* and simply substitute "sisterhood" for "brotherhood"wherever appropriate. Most assemblies followed that advice. Powderly personally initiated Frances Willard and Susan B. Anthony into the KOL's mysteries, and records indicate that St. Louis Knights used the regular initiation ceremony, although they added special songs and handshakes.[93]

The 1881 decision to charter a women's assembly did not resolve matters for two reasons: many men resented women in their assemblies, and women were indifferent to ritual. George Bennie announced that he would rather be a scab than a member of a mixed-gender assembly.[94] Albert Carlton complained of women who divulged secrets, reiterating Stephens's concerns that women could not be trusted with the Order's mysteries. This charge resurfaced in Toronto in 1883, and in New York City in 1886, and passed for conventional wisdom among those male Knights whose sexism included the popular stereotype of women as gossipers.[95] In 1887, Powderly chided Charles Litchman, the Order's General Secretary, "How did you get it into your head that a dispensation was necessary to admit women to an Assembly which had previously admitted none but men?"[96]

The KOL's broad platform and diverse membership spawned Knights who had internalized Victorian beliefs that a woman's proper sphere was the home, not the workplace or lodge (Fig. 5). From such a perspective, the presence of women wage earners was a troubling reminder of the flaws and inequities of capitalism. At best, men saw women as sojourners in the labor movement awaiting freedom from nondomestic toil. Victorian ideology created a double bind for female KOL leaders. On one hand, its penetration into American culture made women hard to organize; on the other, close cooperation with Knights might—if the KOL was successful—push women back into their homes.[97]

The recognition that fraternalism was, at its core, a male preserve put tremendous personal and political pressures on KOL women. Their

92. Powderly, *The Path I Trod*, chap. 28; 1881 *Proceedings*.

93. Powderly, *The Path I Trod*, 289; circular dated February 19, 1882, in *PP*; *Labor Enquirer* (Denver), February 10, 1883.

94. Susan Levine, *Labor's True Woman: The Carpet Weavers, Industrialization, and Labor Reform in the Gilded Age* (Philadelphia: Temple University Press, 1984), 132.

95. A. A. Carlton to Powderly, August 11, 1883, in *PP*; Kealey and Palmer, *Dreaming of What Might Be*, 107–8; C. Hass to Powderly, April 1, 1886, in *PP*.

96. Powderly to Charles Litchman, April 27, 1887, in *PP*.

97. For more on the contradictory pressures facing Gilded Age working women, see Levine, *Labor's True Woman*.

T. V. POWDERLY.

OUR DAILY BREAD.

Fig. 5. Merchant's trade card soliciting KOL business. Though not created by the KOL, it would have appealed to Knights' traditional sensibilities. Courtesy, Smithsonian Institution.

choice was to either accept sexist domestic assumptions or to adopt an antagonistic stance toward those who did. Leonora Barry, the KOL's General Investigator for Women's Work from 1886 to 1890, complained bitterly that many women resisted organization and bought into hearth-and-home assumptions. But she was equally blunt in condemning the sexism she found within KOL ranks, blaming it for retarding her efforts. At the 1887 General Assembly Barry blasted the "selfishness of . . . brothers in toil," whose behavior made a "mockery of the principles intended."[98] Likewise, Charlotte Smith complained to *The Working Woman* that "women have been too much neglected by the founders and advocates of labor organizations who have devoted in many cases their whole time to the education and organization of men, neglecting entirely the claims of their more oppressed and injured sisters."[99]

Smith's remarks underscore the ways that KOL "education" was engendered. Encoding key principles within a ritualistic framework worked well for those experienced in the mysteries of fraternalism, but not as well for women whose associational soil was thinner. In antebellum America, many women feared fraternal orders and some found expression in anti-Masonic movements. It was not until the 1850s that several fraternal orders allowed women to join, and then usually in separate auxiliaries whose primary function was to assist with social events. Actual sororal societies were rare.[100]

Further, the mere substitution of gendered adjectives in KOL ritual paid insufficient attention to the differences between male and female cultures. As men worried about the definitions of "manhood," women thought more of *communitas*. Women were more comfortable with primary relationships rather than with transcendent, quasi-religious mysticism. The record is nearly silent regarding women deriving meaning from ritual. On the other hand, women expressed great enthusiasm for dances, debates, socials, songfests, teas, and trade fairs. As Alice Kessler-Harris notes, men's cultures often stressed "unity, discipline [and] faithfulness," whereas women valued "community, idealism and spirit."[101] Toronto's Katie McVicar argued that male organizing tech-

98. *Report of the General Investigator for Women's Work*, 1887 *Proceedings of the Knights of Labor General Assembly*, in PP.

99. *The Working Woman*, October 15, 1887.

100. By 1890, there were about 500,000 women in auxiliaries and thirty times that number of men serving in fraternal orders. For more on the masculine nature of Gilded Age fraternalism, see Carnes, *Ritual and Manhood*; Clawson, *Constructing Brotherhood*.

101. Kessler-Harris quoted in Ruth Milkman, ed., *Women, Work & Protest: A Century of Women's Labor History* (London: Routledge, 1985), 129. For more on the culture of Gilded Age working women, see Ava Baron, ed., *Work Engendered: Towards a New History of American Labor* (Ithaca: Cornell University Press, 1991), esp. chaps. 1, 2, 4, and 5; Levine, *Labor's*

niques simply did not work with women, while Leonora Barry noted that women complained of male assembly-room habits like smoking and tobacco-chewing.[102]

Women were attracted to the Knights of Labor because of its close link to trade unionism, its rhetorical stance on female equality, and its moral codes, but not its rituals. Although the KOL comprised a sprinkling of teachers, waitresses, housewives, and domestics, the vast majority of female members came from manufacturing.[103] Women created an assembly life that was as practical as it was personally meaningful. Female Knights in Rhode Island set up a "socialistic" nursery for working mothers, and threw themselves heartily into political debates, fund-raising activities, and propaganda efforts directed at expanding KOL membership. They also agitated for suffrage and equal pay for equal work.[104] Chicago women led by the dynamic Elizabeth Rodgers announced, "Let's do like the other assemblies; let us organize a political club."[105] Women demonstrated their practical concerns in times of trouble; few members were as faithful to boycott calls as KOL women. Leonora Barry's 1888 agenda included one hundred speaking engagements, the distribution of 1,900 leaflets, the organization of new assemblies, the appointment of women officers, and a plethora of other administrative duties.[106] With such a demanding schedule it is doubtful she spent much time teaching elaborate initiation rituals.

Neither ritual nor secrecy was common practice among female Knights. They pursued their agendas in public rather than commiserating behind sororal veils. Susan Levine argues that some women Knights viewed their assemblies as alternatives to male saloon culture; doubtless, they also saw them as alternatives to fraternalism.[107] In all, women and the KOL were an uneasy mix, and the lack of common cultural practices helps explain why the Order organized more black men than women.

True Woman; Carroll Smith-Rosenberg, *Disorderly Conduct: Visions of Gender in Victorian America* (New York: Oxford University Press, 1985).

102. See McVicar in Kealey and Palmer, *Dreaming of What Might Be*, 143–44; Leonora Barry in Levine, *Labor's True Woman*, 117.

103. For more details on the work backgrounds of women in the Knights of Labor, see Levine, *Labor's True Woman*; Barbara Mayer Wertheimer, *We Were There: The Story of Working Women in America* (New York: Pantheon, 1977), chap. 10; Mary Blewett, *We Will Rise in Our Might: Workingwomen's Voices From Nineteenth-Century New England* (Ithaca: Cornell University Press, 1991).

104. Paul Buhle, "The Knights of Labor in Rhode Island," *Radical History Review* 17 (Spring 1978): 39–73; Levine, *Labor's True Woman*, 118.

105. *Knights of Labor* (Chicago), February 12, 1887.

106. Wertheimer, *We Were There*, 187.

107. Levine, *Labor's True Woman*, 117.

Whether the product of sexism or choice, cultural isolation made the task of adding "Sisterhood" to Stephens's call for Universal Brotherhood more difficult.

Unhinged Armor: The Decline of Ritual

The varied meanings of fraternalism served mainly to ensure its decline throughout the 1880s. After 1882, the KOL frequently rewrote its ritual, but even Powderly admitted that old practices appealed better to the "heart and intellect" of adherents.[108] In his zeal to make the Order more modern, Powderly threw out the heart and naively trusted intellect. The post-1882 Knights of Labor attracted more members but demanded less of them. After the 1881 convention, the *AK* was shortened. The most salient change was the replacement of the Bible-sworn oath with a simple pledge of honor to the S.O.M.A. code. Welcoming speeches were still rich in symbolism and high-sounding principles, but the demands of an open order began to fray fraternal veils. Notably, initiates were charged to create a favorable public sentiment on the question of labor, and to "harmonize the interests of capital and labor."[109]

Initially, some local assemblies resisted change. Dirigo Assembly in Minneapolis even expanded the ritual by adding a lengthy play featuring the personified characters of "Toiler," "Lobbyist," "Capital," and "Knight" to its initiation ritual. The new Knight also listened to Scripture quotes, a poem, a song, and a lecture based on an article Powderly wrote for the *North American Review*.[110] Most dramatic of all was the response of Brooklyn Local 1562 that ignored every directive to the contrary and continued to practice the ritual as Stephens wrote it.

These small rebellions were the highwater mark for KOL ritual. By 1884, new member requests were reduced to application blanks, a far cry from the high drama Powderly experienced ten years earlier. Explosive

108. Powderly, *The Path I Trod*, 48.

109. *AK*, circa 1883, in *PP.*

110. The ritual for Dirigo Assembly, LA 805, Minneapolis, is located in Powderly's 1883 incoming correspondence, in *PP.* The play was a rather stilted affair. Sample dialogue includes this exchange: Capital declared, "I live by my wits—speculations, rents, and usury—while you work all the time without asking how you might better your condition. . . . God has made me rich and you poor, you had better argue the point with him." After an equally unsatisfactory exchange with "Lobbyist," noble "Toiler" meets "Knight" who explains the Order's principles. When Toiler assents to those, Knight proclaims, "You have begun to think; *you are no longer a machine.*"

growth after 1885 made ritual a less-pressing issue and the central organization lost control of it. A secret circular issued in March 1886 admon-
ished districts and locals to "appoint a competent committee on instruc-
tion to teach our members what the Order was intended for," though
Powderly admitted, "I have no advice as to how they should be taught."
Detroit's *Labor Leaf* worried that local assemblies were "getting into deep
water, as their numbers grow, and . . . will need great skill to prevent
some drowning."[111]

By April 1886, reports of impropriety were pouring into Powderly's
office. In New York, LA 2458 charged that an organizer from LA 5682
"initiated a man his *boss* ordered him to and against free will of initiation
. . . in a room behind a saloon . . . without an anteroom or any other
provision of secrecy." It was further charged that eight women, forced
to join 5682, "immediately after and publicly gave away the signs, and
password." A group of Brooklyn sawyers grumbled that an organizer
was four hours late for an appointment and "we were just as wise when
we got there as when we left."[112]

Fraternalism suffered as ritual declined. A writer using the pseudonym "Old Honesty" insisted that "no man will become a true Knight
without a solemn pledge to be a man at home or abroad. He should
neither drink, gamble, nor swear, and under the protecting shield of
this order of noble and earnest effort may commence an industrious and
thrifty life."[113] However, an 1886 *National Labor Tribune* told of a different
reality in "How Our Members Fulfill Their Pledge":

> Watch the Knight of Labor as he goes to purchase goods; he be-
> longs to the K. of L., yet he never stops to look after the K. of L.
> stamps. He buys boots without the label; his clothes were made
> in a shop by scab labor; he wears a hat without a union label; he
> buys flour in non-union mills; his stove was made in prison for
> aught he knows or cares; he smokes cigars made by Chinese or
> scab labor; he buys cotton cloth made in mills where the notice
> reads, "No Knights of Labor need apply." He reads, but never a
> labor paper; or if he reads one, borrows it from a neighbor so as
> to get rid of helping to support it. He buys the newspaper that
> works 365 days in the year to make a slave of him. He claims to
> be a good K. of L., yet never attends the meetings or pays his
> dues.[114]

111. Secret circular dated March 13, 1886, in *PP*; *Advance and Labor Leaf*, August 25, 1886.
112. Peter Kearney to Powderly, May 8, 1886, in *PP*.
113. *Knights of Labor* (Chicago), August 14, 1886.
114. *National Labor Tribune*, November 20, 1886.

This sad state of affairs encouraged those traditionalists who were seeking to rekindle fraternalism. One effort involved the formation of "The Blue and Gray Association of the Knights of Labor," formally created at the 1886 Special Assembly. Several Civil War veterans decided to create a group "fraternal in its aims and helpful in its spirit, and kindly in its labors, and loyal to humanity." Organizers then transmuted antebellum rhetoric into a modern appeal to fight Northern monopolists.[115] The Blue and Gray Association held annual "encampments" where delegates gathered for fraternity and discussion of common problems. The 1890 event held in Vicksburg, Mississippi, gathered the 1863 battle survivors for fireworks, bonfires, mock battles, rail and river excursions, an opera, horse races, a memorial service, and a banquet.[116]

This was as much a commentary on KOL leadership as it was an exercise in nostalgia. Many Blue and Gray organizers came from the South, where fraternal notions lingered longer. Others included Powderly critics like DA 49's Harry Taylor, a key Home Club figure, and Homer McGraw of Pittsburgh's powerful DA 3.[117] The Blue and Gray attracted many older Knights. The *Powderly Papers* contain a photograph of white-haired Hugh Cavanaugh (Fig. 6) in the full dress uniform of his Arkansas regiment adorned with all of his military ribbons, plus his Masonic badge.[118] Cavanaugh was an important leader, having brought several Knights of St. Crispin assemblies into the Knights of Labor in the early days. He later served as District Master Workman of Cincinnati's DA 48 and was elected an assistant to the GEB in 1886 with the help of the Home Club, from whence he dogged Powderly's heels.

The Association's attempts to add pomp to the declining KOL ritual practices further distanced the old guard from new recruits. In 1888, Knights from Buffalo, New York circulated a pamphlet entitled, "The Purposes and Essential Principles of the Knights of Labor Simplified and Explained." This work reduced principle and ritual to a simple catechism of three questions with one-sentence answers.[119] The LA was called "a school for the education of its members," not a sacred Sanctuary. Notably missing was any mention of the S.O.M.A. ideal. Given that

115. Notes from the 1886 *Special Assembly of the Knights of Labor* held in Cleveland, Ohio, in *PP.*

116. The program of the 1890 Blue and Gray Encampment is located in Powderly's 1890 incoming correspondence.

117. Ibid. Southern Knights who took active roles in the 1890 Encampment include Thomas Green of Pine Bluffs, Arkansas; L. H. Streeter of southern Illinois; L. H. Patterson of Washington, D.C.; F. J. Riley of Richmond; and Henry Buttenberge of Memphis.

118. Photo is on file with the original *PP* at Catholic University, Washington, D.C.

119. *National Labor Tribune,* October 20, 1888.

Fig. 6. Hugh Cavanaugh in full dress uniform of his Arkansas regiment adorned with all of his military ribbons and Masonic badge. Cavanaugh was one of many Knights who joined the Blue and Gray Association of the Order, seeking to rekindle the old fraternalism. Powderly Papers, The Catholic University of America.

each local assembly was allowed only one *AK* and that over two thousand copies of the catechism were printed, it is clear that the latter directed the practices of Buffalo Knights. This was true elsewhere. In 1890, a Baltimore Knight complained:

> I ask myself what induced me to join the Knights of Labor. Did I receive an application blank, read the Preamble, study it, and come to the conclusion that the principles set forth in it are certain to relieve toilers? Did I know that those measures could only be carried into effect by organization, and then conclude to become part of that organization? Right here I discover the first defects. I never saw an application blank, never read the preamble or constitution, and knew nothing of the objects and aims of the Knights of Labor until I was in the order sometime. . . . I knew [only] that there was an assembly of varnishers, and finding a member I gave him the initiation fee, and in due time was initiated. I then found out that a committee of three was appointed on every application; that this committee only reported on the character of the applicant, it was not considered important to know whether he knew the objects and aims of the order or not.[120]

The GEB continued to issue passwords, print circulars of signs and countersigns, and revamp the *AK*, but little was done to revive sagging fraternalism. Directives and changes from the top more closely resembled the Buffalo model of the ritual than Uriah Stephens's original one. The 1891 revision of the *AK* was more political than ritualistic. Instead of being required to accept the mysticism of the early initiation ceremony, a candidate was asked whether he had studied and approved of the Preamble and stood ready to "oppose monopolies, aid co-operation, assist brothers in distress, and remain true to the obligation which you take on being admitted to membership." The candidate pledged the usual things associated with the S.O.M.A. principle but added that he would assist in "abolishing class privileges, monopoly in land and money, [and] the control of railroads and telegraphs by private individuals." Likewise, welcoming speeches were less lofty, the image of the Philosopher's Stone being the sole remnant of the old ritual. The entire ritual was similar in tone to Gilded Age antimonopoly manifestos.[121]

120. *The Critic*, June 22, 1889.
121. *AK*, rev. 1891 ed., in *PP*; 1889 *Proceedings of the Knights of Labor General Assembly*, in *PP*.

Reactions to the new *AK* were officially positive, though many in the Order had reservations. L. P. Wild, the Recording Secretary of LA 3408 (Washington, D.C.) crowed that the new ritual "at once raises [the KOL] above mere trade unionism . . . and places it . . . in the front rank of patriotic organizations."[122] Yet about the time of the *AK*'s release, older Knights petitioned the GEB to authorize a uniformed order within the Knights, a request more reminiscent of Masonic ritualism than labor radicalism.

Despite reconstitution of the Order after 1885, there were still a number of individuals who remembered Knighthood's early days, including cofounder James L. Wright. In June 1892, the circular "Secret Work and Instructions" was reissued, this time using pre-1882 signs in which only verbal challenges and responses were changed. More telling is the decision made at the 1892 General Assembly to reestablish the Philosopher's Stone degree abandoned in 1878.[123]

It was too late to revitalize the Order by turning back the clock, and Powderly sabotaged such efforts when he held the Philosopher's Stone hostage during his 1893 squabbles with Wright and others who ousted him as Master Workman. By 1893, the KOL stood where it had in 1882, a small organization seeking to attract interest. By late 1894, the Order finally wrestled the Philosopher's Stone degree from Powderly, but that act did little to breathe life into the decaying Knights of Labor. Coming full circle, the 1895 General Assembly added the Archeon degree, in homage to the original work of Uriah Stephens. It too had little effect.

The final act was played at the 1896 Rochester General Assembly when General Master Workman James Sovereign returned the KOL to total secrecy. Much of the *AK* was restored to its pre-1881 glory, with both vow and religious metaphors reappearing. It was appropriate that Rochester, New York, was the site for this action, since that city had long produced factions that wished to turn back the clock.[124] Predictably, a new degree order, the Minutemen, was created. Just as predictably, it accomplished little. A long-time Powderly foe, Henry Hicks of DA 49, served as General Master Workman until 1902, when John Hayes assumed total control of the Order. It was Hayes, an ex–Home Clubber, who put the national body to rest in 1917.

122. *JKL*, January 21, 1892.
123. Circulars issued June 4, 1892, and December 26, 1892, in *PP*.
124. Rochester-based revolts included the Improved Order of Advanced Knights of Labor (1883–84), the Independent Knights of Labor (1884), and the Provisional Order of the Knights of Labor (1887).

Fraternalism Reconsidered

Labor fraternalism has fared poorly among critics and historians. In an otherwise optimistic report on the Knights of Labor, Friedrich Engels dismissed ritual practices as one of the Order's "little absurdities." More recently, historian Eric Hobsbawm labeled labor fraternalism "misplaced ingenuity."[125] Yet even today, labor organizations enthrone "solidarity" as their highest ideal but find it difficult to transform rhetoric into practice. Prior to 1880, the KOL used "little absurdities" and "misplaced ingenuity" to achieve remarkable unity. Ritual was cumbersome—even silly at times—but early Knighthood was marked by an internal calm that older members remembered with fondness in the chaotic days that followed.

Critics rightly note that the KOL was a small organization before 1884, thus making solidarity considerably more attainable. The link between quasi-Masonic mysteries and social reform seems so tenuous that one is tempted to dismiss the early Knights as naive, romantic, and irrelevant. But there are compelling reasons to resist such temptations. A sizable chunk of workers' experiences is dismissed if ritual fraternalism is ignored. Labor fraternalism rose in response to the collapse of trade unionism, not because of the mystical musings of men with a predilection for costumed melodrama. For many nineteenth-century workers, trade unionism was ill-adapted to Gilded Age realities. True, the KOL was a small organization, but it survived capital's onslaught in the 1870s. Secret rituals helped keep the labor movement alive during its darkest days, ensuring there would be a labor movement when the climate was more ripe for trade unionism.

Further, labor fraternalism shaped the essential character of the KOL. Ritual was altered in the 1880s, but it was never jettisoned. Much of what the Order became and could *not* become was forged in its early days and is embedded in its ungainly ritual. Solidarity was never confined to class or craft categories. Instead, it was part of the larger package of Knighthood, a loose mix of ideology, unionism, culture, fraternalism, and mysticism synonymous with a transformed society of reformed individuals. Such demands on the self and society guaranteed that the KOL could never conform to "pure and simple" unionism, nor could it put on socialist ideological blinders. Uriah Stephens's vision of a good society was one in which all individuals were bound in fraternal brotherhood grounded in a producerist ethos. To effect this, he called for one big

125. Kenneth Lapides, ed., *Marx and Engels on the Trade Unions* (New York: International Publishers, 1987), 141–42; Hobsbawm quoted in Carnes, *Secret Ritual and Manhood*, 11.

union to create a cooperative commonwealth that would supplant the wage system. Fraternalism was no opiate to deaden the lashes of capitalist oppression, rather it was the sine qua non of organization building that would snatch the whip from capital's hands.

The *AK* was peppered with allusions that found their way into the KOL's platform: an abhorrence of partisan politics, a call for abolition of the wage system, a demand for arbitration of capital/labor disputes, cooperative production, social reform, "equal pay for equal work" across gender lines, and temperance. The call for Universal Brotherhood is directly traceable to the Order's attempts to bridge gaps of ethnicity, gender, ideology, race, religion, and skill. Although it often fell short, the KOL's admirable attempts were predetermined by rhetoric and practices established early on.

Fraternal ideals help us understand the KOL's near obsession with morality. Stephens linked public policy to private morality and created a paradigm in which the destruction of the wage system was a "manly" act, and the adherence to S.O.M.A. an act of practical Christianity. The ideal Knight was chaste, chivalrous, honest, patriotic, religious, temperate, and loyal to labor's cause. A Knight who abandoned his wife or failed to pay his rent endangered brotherhood as surely as the monopolist, rumseller, or scab. Only redeemed individuals could bring about a cooperative commonwealth.

Ironically, ritual served to focus the Order's internal tensions instead of dissolving them. Modernizers like Powderly carried the day but moved too fast for their agenda to be comfortably absorbed. The time that passed from the Reading convention's first discussion of change to the stripped-down Buffalo catechism was a mere ten years. Ritual attracted African Americans to the Knights, but retarded the full integration of women into the Order. More damaging was the coalition between ideological opponents of Powderly and traditionalists. Their battles weakened central leadership at precisely the moment capital moved against the Knights. Far too much time and energy was diverted testing leaders' knowledge of abandoned practices. Rituals were written and rewritten, but most new members found them meaningless. Older Knights longed for days past. Disinterested women angered older Knights who accused them of being untrustworthy comrades, while African Americans discovered that Universal Brotherhood had a white face for some. Still, by the early 1890s, African Americans were among the few Knights who mustered any enthusiasm for KOL practices.

These matters highlight the ways in which a cohesive vision of Knighthood became unglued and confused. Powderly simultaneously eroded fraternal practices and selectively retained their spirit. Once he stripped the actual practices that made the KOL "noble and holy," it was difficult for Powderly to convince members that "something grander" was expected of them." In 1891, Maggie Weir led her women out of Baltimore's Myrtle Assembly after they "derived no benefit from belonging to the order," a conclusion reached by thousands of others.[126] In short, once mystical ties to Knighthood were severed, members were left with an expectation of material payoffs that the KOL was unable to deliver.

Material desires ultimately undid the Knights of Labor. The battle over ritual did not kill the Knights so much as the blows it suffered at the hands of capitalist opponents. By pushing aside the veils of secrecy and taking its crusade for a cooperative commonwealth to the workplace and the street, the Knights attracted attention, but not always the kind it wanted. New members poured into the Order after 1885, though most were unaware that officially the KOL was opposed to strikes. Spurred on by left-wing dissidents, these new members led the KOL into a series of strikes that ended in defeat. If the KOL could not deliver the goods, what was left to keep Maggie Weir in the Order? Certainly not fraternalism.

Ideological differences that were once subsumed by fraternal practice now rose to the fore, and the KOL had no unified identity with which to enculturate the new members that flooded the ranks in 1885 and 1886. Many left the Order from 1887 on. Powderly tried appeals to solidarity as if fraternal structures were still in place. Few issues of the *JUL* failed to include a Powderly pronouncement that Knights were urged to get behind. But divorced from the larger context of ritual, many of Powderly's reformist schemes smacked of small-town moralism. Stripped of ritual, Knights increasingly lost sight of their common problems and pursued parochial agendas. It became increasingly difficult for Knights in New York to assume they had much in common with those in Minneapolis. Local KOL cultures grew creative in the late 1880s, but also more diverse, diffuse, and independent.

Modernizers were correct to assume that the KOL needed to become public to grow, but their hasty attack on secrecy and fraternalism doomed solidarity. Left alone, the KOL may well have evolved into a modern labor organization as Engels predicted it would, but time was not a luxury afforded to the Knights. By the late 1880s, the KOL had been badly mauled in battles with organized capital. The future lay with trade unionism.

But a final word is in order concerning the staying power of ritual. Fraternal practices allowed individuals to find a kernel of common con-

126. *Baltimore Sun*, April 7, 1891, in *PP*.

sciousness amid the tangles of gender, race, ethnicity, and skill. Powderly's brother John remembered of the Knights: "Their ritualism, the secrecy with which their meetings were conducted, the signs and symbols that gave notice . . . as to where and when meetings were to be held, fired my interest and imagination, and in my mind I resolved henceforth my lot was cast with that of the wage earners."[127]

Fraternalism did not disappear with the Knights. Peter McGuire passed youthful days in troublesome Brooklyn LA 1562. Once out of the Order, he became a vociferous critic of the Knights. Yet his own Brotherhood of Carpenters and Joiners practiced a ritual quite similar to that of the KOL. Likewise, Mario Manzardo, an organizer for the Steel Workers Organizing Committee in the 1930s, complained that meetings of the Amalgamated Association of Iron, Steel, and Tin Workers were conducted according to a strict ritual. Manzardo was glad to see the end of ritual, but auto workers found a different reality. After struggling to organize key shops, organizers finally hit upon a winning formula: make converts among fraternal orders like the Masons and the rest will follow.[128]

Fraternalism survived for reasons that had little to do with mummery and mystery; it built community. Even as it declined, the KOL elicited passions and psychic responses the AFL seldom equaled. One should consider how many members stayed in the KOL after 1890 when, objectively, the Order had so little left to offer. Dozens of black assemblies were formed *after* the KOL began its precipitous decline. Likewise, the Order was able to retain about 70,000 members for much of the 1890s, roughly the membership it enjoyed in 1884.[129] They stayed although few "victories" were forthcoming, and past triumphs were too few for residual euphoria to justify loyalty. Once ingrained on the individual psyche, fraternalism put down deep roots. Terence Powderly himself is proof of

127. John Powderly quoted in Kealey and Palmer, *Dreaming of What Might Be*, 3.

128. The carpenters' ritual can be found among the papers of the American Federation of Labor (Microfilm edition: University of Massachusetts). Manzardo's comments are located in Alice and Staughton Lynd, eds., *Rank and File: Personal Histories by Working-Class Organizers* (New York: Monthly Review Press, 1988), 132. For more on the assistance of fraternal orders in United Auto Workers' organizing, see Peter Friedlander, *The Emergence of a U.A.W. Local, 1936–1939* (Pittsburgh: Pittsburgh University Press, 1975).

129. Ware, *The Labor Movement in the United States*, 66; Richard Oestreicher, "A Note on Knights of Labor Membership Statistics," *Labor History* 25, no. 1 (Fall 1984): 102–8. Oestreicher's figures for the KOL in the mid-1890s are probably too low. Usually, the departure of Daniel DeLeon's faction in 1895 is seen as reducing the KOL to about 35,000 members. This does not take into account rural Knights active in the Populist movement, however, and merely reflects the number of dues-paying members. In all likelihood, rural Knighthood remained vibrant until the late 1890s.

this. Years after being dumped from the Order he labored fourteen years to modernize, some forty years after he knelt in William Fennimore's room, Powderly was given an application blank for the Knights of Columbus. Powderly was appalled and told his would-be recruiters, "If it was wrong for the Order of the Knights of Labor to be a secret society in 1879, it cannot be right for the Knights of Columbus to be a secret society in 1917."[130] Powderly abruptly quit the Catholic Church, and at his death, the man who tried to expunge KOL ritual was a Thirty-third Degree Freemason.

130. Powderly, *The Path I Trod*, 370–71.

2 Labor Is Noble and Holy

In June of 1886, the American Congress of Churches gathered in Cleveland. The Congress was one of many Gilded Age forums where clergy debated reasons for working-class distrust of organized religion, and brainstormed strategies for overcoming it. Opinions of causes and suggestions for improvement differed, but most agreed that male workers were deserting churches in droves.

As the Congress met, across town the Knights of Labor were gathered in a special assembly called to address the Order's rapid growth. As a courtesy, the Congress asked Terence Powderly to address its assembled clerics. If workers were not interested in churches, they were quite interested in what Powderly had to say. Powderly declined the invitation, however, when it proved impossible to secure a hall large enough to accommodate the masses who wished to hear his remarks. Instead, several KOL representatives visited, mincing few words in telling God's ministers that workers had good reason for mistrusting them and their institutions.[1]

In retrospect, it is remarkable to think that clerics needed conferences to discuss the obvious: workers distrusted Gilded Age churches because most of them represented the interests of the middle class and business elites, not the concerns of wage earners. Although sincere clerics took up the cause of labor, most who bothered did so only because the issue was trendy. The efforts of early Social Gospel advocates aside, Gilded Age religious hierarchy's commitment to social change vacillated—for the most part—between shallow and hostile. In Detroit, the KOL's Joseph Labadie blasted clerical hypocrisy with such vigor that the Rev. Charles Henderson wrote to the *Labor Leaf* to plead that not all ministers were "tools of the capitalist class."[2]

1. Knights of Labor, *Labor: Its Rights and Wrongs* (Washington, D.C.: Knights of Labor, 1886), 253–60.
2. Labadie's blasts against organized religion can be found in many issues of the *Labor Leaf* in 1886 and 1887. Labadie had a weekly column called "Cranky Notions." For exam-

Labadie's opinions on religion were close to the consensus within the Knights. Had Powderly addressed the Congress of Churches, it is doubtful ministers would have been comfortable with his message. Although Powderly was a deeply religious man, he had little use for most clerics. As he recalled,

> I can find little or no evidence to prove that the ordained teacher and preacher of Christianity has attempted to walk directly in the footsteps of the crucified One in driving the waterer of stocks, the gambler of life's necessities, the despoiler of children, the exploiter of labor, or the grabber of profits from the temple wherein the products of industry are exchanged.[3]

Historians have split over their interpretations of Gilded Age Christianity. Although most would agree that there was much to criticize, some have viewed the late Victorian age as a time in which Social Darwinism weakened, paving the way for the full-blossoming of a Social Gospel movement more sympathetic to labor. Others have echoed Milton Cantor's conclusion that the Social Gospel was little more than a small wave on a sea of clerical hostility that "insouciantly disregarded the changed economic circumstances of American life, and the attendant social misery and parlous conditions."[4]

The Knights of Labor reached Cantor's conclusion a century earlier. But as Powderly's remarks indicate, Knights also distinguished between the message of Christianity and its messengers. While blasting the cant of hypocritical clerics, KOL leaders demanded higher standards from the rank and file. What the Order called True Christianity became the standard by which both individuals and institutions were judged, and the language through which oppression was denounced.[5]

---

ple, see his blast against Episcopal Bishop Samuel Harris on February 17, 1886. For Rev. Henderson's defense of his own conduct and ideas, see *Labor Leaf*, February 24, 1886.

3. Powderly, *The Path I Trod*, 266.

4. Historians sympathetic to the Social Gospel movement include Clifford Clark Jr., *Henry Ward Beecher: Spokesman for a Middle-Class America* (Urbana: University of Illinois Press, 1978); Robert T. Handy, *The Social Gospel in America* (New York: Oxford University Press, 1966); Ronald White and C. Howard Hopkins, *The Social Gospel: Religion and Reform in Changing Times* (Philadelphia: Temple University Press, 1976); and Kenneth Fones-Wolf, *Trade Union Gospel: Christianity and Labor in Industrial Philadelphia, 1865–1915* (Philadelphia: Temple University Press, 1989). Milton Cantor's quote comes from his introduction to George Davis Herron, *The Christian Society* (New York: Johnson Reprint Corporation, 1969).

5. Those who see Christianity as a language through which workers critiqued capitalism include Herbert Gutman, *Work, Culture, and Society in Industrializing America* (New York: Alfred A. Knopf, 1976); Edward P. Thompson, *The Making of the English Working Class*

As we have seen, KOL ritual was imbued with religiosity. By identifying the Order as "noble and holy," some Knights came to see themselves as the saviors of Christianity's true spirit. To that end, their locals functioned as veritable "workingmen's churches" in opposition to established religion. Such Knights and their ministerial counterparts were caught up in mutual caution, suspicion, and distrust. While there were clerics who bravely embraced labor, and Knights who welcomed them into the ranks, the groups constituted minorities within both Gilded Age churches and the Knights of Labor. Ultimately, more sermons were exchanged than plans forged to explore rapprochement.

Sparring with churches had an unintended effect within the KOL. Religion, like ritual, was supposed to be a private, internal cultural expression. Though the term "Christianity" was profusely used, its meaning was as malleable as "Knighthood" or "manhood," having more to do with views on political economy than specific theology. By opening dialogues and debates with clerics, the KOL allowed theology to creep in and open fissures in its ranks. This can be seen by the deepening splits between Protestant and Catholic Knights in the 1880s.

By the 1890s, internal rancor often made mockery of claims to True Christianity and was another of the contradictions the KOL took to its grave. Nonetheless, the KOL's experience with Gilded Age churches contain enough abuse and insult to give pause to even the most fervent defender of the Social Gospel movement. Whatever mollifying effect Social Gospel would bring in the future came too late for the Knights of Labor.

Sons of the Carpenter's Son

Most Gilded Age churches disapproved of secrecy and religion-based fraternal rituals. Thus the earliest contacts between Knights and clergymen were based on distrust and disapproval. In some cases, this began before individuals joined the Order. Powderly recalled a bitter exchange with Father Richard Hennessy of Scranton, who mistook Powderly's machinists and blacksmiths union badge for a Masonic symbol. Hennessy called Powderly a "blackguard" and hurled such invectives that the

---

(New York: Vintage, 1966); and Mary Lynne Mapes, " 'As You Have Ever Been the World's Providers, So Now You Are to Be Its Saviors': A Study of Christianity and the Knights of Labor" (M.A. thesis, Michigan State University, 1991).

shocked future KOL leader finally threatened to thrash the abusive priest.[6]

Catholic clerics were the first to notice the Knights of Labor, and the first to oppose them. As large numbers of Irish became Knights, the Order's sworn oath caused alarm. The Vatican routinely condemned secret orders from the eighteenth century on, and Hennessy's assumption that all unknown iconography was a form of Freemasonry was typical of Catholic prelates. This caused problems in some of the coal-mining regions where the KOL made early inroads, as many were centers of Molly Maguire hysteria in the 1870s. As we have seen, this led Powderly to advocate removing the oath from KOL ritual, and to lead the charge to abandon secrecy. His efforts bore little fruit; in 1884, the Vatican condemned the Knights.

For the most part, however, exchanges between Knights and clerics were few in the early days. Religion was part of the Order's private culture that manifested itself mainly in KOL moral codes. Uriah Stephens dubbed the Order "noble and holy," and infused it with Baptist moralism. It was assumed that Knights would also be Christians, a fact that led Michael Mooney of Leadville, Colorado, to seek advice on what to do about "infidels . . . who do not believe in the God of the Bible." He offered the opinion that anyone who disagreed with biblical injunctions should be denied membership.[7]

Even after the KOL opened its ranks to free-thinkers, atheists, Jews, and non-Christians, a strong code of Christian-based personal morality was expected of members. It was not enough to be a good comrade; a Knight had also to be sober, patriotic, law-abiding, trustworthy, and moral. When a group of Chicago Knights announced the formation of the Non-Swearing Knights to cleanse the stockyards of coarse language, their efforts were greeted with praise, and chapters quickly formed in Boston, Philadelphia, and Pittsburgh. Powderly announced that their efforts would make Knights "the noblest on earth and true gentlemen."[8]

For the most part, KOL morality compared favorably with that of bourgeois bigots, greedy industrialists, and hypocritical clerics. To be certain, the KOL had what one study labeled its "underside": bickerers, brawlers, drunkards, and officers who absconded with funds.[9] But the

---

6. Powderly, *The Path I Trod,* 318–19.

7. For an example of a prayer used in local assemblies, see the report from 300 (glass-workers, Pittsburgh) located in the *PP.* For Mooney's comments see, Michael Mooney to Terence Powderly, January 16, 1881, in *PP.*

8. *JUL,* January 15, 1887; emphasis in original.

9. For more on the "underside" of the KOL, see Kealey and Palmer, *Dreaming of What Might Be,* chap. 5.

KOL tolerated far less than most Gilded Age organizations, and its membership was held to higher standards than that of many churches. One can find evidence for this in the Order's expulsions.

By far the largest number of expulsions were incurred for "violations of obligation" and "conduct unbecoming a Knight." The *JUL* reported 3,754 expulsions from 1880 to 1886, of which 2,326 were for one or both of the aforementioned offenses. (Expulsions were often made for multiple reasons.) An additional 51 were removed for drunkenness, 68 for committing a crime, and 104 for slandering the Order. What exactly was "conduct unbecoming a Knight"? Typical examples chosen from 1885 include Joseph Hurley (Scranton, LA 3671), "for defrauding landlady of board bill"; Mr. Higgins (Troy, N.Y., LA 2639), "for desertion of family and bigamy"; and Henry Allison (Omaha, Neb., LA 2122), "for becoming a professional gambler."[10] More remarkable is the relatively low number (294) of Knights thrown out for scabbing. Although the *JUL* numbers are likely low, it is telling that more reported expulsions occurred for violations of personal conduct codes, than those that directly affected economic livelihood.

An editorialist in Lynn, Massachusetts, wrote, "The Knights of Labor are a moral organization; types of man [*sic*] that all other orders will admit, the Knights of Labor reject." The writer proudly noted that

> the lessons taught by the order on temperance and morality are nowhere more visible to an outsider than in the action of their members while in trouble with their employer. Heretofore a strike meant drunkenness, lawless action, often ending in riots and bloodshed; to-day, the bigger the strike the less the immorality, all through the teachings of the K. of L. We find this lesson, that to gain the esteem and sympathy of your fellow man, you must be a man.

Here the language of manliness is linked with public and private morality in a manner that demanded evangelical action on the part of Knights. The Lynn editorialist advised his readers to "study for some nobler work that is yet veiled . . . [and] after you have learned it, teach it to others."[11]

Such evangelicalism consumed a Knight from Westfield, Massachusetts, who recommended the establishment of a "missionary fund" to

10. *JUL*. My count of expulsions includes all editions from 1880 through 1886 and comes from my painstaking stroke count. It may contain errors resulting from fatigue and attention lapses. Specific examples of expulsions come from the following issues of the *JUL*: June 25, 1885; July 25, 1885; and November 10, 1885.

11. *Knights of Labor* (Lynn, Mass.), May 1, 1886.

send Knights across the country to "preach the new gospel of cooperation," and encourage clergymen to join the Knights of Labor. In his
thinking, "Our order is noble and holy; it makes all men alike, and if
the ministers believe what they preach they will confer a great boon
upon themselves and mankind by coming forward and making them
true and noble brothers without distinction of race, color, or creed."[12] A
similarly inspired Philadelphian compared the KOL's search for truth to
that of the Wise Men who visited the Nativity.[13]

Ritual prayer, personal morality, and evangelism made some locals as
much sects as labor organizations. Central to such formulations was the
essential distinction many made between religion and religiosity. The
bulk of American workers—irrespective of political ideology—assumed
the essential truth of Christianity, but believed its practices were corrupted by monied interests.[14] Powderly expressed the dichotomy well:
"The great power that came to Christianity through the teachings of
Jesus Christ has been largely frittered away through the practice of
Churchianity."[15]

If "Churchianity" was poisoned by corruption, hypocrisy, and greed,
it was incumbent on True Christians to save the Gospel of Christ from
its despoilers. Knights shifted the focus from eschatological theology to
practical Christianity by de-emphasizing Christ's role as heavenly judge
and redeemer, and stressing his earthly ministry. Thus stained-glass
iconography yielded to images of Jesus, the carpenter's son. Workers
were elevated to the status of God's chosen people. Just as the KOL
preamble echoed the biblical injunction, "By the sweat of thy brow shalt
thou eat bread," so Christ toiled as a carpenter to earn his keep. When
John Jarrett addressed the 1886 Church Council, he stressed, "I see in
the audience to-night many who are members of the Knights of Labor;
and they say that labor is noble and holy and they call their order holy.
And why? Because God himself ordained that man should work." Jarrett
was followed by Henry George, who evoked metaphors of Christ the

12. Ibid., September 19, 1885.
13. *JUL,* June 1880; also quoted in Mapes, " 'As You Have Been the World's
Providers.' "
14. Even Gilded Age political radicals often expressed their protests in religious language. Within the KOL, Marxists like Theodore Cuno and committed anarchists like
Joseph Buchanan, Victor Drury, and Dyer Lum uttered religious sentiments on par with
more traditional men like Powderly. Bruce Nelson describes Chicago anarchists as an irre-
ligious group, but those who expressed doubt about the essential truth of Christianity
were a decided minority. For more on the religious views of Chicago anarchists, see Bruce
Nelson, *Beyond the Martyrs: A Social History of Chicago's Anarchists, 1870–1900* (New Brunswick, N.J.: Rutgers University Press, 1988).
15. Powderly, *The Path I Trod,* 66.

carpenter to demand the "kingdom of God on earth" and a church of "justice, not platitudes."[16]

In Massachusetts, Congregationalist minister Jesse Jones joined the KOL in Boston and cofounded with layman Edward Rogers a labor church in a working-class neighborhood. True to the metaphor, Rogers was both a Knight and a carpenter. Likewise, the Rev. William D. Bliss's involvement with Boston-area Knights led him to give up his Congregationalist pulpit to form the Mission of the Carpenter. In Chicago, one writer suggested that Christ's devotion to his trade made him a Knight of Labor.[17]

The imagery of Christ the carpenter was a favorite of George E. McNeill, whose message was simple and direct: "The teachings of the carpenter's Son . . . tend to counteract the bad influences of Mammon." McNeill called labor's demand for justice a "new revelation of the old Gospel," and insisted,

> When the Golden Rule of Christ shall measure the relations of men in all their duties towards their fellows, in factories and work-shop, in the mine, in the field, in commerce, everywhere the challenge will go forth as never before. . . . the promise of the prophet and the poet shall be fulfilled . . . and peace on earth shall prevail, not by the subjugation of man to man . . . but by the free acceptance of the Gospel that all men are of one blood. Then the new Pentecost will come, when every man shall have according to his needs.[18]

In an overt rejection of Social Darwinian imperatives, McNeill insisted that cooperation and Christian charity would replace competitive capitalism. His universalist tone echoed Uriah Stephens, as did his expressed belief that free will, not preordained fates, reigned—be they spiritual or economic. McNeill's beliefs were shaped by the KOL, out-

16. Knights of Labor, *Labor: Its Rights and Wrongs*, 253–60.

17. For more on Jones and Rogers, see Henry May, *Protestant Churches and Industrial America* (New York: Harper Torchbooks, 1967), 74–79. In Clark Halker, *For Democracy, Workers, and God: Labor Song-Poems, and Labor Protest, 1865–95* (Urbana: University of Illinois Press, 1991), Halker incorrectly identified Jones with the Methodist Church. In truth, Jones was a Congregationalist, and Rogers was a Methodist. For more on Bliss, see May, *Protestant Churches and Industrial America*, 241–49. Bliss was also profoundly influenced by socialism. It is worth noting that the notion of a separate workers' church outlived the Knights. In 1894, Lynn, Massachusetts, minister Herbert Casson left the Methodist Church to start the Labor Church in that city. See also *Knights of Labor* (Chicago), August 14, 1886, as quoted in Mapes, " 'As You Have Been the World's Providers.' "

18. McNeill, *The Labor Movement*, 468–69.

lived his involvement in the order, and intensified as he grew older. In a 1903 poem, "The Risen Laborer," McNeill likened organized labor to the triumphant armies of Constantine.[19]

Knights of Labor came to see their quest for justice as a religious crusade. An Illinois miner's wife thought KOL lecturer Richard Trevellick was the "second Jesus Christ" after one of his speeches.[20] Local Assembly 300 bragged that all meetings opened and ended with fervent prayer, while Joseph Buchanan blamed Denver clergy's opposition to the Knights on the fact that "ours was the only genuine Christian society in the city" and thus drew bigger crowds than the churches. One writer asserted simply that it was impossible to be a True Christian unless one was a Knight.[21]

Once again it was Powderly who summed up how many Knights used religion. He called Christ the "world's greatest, most sublime agitator," and fused the languages of social and moral reform. Powderly cataloged all the teachings of Christ that he found applicable to his day, including humility, identification with the poor and condemnation of the rich, commitment to social justice, and honesty.[22] Powderly noted that few of these teachings were practiced by clerics or "so-called Christian" businessmen. What else could Knights do but take up the burden themselves? After all, their platform charged them with making "industrial, moral, and social worth—not wealth—the true standard of individual and national greatness." Thus Knights of Labor came to see themselves as the guardians of true Christianity, embroiled in a holy crusade to save society from Churchianity.

Labor Jeremiads

If the Knights were True Christians, it followed that their clerical opponents were false ones. Powderly remembered,

> Frequently, when at my desk . . . I raised my eyes to a picture of the Crucified Christ on the wall confronting me. Always I won-

19. George E. McNeill, *Unfrequented Paths: Songs of Nature, Labor, and Men* (Boston: James West, 1903), 31–35.

20. See Herbert Gutman, "The Christian Spirit in the Gilded Age," in his *Work, Culture, and Society*.

21. 1886 *Proceedings of Local Assembly 300*, in *PP*; For prayers offered at general assemblies, see any GA *Proceedings*, in *PP*; see also Buchanan, *Labor Agitator*, 258; *JUL*, May 16, 1889.

22. Powderly, *The Path I Trod*, 38, 378.

dered why men who spoke in His name did not walk in his footsteps. Were they His representatives or merely mouthpieces, and was their service but lip service? I often asked myself this question: If Christian teachers had always followed Christ in word and deed would we need such an organization as the Knights of Labor?[23]

John Swinton suggested that most ministers were "jawsmiths" who would be better off listening to KOL lecturers than their own pompous voices. District Assembly 49 went one step further; it added "theologians" to the list of those ineligible for KOL membership.[24]

Knights honored those who valued labor over respectability. An often-cited case was that of the Bishop of London who, in 1888, shocked the religious establishment by resigning his posh post to live among the city's poor. His resignation letter was often reprinted in the *JUL*, and Powderly wrote numerous editorials in praise of the bishop's action. In one such editorial, Powderly noted that, for years, the pulpit was filled with men "who preached the doctrine, 'servants, obey your masters'; but never did they tell who had the right to be master."[25]

Another favorite Christian role model was Wendell Phillips. Scores of KOL locals were named for Phillips, including ones in Springfield, Massachusetts, and Detroit. Phillips was attractive since he, like many Knights, worked out his religious views largely independent of institutional churches. Phillips was also an early friend of labor with ties to the National Labor Union, the eight-hour movement, the Massachusetts Labor Reform party, and the Knights of St. Crispin. He was also an early admirer of KOL activity. Phillips's 1884 death unleashed torrents of praise from the KOL press.[26]

If Phillips was a favorite exemplar, Henry Ward Beecher was the whipping post par excellence. From his Brooklyn pulpit, Beecher won fame and popularity among much of the middle and upper class through the articulation of what one historian called a gospel of "qualitative hedo-

23. Ibid., 378.
24. *John Swinton's Paper*, July 4, 1886; *John Swinton's Paper*, August 8, 1886. Either DA 49 interpreted "theologian" loosely, or its rhetoric was different from actual practice. In truth, numerous clerics joined DA 49, including the Reverend Heber Newton, the Reverend James Huntington, and Father Edward McGlynn.
25. *JUL*, July 5, 1888.
26. For a biographical sketch of Wendell Phillips, see Irving H. Barlett, *Wendell Phillips: Brahmin Radical* (Boston: Beacon Press, 1961); for several of Phillips's prolabor speeches, see *John Swinton's Paper*, October 28, 1883; February 10, 1884; *Labor Enquirer*, February 16, 1884.

nism."[27] Beecher's insistence on equating poverty with indolence won him few friends among the labor movement, and his Social Darwinian defense of laissez-faire—"God has intended the great to be great, and the little to be little"—earned him the scorn of many. In the midst of the 1877 railway strikes he uttered a gross, and often-quoted comment about the low wages that workers complained of: "Water costs nothing; and a man who can't live on bread is not fit to live."[28]

That off-the-cuff remark followed Beecher to the grave. The *Labor Enquirer* could hardly contain its glee when Beecher died in 1887:

> If there is any truth in the Christian religion Henry Ward Beecher is now having brimstone for breakfast, fire and brimstone for luncheon, and good brimstone and hot fire for supper. I rejoice that this man is dead and IN JUDGEMENT. He disgraced even the rotten world in which he lived, and the cries of your starving children will take on a note of gladness when they hear he is gone.[29]

Powderly's suggestion that Beecher made his "bread and water" comment in a moment of passion and was, in fact, a friend of labor was greeted with withering contempt. Jesse Jones pointed out that Beecher "never did get out of the age of individualism," while John Swinton remarked that Beecher's youthful abolitionism "fell under the flatteries of fortune [and] he prostrated himself before the wealthy; he worshipped the golden calf; and his old audience of youthful enthusiasts became a congregation of gilded crabs."[30]

Beecher was emblematic of all that Knights thought was wrong with Gilded Age churches. Even when church leaders discussed the labor problem, a task many turned to in the mid-1880s, labor remained aloof. When several ministers invited John Swinton to hear their sermons, he could hardly contain his skepticism. Swinton asked,

> Where have you been all these years? You have seen the anguish of the masses; you have heard the cries of the sinking multitudes; you have seen the growth of desolating social evils . . . you have

27. Paul Carter, *The Spiritual Crisis of the Gilded Age* (DeKalb: Northern Illinois Press, 1971), 136.

28. Beecher's quote from Carter, *Spiritual Crisis*, 136; May, *Protestant Churches and Industrial America*, 55, 71.

29. *Labor Enquirer* (Denver), March 12, 1887.

30. Powderly, "Speak Well of the Dead," clipping in *PP*; *Labor Leader*, April 2, 1887; *Labor Enquirer* (Chicago), March 19, 1887.

seen the working people trying to grapple with one wrong after another; your ears must have got within sound of their earnest voices pleading for justice. . . . Oh, tell us the news! Where have you been all these years? . . . Eight years ago, when we again had hard times, the only clerical voice heard in hardscrabble was BEECHER'S raucous insult of Bread and Water![31]

Like Swinton, most labor leaders showed little hesitation in lambasting clerics who they thought were ill-informed or antithetical to labor's cause. In Detroit, Joseph Labadie commented on the Rev. Edwin Webb's sermon on socialism: "[It is] a mass of nonsense. . . . If anyone wants to know how foolish and how vicious a man can be he should read it." When the Rev. Rexford vexed Labadie, he devoted three columns of the *Labor Leaf* to personal tirades in response. Under the headline "The Fallacies Preached in the Pulpit: A High-Toned Preacher Talks Nonsense on the Labor Question," Labadie excoriated Rexford's character and warned him of labor's growing impatience: "The pulpit knows little of the subject [of political economy], because it knows little of the laborer. . . . You do not comprehend him. He is fast ceasing to pay any heed to you."[32] When offended, Labadie cared little for the social status of men or institutions. When the YMCA sponsored debates that concluded labor organizations were not beneficial to society, Labadie sneered, "As usual, the YMCA takes the side of capital in the oppression of labor." Likewise, when Samuel Harris, Episcopal bishop for Michigan, released a pamphlet on the errors of socialism, Labadie sarcastically assumed the persona of a "greasy mechanic" to point out to the "learned bishop" that he was "not well acquainted with his subject."[33]

From Denver, Joseph Buchanan unleashed invectives against the church and noted that "with a few exceptions the pulpit took no interest in the labor movement except to lecture it and abuse it, and the exceptions soon lost their charges or found their churches unpopular with those able to pay the minister's salary."[34] A Denver colleague complained in an editorial to the *Labor Enquirer*:

After seeing so much mockery of the meek and lowly Nazarene in our fashionable churches I am forced to the conclusion that

31. *John Swinton's Paper*, April 14, 1886.

32. *Labor Leaf*, January 20, 1886; May 12, 1886; December 2, 1885; August 26, 1885; April 28, 1887. The Reverend Webb hailed from Boston and was a representative of the American Missionary Society. The sermon that rankled Labadie was given by Webb at an AMS meeting in Saratoga Springs, N.Y.

33. *Labor Leaf*, December 2, 1885; February 17, 1886.

34. Buchanan, *Story of a Labor Agitator*, 133.

they are a standing menace to the poor and a flaunting lie in the face of Him they profess to worship. . . . Oh! ye ministers of the gospel! God will call you into account for your remissness of duty in allowing such evils to go unrebuked; the robbed widow and orphan will stand as menacing witnesses against you at the bar of Eternal Justice.[35]

Knights seethed when churchmen dared lecture them on the subject of morality. One Knight found it "strange" that some churches forbade their members to join the KOL, given that it was "far more particular than most churches as to whom it admits for membership." He went on to list those undesirables found not in the Knights but in churches: "liquor dealers, gamblers, lawyers, money-shovers, and stock speculators."[36] In Chicago, Thomas Young suggested that socialists were better Christians than most ministers because he was yet "to meet the first atheist Socialist," though he had met many "Christless" clerics.[37] When news reached Pittsburgh that the Missouri Synod advised Lutherans not to join the Knights of Labor, an outraged editorialist for the *National Labor Tribune* wrote, "The convocation has gone far out of the line of its duty, as that duty is understood in countries where Church and State are independent of one another." The writer suggested that the Synod save its moralizing "for employer's associations . . . [where it is] truly needed."[38]

In Iowa, James Sovereign defended the Knights against clerical attacks. In Cincinnati, the mantle was taken up by Melinda Sissins; in Baltimore by J. G. Schonfarber; and by Phillips Thompson across Canada.[39] Knights like J. H. Amies of Scranton, Thomas Drury of Rutland, Vermont, Jesse Jones of Boston, Heber Newton of New York, and Thomas Van Ness of Denver frequently condemned the hypocrisy of ministers, even though each of them was an ordained clergyman.[40] Van

35. *Labor Enquirer*, February 11, 1886.
36. *JUL*, December 10, 1885.
37. *Labor Enquirer*, June 2, 1886.
38. *National Labor Tribune*, May 21, 1887.
39. For typical remarks on Gilded Age clergy coming from KOL ranks, see *John Swinton's Paper*, esp. July 4, 1886; also *Industrial Leader*, December 18, 1886; *The Critic*, May 18, 1889; *JKL*, June 19, 1990; T. Phillips Thompson, *The Politics of Labor* (Toronto: University of Toronto Press, 1975).
40. See *The Critic*, May 18, 1890. For more on clerics within the KOL, see *PP*, esp. Thomas L. Drury to Powderly, April 21, 1891. This letter contains one of the very few mentions that Drury was ordained. He was quite active in the Rutland Knights, but was known for his role as Master Workman, not his preaching. See also Powderly to J. H. Amies, December 17, 1889, in *PP*. Powderly sent an organizer's commission to the Rev. Amies.

Ness went so far as to accuse fellow clergymen of offering workers "sugar plums" when they "want a steady supply of roast beef."[41]

For sheer vitriol, few Knights could match Alexander W. Wright whose "Spokeshave" columns frequented the *Journal of the Knights of Labor* (JKL) from 1891 through 1893. Wright denounced "canting editors of religious papers," labeled the Rev. Samuel Small of Philadelphia as a "pulpit freak," and dismissed clerical opposition to Sunday openings for the upcoming 1893 Chicago Exposition as the ravings of a "small army of cranks." When the Harrisburg, Pennsylvania, *Church Advocate* attacked a plan for a state lottery and chided workers for their gambling habits, Wright sneered at its hypocrisy:

> If a man plays a game of poker or takes a hand of euchre at five cents a corner, or buys a pool on a race-horse, the religious papers are so cock sure that he is bound for the land of no ice men. But a fellow can speculate in corn or pork, bet on the rise or fall of stocks, he may even gamble on whiskey . . . and no religious paper . . . will ever brand him a gambler. A man may become a millionaire by speculating on town lots and yet, according to the religious papers, bank with certainty upon a celestial corner lot.[42]

Labor jeremiads had their effect; by the 1800s Knights routinely identified more with the Order than with their churches. In Boston, Edward Rogers insisted that "Christ identified himself with working people" but modern churches presented him only as a "personal Saviour." In the absence of a Christ who provided for "secular and social, as well as . . . spiritual and individual wants," churches "have set up a golden calf in his place."[43] A Knight from Allentown, New York, proudly claimed membership in an Order with "more Christianity in it to the square inch than all the modern churches this side of Helena." He claimed that KOL's principles, "if put into practical application, would do more to fill our churches with law-abiding, peaceful, happy, patriotic, God-loving people than all the fat, canting, chicken-eating dominies in Christendom."[44] New York City's "Plutarch" noted simply that the KOL had no place for preachers with "kid gloved minds" afraid "to mingle with the masses."[45] By mid-1892, Plutarch was so fed up that he uttered the unthinkable: "God, so far, has done very little for the labor move-

41. *Labor Enquirer* (Chicago), April 6, 1887.
42. *JKL*, April 26, 1891; April 30, 1891; December 24, 1891.
43. *Labor Leader* (Boston), February 12, 1887.
44. *JUL*, May 16, 1889.
45. *JKL*, May 1, 1892.

ment."[46] Few Knights were willing to go that far but, like Plutarch, still stayed home on Sunday.

Voices in the Wilderness: Protestant Allies of the Knights

The KOL's response to religious hypocrisy was extreme, but was it too much so? Did seeking to become a workers' church stifle would-be progressive clerical allies? Was the KOL so blinded by Beecher-like enemies that it turned away better men? One historian criticized Powderly and wrote, "Of all union men, [he] might have been expected to respond in a friendly way . . . [but instead] told a story of repeated and active hostility on the part of Protestants as well as Catholic clerics . . . [and denounced] organized religion in general."[47]

But critics of KOL policy both ignore the attempts made to appease clerics, and overestimate the power of Gilded Age Social Gospel movements. Powderly made huge concessions to Gilded Age churches by making the KOL public, rewriting the *AK*, denouncing anarchism, and sending envoys to clerical conferences. The little fruit these concessions bore suggests that the KOL's critique of Gilded Age organized religion was on-target, and Powderly's animosity was justified. The Order's battles with the Catholic Church are well-documented, but what of Protestant clerics?[48] Sadly, the record is equally bleak.

Despite mutual suspicion, scores of Protestant ministers either joined or defended the Knights of Labor. Yet as progressive men of God took up the KOL's cause, a painful, but obvious, fact emerged: their numbers were too few and their voices too weak to convert their antilabor colleagues, sway their hostile congregations, or transform the institutions they represented. Whatever the Social Gospel movement became emerged too late to help the Knights of Labor.

By the mid-1880s, scores of theologians debated the "labor question," pondered the absence of workers in the pews, and issued reams of tracts, sermons, and lectures on the pressing social issues of the day. Frederic Dan Huntington and his son James show both the potential and limits of Gilded Age bonds between the church and labor. Both men

46. Ibid., June 9, 1892.
47. May, *Protestant Churches and Industrial America*, 216–17.
48. For more on Powderly and the Catholic Church, see Powderly, *The Path I Trod*, 317–82; and Browne, "The Catholic Church and the Knights of Labor."

were Episcopalians, the Gilded Age's most sympathetic church toward the working class. In 1869, Frederic Dan was made bishop of central New York and moved his family from Hadley, Massachusetts, to Syracuse. A man who experimented with numerous religious traditions as a youth, Bishop Huntington noticed that none captured the imagination of workers. He began an inquiry into conditions of labor that culminated in 1887, when he and his son James founded the Church Association in the Interests of Labor (CAIL). Bishop Huntington served as CAIL president from 1887 until his death in 1904.

Frederic Dan Huntington was an ardent and moralistic reformer. Much like Powderly, the elder Huntington immersed himself in a variety of reform movements, including those involving labor. The KOL first attracted his attention in 1883, and Huntington offered tentative praise.[49] He also upheld the KOL as an alternative to more dangerous groups such as the socialists and communists. The Knights, he wrote, "breathe a spirit . . . in consonance with the laws of Christian ethics."[50]

When Huntington threw his support behind CAIL, he authored a carefully worded pamphlet to counter objections from within Episcopal ranks. He asked the church's affluent members to recognize their responsibility to labor, to reject laissez-faire economics, and to recall Christ's own ministry to the poor. He reminded them of "how [Christ] lived . . . how He invariably treated social distinctions, on what social classes He pronounced benedictions . . . and at the hand of what class he was crucified." Huntington found distressing parallels in his own time, and age marked by "turmoil and violence, strikes and lock-outs, hung-up wheels of factories, and stalled railway trains." Like Uriah Stephens, he assigned blame to "legislators and manufacturers and millionaires" who showed contempt for the "brotherhood of man."[51]

By 1890, Bishop Huntington had convinced forty other bishops to join CAIL. He declared "Labor Sunday" once each year, a day given over to an exploration of how the church could aid the working class. New York City's 1891 Labor Sunday enjoyed the full cooperation of the KOL. More

49. Frederic Dan Huntington, *Memoir and Letters of Frederic Dan Huntington*, ed. Aria S. Huntington (New York: Riverside Press, 1906), 165, 196; Ruth Huntington Sessions, *Sixty Odd: A Personal History* (Brattleboro, Vt.: Stephen Daye, 1936); F. D. Huntington, "The Church and the Labor World," *Iron Cross*, 1883, Porter-Phelps-Huntington Papers, Amherst College [hereafter cited *PPHP*].

50. F. D. Huntington, "Some Points in the Labor Question," *The Church Review*, July 1886, in *PPHP*.

51. F. D. Huntington, "Open Letter to the Living Church," publication of the Church Association in the Interests of Labor, no. 1, 1887, in *PPHP*; F. D. Huntington, *Memoir and Letters*, 353–55.

important, CAIL lobbied for reformed tenement labor laws, mandatory arbitration of labor disputes, the abolition of child labor, and a shorter work day. CAIL was even successful in diverting all of the Episcopal church's printing needs to union shops. Not surprisingly, the KOL praised Huntington. *The Critic* printed the CAIL platform side-by-side with the KOL's own, and the Order's official journal frequently excerpted Huntington's sermons.[52]

If Frederic Dan Huntington showed the reform possibilities of a circumspect rhetorician, his son James exemplified the spirit of direct action. In Syracuse, James found himself working in institutions for which his father was an overseer. These experiences, studies of Episcopal monaticism, and his friendship with Leonora O'Reilly, led to a decision to become actively involved with the poor. In 1884, he and two other priests went to New York City's Lower East Side and formed the Brothers of the Holy Cross, the first American order of Episcopal monks. They lived in a sparsely furnished tenement in one of New York's poorest working-class neighborhoods. O'Reilly introduced James to the Knights of Labor and he joined DA 49, its prohibition against clerics notwithstanding.[53]

James Huntington's pronouncements show influences from DA 49's more radical side. In an address to the Anti-Poverty Society he thundered:

> There are workingmen in this country who have paid for themselves not three but thirty times, and they do not belong to themselves yet. Why? Because a number of men get hold of labor by declaring that they have a right to the bodies of men; that they have a right to make other men use their powers to minister to their advantage and comfort. Then you have slavery.

The younger Huntington surfaced in Streator, Illinois, to help local Knights negotiate an end to a coal strike, led boycotts against sweated goods in New York City, and was among the most tireless workers for Henry George's 1886 mayoral campaign.[54]

52. F. D. Huntington, "Causes of Social Discontent," *The Forum*, September 1888, in *PPHP*. Also see Huntington's address to the Evangelical Alliance (Boston, December 5, 1889), in *PPHP*; May, *Protestant Churches and Industrial America*, 184–85; *National Labor Tribune*, April 25, 1891; *The Critic*, June 21, 1890; *JKL*, December 3, 1891.

53. F. D. Huntington, *Memoir and Letters*, 338; Sessions, *Sixty Odd*, 303–4; *The Standard*, July 23, 1887, in *PPHP*.

54. James Lincoln Huntington, "James Otis Sargent Huntington," pamphlet, 1937, in *PPHP*; May, *Protestant Churches and Industrial America*, 239–41; Vida Dutton Scudder, *Father*

Huntington initiated others—including Vida Scudder—into the Knights of Labor. In 1891, he went to Toronto on the Order's behalf, and was an honored speaker in Philadelphia at the KOL's twenty-third anniversary celebration. Before an assembly of KOL women, Huntington praised the Order's commitment to "human brotherhood." He bitterly denounced Andrew Carnegie for the savagery of the 1892 Homestead Steel lock-out. Everywhere he went, he reminded his audiences that he was simultaneously a priest, a "Free-Trader, a Single-Taxist, and a Knight of Labor."[55]

The Huntingtons meant, and did, well. As Episcopalians, they were the best representatives of the Gilded Age's most sympathetic church toward labor. Other leaders who were at least willing to consider the merits of labor's social cirtiques included Thomas Clark, bishop of Rhode Island; Phillips Brooks, bishop of Massachusetts; the Rev. Heber Newton, a member of DA 49; William Porter Bliss, a member of DA 30 in Boston and cofounder of the Church of the Carpenter; and layman economist Richard Ely. Not even J. P. Morgan could escape in the Episcopal Church; the rector of his St. George's Church of New York City was W. S. Rainford, a man profoundly influenced by Christian socialism, and his bishop and good friend, Henry Codman Potter, was the second president of CAIL.[56]

Yet it is fair to ask what good this did the Knights. For all of its well-intentioned leaders, Episcopalianism was also the Gilded Age's wealthiest church. Morgan may have squirmed uncomfortably during Rainsford's sermons, but he remained unconverted. Alfred Thayer Mahan simply quit the church because of its Social Gospel leanings. Many leaders—including Samuel S. Harris, the bishop of Michigan—were openly hostile to labor. Ultimately, Episcopal rhetoric outdistanced its achievements. Organizations like CAIL presaged Progressive era reform in areas like sweat shop reform, child labor laws, and factory inspection

Huntington: Founder of the Order of the Holy Cross (New York: E. P. Dutton, 1940); *The Holy Cross Magazine*, August 1935. Vida Scudder was a delegate to the Knights of Labor 1886 General Assembly held in Richmond, Virginia.

55. Scudder, *Father Huntington*, 148, 160; *The Critic*, October 5, 1889; *JKL*, February 12, 1891; *JKL*, January 7, 1892. Scudder claims that Huntington addressed Knights in Toronto, Minneapolis, Memphis, New York, and Brooklyn during 1890 alone.

56. For more on Episcopalians and the labor movement, see *JUL*, January 10, 1889; John Rutherford Everett, *Religion in Economics* (New York: King's Crown Press, 1946), 75; Richard T. Ely, *The Labor Movement in America* (New York: Thomas Y. Crowell, 1886), v; *John Swinton's Paper*, September 6, 1886; *The Christian Union*, January 1, 1890; May, *Protestant Churches and Industrial America*, 242–45; W.D.P. Bliss, *American Trade Unionism* (Boston: Church Social Union, 1896); Ely, "Land, Labor, and Taxation," *The Independent*, December 29, 1887; *The Independent*, August 28, 1890.

codes—impressive changes, but pale when compared with KOL demands. Social Gospel advocates were seldom willing to question the basic assumptions of capitalism, and most Episcopalians, if they thought of labor at all, were likely more comfortable with the rhetoric of Frederic Dan Huntington than with the social activism of his son. Richard Ely was one such man, and his writings were arguably more influential than most of the sermons of Gilded Age Episcopalianism.

Like Frederick Dan Huntington, Ely praised the Knights of Labor for being "in line with the precepts of Christianity" and fostering the "good opinion" of employers who truly wished "their laborers well." That said, he criticized several of the Order's principles, including any that smacked of public ownership. He cautioned Knights to eschew socialism in favor of "the doctrine of human brotherhood," an appropriation of Uriah Stevens's vision that rejected the structural base upon which the precept rested. When Ely repeated these thoughts before a gathering of Baltimore Knights he was politely, but unenthusiastically, received.[57]

Another striking fact about Episcopal support for the Knights of Labor is that so much of it came when the Order was in decline. Frederic Dan Huntington was virtually alone among Episcopalians in supporting the KOL in 1883, when the Order needed a boost. By the time CAIL was formed in 1887, the KOL was sinking; when it was effective in the late 1890s, the Order was nearly dead. Swinton's charge that clerical interest in labor was driven more by trend than commitment rings disturbingly true.

James Huntington's career shows still another limit to Episcopalian reform efforts. Shortly after his bitter denunciation of Carnegie at the Knights' 1892 anniversary celebration, Huntington abruptly retired from public life. His Holy Cross monastery on the Lower East Side of New York City was closed, and reopened in Westminster, Maryland, a rural town far from the rumblings of industrial strife. In 1904, the monastery was moved to its current home in West Park, New York, a scenic village on the Hudson River, north of Poughkeepsie. From 1893 to his death in 1935, James Huntington's social opinions were confined to his prayers and his writings.

A big problem for the KOL was that Episcopalianism was the best that Gilded Age organized religion could offer; most churches showed significantly less sympathy. Though some churches produced men of the caliber of the Huntingtons, few were able to convince many of their colleagues. Once one strays from Episcopalianism, religious support for

---

57. Ely, *The Labor Movement in America*, 75–84; *Labor Leader*, February 1, 1890; *The Critic*, January 31, 1891.

the KOL was countermanded by powerful opposition. Lutherans, Baptists, and Reformed Presbyterians cautioned their flocks to avoid the KOL, with the Presbyterians condemning the Knights as a "Christless society." In Chicago, Ezra Asher Cook used the National Christian Association and its nationwide publications to condemn all fraternal societies including the KOL.[58]

Influential journals like the *Christian Advocate, The Christian Union,* and *The Independent* at best damned the KOL with faint praise; at worst, they launched savage attacks on the Order. When the KOL struck Jay Gould's railroads again in 1886, the *Advocate* accused the Order of hoarding vast sums of money in order to "deprive thousands of workers, not Knights, of their right to work for whom they please [and] to cripple the commerce and manufactures of the nation."[59] The *Union* responded with attacks on Joseph Buchanan and George McNeill, while *The Independent's* editor, Henry C. Bowen, published articles from critics like Arthur C. Hadley and Simon Newcomb. Not that Bowen needed help. Simply detesting the KOL, he did not hesitate to label Powderly a "king [who makes] individual liberty a thing of the past . . . [and] rules with all the moderation . . . of a sultan of satraps and slaves."[60] Bowen took great glee in reporting the KOL's demise in the late 1880s. In 1888, he wrote, "The simple truth is that, by reason of lack of brains, as well as false principles, the organization started with its final doom distinctly impressed upon it. . . . It has done no real good for the cause of labor; and

---

58. *John Swinton's Paper,* May 29, 1889; *Labor Enquirer,* February 28, 1885; see also Chapter 7 of this work; also *Labor Enquirer,* February 13, 1886; *Knights of Labor* (Chicago), December 4, 1886.

One of the few Presbyterians to support the KOL was Myron Reed of Denver. For a list of those ministers hostile to the Knights and the KOL's reaction, see *Labor Enquirer,* January 22, 1884; *The Presbyterian Review,* April 1887; *JKL,* February 6, 1890; *JKL,* February 13, 1890; *JKL,* March 30, 1893. Among the Baptists, the following ministers were sympathetic to the KOL: Charles R. Henderson (Detroit), J. C. Allen (Brooklyn), W. W. Everts Jr. (Haverhill, Mass.), Philip Moxom (Boston), C. Herber Woolston (Philadelphia), and Walter Rauschenbusch. For Baptist friends and enemies of the Order, see *John Swinton's Paper,* April 11, 1886; May, *Protestant Churches and Industrial America,* 190–92; *JKL,* May 21, 1891; *Boycotter,* October 24, 1885; *Labor Leaf,* February 24, 1886; *Labor Leaf,* December 22, 1886. See also Ezra A. Cook, *The Knights of Labor Illustrated* (Chicago: Ezra A. Cook, 1886), located in *PP.* This booklet was one in a series that "exposed" secret societies. Other booklets attacked Freemasons, Odd Fellows, Knights of Pythias, and Grand Army of the Republic.

59. *Christian Advocate,* April 29, 1886; May 6, 1886; May 20, 1886; June 24, 1886.

60. *Christian Union,* March 26, 1885; June 3, 1887; *Labor Leaf,* April 3, 1886; *The Independent,* February 19, 1885; July 21, 1885; May 14, 1885; May 25, 1885; March 25, 1886; August 12, 1886; July 15, 1886; June 3, 1887; July 15, 1886; April 18, 1886. For an example of attack on Newcomb, see C. P. Ridenour, "A Plain Man's Talk: Questions," *The Independent,* July 1, 1886; also *The Independent,* June 10, 1886; July 15, 1886; November 4, 1886.

when it shall be dead and gone, no laboring man will have the least cause for regret." When that obituary proved premature, Bowen served the ultimate indignity by encouraging William Vanderbilt to crush the Order during the 1890 New York Central strike.[61]

In each of the three cases, what the journals offered workers was pious pap on the need for patience, moral rectitude, and the promise of reward in the afterlife. Anything that smacked of collective activity was branded as "dangerous socialism." To be fair, each journal ran an occasional piece by sympathetic writers like Frederic Dan Huntington, Lyman Abbott, and Washington Gladden, but as a whole, they mirrored most Gilded Age religious journals by standing closer to Social Darwinism than the Social Gospel.

One is hard-pressed to find a single denomination in which supporters of the Knights outnumbered the critics. Among the Congregationalists, Jesse Jones of Boston, the Rev. E. Fales of Houston, and Hugh Pentecost of Newark, New Jersey, joined the KOL and were quite active. Yet Jones complained, "There are 3,000 Congregational ministers in this land, and Lyman Abbott, [F. A.] Noble, my friend and myself—five [sic] souls out of 3,000—are all those who have ever lifted a volice on this subject [labor], unless you count Beecher's 'bread and water.' " When the Rev. A. H. Bradford protested, he was able to name only eleven others who favored labor, and several on his list—like Josiah Strong and A.J.F. Behrends—were dubious choices.[62]

More typical of Congregationalism were Henry Ward Beecher and Joseph Cook. From 1875 to 1895, Cook used his "Monday Lectures" in Boston to denounce socialism, strikes, and the Knights of Labor.[63] The fates of Jesse Jones and Hugh Pentecost are suggestive of how little support Congregational labor advocates could expect. Jones found himself without a pulpit and spent the three years before his death in 1893 preaching mostly to labor gatherings. The same fate would have likely befallen Pentecost had not he beaten church hierarchy to the task. The Great Upheaval of 1886–87, the Haymarket riots, and Henry George's campaign caused Pentecost to undergo a secular conversion that led him

---

61. *The Independent*, November 22, 1888; September 12, 1889; December 19, 1889; August 28, 1890; October 2, 1890; H. K. Carroll to Terence V. Powderly, September 15, 1890, in *PP*.

62. *Christian Union*, March 25, 1886; July 29, 1886; January 21, 1886; February 5, 1886; April 21, 1887; March 3, 1887; August 25, 1887. *The Haverhill Laborer*, April 24, 1886; May 1, 1886. *John Swinton's Paper*, December 13, 1885. For Washington Gladden's remarks on the labor movement, see *Christian Union*, July 23, 1885; Washington Gladden, *Tools and the Man: Property and Industry Under the Christian Church* (Boston: Houghton-Mifflin, 1893), 13–14, 79–86, 123; Washington Gladden, *Social Salvation* (Hicksville, N.Y.: Regina Press, 1975), 14.

63. Cook's 1882 lecture on the KOL was reprinted in *The Independent*, March 4, 1886 and *Our Day*, December, 1888. The latter reprint is located in *PP*.

to agnosticism and anarchism. Pentecost quit the church and exchanged the Gospel of Christ for that of Kropotkin.[64]

The Knights fare no better with the Unitarians or Universalists. Unitarian friends of the Order included the Reverends J. Coleman Adams of St. Paul, Minnesota; E. M. Clark of Sedalia, Missouri; F. McKinney of Manchester, New Hampshire; and layman Carroll Wright, head of the U.S. Bureau of Labor Statistics. These men raised their voices in support of the KOL, but in Boston, a stronghold of Unitarianism and the base of the KOL's largest district assembly, few clerics were moved. Ministers and writers like Howard Brown, Kate Gannett Wells, and Joseph Ely bitterly denounced the Order.[65] The Knights fared no better at the hands of Universalism. Dr. Cantwell, the editor of the sect's most important journal, *The Universalist*, claimed there was no difference between the KOL and anarchism.[66]

There is little evidence to suggest that Gilded Age Protestantism extended a fraternal hand for the Knights of Labor to grasp. At best its record toward labor was mixed, mostly hostile. It mattered little whether the denomination was high church or low church, theologically conservative or liberal. Despite the outstanding champions of labor each church produced, they were neither numerous nor particularly effective in converting others. Only Episcopalianism produced more than a handful of broad-minded reformers, and even it did little to help the Knights until the Order was in decline. Two typical Protestant clerical champions were Walter Vrooman and C. Herbert Woolston.

Vrooman was popular in Rocky Mountain mining towns where he was nicknamed the "boy-preacher socialist." Knights in Kansas and Colorado enthusiastically reported his sermons, and Vrooman even started a paper in Kansas City in support of the Order and Christian socialism.[67] Yet one is hard-pressed to find another member of Vrooman's Disciples of Christ who was supportive of the KOL. Like Vrooman, Baptist minister C. Herbert Woolston was a firm supporter of

64. May, *Protestant Churches and Industrial America*, 74–79; *Dawn*, April, 1893. For information on Pentecost's support of Henry George, see *Labor Enquirer* (Chicago), July 23, 1887. On Pentecost's decision to leave the church, see *Christian Union*, February 9, 1888. See also May, *Protestant Churches and Industrial America*, 238–39; *Labor Enquirer* (Denver), January 21, 1888; *JUL*, July 15, 1888; Hugh O. Pentecost, "Evolution and Social Reform: The Anarchist Method," in his *Sociology: Popular Lectures and Discussions Before the Brooklyn Ethical Association* (Boston: James West, 1890).

65. *Knights of Labor* (Chicago), December 4, 1886; November 20, 1886; September 18, 1886. *Unitarian Review*, January, 1883; March 1884; November, 1885; March, 1886; April 1886; December, 1886.

66. For the KOL's response to Cantwell, see *Knights of Labor* (Chicago), September 18, 1886.

67. *Labor Enquirer*, July 31, 1886; October 2, 1886.

the Order. When Woolston defended the Knights against a vicious attack on its character, the *Journal of the Knights of Labor* (*JKL*) thanked him, but correctly labeled him "a voice crying out in the wilderness."[68]

All too frequently men like Vrooman and Woolston were prophets without honor among their flocks. Reform-minded ministers joined the Knights, but their voices were whispers, while those of Gilded Age Henry Ward Beechers thundered from the pulpit. In 1891, Powderly received a flyer from John Merritte Driver, a Methodist minister from Fort Wayne, Indiana, who wished Powderly to promote his book favorable to unions and the Knights. Powderly stamped Driver's letter "No Answer Required," and ignored it.[69] In England, Methodism was an integral component of class consciousness, but not in America.

Exchanging Sermons

The antichurch tirades of Labadie, Wright, and Plutarch were standard fare in KOL journals. By the 1890s, even pious, moralistic men like Powderly held out little hope for "Churchianity." This suggests that no attempt at finding common ground was ever considered. Between 1878 and 1892, four important debates occurred within the KOL over its relationship to mainstream Protestantism. The KOL and Protestant churches took a serious look at one another before parting company, particularly during vulnerable moments when one party or the other weighed the potential advantages of an alliance. In the end, neither side was willing to make the sweeping compromises necessary for permanent rapprochement. When the dust settled, both the KOL and the churches resorted to time-tested practices: they exchanged sermons.

68. *JKL*, May 21, 1891. The *JKL* was overly harsh on the Baptists. For other Baptist supporters of the KOL, see note 53, above.

69. J. M. Driver to Powderly, July, 1891, in *PP*. There were a few Methodists who allied themselves with labor. See C. C. McCabe to Powderly, March 27, 1886, in *PP*. McCabe was the recording secretary of a Methodist church on Broadway in New York City. His letter was one of general support for the KOL.

For a decidedly radical Methodist, see *Boycotter*, June 22, 1886. This issue printed segments of sermons from the Reverend Strobridge of New York City's 18th St. Methodist Church that implied that machine-smashing might be necessary on occasion, and one from I. J. Lansing of Brooklyn that compared wage-earners to chattel slaves. Another KOL supporter was William E. Mitchell. See *JKL*, October 8, 1890. The Reverend Mitchell was pastor of New York City's 43rd St. Methodist Church and the editor of *Lyceum Herald*. He praised Powderly for his agitation on behalf of the antimonopoly movement. Perhaps the best-known Methodist reformer was laywoman Emma Willard. For a synopsis of Emma Willard's career as a Methodist reformer, see *Christian Union*, January 30, 1890.

The earliest attempts to make peace were initiated by the Knights in the late 1870s, culminating in 1882 when the Order abandoned secrecy, removed offending scriptural references from its ritual, and replaced its oath with a vow. Much of this was designed to appease Catholic prelates, not Protestant ministers. Nonetheless, it bears noting that Powderly's efforts to appease Gilded Age churches was dramatic and substantial. We have seen the heavy price he paid in terms of opposition and factionalism.

Those Protestant ministers and Catholic priests who noticed applauded Powderly's reforms; few of them did, however. Powderly's enemies wanted to see results in exchange for the KOL's efforts to become more palatable to clerics, and restive elements served notice of their displeasure at the 1882 Grand Assembly. Theodore Cuno introduced a resolution that was referred to the Committee on the State of the Order. Cuno noted that his assembly, Brooklyn's secretive LA 1562, "has resolved to take an active part in the 'spreading of the light,' " which he defined as "truth and science." Cuno suggested that ministers be invited to preach sermons on the "abolition of private property" and on the recovery of "man's natural inheritance . . . from the land-thief class." He drafted an appeal to ministers that was decidedly confrontational in its demand that they follow the KOL's lead or be denounced as hypocrites. One part read:

> Rev. Sir:—You are a professed minister of revealed religion, and we hold you to be such. You proclaim to the world that the Bible, or Holy Scriptures, is your rule and guide of Faith. We assert that Religion is either a grand harmonious, and divine system of truth and justice, or a conglomeration of falsehoods and supersitition. Which is it?
>
> We press you for an answer, and therefore ask you to preach from your pulpit, at the earliest possible moment, sermons based upon the following texts.

Cuno peppered his circular with Scripture texts and ended with Matthew 6:24: "You cannot serve God and Mammon."[70]

For the most part, little came of Cuno's proposal, since his LA 1562 was embroiled in the Duryea scandal, and the Order was still small enough for most churches to ignore. Several toned-down appeals to

---

70. 1882 *Proceedings of the Knights of Labor Grand Assembly,* in *PP.* Cuno also recommended that ministers use the following texts in their sermons on behalf of labor: Lev. 25:23–37; Amos 9:15; Matt. 6:24.

clerics left KOL headquarters, but there is little evidence of any clerical response. The lack of clerical attention was parodied in an 1884 *JUL* poem in which preachers sermonized about the need to collect money to send missionaries to the far-off land of "Borroboola Gha," where starvation, immorality, and injustice were a short walk from even the most posh church.[71]

Neglect vanished when the KOL defeated Jay Gould in 1885. The third phase of KOL/church relations found the Knights playing hard to get. In 1886, churches extended a fraternal hand, and the KOL was strong enough to demand concessions. As we have seen, the 1886 ecumenical Church Congress coveted Powderly's blessing for its discussion, "The Workingman's Distrust of the Church; its Causes and Remedies." Powderly authorized surrogates to represent the KOL, including civil service reformer Everett Wheeler, president of the Amalgamated Association of Iron and Steel Workers John Jarrett, Henry George, and Dr. Wayland Hoyt, a Philadelphia clergyman.[72]

None of these men minced words in telling clerics what was wrong with Gilded Age churches; all of them sang the KOL's praises, and insisted that it was a refuge of true Christianity. This time, ministers listened with respect as the Order's strength could not be ignored. Abandoning their customary defensiveness, many clerics reacted with an enthusiasm that threatened to transform the conference into a KOL pep rally. The Rev. T. DeWitt Talmadge, normally cautious in his support of labor, promptly joined a Brooklyn local assembly, while the Rev. William Wilforce Newton of Pittsfield, Massachusetts, gushed, "I don't know whether the Knights of Labor have captured us or we the Knights; but thank God we are beside them."[73] Even the cautious Lyman Abbott was moved. Shortly after the Congress he came out in favor of the eight-hour work day, denounced a Methodist minister who supported Jay Gould, called the Knights of Labor the most "just and reasonable" of all labor organizations, and counseled capitalists to "make common cause" with the KOL.[74]

Organized religion's 1886 praise of the KOL proved ephemeral. It was not long before Lyman Abbott tempered his support for the Knights, first by pointing out flawed ideas, and then by attacking it outright. By mid-1887, his *Christian Union* magazine declared itself "very doubtful

---

71. Most *JUL* issues contained lists of books recommended for local assembly purchase and available through the general secretary's office. For the poem "Borraboola Gha," see *JUL*, October 25, 1884.

72. Knights of Labor, *Labor: Its Rights and Wrongs*, 230.

73. Ibid., 268–72.

74. Ibid., 63–65.

about the perpetuity of the Knights of Labor," and "more than doubt-ful" about "some of its principles" and actions. Other religious papers, like *The Independent*, rejoiced when the Knights lost the 1887 Reading strike.[75] Clerical support for labor was shallow, and could not transcend the euphoria of moments like those in Cleveland. Generally, the Great Upheaval proved too great a challenge for most clerics, and it crystalized opposition to the Knights rather than win the Order new friends.

The highwater mark in KOL/Protestant church relations proved to be 1886. Once the Knights of Labor began to decline, ministers began to attack or ignore it. For an Order in desperate need of allies, church at-tacks were another measure of perceived hypocrisy, and a justification for the harsh counterattacks of Labadie, Wright, and Plutarch. Still, the KOL made a final attempt at rapprochement, a feeble gesture on behalf of John Hayes to rekindle the church's flagging interest in the KOL, and boost the circulation of the *JKL*. In 1892, Hayes pulled a page from Cuno's book and addressed a general letter to clergymen. He reminded them of the importance of the labor question:

> He who would preach the gospel to the poor, and who would preach it so that the common people will hear him gladly, must not only be able to tell them of theological and spiritual matters, but he must be able to sympathetically speak to them on those social and industrial questions, on the right solution to which their material welfare so greatly depends; questions which . . . will help or hinder the moral growth of the people.

Hayes disingenuously claimed the KOL was "the most numerous of all labor organizations," and representative of "the aims and objects of labor organizations generally."[76]

Few ministers responded to Hayes's call, just as few responded to Cuno eleven years earlier, and it is doubtful that many Knights took Hayes seriously either. A church/KOL alliance never materialized be-cause rhetoric passed for action in rapprochement efforts. Rather than genuine attempts to fuse interests, each side courted the other in its own interests. Courting gave way to sermonizing, which soon degenerated into rancor.

From Knighthood's earliest days, individual Knights viewed religion as a private matter. By viewing their Order as a workingman's church,

---

75. *Christian Union*, August 25, 1887; *The Independent*, January 19, 1888, November 22, 1888.
76. Letter located in *PP*. It is also reprinted in several 1892 editions of the *JKL*.

Knights saw no reason why they should not air their own views on religious matters. *The Critic* ran articles on "Sunday Discourse," a series of labor lectures held in Baltimore, that had all the earmarks of labor sermons. One afternoon featured A. W. Wright and Thomas McGuire. Wright joked that he was uncomfortable speaking on Sunday because he didn't "wish to scab on clergymen." He proceeded to harangue the audience with his views on man's place in the cosmology, the sanctity of toil, and the hypocrisy of Lyman Abbott. McGuire used the Lord's Prayer to argue that the brotherhood of man demanded the destruction of the "present commercial system."[77]

In the 1890s, the Knights of Labor conducted its own religious affairs. Incredibly, after decades of betrayal and hostility, Protestant clerics still wondered why workers stayed away, an issue explored by Francis Douglas for readers of *The Christian Union*. When the Rev. E. P. Foster of Cincinnati wrote to the *JKL* to complain of Melinda Sissins's attack on Protestant defenses of the rich, suggesting that labor's hostility was hurting its chances of changing denominational attitudes, it was Sissins who engendered sympathetic letters.[78] The stage was set for zealots like Plutarch to spew their venom with impunity as fewer and fewer Knights clung to the belief that churches had much to offer beyond hollow sermons.

No Roads Lead to Rome

The KOL underwent three major demographic shifts that affected the Order's religious orientation. The craftsmen who founded the KOL were mostly native-born and Protestant, as were the bulk of their early recruits. As the Order moved beyond Philadelphia and attracted miners, shoemakers, and textile workers, membership composition changed. By the time he assumed control of the Knights, Terence Powderly, the son of an Irish immigrant, was representative of the new rank and file. Irish Catholics like Powderly controlled most of the leadership positions by the early 1880s.

We have seen how pressure from Catholics led to changes in the KOL ritual. So too we have witnessed the way in which KOL leaders battled Protestant clerics and developed practices and beliefs that stood in opposition to established Gilded Age churches. Irish Catholic leaders led the

---

77. *The Critic*, May 18, 1890.
78. *Christian Union*, June 16, 1890; *JKL*, June 19, 1890; July 10, 1890; July 17, 1890.

KOL as it underwent its third demographic shift: an influx of new members in the mid-1880s, the bulk of whom were non-Irish and non-Catholic. KOL leaders erred in adopting a highly public profile in battles against organized religion. The move from private to public belief led to the politicization of religion within KOL ranks, allowing theology to rear its read and exacerbate tensions between Catholics and non-Catholics within the Order. KOL leaders were unable to escape the suspicion that they opted for hard-line policies for Protestants, but appeasement toward the Church of Rome.

This became problematic during the mid-1880s, when the relative percentage of Catholic Knights declined. Powderly assumed control in 1878, when Catholics were in the majority. By 1884, Powderly estimated, they constituted about half of the rank and file. That percentage was destined to decline further as the Knights expanded into new areas. For example, Joe Buchanan helped organize 25,000 employees of the Union Pacific Railroad into DA 82. Although some of these western Knights were in occupations that historically drew on Irish labor, this was not uniformly so, and Irish enclaves were not as concentrated as they were in the industrial northeast.[79] A break-down of Illinois' 37,974 Knights shows that in 1886 45 percent were native-born, 16 percent German, 13 percent Irish, 10 percent British, and 5 percent Scandinavian.[80] Of these groups, only southern Germans and Irish were traditionally Roman Catholic. Numbers are similar in New Jersey where, in 1887, only one-fifth of the state's 40,172 members claimed Irish ancestry. There was even a small number of Jews in the Order.[81]

Catholicism was on the rise in Gilded Age America, but so was nativism and anti-Catholicism. Despite a 500 percent increase in their numbers, between 1840 and 1860 Catholics remained a religious minority. As the composition of KOL rank and file changed in the 1880s, the Order's Catholic leaders often confronted members who had internalized the anti-Catholicism of popular culture. For these members, efforts to win papal approval of the Knights were misguided. In 1891, Pope Leo XIII issued the encyclical *Rerum Novarum*, which removed Rome's objections to organized labor. Powderly's lobbying was influential, but it raised the ire of Protestant Knights who resented the time and energy involved.

79. Powderly to Patrick Ryan, October 24, 1884, in *PP*; Stromquist, *A Generation of Boomers*, 61–69, 188–89.

80. John R. Commons et al., *History of Labour in the United States, vol. 2* (New York: Macmillan, 1936), 382.

81. The information on New Jersey Knights comes form C. Kim Voss, "Working Class Formation and the Knights of Labor, 1875–1895" (Ph.D. diss., Stanford University, 1986), 75. For more on Jews within the KOL, see Herbert Gutman, "The Knights of Labor and Patrician Anti-Semitism," *Labor History* 13 (1972): 63–67.

Powderly's inconsistency contributed to Protestant complaints. In 1881, he signaled that he was weary of courting the Catholic Church:

> If the workingmen don't know enough to stay in the order and help themselves in this world then go to hell when they die in preference to leaving it to accommodate the church, remain in poverty all their lives and go to hell when they die, then I can't help them one bit. I believe that if God is anything of a labor man at all he'll remember these cowardly scoundrels who flee from us to save their souls (if they have souls).[82]

Powderly was already feeling the heat from disgruntled Protestants who were upset over changes in the ritual. He also felt pressure from radicals—like those of DA 49—who cared little what any clergyman thought of the Order.

Protestations to the contrary aside, Powderly did care. When Roman Catholic bishops gathered in Baltimore in 1884 to discuss the Knights, Powderly begged them not to condemn the Order: "Turn us out of this organization and it becomes a Protestant association with a return to oath-bound secrecy, and instead of a blessing to us it will prove a curse."[83] Powderly reminded the bishops that only one-half of KOL membership was Catholic, but that most of its leaders were. His appeals were for naught as both the bishops and Rome denounced the Knights.

Powderly's concern for church opinions can be seen in his battles with Quebec's intransigent Archbishop Elzear Alexander Taschereau, who denounced the Knights in 1885. Powderly enlisted the aid of the sympathetic James Cardinal Gibbons of Baltimore, who likewise failed to move Taschereau. Powderly's own trips to Quebec in 1885 and 1886 proved equally unsuccessful. Only two of Quebec's thirty-six KOL locals were French-speaking, and since most English-speaking Quebecers were Protestant, it is unlikely many Knights were affected by Taschereau's ravings.[84]

The clash with Taschereau led to a rumor that Powderly planned to seek papal approval in a trip to Rome. This caused outrage among Protestant Knights who had applauded Powderly's earlier chastisement of Catholics. In early 1885, Powderly appeared to agree with his critics. To Robert Layton he confided:

> We have such damn good Catholics in the Order that they confess not only their sins but their virtues. If they want to get drunk, if

---

82. Powderly to Charles Litchman, May 18, 1881, in *PP.*
83. Powderly to Patrick Ryan, October 24, 1884, in *PP.*
84. Garlock, *Guide to Local Assemblies of the Knights of Labor.*

they want to fight, to lie, to steal, to libel, to cheat or act the rogue
or scoundrel in any way they *act* and never consult the priest. But
if they are asked to do something to improve the condition of
their fellow man their conscience troubles them. . . . Now some
of them are finding fault with the A. K. [*Adelphon Kruptos*] because
the words "except to my religious confessor" was left out of the
pledge. If my memory serves me right it was a Catholic who objected to that clause. . . . I know no Protestant objected to it.[85]

When rumors surfaced that Powderly was again considering a direct
papal appeal, he was inundated with letters urging him not to go to
Rome. The backlash was so severe that Powderly was forced to inform
Montreal's Bishop Fabre:

> *I will never go to Rome.* I am an *American.* I have made every honor-
> able proposition to the clergy . . . and I am positive I know more
> about the condition of the laboring people and their wants than
> the Pope. . . . God it makes my blood boil. Go to Rome? *Never* I
> will not leave *America.* And if the Church wishes to array herself
> on the side of Anarchy [in Quebec] let her do so. . . . I am not a
> wealthy man, and the history of the past proves that a poor man
> representing a *poor man's cause* need not knock on the gates of
> Rome.[86]

But the damage was done. Powderly spent much of the remainder of
the decade deflecting allegations that it was rank-and-file outrage that
led him to speak out. Joseph Buchanan used that perception to attack
Powderly, and the angry Master Workman responded: "Your insinua-
tion that the Catholic Church in any way dictates the policy of the Order
is unworthy of you. . . . You know as well as any man that it never
influenced me in my dealings with the Order. . . . I belong to no other
organization on the face of the earth than the KNIGHTS OF LABOR."[87]
Noble words, but when Powderly visited heavily Protestant Denver, he
faced fifty prepared questions including: "Did you not reveal to Cardinal
Gibbons the whole of the secret work, and furthermore say to the Catholic Church that if there was in the order anything which It desired altered or changed, that should be done?" and "Is it not a fact that you

85. Powderly to Robert Layton, April 25, 1885, in *PP.*
86. Powderly to Bishop Fabre, February 24, 1886, quoted from Browne, "The Catholic
Church and the Knights of Labor," 149–50.
87. Powderly to Joseph Buchanan, December 22, 1886, in *PP.* Emphasis in original.

attend mass, sometimes as often as three times a day; that you fully confess even the secrets of the order to the Catholic priesthood, and that you are pledged to them to bend this order as they may wish to break it?" He also was accused of allowing Rome to rewrite KOL policy, a charge he denied, but that would not go away.[88]

The timing of this controversy was unfortunate. In consonance with Protestants who saw KOL locals as workingmen's churches, many Catholics embraced the Knights in defiance of clerical opposition.[89] Conceding as much when he ventured to Rome in 1887, Cardinal Gibbons asked the pontiff to reconsider the church's condemnation of the Knights. He argued that the ban was a "cruel blow to the authority of the bishops [who] would be powerless to compel the obedience of our Catholic workingmen who find [the condemnation] false and iniquitous." He further warned that failure to remove it would force "sons of the Church to rebel against their mother," ultimately resulting in "doubt and hostility" toward the Holy See.[90] In 1891, the pope acquiesced.

But members did not foresee a shift in church policy, but rather saw public behavior suggesting that KOL policy was dictated by Rome (Fig. 7). Another dimension of the controversy manifested itself in the figure of Father Edward McGlynn, a radical priest and associate of Henry George. McGlynn's excommunication from the Catholic Church — largely for political reasons — made him the darling of many labor agitators, although Powderly was not among his admirers. When Powderly arrived at Denver, another question awaiting him was, "Do you approve of the church persecution of Dr. McGlynn? If not, why has not your voice been raised in protest?"[91]

To make matters worse, Powderly became embroiled in a petty conflict with McGlynn that spilled into public view and inference. When George and McGlynn formed the Anti-Poverty Society in March 1887 and began publishing the *Standard* as its official journal, McGlynn asked Powderly for the *JUL* mailing list. When Powderly explained that he lacked authority to release the list, McGlynn charged that Powderly opposed him for

88. "Concerning the Trip of G.M.W. Powderly to Denver," in *PP*; *JUL*, January 31, 1889. In this issue of the *JUL*, Powderly had to repeat his claim that Rome did not dictate policies of the Knights of Labor.

89. Browne, "The Catholic Church and the Knights of Labor," 134. Those Catholic prelates who feared that, given a choice between the Church and the labor movement, workers would choose the latter had some grounds for fear. In a related vein, the Catholic Church's decision to charter the Knights of Columbus in 1882 is often seen as a concession to its inability to get workers to give up secret and fraternal orders.

90. Powderly, *The Path I Trod*, 349.

91. "Concerning the Trip of G.M.W. Powderly to Denver," in *PP*.

THE NEW ALLY OF THE KNIGHTS OF LABOR—DOES THE CATHOLIC CHURCH SANCTION MOB LAW?
What Cardinal Gibbons Calls "Taking the Part of the ——— the Knights of Labor — "against the Stronger" — the Scab.

Fig. 7. Catholics were heavily represented in both the leadership and rank-and-file of the KOL at a time when anti-Catholicism was rife in America. Powderly's efforts to court Rome were resented by many inside and outside the Order. This *Puck* cartoon suggests that Cardinal James Gibbons of Baltimore sanctions "mob law" by sympathizing with the Knights. Courtesy, Neilson Library, Smith College.

religious reasons. He also resurrected the canard that Powderly sent an emissary to Rome to argue on behalf of the Knights. Powderly was furious, but McGlynn repeated his charges in the *Irish World* and kept suspicions alive.[92]

Once again Powderly faced a barrage of angry anti-Catholic letters. In both the *Journal of United Labor* and the *Irish World* he was forced to address charges that he packed the executive board of the lecturer's roster with Catholics.[93] In Pennsylvania, a Knight accused Powderly of revealing secrets to the Catholic Church. The Knight went on to condemn Catholicism in general for its censorship policies, its persecution of the Masons, its destruction of "freedom of thought," and its plot to take

92. *Irish World*, February 4, 1888.
93. *JUL*, January 31, 1889; February 19, 1889; January 26, 1889.

over the KOL. He boldly declared, "I would prefer being a meek Protestant, rather than a good Catholic . . . knowing as much about their workings as I do. I don't object to you being one, but I do object to being governed by Catholicism."[94] To his Milwaukee friend Robert Schilling, a distraught Powderly wrote that "I am a Roman Catholic, and whether a good one or not makes no difference. The fact has been published that I am only a spoke in the Pope's wheel." He lamented that he could do nothing to "change the minds of these bigots."[95]

He was right. Anti-Catholicism split the Order. A 1889 fight for the post of District Master Workman of Pittsburgh's DA 3 was won by the Catholic John F. Doyle over Protestant J. M. Ross by a 37 to 27 vote along strict religious lines.[96] By mid-1891, not even Cardinal Gibbons was safe from attack. When he delivered a sermon in which he claimed that God "made the poor and always intended they should be poor," Alexander Wright responded with his own homily on political economy and accused Gibbons of hypocrisy. He enjoined laborers to reject "the dole of cant and hypocrisy, the smooth-tongued orations of sleek-fed priests, the lying pretenses of selfish, sensual, greedy, heartless humbuggery that besmirches the sacred justice of an all-wise and beneficent Creator."[97]

Terence Powderly served as General Master Workman of the Knights of Labor for the last time in 1893. In his address to the General Assembly that dislodged him, Powderly gave an account of his dealings with Catholic hierarchy in a final attempt to derail "bigotry and religious intolerance" within the Order. After laying open his files, Powderly warned that "there is an anti-Catholic crusade sweeping over the land . . . and, like all other crusades of its kind, it carries with it more malice than reason, more of bitterness than love of right, more of ignorance than knowledge of religion, more of a belief in wild rumor than a desire to know the truth." He implored Knights not to let bigotry obscure the "grand and noble" action taken by Leo XIII.[98]

By the end of the convention, Powderly was gone and with him went the last vestiges of 1870s-style Knighthood. The Order was about the same size as it was when Powderly assumed its reins in 1878, but its composition was quite different. Daniel DeLeon spoke for a faction of urban socialists who cared little for organized religion when he told

94. [Arnie?] Lamp to Powderly, February 6, 1889, in PP. [Signature is smudged.]

95. Powderly to Robert Schilling, June 23, 1891, in PP.

96. *Irish World*, February 4, 1888. The *Irish World* claimed there was "no evidence of bitterness" in the election, an assessment that seems unlikely.

97. *JKL*, May 21, 1891; May 28, 1891.

98. 1893 *Proceedings of the Knights of Labor General Assembly*, in PP.

Powderly, "The K. of L. under you stands in the way of progress. We have to get rid of you and supplant the order with a more radical form of organization."[99] Equally fed up with Powderly were rural Protestants mildly sympathetic to socialism, but wildly fearful of Catholicism. In an 1893 article, "The Rise and Fall of Terence Powderly," the *Brooklyn Citizen* noted that the Grand Master Workman's decision to seek peace with Rome was one of the policies for which he most widely criticized.[100] The convention also swept aside many of Powderly's long-time Catholic friends. The Catholic hold-overs were two men whose religion never got in the way of their ambition, John Hayes and Thomas McGuire. Typical of the new leaders were newly elected Master Workman James Sovereign, an Iowa Protestant, and executive board member James M. Kennery of Nebraska, "a member of several secret organizations."[101] Appropriately, Sovereign dealt the final blow to Catholic rapprochement; in 1895 he led the KOL back to ritual secrecy.

Conclusion: A Noble and Holy Order

The Knights of Labor was imbued with religiosity. It was found in the Order's ritual, its oath, the speeches of its members, and in the pronouncements of its national leaders like Uriah Stephens and Terence Powderly. Members were told that labor was "noble and holy," and that Knights were on a crusade to usher in labor's millennium. Knightly religion was more than a matter of individual belief; it was part of the psychic foundation on which the Order rested.

Knights associated themselves with True Christianity and though the Order was not uniformly Christian, it was so much so that it is nearly impossible to articulate a definition of Knighthood that does not involve Christian precepts.[102] KOL locals functioned as working-class alternatives to Gilded Age churches. Despite the scorn with which most Knights held doctrinal disputes, a vaguely articulated KOL theology emerged through actual practices.

The first aspect of KOL theology involved a distinct interpretation of

99. Powderly, *The Path I Trod*, 262.
100. *Brooklyn Citizen*, December 3, 1893, in *PP.*
101. *JKL*, January 4, 1894.
102. Other historians who have noted the propensity of Gilded Age laborers to develop their own theological codes include Gutman, *Work, Culture and Society,* chap. 2; and Halker, *For Democracy, Workers, and God.* In Fones-Wolf, *Trade-Union Gospel,* the Knights are called a "sect." See chap. 3 of that work.

the life and passion of Jesus. Most Knights simply assumed essential tenets of Christianity, such as Christ's divine nature and his redemptive powers. More important to Knights was the ideal of the earthly Christ— the "Carpenter's Son"—who set the standards for social and individual morality. Knights saw Gilded Age clerics and their middle-class congregations as idlers who were devoted to Mammon and contemptuous of the poor. This life compared badly to that of Jesus, who himself toiled, eschewed material riches, and spent his time among the poor.

Emphasis on Christ's earthly nature rooted in a *communitas* interpretation of primitive Christianity led to full-scale assaults on Social Darwinism. Knights saw God as a benevolent deity with a temporal and material plan for His creation, as well as an eternal and spiritual one. Discrepancies between rich and poor were not "natural," as Social Darwinists insisted, rather they were the product of sinfulness, greed, and the abandonment of the principles of Universal Brotherhood. Knights rejected utterly the much-quoted command "Servants, obey your masters," because ministers never addressed the process by which masters were created. They accused ministers and capitalists of creating a cult of individualism, out of sync with the life of Christ and the apostles whose practical religion involved a form of cooperation and a vision of a cooperative commonwealth.

Knights also believed in free will and moral perfectionism. Their belief in free will led them to skewer clerics who presumed to tell workers what to believe, or who offered Social Darwinist explanations for poverty. As Knights saw it, belief, hypocrisy, and sin were acts of free will. From this it followed that so too was the choice for morality. The KOL was selective about whom it admitted, and insisted on strict codes of personal ethics. Only upright, autonomous individuals could build the community bonds necessary for a moral commonwealth. The KOL's emphasis on morality was not an attempt to ape middle-class values, rather it was a strain of working-class respectability that Knights thought set them above bourgeois hypocrites.

Finally, KOL theology involved a crusading zeal that led to proselytizing. Knights of Labor tried to lead by example in their quest to make the world anew. They did not hesitate to tell others that the KOL's way was the proper route to moral, as well as social, renewal. They did not shy away from telling ministers to jump aboard the KOL bandwagon if they truly believed they were agents of God. The letters sent by Theodore Cuno and John Hayes, demanding that clerics honor biblical injunctions regarding the poor, were presumptuous, but they were also sincere.

Of course, Gilded Age churches were too powerful to ignore altogether. Labor jeremiads were preached in the press, on the streets, and from the pulpit. Sometimes the Knights won allies, and a few of them labored long and nobly on behalf of the Order. For the most part, however, KOL sermons fell on deaf ears. Most clerics saw the KOL as a competitor for working-class souls and felt threatened. The Order's social message was too radical for those for whom the age of the Social Gospel had not yet dawned. There were several attempts at alliance building, but neither the churches nor the Knights were willing to find common ground. Churches demanded that the Knights make changes in its ritual as a precondition for even considering the merits of its cause. Likewise, the KOL made changes when it was in its best interest to do so, but came to the 1886 Church Congress in a defiant mood only when it held the upper hand. In the end, Gilded Age churches were among the external forces that conspired to crush the Knights of Labor.

Public battles created internal conflict that weakened the Order. This was most obvious in the attempt to win the Catholic Church's approval of the Knights. Religion unified members best when doctrinal differences were subsumed by True Christianity. Dalliances with Catholic prelates opened the question of whether True Christianity had a denominational component, a process at odds with the very notion of a workers' church. These battles revealed a vicious intolerance within the KOL. While members spoke of the brotherhood of all, they were not above cruel anti-Catholic smears, which Protestant ministers like Josiah Strong would have approved.

The Knights of Labor struck its most responsive chord by maintaining itself as a working-class alternative to organized religion. Despite the KOL's un-Christian bickering and nonfraternal factionalism one is tempted to agree with the Allentown, New York, Knight who claimed the Order had more true Christians than "all the churches this side of Helena."[103] Its critique of "Churchianity" lingered in the minds in workers long after the KOL faded. The KOL's successors avoided the pews for the same reason many Knights did: the organized church was no friend to organized labor. Knights internalized the message of the "Carpenter's Son" and worked it out in their assembly halls. By integrating religion with ritual, personal morality, and KOL principles, a strain of practical Christianity evolved among members that shamed Gilded Age "Churchianity." By the mid-1890s, the KOL was a dying organization. In its waning days it retreated to the practices of its secret period. The Knights' last Master Workman was a lukewarm Catholic, John Hayes. In 1917, Hayes disbanded the oath-bound, secret organization. The Knights of Labor was born "noble and holy" and died in the same state of grace.

103. *JUL*, May 15, 1889.

3 Storm the Fort

The Knights of Labor in Song

Toiling millions now are waking,
See them marching on;
All the tyrants now are shaking,
Ere their power is gone.

Chorus
Storm the fort, ye Knights of Labor,
Battle for your cause;
Equal rights for every neighbor,
Down with tyrant laws!

Lazy drones steal all the honey
From hard labor's hives;
Bankers control the nation's money
And destroy your lives.

Chorus

Do not load the workman's shoulder
With an unjust debt;
Do not let the rich bondholder
Live by blood and sweat.

Chorus

Why should those who fought for freedom
Wear old slavery's chains?
Workingmen will quickly break them
When they use their brains.

Chorus[1]

In 1887, Frances Willard wrote to Terence V. Powderly with what she feared was a "trivial" concern. Why, she wondered, did the "Knights

---

1. Philip S. Foner, *American Labor Songs of the 19th Century* (Urbana: University of Illinois Press, 1975), 154.

have no songs of their own?" She ventured, "I think they will get on better if they can march to music and so suggest to you."[2] Mrs. Willard thought KOL songs rare because she looked for them in the wrong place. Instead of writing to Powderly, she should have visited her local assembly hall. Someone would have told her that "Storm the Fort Ye Knights of Labor" was one of the century's best-known songs. Perhaps an old-timer would have informed her that the song tradition within the KOL was deep and sacred.

KOL music developed along with the Order, and was central to its oral culture during early days in which many Knights were barely literate. Like ritual, music could be memorized, and no meeting was complete without several flights into song. Since Willard's tastes were more literary, members could have provided her with copies of published songbooks, broadside sheets, and clippings from KOL newspapers devoted to song. Virtually no one would have thought Mrs. Willard's desire for more songs "trivial."

Part of Mrs. Willard's confusion resulted from the private nature of KOL singing. Although music took on new importance in Knighthood's more literary post-1882 period, it was, like ritual and religion, performed most frequently in private. Even as the Order opened its doors and songs appeared in print, few songs other than "Storm the Fort" and a few others ever ventured far from the assembly room.

Why then bother with songs sung in private to tunes (mostly) forgotten? Because song helps unlock practices and values within the KOL. Singing had many functions, the primary one being to foster solidarity among the rank and file. The act of group singing was similar to that of performing common rituals; that is, it muted individual identity in favor of a collective one. Not surprisingly, the favorite topic of KOL songs was the Order itself. The earliest songs were assembly odes integrated into the ritual and touting the virtues of fraternalism. Gradually these were supplemented with other lyrics that sang the Order's praises.

The act of celebrating the KOL in song was also an act of socialization. Embedded in the lyrics were principles, values, and beliefs essential for the proper practice of Knighthood. Music also kept Knights focused on both the forces that threatened them—corruption, greed, hypocrisy, tyranny—and the virtues that would transform society. Familiar constructs such as True Christianity and True Patriotism were reinforced through singing.

All of this came about through lyrics that may strike the modern reader as vague and undirected. With several notable exceptions, ene-

2. Frances Willard to Terence V. Powderly, April 25, 1887, in *PP.*

mies were not mentioned by name, and generalized platitudes were more common than specific politics or policies. By focusing on broad principles, music—like ritual and religion—created a psychic dimension of Knighthood that nurtured and sustained members. It also meant that songs had a better chance of staying in the KOL repertoire than those that were more specific. In this sense, principles survived both victory and defeat in order to fight another day.

Music was one of the most resilient of the KOL's cultural practices. Songs written after 1882 showed the Order's new concerns for public reform, but singing patterns remained wedded to local traditions for much longer than other practices. Nonetheless, singing eventually began to show signs of outside influences. Although Victorian constructs were often adapted for the KOL's own use, their very presence opened the possibility of contamination that might lead to co-optation. By the 1890s, KOL song had lost much of its earlier power, but before it faded it bequeathed a legacy of social protest singing that was passed to future generations, a final reason for studying the Order's music.

Several notes of caution before opening the musical treasure trove: Any analysis of song inevitably probes lyrics and analyzes themes in a discrete manner that would alarm singers and composers. This by its nature, is arbitrary and misleading. I will focus mostly on lyrics, ignoring the fact that the tunes themselves often had great relevance. One must also be cautious before judging the artistic merits of songs. By critical standards, many KOL lyrics use forced rhymes, employ too many (or too few) syllables to conform to meter, or are simply bad poetry. In the age of the KOL, however, the theme—not the medium—was the message.

Further, the same song might have multiple themes, from which I choose to analyze but one. Knights of Labor saw their songs as part of an overall repertoire, not individual units to be dissected. Moreover, music was only one part of a larger set of cultural practices designed to help Knights in their larger task of rebuilding society. What are today historical documents were, in their own time, part of a living culture and an ongoing struggle.

Sing! Brothers, Sing!

The late folksinger Lee Hays once wrote:

> Good singing won't do;
> Good praying won't do;

Good preaching won't do;
But if you get them all together
With a little organizing behind it,
You get a way of life
And a way to do it.[3]

The KOL understood that music, religion, and organizing went hand in hand. The KOL singing tradition was part of nineteenth-century working-class culture, and a link in the unbroken chain of social protest singing that connected life and the workplace.[4] The Order inherited a rich social protest tradition from groups such as the Philadelphia carpenters, New England textile operatives, the Ten-Hour Movement, the Greenback Labor Party, and the Grand Eight-Hour League. Much of KOL song was simply built on existing form and convention: broadsides, folk song structure, and parodies of familiar tunes.[5] Of the 151 KOL songs I sampled for which a tune can be determined, 132 (87.4 percent) used existing rather than original music—most often religious airs, parlor standards, and popular songs. Despite full-scale borrowing, however, the Knights improved on its inheritance and bequeathed a richer trove to such movements as the Populists, trade unions, the IWW, and the CIO.

Singing is an ephemeral expression. Who sang, and how many voices joined in the chorus? What did it mean to those who lifted their voices in song? Of what lasting importance was it? It is possible to infer several things. First, social protest singing provided Knights with a psychological outlet for internalized bitterness. A recent study links labor singing to movement culture ideology and notes that lyrics typically represent an "oppositional, offensive, resistant strand of workers' cultural fabric."[6] Structurally, most KOL songs employed a simple pairing scheme that contrasted good and evil themes such as Knighthood versus parochialism, solidarity versus individualism, true Christianity versus hypocrisy, or true Patriotism versus subversion. KOL songs thoroughly skewer targeted injustices, tar those who perpetuate them with betrayal of God and country, and end with the promise of a coming golden age. Such messages steeled the resolve of Knights in the midst of protracted battles against Gilded Age monopolists.

3. Pete Seeger and Bob Reiser, *Carry It On!: A History in Song and Picture of the Working Men and Women of America* (New York: Fireside Books, 1985), 10.

4. John Greenway, *American Folksongs of Protest* (New York: A. S. Barnes, 1960), 225.

5. Most working-class songs conform to the process of borrowing. For more on this, see Greenway, *American Folk Songs of Protest*; see also Hazel Arnett, *I Hear America Singing!: Great Folk Songs from the Revolution to Rock* (New York: Frank Taylor, 1975); Clark Halker, *For Democracy, Workers, and God*.

6. Halker, *For Democracy, Workers, and God*, 13.

Second, it is clear that singing was widespread within the Order. In 1914, Powderly reminisced:

> In the early days of the Knights of Labor, many a man poured out his heart in songs about the rights and wrongs of labor. . . . No one member was selected to sing alone; all joined in; someone led, of course, but we all tried to sing and if all didn't do it right the volume of sound enabled us to escape detection and, being a forgiving lot of mortals, no effort was made to ferret out and punish the offenders against harmony.

He added that his office received numerous song submissions, some "excellent, some good, others indifferent, many atrocious." He joked of destroying some, "The law intervening between the poets and well merited punishment, [I] burned a few instead of their guilty authors."[7]

Many unsolicited songs were forwarded by enthusiasts like Tom O'Reilly, himself a singer and songwriter of some renown. O'Reilly frequently wrote to recommend a "stirring song" for wider distribution.[8] "Caractus" of Altoona, Pennsylvania, thought the Order needed a song about scabs: "Why not have the 'Scabs' March?' . . . It should become more popular . . . than the 'Rogues' March.' I trust that some political and musical genius may consider this matter and carry it out."[9]

The *AK* mandated that "appropriate odes" be sung during the opening and closing ceremonies of each assembly meeting.[10] Most assemblies determined for themselves what "appropriate" meant until 1881, when the opening ode for LA 1626 of Ottumwa, Iowa, was printed in the *JUL*. Soon, it was widely emulated. Sung to the tune of "O That Will Be Joyful," the Ottumwa ode was rich in references to ideal Knighthood:

> Once more within the sacred veil,
>   Our hearts in union sweet,
> Let each one strive in peace to work—
>   No discord may we meet.
> May social love prevail,
>   To give us harmony;

7. Emily Balch, "Songs For Labor," *The Survey* 3 (January, 1914): 408–28.
8. For example, see Thomas O'Reilly to Powderly, July 22, 1887, in *PP.*
9. Caractus to Powderly, September 1, 1892, in *PP.*
10. *Adelphon Kruptos*, 1886 edition. Earlier editions of the *AK* also mention the use of music in assemblies.

> That right may triumph over wrong
> When labor shall be free.[11]

By picturing the assembly as a haven of harmony, the Ottumwa ode evoked the Stephens model of fraternalism.

Such images are even more explicit in an opening ode used by Kansas Knights. The Order's S.O.M.A. code echoes throughout:

> Knights of Labor, all fraternal,
>   Meet we here for mutual help;
> Guarded each by truth and justice,
>   All our thoughts are not on self;
> For the ones who hold the power
>   Rob us of our every need.
> Needy brothers all around us,
>   Suffering from old Shylock's greed.
>
> Hear the pleadings of the workers,
>   As they toil from day to day;
> Let it be our aim and object
>   To drive the hungry wolf away;
> Extending to our toiling brothers,
>   Everywhere a helping hand.
> Give protection to the workers,
>   Needy ones all o'er the land.[12]

Not all odes evoked early Knighthood. Despite the proliferation of the Ottumwa ode and a growing move toward sharing songs in the *JUL*, locals continued to respond to regional preferences. Politicized Knights, like those of Pioneer Assembly in Colorado, were less romantic than their Iowa and Kansas brothers. Their ode, composed to the tune of "America," defiantly proclaimed Knighthood's goal: "To elevate humanity/Our end and aim shall be/To break the shackles from their limbs/ And set the wage slaves free."[13]

Several assemblies added musical intervals beyond opening and closing odes. Both the Knights of Beatrice, Nebraska, and East Saginaw, Michigan, had initiation songs. The latter not only welcomed the initiate, but also musically advised him that he was among "MEN" and that

11. *JUL*, March 15, 1881; reprinted in Foner, *American Labor Songs of the 19th Century*, 146.
12. Foner, *American Labor Songs of the 19th Century*, 147.
13. *Labor Enquirer*, July 3, 1887.

"honor's work is here."[14] Knights reported joyous singing interludes scattered throughout their meetings. In fact, Knights could not escape music in their assembly halls. Several locals, including three in Toledo, one in Balitmore, and the all-female Helping Hand Assembly (LA 3684) of Marlboro, Massachusetts, had glee clubs, and many assemblies had their own bands. Special meetings employed even more than the usual complement of music prescribed by the *AK*. An 1884 Knights of Labor reception held in Burlington, Iowa, included five musical interludes and solos from a quartet of local Knights. An 1886 meeting in Murphysboro, Illinois, was opened to the entire community—a rare, but by no means singular, event. Before settling down to listen to a two-hour lecture, a choir led all in the singing of "Storm the Fort, Ye Knights of Labor."[15]

Closing odes were usually the KOL's most sentimental songs. The 1881 Ottumwa closing ode appealed to fraternal brotherhood and to God, "who knows each heart/Who has ever been our friend." Another reminded members that their meeting united hearts "as one" and that, "our sacred pledge is strengthened/Our duties lighter grow." It implored workers to return to their homes and work, strengthened by their mutualism: "Then pledged to one another/Our course we will pursue/ Here each one meets as brother/Nor elsewhere proves untrue."[16]

Although little-known to scholars, there were even official Knights of Labor songsters. By the 1880s, J. D. Tallmadge's *Labor Songs Dedicated to the Knights of Labor*, and Mons Samuel "Monssini" Baker's *The Songs of Monssini* were widely available.[17] As late as 1892, new songsters appeared with the publication of Phillips Thompson's *Labor Reform Songster*, a songbook touted as a "liberal education upon economic questions set to popular and stirring airs."[18] Further, KOL journals printed scores of lyrics with testimonials of how popular particular songs were in given locals, and few KOL socials failed to include music on their programs.

14. John A. Cotter to Powderly, February 2, 1886, in *PP*; see also initiation ceremony of LA 1867 located in *PP*.

15. 1887 *Proceedings of the Knights of Labor General Assembly*, in *PP*.

16. *JUL*, March 15, 1881; Foner, *American Labor Songs of the 19th Century*, 146; Monssini Baker, *The Songs of Monssini or the Cry of Labor Defrauded* (Minneapolis: Thomas A. Clark, 1889), 17.

17. J. D. Tallmadge, *Labor Songs Dedicated to the Knights of Labor* (Chicago: J. D. Tallmadge, 1886); Baker, *The Songs of Monssini*; Phillips Thompson, *The Labor Reform Songster* (Philadelphia: Knights of Labor Press, 1892). Tallmadge was a Chicago printer. One of his motives may well have been to promote his wife Emily's songs, two of which were included in his songster. Monssini Baker was a pseudonym for Thomas Clark. Clark worked out of Minneapolis and was a self-promoter who was probably partially motivated by a desire to realize some profit. Thompson was a reformer from Ontario.

18. *JKL*, June 16, 1892.

Irrespective of the source of their songs or the occasion for singing them, Knights loved little better than singing their own praises. Many songs discuss aspects of the Order's principles, or symbolically evoke the experience of Knighthood. A few relate aspects of the Order's history. "The Noble Knights of Labor" contains lines such as, "In the year of sixty-nine they commenced to fall in line/The great Knights, the noble Knights of Labor." The chorus notes the medieval chivalric traditions upon which Knighthood rested—"Like the good old Knights of old, they cannot be bought or sold"—and credits the Order's founder with its high principles:

> U. S. Stephens was the man this great order once began
> The great Knights, the noble Knights of Labor
> And he started what they say is the strongest band today
> The great Knights, the noble Knights of Labor
> Bless the mind that gave them birth, they're the finest men on
> earth.[19]

Labor poet Gerald Massey also evoked medieval ideals in his "The Chivalry of Labour." He ended his song with a vision of the future that harks back to the past:

> Work, Brothers mine; work, hand and brain;
> We'll win the Golden Age again;
> And Love's Millennial morn shall rise
> In happy hearts and blessed eyes.
> Hurrah! hurrah! true Knights are we
> In Labour's lordlier chivalry.[20]

The future was usually vague in KOL songs, seldom more specific than hopes for a coming "Golden Age" like that found in Massey's composition. Nonetheless, Knights believed that their efforts would light the way. In 1885, Charles Mackay cautiously wrote, "There's a good time coming, boys/A good time coming/We may not live to see the day/But the earth shall glisten in the ray/Of the good time coming."[21] One year later, Eugene Geary boldly announced that the new era had begun. His

---

19. Foner, *American Labor Songs of the 19th Century*, 148.
20. Balch, "Songs For Labor," 422. Gerald Massey was an English proletarian poet associated with Christian socialism and the circle of F. D. Maurice and Charles Kingsley. For more, see Brenda Colloms, *Victorian Visionaries* (London: Constable, 1982).
21. Foner, *American Labor Songs of the 19th Century*, 150.

song, "The March of Labor," was one of the more popular labor songs
of the day. Geary's opening verse proclaimed,

> Hurrah! the dawn is breaking;
>   Ye toiling hearts arise;
> The despots now are quaking;
>   Hear not their frantic cries?
> Too long they've on us trampled;
>   White slaves oppressed we were;
>   The galling chain
>   We'll rend in twain
> And gain our victory.
>   March, march, march,
>   From sea to rolling sea;
> Ten million strong we'll march along
>   To labor's victory.[22]

Despite the Knight's imprecise notions of the future, their songs offered wage-slaves the sort of hope embedded in antebellum slave songs.
Like the latter, Knight songs looked forward to a future victory that resembled the second coming of Christ and the 1,000-year reign of peace
that would ensue.[23]

If KOL songwriters disagreed over the timing of the coming golden
age, they were in accord over the need to educate and recruit members
in the present. Many Knights' songs exhorted members to organize. In
"Come, Brothers, Come," organizing is equated with manliness: "Come
rally, noble Knights of Labor/Come forth and prove your manliness/No
longer more, in spite your toiling/Live in starvation and distress."[24] If
organization was universal, labor's enemies would fall. Kansas Knight
Francis Goodwin expressed this in "Knights of Labor Song":

> Ye valiant Knights of Labor, rise,
> Unfurl your banners to the skies,
> And go to work and organize,
>   Until the world is won.

---

22. *The Boycotter* (New York City), July 3, 1886.

23. See Lawrence Levine, *Black Culture and Black Consciousness: Afro-American Folk Thought
From Slavery to Freedom* (New York: Oxford University Press, 1977), esp. chap. 3: "Freedom,
Culture, and Religion."

24. Foner, *American Labor Songs of the 19th Century*, 150. David Montgomery argues that
"organization" was one of the key words of the nineteenth century, a term implying panacean relief for labor's ills. See Montgomery, *The Fall of the House of Labor*, esp. chaps. 1–3.

> See the lordly nabobs quake,
> See the politicians shake,
> Labor now is wide awake,
> Justice will be done.[25]

The universality of labor's cause was a favorite ploy to encourage membership in the KOL. In a variant of Geary's "The March of Labor," Marlboro, Massachusetts, Knights sang of how the Order battled oppressors for all toilers, a fight the song identifies with "true Knighthood" three times.[26] Thomas Leahy of Keene, New Hampshire, was even more explicit. In a long song composed to the tune of "Rally Round the Flag," Leahy exhorts,

> Come join the K. of L. boys, come each toiling swain,
> All men and women who labor,
> Come join the K. of L., from Oregon to Maine,
> For the wrongs and the rights of labor,
> Labor forever hurrah! boys, hurrah!
> For the life of the nation and prop of the law,
> And we'll rise it to that station where no man can draw,
> Millions from our labor, hurrah! boys, hurrah![27]

Leahy's next five verses identify labor's foes—greedy capitalists, bankers, brokers, usurers, and landlords—and promises victory if all workers join the Knights of Labor.

Iowa coal miner Will Minnick was even more eloquent in "Organize the Hosts of Labor." The first verse repeats the theme of universal organization, while the last is specific to the KOL:

> Organize the hosts of labor
>   In one common brotherhood,
> He who drives the locomotive
>   And the one who turns the sod;

25. *JUL*, April 16, 1887.
26. *Haverhill Laborer*, April 3, 1886.
27. "Come Join the K. of L. Boys" was sent to Powderly by Thomas Leahy on May 19, 1886, in *PP.* One should not make too much of terms like "boys," "men," and "brothers." In most of these songs the three are used interchangeably without reference to age, maturity, or status. Often one term is used over another simply because of its metrical superiority. In these songs Knight songwriters also employed a variant form of "Come-all-ye" ballads in order to evoke comradeship. For more on "Come-all-ye" ballads, see Roger Abrahams and George Foss, *Anglo-American Folksong Style* (Englewood Cliffs, N. J.: Prentice-Hall, 1968).

Those who dig the dusky diamonds,
    And produce the shining gold.
Those in factory and in workshop,
    Bring them to this shepherd's fold. . . .

Give them through united effort,
    Organize and drill with care
In the tactics of our Order
    Knighthood teaches everywhere.
Moving on in one direction,
    Labor's cause to guard and guide,
By the wise and wholesome council
    Each assembly shall provide.[28]

Minnick sounded a theme that the Order officially trumpeted: the assembly as educator of labor. Knights of Labor songwriters often put the Order's principles into verse. Mrs. Bulah Brinton, one of the few female songwriters of the Knights, mentioned several principles in her "All Hail Labor Knights!!!" including the boycott: "They came not with dynamite, with saber or with shot/Nor weapons of plunder or of carnage have they got/Just labor's defence is the peaceful boy-cott." She also mentions the organization of women and the fight for the eight-hour day: "Fair ladies of honor come crown these brave Knights/God help them to gain men and women their just rights/The eight hour law, for the day, and workmen's nights."[29]

It is difficult to know how many local assembly favorites were sung elsewhere, but there were at least several KOL "standards," such as the Ottumwa ode, that disseminated widely. Probably the earliest to travel were songs written by the respected literary figure and labor sympathizer Augustine J. H. Duganne, who joined the KOL shortly before his death. Duganne's *Fellowship Songs* is sometimes considered the first collection of American labor songs. In 1878, Duganne honored Powderly with one of the two hundred printed copies of that work. Duganne died in 1884, but his songs and poems appeared often in the *JUL* between 1880 and 1884, outnumbering most others in the early days of the *Journal*.[30] As the Order expanded and *JUL* circulation grew, local songwriters like Tom O'Reilly of New York, George McNeill of Boston, and Arthur and Charles Cheesewright of Denver grew in renown.

28. *JUL*, August 2, 1888; Foner, *American Labor Songs of the 19th Century*, 151. William H. ("Will") Minnick also spelled his name "Minnich."

29. Bulah Brinton to Powderly, March 10 (?), 1886, in *PP*. (Date is smudged on original letter.)

30. Balch, "Songs For Labor."

One of O'Reilly's compositions created a stir. No particular song was used to close general assemblies until 1887, when O'Reilly unveiled his "Song of the Proletaire," also known as "If We Will, We Can Be Free." O'Reilly had a fine singing voice, and the song became a minor sensation. Both Powderly and the *JUL* were besieged by requests for it. The first verse of this song proclaims:

> Base oppressors, cease your slumbers,
>   Listen to a people's cry,
> Hark! uncounted, countless numbers
>   Swell the peal of agony;
> Lo from Labor's sons and daughters,
>   In the depths of misery,
> Like the rush of many waters,
>   Comes the cry, 'We will be free,'
>   Comes the cry, 'We will be free.'[31]

"Song of the Proletaire" is an example of a local song that passed into general use. O'Reilly wrote the song in the early 1870s, and New York City Knights sang parts of it in the 1880s. (O'Reilly did not bother to copyright it until 1887). On October 1, 1887, the song appeared on the front page of the *JUL* complete with musical score. It was used again at the 1888 Minneapolis General Assembly, and soon became known as the "Convention Ode," closing all GAs thereafter.[32]

"Song of the Proletaire" was a show piece for the Order and an example of mature KOL song tradition. But it never dislodged "Storm the Fort" in popularity. The signature song for the "Noble and Holy" Knights of Labor began life as a gospel song penned by Philip Bliss. The Knights transformed it in a labor standard that out-lived the Order; it was one of the few songs performed outside of assembly halls. Joseph Buchanan called "Storm the Fort" "the battle hymn of organized labor in the West." During the 1885 Gould strike, "nearly two thousand" Denver Knights used it to serenade jailed comrades, harass boycotted merchants, and buoy spirits during parades and rallies. With only slight

---

31. 1887 *Proceedings of the Knights of Labor General Assembly*. O'Reilly's reference to "daughters" is one of the few found in KOL songs, a cultural form much more male than poetry. As I will argue in the next chapter, women found much more expressive freedom in poetry. Poetry, of course, became much more important when the Knights abandoned secrecy and provided journals for its publication. Music, by contrast, was part of earlier KOL practices and retained more residual sexism.

32. *JUL*, October 1, 1887, December 6, 1888; *JKL* November 26, 1891. (The *JUL* changed its name to *Journal of the Knights of Labor [JKL]* in 1890.)

hyperbole, Buchanan recalled hearing "Storm the Fort" forty times in a single day.[33] As I show later, variants of "Storm the Fort" have been sung many times since Buchanan heard it outside the Denver jail.

By the mid-1880s, KOL songwriters and sympathizers were interested in spreading the Order's musical message beyond the assembly room. Doubtless some dreamed of winning renown, or perhaps of making a profit on their enterprise. Knight Budd Harris borrowed from the broadside tradition and printed his "Knights of Labor" on small cards that he hawked to individuals and assemblies. He enjoyed modest success with a song that included sentiments such as these:

> They ask nothing wrong you can plainly see,
>   All that they demand is but fair,
> A lesson they'll teach with me you'll agree,
>   To every purse-proud millionaire.
> Fair wages they want, fair wages they'll get,
>   Good tempered they wage all their fights,
> Success to the cause may the sun never set
>   On each brave Assembly of Knights.[34]

J. D. Tallmadge's *Labor Songs Dedicated to the Knights of Labor* (1886) opened with a dedication page that excerpted a Powderly speech, and contained twenty-nine songs, including labor standards such as "Labor's Ninety and Nine" and "The Workingmen's Marseillaise." His small booklet sold for 10 cents, and the cover was emblazoned with the exhortation "Sing, Brothers Sing!"[35]

Monssini Baker was a self-promoter who inflated his reputation as a composer by putting his name on existing songs to which he, in fact, made only minor alterations. Nonetheless, his collection includes "Workingmen's Marseillaise" and two familiar assembly odes. Despite Baker's egoism, many songs in the Baker songster actually espouse KOL principles more directly than those of Tallmadge. Baker, like Powderly, had a penchant for causes of all sorts. Song topics explore issues such as elections, Irish Home Rule, German nationalism, temperance, and women's suffrage. His songster did well enough to go into a second edition.[36]

Ontario reformer Phillips Thompson's songster did not appear until

---

33. Buchanan, *Story of a Labor Agitator*, 194–97.
34. Foner, *American Labor Songs of the 19th Century*, 48.
35. Tallmadge, *Labor Songs Dedicated to the Knights of Labor*.
36. Baker, *The Songs of Monssini*.

1892. It was intended to boost the sagging Order, but Thompson covered his bets by giving most of the songs a more general reform nature.[37] His songster—devoid of songs singing KOL praises—stands as a metaphor for the decline of the KOL. It did not, however, mean the end of the labor protest singing. Knights preferred to sing about themselves, but their songs also exposed the social evils of their day and promoted the importance of solidarity, ideas that outlived the Order, and themes to which I now turn.

True Christians/True Patriots

Many KOL songs dealt with oppression because Knights felt they held the moral capital through which to expose it. Songs did more than critique existing society; they offered redemption to both individuals and the nation. Personal and national salvation could only emerge in a world in which moral and political power lay in the hands of those best able to make productive use of them, the noble and holy Knights. KOL songs offered truly oppositional versions of religion and patriotism consonant with the Order's ritual practices, rhetorical flourishes, and private beliefs. Music reinforced the call to remake American society and place producerist Christians in charge.

"Noble and holy" themes are common in KOL songs. Although some degenerated into sentimental and vague millennialism, most remained rooted in an earth-bound reading of Christianity grounded in social justice. Songs echoed motifs of Jesus the carpenter, the sanctity of toil, and Christ the condemner of Mammon worship. Just as Christ cleansed the temple to prepare for his own Passion, so too would the Knights cleanse American society to prepare it for labor's dawn. The most famous song that links worldly and other-worldly is "Eight Hours," co-written by Jesse Jones, a Knight who was also a minister. The song demands "Eight hours for work, eight hours for rest, eight hours for what we will!" under the straight-forward logic that "God has will'd it."[38]

Knights celebrated True Christianity, and the Reverend Jones felt comfortable inside KOL despite musical attacks on established churches that

---

37. Thompson, *The Labor Reform Songster*.

38. Foner, *American Labor Songs of the 19th Century*, 217. Jones and James Blanchard co-wrote the song before Jones joined the KOL. It began as a poem written by Blanchard in the 1860s, with Jones adding the music. It was already a labor staple when the Knights appropriated it sometime in the early 1880s. It quickly became a favorite among Knights.

echoed KOL editorialists. For example, Denver Knights sang, "The people they are waking and the church is losing ground/ For they're tired of tending places where the truth is never found."[39] An even more defiant spirit permeated "Modern Missionary Zeal," which not only attacked churches as "heathen temples" that "substitute for sermons/adulterated rum," but skewered theologically ignorant preachers and accused the church of promoting imperialism: "Onward! Christian soldiers/On to heathen lands!/Prayer book in your pockets/Rifles in your hands."[40]

Most KOL songs were less harsh than the aforementioned offerings, but none shied away from attacking hypocrisy. An ode from Cambridge, Massachusetts, accuses "tyrants" and "gold-hoarding knaves" of stealing from workers while hiding "beneath religion's cloak." The chorus of this song describes labor's struggle in terms symbolic of a crusade:

> We'll fight in this great holy war till we die;
> No longer in silence we'll whimper and sigh;
> No longer we'll cringe at the proud tyrant's nod.
> But defy him, and fight 'neath the banner of God.[41]

Crusading zeal also found its way into James Barrett's "The Labor Battle Song," a song that describes labor's struggles with capital in apocalyptic terms. The opening line promises that "the Christ of Labor" will come to lead workers to victory. The second verse continues this vision:

> Hear the tramp of resurrection that's awakening alarms,
> Like the charges of the angels when they order us to arms—
> From the clutches of the despots save your country, homes,
>   and farms,
> As we go marching on.[42]

The song was a favorite of Baltimore Knights, and made its way into the Tallmadge collection. Another tune from that songster, "God Speed the Right," equates labor's battle with "truth" and "glory," while the prayerlike lyrics assure workers that God supports their "noble cause."[43]

39. *Labor Enquirer* (Denver), March 31, 1888.

40. *JKL*, July 3, 1890.

41. *JUL*, March, 1882.

42. Tallmadge, *Labor Songs Dedicated to the Knights of Labor*, 6; reprinted in the *Baltimore Critic*, August 4, 1888. Like many KOL reformers, Barrett was grounded in antebellum reform movements, especially abolitionism and revivalism. He wrote for several religious journals, and later started his own newspaper dedicated to the general cause of reform. For more, see Halker, *For Democracy, Workers, and God*, 118.

43. Tallmadge, *Labor Songs Dedicated to the Knights of Labor*, 18.

Monssini Baker's collection contains similar songs. In "The Laborer Defrauded," Moses appears as a metaphor for labor, and the Egyptian pharaoh symbolizes monopolists. Baker also included two songs that implored Christ to establish his reign and save labor from its oppressors.[44] Likewise, Phillips Thompson's songster contains fleeting references to religion, although it mostly consists of promises of better times "in the sweet by(e) and by(e).[45]

But even that seemingly innocuous sentiment was an expression of defiance. "Sweet Bye and Bye" was one of the more popular hymns of the late nineteenth century and many Knights would have read irony into Thompson's lyrics. Thompson relied on one of the oldest protest song traditions: setting new lyrics to established tunes. The KOL sang at least five rewritten songs to the tune of "Sweet Bye and Bye"; in all, at least 22 of the 151 tunes (14.6 percent) in my sampling were lifted from popular religious airs, including two of the Order's most famous songs, "Storm the Fort" and "Ninety and Nine." KOL songwriters no doubt appropriated hymn tunes in a conscious attempt to seize the moral high ground.

The manner in which KOL songwriters attacked their oppressors suggested an alternative hegemony. As a direct offshoot of a belief that practical Christianity is the antidote to social injustice, Knights viewed themselves as guardians of True Patriotism. These sentiments were expressed in speech, writing, and song. In 1887, Powderly encouraged Knights to celebrate the Fourth of July and remind "the common people . . . that we have a country [and] a flag. The monopolist and the anarchist care nothing for American liberty or institutions."[46] An 1888 *Journal of United Labor* editorial compared corporations to King George III: both showed their "contempt of the law." According to the editorialist, only the "trades unions and K. of L. stand as stood the founders of American liberty—against King Monopoly, that, like a leech, sucks the blood of labor."[47] Denver's Charles Cheesewright made that connection in song: "Now let us emulate/The olden patriots great/And stand for right/Never let us forget/The example they have set."[48]

These examples illustrate basic tenets of KOL patriotism. First, there is the notion that entrepreneurial elites were morally bankrupt and antidemocratic. The values of greed, individualism, and the profit motive

44. Baker, *Songs of Monssini*, 5, 19.
45. Thompson, *The Labor Reform Songster*.
46. *JUL*, May 14, 1887.
47. *JUL*, January 4, 1888.
48. *Labor Enquirer* (Denver), July 3, 1887.

were seen as inherently at odds with older republican traditions of production, community, and cooperation. Second, advocates of the new order were un-American, and more akin to despots like George III or the Russian czar than American "olden patriots" like Thomas Jefferson. Finally, the proponents of laissez-faire capitalism were a threat to the very survival of the Republic; Powderly put them in the same category as anarchists.

Emily Tallmadge's "Rouse! Americans, Rouse!" captures the anxiety that Knights felt for the future of the Republic:

> Americans, rouse! or sleep forever;
> Rouse! Americans, rouse!
> Strike for freedom, now or never!
> Rouse! Americans, rouse!
> A golden scepter waves above you,
> Strike if freedom's call can move you.
> For those you love, for those that trust you,
> Rouse! Americans, rouse![49]

The Tallmadge collection returns often to the theme that only labor can save the nation. The second verse of "Ring the Bells of Freedom" proclaims the KOL's victory over wage slavery: "Ring the bells of freedom! there is joy to-day/For the victory of each noble Knight/Yes, a slave is rescued from the birds of prey/And lab'rers hold the ransomed seat." "Our Battle Song" upholds the KOL as crusaders of "brawn and brain against injustice" and the vanguard of victory against enslaving "grabbers, thieves and traitors."[50]

The aforementioned songs resonate with long-standing republican traditions and critiques of social privilege. But True Patriotism took even more radical turns. John Cosgrove's version of the "The Red Flag" appears in the same column of the Denver *Labor Enquirer* as William Morris's socialist anthem "No Master," and suggests a new banner around which labor should rally: "O, the Red Flag, the Red Flag is flying/Its scarlet shall flame o'er the free." Cosgrove's text is alive with imagery of groaning toilers and robber barons. On the same page, a song from Xavier H. Leder was even more direct, "On Mammon's sad ruins the Old Red unfurling/The torch of Redemption is spreading its glare."[51] Since the *Enquirer* served as the official organ for both DA 89 and the

---

49. Tallmadge, *Labor Songs Dedicated to the Knights of Labor*, 3.
50. Ibid., 13, 15.
51. *Labor Enquirer* (Denver), July 3, 1887.

Rocky Mountain Social League, it was long a repository of radical sentiment inside the KOL. Even before the Cosgrove and Leder songs appeared, the *Enquirer* printed Arthur Cheesewright's "Social Freedom," whose second verse proclaims:

> The Black and Red united and climbing with a will,
> Mounting the heights of Social Freedom;
> And we'll never get aweary until we've climbed the hill,
> Shouting the cry of Social Freedom.[52]

The colors in Cheesewright's verse referred to an ongoing struggle convulsing Denver between anarchists following the model Michael Bakunin's Black International, and socialist factions split between Lasalleans and Marxists. All of Denver's left-wing factions agreed, however, on their common dislike of capitalism.

Knights' songsters are pregnant with images of the Order as the protector of the Republic. Tallmadge included "Fling to the Breeze Our Banner," the first verse of which runs: "Come brothers, come, our country calls you/Dare you your dearest rights maintain?/Let us dethrone presumptuous leaders/Let labor and true Knighthood reign." A variant of this song turned up in Denver in 1887, calling on workers to cast "frauds" out of the Senate, while "To the Polls!" calls for labor to reclaim the rights for which the nation's founders fought.[53] Thompson's collection included "Spread the Light," a call to political education, and "Awake and Be Free," a favorite among radicals.[54]

Ultimately, KOL songs of politics and patriotism were like those that employed religious themes. Both forms upheld the Order and its supporters as true models by which others should be measured. In truth, it is unlikely many Knights saw a difference between religious and patriotic song imagery, since the main purpose of each was to cultivate an "us/them" mentality that strengthened rank-and-file resolve. All KOL songs were imbued with a crusading zeal that was equally moral and political. In the ultimate marriage of these themes, songwriter John Thompson added his own version of "The Red Flag," wherein the banner was a symbol of Christian brotherhood, not radical politics.[55] It mattered little whether the focus was on religion or on politics. The most promising vision for Americans and their nation remained the one ex-

---

52. Ibid., June 1, 1887.
53. Tallmadge, *Labor Songs Dedicated to the Knights of Labor*, 3; Baker, *Songs of Monssini*, 4.
54. Thompson, *The Labor Reform Songster*, 18, 19, 22, 23.
55. Foner, *American Labor Songs of the 19th Century*, 153.

pressed by Uriah Stephens: a Christian brotherhood that redeemed individuals and institutions. In this sense, John Thompson's tamer "Red Flag" links with Cheesewright's more revolutionary "Social Freedom," just as Phillips Thompson's "Sweet Bye and Bye" links with the defiant "Modern Missionary Zeal." Each songwriter differed on means, but they agreed that the goal was to produce a commonwealth in which True Christianity and True Patriotism reigned supreme. With the ultimate goal firmly in mind, Baker's "Pledged to the Right" is pure KOL:

> With willing heart and mind,
> Workingmen now combine,
>   For Freedom's cause;
> Let every sound proclaim,
> In our Creator's name,
> That we henceforth maintain,
> His righteous laws.[56]

Chivalry Versus Tyranny

Having identified themselves as True Christians and True Patriots, KOL songwriters created a vast repertoire of songs about oppression that identified the enemies of labor whom chivalrous Knights would overcome. To the modern ear, many of their songs seem vague, sentimental, and trite. Quite a few show signs of Victorian contamination within KOL ranks, an often-cited charge by the Order's critics (and, later, by historians). But many of these songs have mixed messages that require subtle disentangling. One must take caution to differentiate real Victorian sentimentality in the Knights—which existed in abundance—from that which was tactical.

On occasion, KOL songwriters found it effective to condemn bourgeois society in its own language and style. Consider "Only a Crust of Bread":

> Give me a crust of bread mother;
>   Only a crust of bread.
> 'Twill serve to help you think of me,
>   Think of me when I'm dead.
> I'm starving mother, the life I've left

---

56. Baker, *Songs of Monssini*, 4.

> May last a day or two
> If I can get a crust of bread,
> A crust to carry me through.

The child dies of starvation and the tragedy reaches its soppy climax with a short lament from the mother, who takes solace that her son will go to heaven where "rich and poor do meet" and where "all the same price get."[57]

On the surface this looks like fluff and drivel, but it is more than a surrender to mawkish Victorianism. "Only a Crust of Bread" is a musical version of a well-known poem, and was similar in tone to the "factory girl" fiction of popular periodicals. But whereas abused factory operatives were always rescued in Victorian fiction—usually by a middle-class suitor who sets things right—no such happy ending is in sight in "Only a Crust of Bread." The song uses Victorian sentimentality to expose class injustices.

KOL songwriters like Charles Cheesewright were adroit at using the oppressor's own language, logic, and style to argue for change. In "The Factory Girl," Cheesewright drew on formulas dating from the early 1800s. He even set the lyrics to the tune of the parlor standard "The Orphan Boy." This song takes up the plight of a young girl who declares, "I am a poor little factory girl/I toil from early morn to night/My sisters and brothers do the same/For us the factory is aught but bright." As the piece unfolds, one learns that her father was displaced by a machine, and that her mother died in the very factory where the girl now labors: "My poor, dear mother sank at last/The factory lord heard not her moan/But into wealth he still does coin/Our lives, our flesh, our blood, our bones."[58]

Cheesewright was no Victorian but rather a devoted member of the anarcho-syndicalist Rocky Mountain Social League. The tone of "The Factory Girl" is ironic, and skewers bourgeois society on its own terms. Cheesewright experimented with various styles, and was best known for his biting sense of humor, as in "The Hurrah Wagon," a satire on class and drinking. The "hurrah wagon" was the nickname given to the police van that collected drunks and deposited them in the local lockup. Cheesewright wryly noted the class dimensions of this practice:

> But if a dude or banker
> Gets out upon a tear,

57. *Labor Leaf*, November 18, 1885.
58. *Labor Enquirer* (Denver), July 16, 1887; Foner, *American Labor Songs of the 19th Century*, 155.

And raises Ned upon the street
The wagon isn't there;
A copper takes him gently home,
Next day the papers state,
Lord Vere de Vere was overcome
By the sun's extreme heat.[59]

This set of Cheesewright lyrics also had a hidden agenda, namely attacking what he thought was the real Victorian contamination inside the KOL: Powderly's zealous temperance policies. "The Hurrah Wagon" was actually a tongue-in-cheek swipe at Powderly. By 1887, Joseph R. Buchanan and Burnette Haskell, editors of *The Labor Enquirer*, the paper in which "The Hurrah Wagon" appeared, were bitter enemies of the General Master Workman whom they thought hopelessly bourgeois in outlook. Cheesewright's satirical ditty on worker binges coincided with Powderly's visit to Denver in order to answer charges drawn by Haskell and Buchanan. Haskell printed "The Hurrah Wagon" to irk Powderly on the eve of his visit, underscoring their political and cultural differences.[60]

Still, it would be foolish to deny that Victorian ideology was nonexistent within the KOL. "The Runaway Banker" from the Tallmadge collection lampoons bankers, but ridicules African Americans in the process. Written in mock-black dialect, it tells of a banker who oppressed the locals but fled town when he heard the KOL was on its way. In the interim, his property and wine cellar were taken over by the local black population:

De victims are so lonesome libbin
In de log house on de lawn,
Day move dar tings to Banker's parlor
For to keep it while he's gone.
Dar's wine and cider in de kitchen,
An de victims dey got some;

59. *Labor Enquirer* (Denver), April 2, 1887.
60. Buchanan learned the hard way that temperance was a losing issue in Denver. After embarrassing himself by getting drunk at the 1885 General Assembly in Hamilton, Ontario, Buchanan renewed his temperance pledge and was briefly a zealot. Temperance proved to be the political undoing of Buchanan's slate of candidates in Denver elections during 1886 and 1887. By the time Powderly arrived in Denver, the temperance movement was weak and there was more political hay to be made condemning it than supporting it. For more, see David Brundage, "The Producing Classes in the Saloon: Denver in the 1880s," *Labor History* 26 (Winter 1985): 29–52.

I s'pose dey'll all be confiscated
When de Knights of Labor come.[61]

The dialect is certainly not accurate, and although it is plausible that Tallmadge collected the song and mistranslated speech patterns, the song's drinking and vandalism present an unsavory image of African Americans more in line with Victorian stereotypes than the KOL's official position on race.

Many of the Victorian ideals that found their way into KOL songs were tempered by class, however. Women in KOL songs are often closer to bourgeois notions of *kinder, kirche,* and *kuche* than to those of nineteenth-century feminism. Nonetheless, they departed from hegemonic Gilded Age gender norms. For example, Phillips Thompson's "Thirty Cents a Day" contains troubling themes:

In a dim-lighted chamber a dying maiden lay,
The tide of her pulses was ebbing fast away;
In the flush of her youth she was worn with toil and care
And starvation showed its traces on the features once so fair.

No more the work-bell calls the weary one.
Rest, tired wage-slave, in your grave unknown;
Your feet will no more tread life's thorny, rugged way,
They've murdered you by inches upon thirty cents a day![62]

All the elements of popular stereotypes are here, and one is hard-pressed to find a KOL song in which a man dies of hard work. Young women and children are frequently cast as victims, with starving children usually fatherless, and dying women widowed or orphaned. But again, these stereotypes indict middle-class society through its own logic. Working women symbolized the bourgeois oppression of low-wage labor that supported a system of exploitation that made it impossible to survive on a single wage. In a curious manner, the songs condemned capitalism for forcing women to assume roles for which they were thought to be unsuited. Even women Knights reinforced the notion that women forced to labor led to tragedy. In "Labor In Want," Melinda Sissins took on greedy factory owners, loan officers, "Shylocks," and antigreenbackers with gusto and zeal. Sissins adds pathos by including a woman who is forced to work after her mother's death and a bank foreclosure on their house.[63]

61. Tallmadge, *Labor Songs Dedicated to the Knights of Labor,* 16.
62. Thompson, *The Labor Reform Songster,* 15.
63. *JKL,* November 2, 1893.

Some Knights held such progressive views of women. By the mid-1880s, the KOL was committed to women's suffrage, called for an equal rights amendment to the Constitution, and counted Susan Anthony, Elizabeth Cady Stanton, and Frances Willard among its members. The Baker songster contains an anthem supporting votes for women. "Woman Suffrage" upholds the KOL's rhetorical stance on equality and—in deference to Mrs. Willard—links votes for women to its moral stand on liquor:

> If a social question is to be solved,
> Where man and woman alike are involved,
> Their mutual welfare we best may promote,
> By giving each of them the privilege to vote. . . .
>
> Then give her a chance on the question of liquor,
> And soon he will cease to starve and kick her,
> And our youth will grow up in knowledge and health,
> And our nation be strong in wisdom and wealth.[64]

Most KOL songs of oppression were more direct. Songwriters were fond of dividing the world into noble toilers and those who robbed them, pitting chivalrous Knights against the forces of tyranny. These offerings dominate the songsters. "The Runaway Banker," with all its racial stereotypes, was an aberration in the Tallmadge collection; other songs attacked bondholders, brokers, antigreenbackers, and false politicians. In such songs, salvation from tyranny came from chivalrous Knights of Labor. In "Our Battle Song," would-be oppressors are thwarted when they see "How the mighty host advances/Labor leads the van/The Knights are rallying by the thousands/On the labor plan." Greenbacks and sound currency triumph over bondholders and corrupt politicians when "Labor and true Knighthood reign."[65]

The monetary system is also the subject of a song written by ardent Greenbacker and agrarian radical B. W. Goodhue in the Tallmadge collection:

> The greenback, the hope of the nation,
> The money the people demand;
> It saved us from war's desolation,
> And shall be supreme in the land.

64. Baker, *Songs of Monssini*, 14.
65. Tallmadge, *Labor Songs Dedicated to the Knights of Labor*, 18, 21.

A later verse adds:

> It will open the workshop and foundry,
>   Many ships it will send from our shore;
> It will bless ev'ry home in the country,
>   And save us from tramps by the score.[66]

The greenback songs in the Tallmadge collection are suggestive of the transformation of the KOL after 1887. The Order grew slowly in rural America, even as it declined in urban areas. By the early 1890s, much of the KOL was indistinguishable from Populism, and Knights' songs reflected this. Tallmadge's "Labor's Cry For Freedom" attacks stock gamblers, monopoly, "money kings," and "vampires that live on ill-paid labor." Baker includes a similar song in his 1889 songster. By the mid-1890s, a variant of "Labor's Cry" surfaced as a Populist party rally song. "The People's Cry For Freedom" retained Tallmadge's call to end wage slavery and mentions "workingmen" several times, but the enemy changed. The final verse of the song proclaims:

> So we're forming everywhere—North and South and East and
>   West
> To give the slave of wage his freedom;
> And we'll hurl the Idol GOLD from the land that we love best
> And give every soul his freedom.[67]

Greenbacker concerns notwithstanding, the most important song included in the Tallmadge collection was "Labor's Ninety and Nine," one of the most popular labor songs of the nineteenth century. Though its authorship is uncertain, it appears that the earliest version was penned by Mrs. S. M. Smith of Kewanee, Illinois, for Greenbacker Peter Cooper's 1876 presidential bid, with an updated version by E. H. Gillette, a Congressman from Iowa who joined the KOL, appearing in the 1880s. By the time Thompson's songster appeared in 1893, "Ninety and Nine" was so well known that it had entered the folk process. Variants abounded, as did new songs using its music. (It even enjoyed life into the twentieth century: Charles Kerr published a version in his *Socialist Songs with Music*.) Each of its four verses is similar in content to its opening:

> There are ninety-and-nine who live and die
>   In want and hunger and cold,

---

66. Ibid., 12–13; see also 26, "Labor's Yankee Doodle."
67. Tallmadge, *Labor Songs Dedicated to the Knights of Labor*, 31; Baker, *Songs of Monssini*, 7; Greenway, *American Folksongs of Protest*, 61.

That one may live in luxury
    And be lapped in its silken fold;
The ninety-and-nine in their hovels bare,
    The one in a palace in riches rare.[68]

The message of "Ninety and Nine" was clear: the masses were being exploited by a greedy few. Monssini Baker added land speculators, usurers, and scabs to the list of villains. One song promised the rising of chivalrous Knights to the rescue of debased labor:

Arouse, ye Knights of Labor, rise and stand
Emancipate the laborer in every land.
No other knight can his cause compare,
To that for which our lives we swear,
Called by humanity's cry to do or dare![69]

In "Yankee Doodle Now-a-Days," Baker took on land monopolists and mortgage-holders to the jaunty tune of America's most popular air:

Yankee Doodle Dudes and Drones
    Are getting rather plenty.
They live in style while labor groans
    In garret, street and shanty.

Yankee Doodle Dudes and Drones
    Boom your land and money.
But stay your mortgages and loans
    Or things will turn out funny.[70]

The choice of tune was wistful, but also provocative. Throughout much of the nineteenth century, "Yankee Doodle Dandy" was the anthem of choice for the masses ("The Star Spangled Banner" did not become America's national anthem until 1931), thus making Baker's parody shocking and effective.

Baker also reminded Knights that one of the duties of True Patriots was voting, an act that would help workers rid themselves of politicians

68. Tallmadge, *Labor Songs Dedicated to the Knights of Labor*, 25; Foner, *American Labor Songs of the 19th Century*, 142–43; *Labor Enquirer* (Denver), February 23, 1887; *Labor Enquirer* (Chicago), July 2, 1887; *The Boycotter*, July 10, 1886.
69. Baker, *The Songs of Monssini*, 10.
70. Ibid., 9.

in the pockets of monied interests. Typical is "Workingmen's Campaign Song":

> But if might is right, then fight is right
>   And victory is ours;
> We'll to the polls no more like fools,
>   To vote away our powers;
> For Dives and his hirelings
>   Can be counted with the few,
> While working men are everywhere
>   Where'er there's work to do.
> Of the sixty millions they can say
>   Who shall our country rule,
> Who shall legislate or sit him down
>   In the presidential stool;
> For thieves and robbers hitherto
>   Have chiefly made our laws;
> Their grants and privileges at last
>   Must have their final clause.[71]

Phillips Thompson also printed songs of oppression, including a variant of "Ninety and Nine." In "The Bitter Cry," Thompson attacked capitalism: "From dawn to dark we toil/To earn wealth for others/The men who reap the spoil/Forget we're their brothers."[72] His "March! March! March!" appropriated the tune of one the age's most popular songs, "Tramp! Tramp! Tramp!" in order to attack poor working conditions, landlords, and usurers. In "The Factory Slave," he employed the tune of "Swanee River" to complain of low wages.

Many KOL songs about oppression seem tame and outmoded by today's standards, a condition that adds fuel to (often misplaced) charges of Victorian sentimentality. To be certain, KOL song lyrics were filtered through residual racism, sexism, and Victorianism, but they were still radical by the standards of the day. If the lyrics seem oblique and elliptical today, we would do well to remember that the lyrics, style, and form are those of another time, with the villains and victims quite real and recognizable to the Knights who sang of them. Far from being oblique, the song messages were disarmingly direct. The world was di-

71. Baker, *Songs of Monssini*, 11; Kealey Palmer, *Dreaming of What Might Be*, 221–22. Kealey and Palmer also note how the popular song "Only a Brakeman" was worked into a specific campaign song in Ontario.
72. Thompson, *The Labor Reform Songster*, 5.

vided into two clear categories: those who labored and those who exploited. This simple good-versus-evil paradigm of chivalrous Knights and heartless tyrants allowed the songs to communicate their message despite bad poetry, forced meter, and surface sentimentality.

Come, Brothers All

Although Knights of Labor preferred to sing about themselves, the Order's critique of capitalism, in consonance with principles of Universal Brotherhood, opened their gaze toward broader horizons. Another genre of KOL songs dealing with the unity of working-class interests emerged promoting solidarity. Solidarity, as expressed in song, contains elements of class consciousness, but of a transcendent strain in which ideology is suffused and vague.

If capitalists, proprietors, and politicians occasionally joined KOL locals, they nonetheless took a beating in songs of solidarity. Most non-wage earners were dismissed as "idlers," and songs served as clarion calls for working-class defiance and unity. Typical is Mrs. Jacief's 1882 song "Come, Brothers All":

> Come Brothers all, attend the call,
>   Kill politics and party!
> Oh come and join our noble throng,
>   With courage true and hearty.
> Bring fathers and mothers, bring sisters and brothers,
> To help resist oppression,
>   And swell our ranks till all shall see,
> We truly mean Progression![73]

Likewise, Thomas McGuire reported that New York City Knights regularly sang "Song of the Proletaire," but only its chorus, which warned "tyrants" and "despots" that "iron bands are giving way."[74]

Songs of solidarity increased after the Order's membership was reconstituted after 1885, while the number specifically about the Knights declined, a trend in keeping with the Knights' attempt to evolve from a narrow fraternal organization to a broader labor advocacy order, and reflective of its later decline. The shift in lyrical theme was never formal-

---

73. Foner, *American Labor Songs of the 19th Century*, 156.
74. *JUL*, December 10, 1884.

ized, but Powderly's office became a repository for new songs, and beginning in 1886 one sees a dramatic increase in the number of songs printed in the *JUL*.[75]

A song from Colorado, "Labor Free For All," is typical of KOL solidarity compositions:

> Start the music comrades, we'll sing a labor song,
> Sing it with a spirit, that will speed the Cause along:
> Let it ring throughout the world, in chorus full and strong.
> Now we are fighting for Labor.
>
> Hurrah, hurrah, Labor is free for all:
> Hurrah, hurrah, hasten to the call;
> Shout the joyful tidings, King Capital must fall.
> Now we are fighting for Labor.[76]

The song apparently enjoyed popularity, and was reprinted in the *Labor Enquirer* more than a year after its debut. Patrick Molony's "Freedom" was similar in content. His second verse includes the lines, "Let the sons of Labor/Take the rightful yield/Let the freehold saber/Rule the battlefield."[77]

The Tallmadge songster included numerous songs on the theme of solidarity, including a composition by his wife, Emily, and a reprint of "Labor Free For All." In "Labor's Bye and Bye," the vision is of a future where "all trades and producers" control both the political and economic structures of the land, while "When Workingmen Combine" promises that united toilers can defeat "banks," "railway kings," and "idle drones."[78] The most important song of solidarity in the Tallmadge collection is "The Workingmen's Marseillaise":

> Downtrodden millions, rise victorious,
>   For Truth and Justice firmly stand;
> God is your shield, your cause is glorious,
>   The freeman's hope in every land.
> Long have we pled, our wrongs recalling,

75. For example, see Powderly circular of December 1887, disseminating "The Brotherhood of Man" by Ida Hunt and J. Harris, in *PP*; Thomas O'Reilly to Powderly, July 22, 1887, in *PP*; *JUL*: June 10, 1886; April 11, 1887; September 3, 1887; October 1, 1887; December 20, 1888; December 27, 1888.

76. *Labor Enquirer* (Denver), February 27, 1886; reprinted July 3, 1887.

77. The song by Patrick Molony is found in *PP* among miscellaneous incoming correspondence. The date is illegible.

78. Tallmadge, *Labor Songs Dedicated to the Knights of Labor*, 5, 11, 22.

But Freedom leads a valiant band;
With swords of victory in hand,
A hireling host before them falling.

Arise! ye friends of truth!
Gird on the sword of right!
Work on, work on; all hearts resolved
To live for Liberty.[79]

When one encounters a text whose authorship is disputed, it is often a tip that the song was popular enough to enter the oral tradition. This is certainly true of the "The Workingmen's Marseillaise." Philip Foner claims the song was copyrighted by Charles Thompson in 1877, while *John Swinton's Paper* credited New York Knight David Healy with writing it. The song seems to have been around long before Healy's active involvement with the labor movement, and Thompson may well have been the author. But Tallmadge did not attribute the piece, an indication that it was standard fare. Typically, Monssini Baker tried to pass it off as his own.[80] In any event, among Gilded Age workers, the song was surpassed in popularity only by "Storm the Fort" and by variants of "Labor's Ninety and Nine." It was also a favorite of anarcho-socialist movements, despite its sentimental Christianity. It probably came to the KOL's attention through Healy, a member of DA 68 in Troy, New York, a district suffused with radicals.

Baker also included songs of solidarity in his collection. "Union Rallying Song" upholds solidarity as a way of eliminating scab labor: "Our Union forever, hurrah! boys, hurrah!/Down with scab labor, uproot it near and far."[81] Noteworthy in the Baker collection is that the call to union is not specific to the Knights of Labor. His booklet contains separate KOL rallying songs and, though he billed himself a Knight, he nonetheless offered songs that even a trade unionist feuding with the Knights could have sung in good conscience.

Knights of Labor solidarity songs were fluid, with the lyrics rewritten according to local needs, shifting political climates, and the fortunes of

79. Ibid., 22.
80. Foner, *American Labor Songs of the 19th Century*, 129; *John Swinton's Paper*, July 5, 1885, March 11, 1886; Baker, *The Songs of Monssini*. In fairness to David Healy and Monssini Baker, their versions of "The Workingmen's Marseillaise" contain different lyrics than the Thompson piece. In the loose world of nineteenth-century musical copyright laws, and the common practice of using the same tune for numerous sets of lyrics, it may be accurate to say that each man wrote original lyrics.
81. Baker, *The Songs of Monssini*, 7.

the Order. In 1887, Charles Cheesewright wrote new lyrics for "America" that contained only a few changes:

> Our cause it is of thee,
> Sweet Cause of Liberty,
>   Of thee we sing;
> For thee our fathers died,
> For thee we fight with pride,
> For thee we're all allied;
>   Thy reign to bring.[82]

But by 1890, following the execution of the Haymarket anarchists, a precipitous decline in the Knights, and general oppression of labor movements everywhere, Los Angeles Knight Ralph Hoyt felt less charitable:

> Our country, 'tis of thee
> Sweet land of knavery,
>   Of thee we sing!
> Sweet land of Jobs and Rings,
> And various crooked things
> Our social system brings
>   Full many a sting.

Hoyt didn't stop there; he identified the nation with "great defaulters," gold hoarders, "demagogues," and monopolies. He ended with a call to revolution.[83]

By the time Phillips Thompson's collection appeared in 1892, all the Knights of Labor had to offer the labor movement was the idea of solidarity, so it is not surprising to find many such songs in his songster. Most of them glorified workers ("Hurrah for the men who work/Whatever their trade may be") and encouraged them to organize: "Rouse, ye sons of labor all, and rally in your might!/In the Eastern heavens see the dawning of the light,/Fling our banner to the breeze, make ready for the fight."[84] Thompson realized that the KOL had lost its leadership of labor's struggle, and many of his songs used the generic term "union" rather than referring to the Knights. Thompson even reworked Baker's "When K. of L. Men Shall Rule," with new lyrics appearing under the title, "When Labor Has Come To Its Own" and substituting that title

---

82. *Labor Enquirer* (Denver), July 3, 1887.
83. *JKL*, July 3, 1890.
84. Thompson, *The Labor Reform Songster*, 6, 9.

line where Baker had written "when K. of L. men shall rule that day."
Further, Thompson expunged Baker's references to temperance, the
eight-hour movement, and cooperation, in favor of threats against Wall
Street and Jay Gould and the hope that "farmers and laborers [will] all
combine."[85]

Songs of the KOL made tentative forays into the possibility of working-class solidarity, a theme destined to become a guiding force in the
future labor movement. In 1915, a young songwriter for the IWW, Ralph
Chaplin, did as so many KOL songwriters before him had done: he
penned new lyrics to fit the familiar tune "John Brown's Body." (The
KOL sang at least seven songs to that tune.) His "Solidarity Forever"
became an instant hit and remains a labor song staple.

What Chaplin tapped into is often ignored: it was the KOL that kept
alive the dream of solidarity as an alternative to the particularist agendas
of most trade unions. As the first broadly based labor organization to
survive long enough to make a difference, the KOL offered the possibility of an oppositional working-class culture in which craft, ethnicity,
gender, ideology, and race could be subsumed for the larger good.[86] The
Knights reminded workers that "an injury to one is the concern of all."
It was no accident that Ralph Chaplin wrote of solidarity for an organization whose own motto was a recognizable variant of the once-defiant
Knights of Labor.[87]

Holding the Fort: The KOL's Musical Legacy

The link between Ralph Chaplin, the IWW, and the KOL may strike
some readers as tenuous, even contrived. But if one considers the many

85. Baker, *The Songs of Monssini*, 151; Thompson, *The Labor Reform Songster*, 30–31.

86. Both the IWW and the CIO also contained impressive collections of songs whose
general theme is solidarity. Although the direct link between most of these and the KOL
songs is tenuous, the KOL nonetheless deserves credit for revitalizing the notion of solidarity songs. The IWW's 1984 songbook contains a host of solidarity songs: "Solidarity
Forever," "The International," "Workingfolk Unite," "Hold the Fort," "Workers of the
World Awaken," and "There is Power in a Union." All of these were in vogue by or before
1915. See *Songs of the Workers: To Fan the Flames of the Discontent* (Chicago: Industrial Workers of the World, 1984). Many of these were also CIO favorites, especially "Solidarity Forever," "There is Power in a Union," and "Hold the Fort." Other popular CIO solidarity
songs include the many variants of "Which Side Are You On?" "Union Maid," "We Shall
Not Be Moved," "Step By Step," and "Roll the Union On." Examples of these can be
found in Seeger and Reiser, *Carry It On!*

87. The IWW's motto was "An Injury to One Is an Injury to All."

dimensions in which legacies are formed and operate, it assuredly is not. In the remaining pages of this chapter, I turn to how the KOL's efforts outlived the Order. Central to appreciating the Knights' musical legacy is an understanding of tradition and inspiration. While a few specific songs remain from the KOL era, the bulk of the Order's legacy lies in its role in keeping alive the tradition of social protest singing, and in inspiring future labor singers and songwriters to continue that tradition.

One of the most astute observers of the social protest tradition was folklorist John Greenway. When he researched protest songs in the 1950s he remarked, "In labor these days, everyone sings."[88] By his reckoning, the KOL played a big role in making that scenario possible. The KOL stood in the middle of a labor song tradition that began in colonial times and stretched through the CIO. The KOL bequeathed a rich musical treasure trove to which organized labor added, especially the IWW and the CIO. Had not the KOL sung, labor's song heritage would likely have been a far poorer one. As Greenway noted, the AFL was "virtually barren" of songs marking "the progress of unionism."[89] Those few songs of importance in the AFL repertoire—like "When Workingmen Combine" and "The Workingmen's Marseillaise"—came to the organization through the Knights. AFL unions sang, but their craft exclusiveness blunted the development of class-wide solidarity. Lyrics like "World-honored craftsmen, your weapons of pow'r/Never gleamed brighter than in this great hour" and "Hurrah for the noble carpenter" ring hollow beside the KOL's motto of "An injury to one is the concern of all." One of the better AFL musical offerings is Thomas Confare's "The March of Union Labor":

> The march of union labor should be welcomed ev'rywhere
> From the humble little cottage to the door of the millionaire;
> From the science of the universe is made by brain and brawn,
> And the wisdom of the unions long ago began to dawn
> Upon capital advancing and now in full command;
> All we ask for is to show us a kind and generous hand;
> For industries of this country demand of you the call,
> The march of union labor should be welcomed by you all.[90]

Nonetheless, Confare's song—a reworking of several KOL songs— has all of the bland sentimentalism of Victorian parlor pieces, with little

88. Greenway, *American Folksongs of Protest*, 225.
89. Ibid., 9, 11.
90. Foner, *American Labor Songs of the 19th Century*, 137, 168–80; Balch, "Songs For Labor," 411.

of the pathos that made those pieces successful. Its appeal was wider than those songs that were craft-specific, but only marginally so.

Emily Balch was not impressed by AFL singing. In 1914, she wrote, "[Perhaps] the craft union is too practical a work-day organization for song; it has been difficult to find words or music of special originality or permanence growing out of [the AFL]."[91] To find examples of stirring labor songs Balch did the sensible thing: she wrote to Powderly and asked him about old KOL songs. Balch may have been overly harsh in her assessment of AFL singing, but there is little doubt that labor singing declined with the KOL in the 1890s, and was in the doldrums until revitalized by the IWW. Not coincidentally, the most musical AFL crafts were those headed by ex-Knights such as Thomas Armstrong, William H. Foster, George McNeill, and the United Mine Workers, once a KOL union.[92]

Of the trade unions, miners sang far more than most. This is largely due to the unique nature of mining and the communities that the industry supported. Most mine patches were secluded, and mine work was dangerous and tedious. These forces combined to create a subculture that was distinctively rough, male, expressive, resilient, and self-contained. Miners were quick to lash out against perceived injustices and, if pushed too far, did not shrink from violence. The isolation of mining hamlets hampered efforts at national organization, but miners proved adroit at combining on the local level. Since their lives were hard already, miner strikes were difficult to break quickly. It was not easy to import scabs into small hamlets whose entire institutional life revolved around the portal and pit.[93]

Music was an integral part of mining-town culture. Ethnic music predominated and the air was often filled with Irish jigs, Scottish reels, and Polish polkas. But KOL miners also wrote about current conditions and concerns. Phillips Thompson collected "The Pennsylvania Miner," written in response to the bloody 1887–88 anthracite strikes broken by scabs, starvation, and Pinkerton detectives:

Come, listen, fellow-workingmen, my story I'll relate,
How workers in the coal-mines fare in Pennsylvania State;

91. Balch, "Songs For Labor," 411.
92. Halker, For Democracy, Workers, and God; Balch, "Songs For Labor."
93. Archie Green, Only a Miner (Urbana: University of Illinois Press, 1972), chap. 5; Montgomery, Fall of the House of Labor; Altina Waller, Feud: Hatfields, McCoys, and Social Change in Appalachia, 1860–1900 (Chapel Hill: University of North Carolina Press, 1988); Anthony F. C. Wallace, St. Clair: A Nineteenth-Century Coal Town's Experience with a Disaster-Prone Industry (New York: Alfred A. Knopf, 1987); Katherine Harvey, The Best-Dressed

Come, hear a sad survivor, from beside his childrens' graves,
And learn how free Americans are treated now as slaves.

They robbed us of our pay,
They starved us day by day,
They shot us down on the hillside brown,
And swore our lives away.

Pinkerton detectives and ruffians turned the song's protagonist and his family out of their humble cabin, his wife and children freezing to death. Like many miners, the hero of this song did not stoically accept his fate:

Half-crazed I wandered round the spot, and just beyond the town
I met a dastard Pinkerton and struck the villain down;
My brain was frenzied with the thought of children, friends, and
    wife
I set my heel upon his throat and trampled out his life.[94]

KOL miners wrote many songs, including "Our Brave Little Band," the unofficial theme song of National Trade Assembly 135. It is a ten-verse song the chorus of which ("Three cheers for our brave little band/ Three cheers for our brave little band/A just recompense for our labor/Is all poor miners demand") was sung after the first nine. The last chorus added a slight twist: "Three cheers for our brave little band/Three cheers for our brave little band/By the united Knights of Labor/Oppression must cease in our land."[95] Another popular song was "Coal Creek Troubles," a song commemorating the 1891 Coal Creek, Tennessee, strike. There, miners were especially venomous in their scorn for Governor John P. Buchanan, a Democrat who was elected with the help of the Tennessee Farmers' Alliance, and who betrayed his allies by supporting convict labor in the mines and sending state policemen to guard the

Miners: Life and Labor in the Maryland Coal Region, 1835–1910 (Ithaca: Cornell University Press, 1969); George Korson, *Songs and Ballads of the Anthracite Miner* (New York: Grafton Press, 1927); Korson, *Coal Dust on the Fiddle* (Philadelphia: University of Pennsylvania Press, 1943).

94. Thompson, *The Labor Reform Songster*, 7. Thompson's authorship for this song is unlikely. The song was popular from the 1890s into the 1930s and I suspect it was already a staple by the time Thompson included it in his songster. Its themes are quite unlike any in the Thompson collection, especially its espousal of violence. Further, nowhere else does Thompson employ a "come all ye" opening stanza, standard fare in miner songs. Thompson's claim of authorship perhaps rests on the possibility that he was the first to print the musical score.

95. Foner, *American Labor Songs of the 19th Century*, 200–201.

pits. Disgusted Knights sang, "The corruption of Buchanan/Brought the convicts here/Just to please the rich man/And take the miners' share."[96]

By the time folklorist George Korson collected miner stories and songs in the 1930s, few workers boasted of as rich a musical heritage as coal miners. By then, miners were at the fore of labor singing traditions. It was no accident that the AFL's most musical trade was one that five decades earlier was heavily organized by the KOL.

For the most part, twentieth-century labor songwriters drew on the KOL indirectly, though not entirely so. Folklorists have debated fiercely the definition of a true "folksong."[97] By most standards, however, two KOL favorites—"Storm the Fort" and "Ninety and Nine"—qualify. "Storm the Fort" was destined to outlive the Order. It even made its way to England and was sung during a nineteenth-century transport workers' strike. In 1912, a variant was sung during the Lawrence textile strike.[98] Reworked as "Hold the Fort," the song became a favorite of the IWW. The IWW 1914 songbook includes the following lyrics:

> We meet today in freedom's cause
> And raise our voices high;
> We'll join our hands in union strong
> To battle or to die.
>
> Chorus:
> Hold the Fort for we are coming,
> Unionists be strong.

96. Green, *Only a Miner*, 176. This song was popular in the 1930s and was recorded by Mike Seeger in the 1970s.

97. For an overview of folksong scholarship, see Jan Brunvand, *The Study of American Folklore* (New York: W. W. Norton & Co., 1978), chap. 10; Richard Dorson, *American Folklore and the Historian* (Chicago: University of Chicago Press, 1971); Greenway, *American Folk Songs of Protest*, 7, 9.

Not all folklorists agree with Greenway that social protest songs are folksongs. Tristram Coffin was especially vigorous in his attacks on Greenway. For the purposes of determining the legacy of KOL singing, however, the debate over folksong criteria is irrelevant. Those interested in the debate should see Edward P. Ives, *Joe Scott: The Woodsman-Songwriter* (Urbana: University of Illinois Press, 1978); also Ives, *Larry Gorman: The Man Who Wrote the Songs* (Bloomington: University of Indiana Press, 1964); and Ives, *Lawrence Doyle: The Farmer Poet of Prince Edward Island* (Orono: University of Maine Press, 1971). See also Abrahams and Foss, *Anglo-American Folksong Style*, 5; Henry Glassie, Edward Ives et al., *Folksongs and Their Makers* (Bowling Green: Ohio University Press, 1978); Barre Toelken, *The Dynamics of Folklore* (Boston: Houghton-Mifflin, 1979), chaps. 1–4.

98. Foner, *American Labor Songs of the 19th Century*, 130; *I.W.W. Songbook*, 28th ed. (Chicago: Industrial Workers of the World, 1946); Pete Seeger to Robert E. Weir, personal correspondence, November 29, 1987; William Cahn, *Lawrence 1912: The Bread and Roses Strike* (New York: Pilgrim Press, 1977), 131.

Side by side we battle onward,
Victory will come.

Look my comrades, see the union
Banners waving high.
Reinforcements now appearing,
Victory is nigh.

See our numbers still increasing;
Hear the bugles blow.
By our union we shall triumph
Over every foe.

Fierce and long the battle rages,
But we will not fear,
Help will come whene'er it's needed,
Cheer, my comrades, cheer.[99]

The IWW was not the only organization to sing the reworked "Hold the Fort." Pete Seeger knew it as "a favorite union song of the 1930s" and it surfaced in both the CIO and the Young Communist League. As a member of the Almanac Singers, Seeger recorded the song. In 1959, it even appeared as a parody. Dave Van Ronk and Richard Ellington changed it to "Hold the Line" in their send-up of the IWW songbook, *The Bosses' Songbook: Songs to Stifle the Flames of Discontent*. More recently a new variant emerged in a collection of labor songs assembled by Seeger and Rob Reiser. It is still included in the official IWW songbook.[100]

"Labor's Ninety and Nine" also enjoyed a long life. As we have seen, "Ninety and Nine" predates the KOL as a metaphor, poem, and song. But once appropriated, only "Storm the Fort" and "Song of the Proletaire" made their way into more journals than "Ninety and Nine." Another measure of the popularity of "Ninety and Nine" is the number of variants it inspired. I collected only one version that exactly matched another; only its central theme remained constant: ninety-nine workers toil to produce the idle leisure of one millionaire. Variants abounded in the 1890s. Although the song's popularity waned in the twentieth century—its pathos was too Victorian for twentieth-century sensibilities—the metaphor of the masses slaving for idle masters became a sta-

99. *I.W.W. Songbook*, 8th ed., 1914; reprinted in 28th ed., 1946, and 35th ed., 1984.
100. Seeger to Weir, November 29, 1987; Seeger and Reiser, *Carry It On!*; *I.W.W. Songbook*, 1984.

ple of IWW songs like "We Have Fed You All For a Thousand Years" and "Fifty Thousand Lumberjacks."[101]

"Ninety and Nine" illustrates another aspect of the KOL's musical legacy: it was a conduit for social protest songs it did not originate. Two twentieth-century favorites passed on by the Knights were "The Workingmen's Marseillaise" and "Eight Hours." The original "Marseillaise" was written by Rouget de Lisle during the French Revolution and became the national anthem of France. The author gained fame, and his song appeared in numerous radical and labor publications. By the 1870s, variants of the song were produced, and the Knights of Labor contributed several. Both Tallmadge and Baker included the following version in their songsters:

> Downtrodden millions, rise victorious,
>   For Truth and Justice firmly stand;
> God is your shield, your cause is glorious,
>   The freeman's hope in every land.
> Long have we pled, our wrongs recalling,
>   But Freedom leads a valiant band;
> With swords of victory in hand,
> A hireling host before them falling.
>
>> Arise! ye friends of truth!
>> Gird on the sword of right!
>> Work on, work on; all hearts resolved
>> To live for liberty.
>
> Oh, glorious work! can man resign thee,
>   Or scorn repay thy generous hand?
> Creation's Lord to men consign thee,
>   Thou conqueror o'er sea and land!
> Shall workmen blush thy worth revealing,
>   Or men scorn him by labor soiled?
> Naught won had we not fought and toil'd,
> All other arts are unavailing.[102]

101. In all, I collected seven other variants of "Ninety and Nine." See *Labor Enquirer* (Denver), February 23, 1886, July 2, 1887, July 19, 1887; *Labor Enquirer* (Chicago), July 2, 1887; *Boycotter* July 10, 1886; Tallmadge, *Labor Songs Dedicated to the Knights of Labor*, 25; Thompson, *The Labor Reform Songster*, 23–24. For IWW songs that modify this theme, see Joyce Kornbluh, ed., *Rebel Voices: An IWW Anthology* (Ann Arbor: University of Michigan Press, 1968), 27, 267.

102. Tallmadge, *Labor Songs Dedicated to the Knights of Labor*, 8; Baker, *The Songs of Monssini*, 3–4.

Likewise, the Knights of Labor perpetuated "Eight Hours," a song penned in the 1870s by J. G. Blanchard and future Knight Jesse Jones. "Eight Hours" enjoyed modest popularity until 1886, when it captured the imagination of planners for the nationwide May 1 strike for the eight-hour work day. The song survived into the twentieth century until, ultimately, it became more important as a symbol than as a song. Musically, the tune and lyrics belong to the nineteenth century, but the sentiments expressed became a rallying cry for labor, especially the final lines: "Eight hours for work, eight hours for rest, eight hours for what we will." Those final phrases captured the working-class imagination in ways the rest of the song did not. Parading Knights carried that slogan aloft on their banners and when the KOL faded, others took up the burden. In 1897, striking mine workers sang a different version of "Eight Hours," and in 1912, Wobbly songwriter Richard Brazier penned still another version. Since the eight-hour work day was not yet legally established (1938), other songwriters, banner-wavers, and propagandists were afforded ample opportunity to improvise with the symbolism that was invented by Blanchard and Jones and perpetuated by the KOL.[103]

The lingering imagery of "Ninety and Nine" and "Eight Hours" was joined in the twentieth century by at least one other staple from the pen of KOL songwriters: the red flag. The KOL is yet to receive its due from historians of Gilded Age radicalism for its role in energizing socialist and anarchist movements. The red flag came to the KOL through its more radical members, especially in locales like Denver and New York City where the leadership of the Knights and radical groups often interlocked. Both the KOL and radical movements were small in the 1870s, but the KOL's huge membership upsurge in the 1880s gave radicals of all stripes a voice that was unthinkable a few years earlier. It is likely that many workers first became aware of red flag symbolism through KOL journals.

By 1886, various songs, each titled "The Red Flag," appeared in KOL journals. By the 1890s, the red flag metaphor was commonly used by labor songwriters, paving the way for the most famous song version, penned by British socialist James Connell. Connell cited the execution of Haymarket radicals, the 1889 London dockworkers' strike, the repression suffered by the Irish Land League, and his personal beliefs in philosophical nihilism as the sources of his inspiration. Connell's version became the official anthem of the British Labour party, and soon found its way to America. It was printed in the IWW's first songbook, and labor radical Len DeCaux recalled it as a favorite in the early days of the CIO.[104]

103. Balch, "Songs For Labor," 411; Kornbluh, *Rebel Voices*, 178–79.
104. Len DeCaux, *Labor Radical: From the Wobblies to the C.I.O.* (Boston: Beacon Press, 1970).

Connell never credited the KOL with inspiring him, even though most of the sentiments he expressed were echoed in earlier KOL songs of the same name. Such is the power of the oral tradition. Connell appropriated a symbol that was so popular that he thought little of its origin or history. But at least one old-time Knight found that Connell's song struck a familiar chord. When Victor Drury, the firebrand anarchist of New York's DA 49, died in 1918, Leonora O'Reilly found Connell's "The Red Flag" among his personal effects.[105]

The KOL's final legacy was that it had established norms of musical style for the labor movement. Of particular note was the Order's use of popular and hymn tunes as musical scores for labor lyrics. In my survey of 166 KOL songs, only 19 employed original tunes. Subtracting the 15 for which I was unable to find a reference to tune, 132 songs (87.4 percent) set new lyrics to familiar tunes, such as "Marching Through Georgia" (10), "America" (8), "Auld Lang Syne" (7), "John Brown's Body" (7), "Tramp! Tramp! Tramp!" (6), "Sweet Bye and Bye" (5), and "Red, White, and Blue" (5). The 1945 edition of the *I.W.W. Songbook* contained a dozen songs written to tunes that the KOL also used. Though one might argue that the popularity of "Auld Lang Syne" and "John Brown's Body" make this crossover predictable, one is hard-pressed to explain why the tune to "Tramp! Tramp! Tramp!" remained decades after the song's heyday. As late as 1984 the IWW's songbook still contained five tunes the Knights used.[106]

Clear stylistic parallels exist between KOL songwriters and Joe Hill, the most famous IWW songsmith. Since Hill was born in Sweden and emigrated to America only after the KOL was all but defunct, its influences on him are indirect. Nonetheless, Hill used gospel tunes for many of his most famous songs, including "Nearer My Job to Thee" and "There is Power in a Union." His most famous song, "The Preacher and the Slave," employed the tune of "Sweet Bye and Bye," one that inspired at least five KOL songs. Hill spent most of his time among West Coast dockhands, and perhaps heard parodies of "Sweet Bye and Bye" there. His base in San Pedro, California, put him in the backyard of Ralph Hoyt, a Los Angeles Knight with a reputation for parodying religious and patriotic songs.

Another source for Joe Hill's tunes was Tin Pan Alley, from which he borrowed to create IWW standards like "Casey Jones, the Union Scab," "It's a Long Way Down to the Soupline," and "Mr. Block." Again, this

---

105. Some of Victor Drury's writings and effects are found in the collection *Leaders of the Women's Trade Union League: Leonora O'Reilly* (Schlesinger Library, Radcliffe College).
106. *Songs of the Workers.*

parallels KOL standards. Of 151 identifiable tunes used by the KOL, 78 (51.6 percent) used popular tunes of the day.

The most famous song in U.S. labor history, "Solidarity Forever," was likewise penned to a popular tune by IWW editor Ralph Chaplin, who chose the tune "John Brown's Body." By then, Chaplin and most Americans knew the tune best through Julia Ward Howe's "Battle Hymn of the Republic." The tune was a favorite of Knights of Labor songwriters. No fewer than seven songs were written to "John Brown's Body," including several parodies of Howe's American classic. Chaplin claimed "revolutionary fervor" as his inspiration, but again the style and content of his masterpiece fell solidly within parameters of labor singing already established by the Knights.[107]

Not even the IWW's much vaunted radicalism was free of KOL musical influence. The KOL rank and file was often more radical than its leaders, and the Order in general was more ideologically left of center than is often appreciated. KOL songwriters were capable of vitriolic outbursts worthy of any radical organization. Ralph Hoyt's parody of "America" has already been noted (see 132, above). Verse three adds these thoughts:

> Land of the great defaulter,
> Of knaves that need the halter,
>   Where gold is king.
> Land where fond hopes have died,
> Where demagogues reside,
> Monopolies reside,
>   And misery bring.[108]

Phillips Thompson included an equally radical song set to "America": H. W. Fusion's "Awake! Be Free," which attacks trusts, "Mammon's reign, sordid knaves," and landlords.[109]

Organized religion and religious hypocrisy were skewered by KOL songsmiths with the same gusto that Alexander Wright exhibited in journal editorials. Nearly 10 percent of the songs in my sample used religious tunes and contained attacks on religious hypocrisy. Hoyt's "Modern Missionary Zeal" parodied "Onward! Christian Soldiers." He lampooned war-mongers who marched into battle with prayer books and Gatling guns. The message and style of "Modern Missionary Zeal" closely parallel that of Wobbly songwriter John Kendrick, whose 1917

107. Tallmadge, *Labor Songs Dedicated to the Knights of Labor*, 6; Bulah Brinton to Powderly, undated latter, in *PP*; Kornbluh, *Rebel Voices*, 26.
108. *JKL*, July 3, 1890.
109. Thompson, *The Labor Reform Songster*, 22–23.

song opens "Onward, Christian Soldiers/Marching into war/Slay your Christian brothers/As you've done before."[110]

There were, of course, important ideological differences between the KOL and the IWW. Even at its most radical, the KOL saw itself as the guardian of True Patriotism and True Christianity, whereas the IWW saw itself as a challenge to both. The IWW jettisoned patriotism for its vision of an internationalist "one big union." The KOL also saw itself that way, but did not exclude nonworkers or call for the end of national distinctions. The IWW also tended to see organized religion as hypocrisy at best, Marx's "opiate" at worst, whereas the Knights thought Christianity was the basis for utopia.

But one need not establish ideological consonance between groups to make a case for cultural borrowing. Knights of Labor songs emerged within a specific labor community with its own values, rituals, and beliefs, but nonetheless a style evolved that circulated through contemporary and future worker cultures in both oral and written sources. The Knights drew upon an established tradition of social protest singing, enriched it, and passed it on. Social protest singing would have survived had the KOL never appeared, but the Knights gave it a vitality that could not have existed without an organization as large and as filled with possibilities as the Knights. Len DeCaux once expressed amazement that many CIO unionists did not realize that the songs they sang were passed down from the IWW.[111] One wonders what DeCaux's reaction would have been if told that his Wobbly favorites owed a debt to the Knights of Labor.

In specific form, little of the music or of the KOL itself survived. In the realm of ideals, lyrical imagery, and musical style, however, the KOL's legacy is impressive. As organized labor still searches for solidarity, it frequently falls back on the power of music. Even today the AFL-CIO sponsors "labor jams" and music workshops, while singer/songwriters like Si Kahn, Tom Juravich, Bruce Phillips, and Pete Seeger manage to both keep the old traditions alive and add to the social protest repertoire.[112] "Storm the Fort" is now sung as "Hold the Fort," an appropriate metaphor for organized labor's fate in recent years. The torch of social protest once borne by the Knights of Labor still burns, though with a cooler flame.

110. Foner, *American Labor Songs of the 19th Century*, 152; Kornbluh, *Rebel Voices*, 326–27.
111. DeCaux, *Labor Radical*, 270–72.
112. Numerous labor and union publications print song tunes and lyrics and carry news of songfests and labor recordings. Before it ceased publication in the late 1980s, one of these was *Talkin' Union*, Takoma Park, Maryland. The IWW still publish songs in its offical journal, *Solidarity*. Every year the AFL-CIO sponsor song workshops and other cultural events at the Meany Center. Its 1983 *Songs for Labor* booklet contains a version of "Hold the Fort." Labor songs also appear in abundance in Peter Bloodstone, ed., *Rise Up Singing* (Bethlehem, Pa.: Sing Out Publications, 1988), a mass market publication that has sold thousands of copies.

4 Solidarity, Segmentation, and Sentimentality

The Knights of Labor in Poetry

The following poems are so different in style, sentiment, and content that we must remind ourselves that the same organization produced them. How do we account for such differences? The first poem came out of Chicago and was published in late 1886 when the city's anarchist community was seething with rage in the aftermath of the Haymarket riots. The second was penned by Thomas O'Reilly, a Powderly crony and a staff employee at KOL headquarters, where he worked as a printer for the Order's journal. This is the same Thomas O'Reilly who wrote "The Song of the Proletaire," a composition far more radical in content, and far less sentimental in tone. Thus it is difficult to dismiss these poems merely as the products of different poets writing in different places at different times.

Address to the Statue of Liberty

Hail to thee, statue! humbug gigantic!
Metallic misnomer, protuberance vast.
Sculptural gush! to thee all hail!
Liberty! chained art thou to ocean rock,
With arm aloft, bearing a flameless torch,
Lighting, by subterfuge electric,
A rod of dreary wave . . .

Thy whole a grim, colossal lie,
Internally a void, externally paralytic.
Useless, absorbent of wealth and skill,
Vain boast of only partial fact
Of freedom not yet gained.
Irony's embodiment; quintessence of satire . . .

Man's rights suppressed, policeman's club supreme,
In direful straits are thy disciples,
Who, trusting thee, false liberty,
Have learned thou art a lie,
That thy vast mouth, profoundly dumb,
Is closed, hermetically sealed;
Nor hope's in freedom's cause
While two-inch mouths with heart and brains attached,
Are lured by deceptive light,
To rocks deceptive—to hangman's noose.[1]

One More Unfortunate

I'm so hungry, sister darling!
    I'm so hungry Lilly, dear!
Sobbed a little half-clad orphan
    In a chamber damp and drear.

Cold without—the lamplight's flicker
    Threw strange shapes upon the wall—
On the bed—where lay the child-babe
    Wrapped within her sister's shawl.

When at length the hungry baby,
    Moaning, cried herself to rest,
Lo! her sister, pretty Lilly,
    Rising softly, quickly dressed.

In her eyes there gleamed a purpose—
    'I'll not see you starve,' she cried.
God above! now You desert us,
    Since our darling mother died.

'O my God! I crave Thy pardon;
    Troubled billows o'er me roll;

1. *JKL* (Chicago), December 11, 1886.

Hunger maddens!—Look at the baby
Feed her Jesus! Save my soul.'

Then she listened, scarcely breathing,
Trusting, hoping for a sign;
But without the cold winds whistled—
'Jesus feed me!—Lord divine!'

Thus she cried; but when no answer
Came to her maddened prayer,
From her knees she rose up quickly—
Left her sister sleeping there.

'He will give me gold,' she muttered,
'If he hasn't changed his whim;
He shall have me—yes, the villain!
Though I sell my soul to him.'

When next morning Lilly entered,
Sobbing, shuddering with dismay,
There upon the cold straw mattress,
Dead, her sister lay!

A hurrying step on a lonely wharf,
Where the gray waves moan in the gathering gloom;
A stifled sob—and with never a prayer—
A desperate woman has met her doom.[2]

What is written is a matter of personal expression, but what is printed involves an editorial decision. Despite their competing sentiments and contradictory impulses, these two poems are representative of the KOL's inner dynamics. As we have seen, Knights used surface sentimentality for other purposes. O'Reilly's poem is a variant of the song "Only a Crust of Bread," which Charles Cheesewright used to great advantage. Nonetheless, the O'Reilly poem is as Victorian in style as the Chicago poem is direct in its challenge to constituted authority. There is an important contextual difference between Cheesewright's song and O'Reilly's poem. Singing was a collective act done in assembly halls, whereas reading a poem was usually a solitary one done in private. Stripped of the reinforcement of ritual and comraderie, the reader of a poem was less likely to understand stylistic parody—if that is what O'Reilly intended—than those who sang "Only a Crust of Bread."

Why then was poetry a staple of KOL publications, and why did it

2. *JKL*, April 30, 1891.

put forth such ambiguous messages? The answer lies in the changing nature of KOL culture. The cultural forms discussed so far—ritual, religion, and music—were largely internal expressions of Knighthood, the roots of which were planted before 1882, the year the Knights abandoned secrecy. Although Knights wrote poetry before 1882, it was mass produced only after that year. Pre-1882 KOL culture was private, fraternal, ritualistic, and oral; post-1882 culture was increasingly public, individualistic, formulaic, and literate. In addition, notions of class-bound (or at least producer-bound) solidarity began to replace more restrictive, but better defined, images of fraternal brotherhood. Despite the universalist rhetoric of early Knighthood, ritual practices made membership highly selective. As the KOL went public, its culture underwent a transformation. Whereas the pre-1882 Knights sought individuals deemed worthy of Knighthood, the post-1882 Order assumed all toilers were worthy and needed only a modicum of education to affirm their self-worth.

KOL culture changed after 1882, but the shift was not a smooth one. As the KOL jettisoned fraternalism, its culture became more varied and diffuse. Locals often evolved independent practices that sometimes complemented and sometimes conflicted with officially sanctioned ones. In poetry, this surfaces in the large number of offerings that praise Powderly, and in the impressive corpus of those that damned him. In some respects, post-1882 KOL culture was an experiment that ended badly. New forms of expression evolved, but they seldom had the cohesive influence on the Order that ritual, religion, and music once had. As the poems above indicate, consistent content, direction, and style were lacking. In the end, KOL poetry offered members equal doses of solidarity, segmentation, and sentimentality.

Spread the Light

Poetry appeared more often after 1882 because emergent KOL culture was more print-bound than it had once been. Pre-1882 Knights believed in self-improvement. One was supposed to be able to write one's full name in order to gain admittance beyond the assembly's Inner Veil, yet perusal of the General Master Workman's incoming correspondence reveals that many Knights of the 1870s were barely literate.[3] The campaign

3. See *PP.* Compare Uriah Stephens's incoming correspondence contained in reels 1 through 4 with that which reaches Powderly's office in the 1880s. Many of the letters Stephens received were scarcely literate.

for literacy began in 1880 with the creation of the *Journal of United Labor* and it was in full swing by 1884, the year the *JUL* became a weekly, rather than monthly, paper. Although literary sources such as poetry and fiction were sometimes mere column fillers, for the most part they were designed to "spread the light" and educate the rank and file.

Education was seen as a two-front struggle with both the working class and the general public in need of enlightenment. Several KOL papers were disseminated in the open marketplace, and most KOL editors were aware that their publications were read by those outside of the Order. (The "open letter" to politicians, employers, and the public was a frequent feature in KOL journals.)

This nonetheless made poetry's scope more limited than that of music, even though songs seldom surfaced outside of assembly halls. Though poems circulated widely in print, they normally were read in private. Favorite songs passed into a canon that reemphasized the same values every time they were sung. By contrast, one poem quickly yielded to another. Both music and poetry inspired members, but the stimulation derived from individual poems tended to be of shorter duration and seldom was reinforced collectively.[4]

Although few poems enjoyed more than mementary fame, members nonetheless were moved by them. In 1889, a Virginia Knight advised the *JUL* that he had just read Charles E. Darling's "The Tidal Wave of Liberty," and was deeply affected: "It seemed that I could realize facts as they are and facts as they will be more than I had ever done before."[5] This was precisely the effect labor poetry was supposed to have. For the correspondent, the poem did not reinforce a fully developed consciousness, but rather induced an awakening, a moment of revelation.

KOL leaders recognized the power of poetry to inspire readers. A month before the letter from Virginia, Powderly wrote to John Hayes, complaining that "for some time there has been a lack of poetry in the Journal and I think the effect is bad. It directs the attention of the readers to [sic] closely to the hard, every-day matter of fact existance [sic] we lead and they become soured. Let us have more poetry even though we have

4. The differences between poetry and music lead me to take exception with Clark Halker's recent study dealing with these forms of expression in the nineteenth-century labor movement. Halker uses the concept of "song-poem" and treats his material as written text. Although I agree it is difficult to determine whether a given set of verses is a poem or a song, I have chosen to eliminate questionable compositions from my analysis. Songs and poems can have similar functions, but their differences are worth nothing. See Halker, *For Democracy, Workers, and God*.

5. *JUL*, September 5, 1889. Charles E. Darling was a member of KOL Local 7349. His poem, "The Tidal Wave of Liberty," appeared in the *JUL* on January 15, 1887.

to make it ourselves."[6] Powderly saw poetry as a means of rekindling hope in the minds of the dispirited, and he recognized its power as a propaganda tool. He realized that unless more workers like the Virginia Knight were awakened, they had little hope of transcending degraded social and economic circumstances.

KOL poets, editors, and leaders used poetry to put forth immediate concerns, offer amelioration, and arouse sentiment. But the KOL suffered no illusions that verse could substitute for action. The Knights used poetry to arouse members in hopes that they would build a practical organization capable of attaining concrete gains on labor's behalf. In retrospect, KOL leaders were overly naive about the transformative value of education, but even the cautious Powderly realized that more than enlightenment was needed to change society.

KOL poetry usually communicated a single message. Much of it was written and printed in response to immediate concerns. As Marcus Graham observed, "Poetry and propaganda are two sides of the same shield." But as Graham also noted, poetry can be either an escape from or an affirmation of the world.[7] KOL editors exposed readers to both visions. Those who searched for a master plan in Knights' poetry do so in vain; for every position, one quickly located its contradiction in print or deed. Women, for example, were elevated as comrades in the workplace, *and* depicted as mere Victorian homemakers. Likewise, they were praised for their moral guardianship of society in the same journals that printed insulting anecdotes and stories in which women appear as helpless and incompetent. Many other messages were mixed: some poems urge cooperation with capitalism, others urge its overthrow; religion is held up as a liberating ideal in one verse, as an enslaving power in another. Unlike its songs, one does not even find consistent messages about the KOL itself: one poem praises the Order for practicing perfect brotherhood, while another bitterly complains of fragmentation and disunity; one poet cheers readers with the hope of an emergent new age, while the next depresses them with woes of labor being crushed.

While trying to forge a new culture, KOL editors walked a tightrope between the Order's factions, the pulls of divergent cultural expressions, and reader expectations that KOL papers resemble the popular press. An 1887 editorial in the *JUL* makes this clear. While bragging that "every shade of opinion—political, religious, and social—is represented by our members," the *JUL* announced the unveiling of a new six-column format

6. Powderly to John Hayes, July 28, 1889, in *PP.*
7. Marcus Graham, ed., *An Anthology of Revolutionary Poetry* (New York: Active Press, 1929), 35–37. Marcus Graham was a pseudonym for Schmuel Marcus.

with expanded features, whose "mission must necessarily be educational." The most notable changes in the *JUL*, however, were the inclusion of more serialized stories, pithy proverbs, discussions of religion with moral sermons from Powderly, the appearance of a "woman's page," and an increase in the space devoted to poetry. As the *JUL* explained, the paper wanted to devote more attention "to matters of interest in the family circle" to make the paper "a welcome visitor at the fireside as well as in the workshop."[8]

Whatever the message, a reader of KOL journals always had plenty of poetic input to contemplate. The chart below is my count of entire poems or substantial excerpts printed in the *Journal of United Labor* (after late 1889 called the *Journal of the Knights of Labor [JKL]*) from 1880–93:

Poems in the Journal of United Labor

Year:	Poems:
1880	14
1881	15
1882	8
1883	10
1884	41
1885	30
1886	29
1887	148
1888	59
1889	19
1890	23
1891	30
1892	57
1893	47

Relatively few poems were published from 1880 through 1883 because the *JUL* was a monthly paper. It became a weekly in 1884, the first year one sees a substantial increase in column space devoted to poetry. The decline in 1885 and 1886 coincides with the KOL's period of rapid growth, a time in which the Order was trying to sort out its fortunes and redefine itself. The peak year for KOL poetry was 1887, and reflected that brief moment (already slipping away) in which the Order hoped to speak for the entire working class. Reality dawned in 1888, and less poetry appeared. The statistical low point came in 1889 (if one ignores the

8. *JUL*, July 9, 1887.

1880–83 monthly journals) and reflects the chaotic condition of both the Order and its journal, which most KOL members agreed was being mismanaged by A. M. Dewey. Dewey's resignation brought forth A. W. Wright as editor, as well as a clamor for more poetry. Poetry became a standard feature under Wright's editorship.

Poetry was also an integral part of local journals. From July 1883, to May 1888, Denver's *Labor Enquirer* printed 144 poems; Baltimore's *Critic* published 68 in 1889. The *Haverhill Laborer* included 124 poems in 1885 and 1886 alone, a number suggesting that local papers responded to the Order's rapid growth and expanding needs much faster than did the *JUL*. Another paper from Massachusetts DA 30 indicates the centrality of poetry in that district. Boston's *Labor Leader* was a KOL paper until editor Frank Foster left the Order in 1888. When he was in the fold in 1887, the *Labor Leader* contained 42 poems; 1888 editions printed only 30.

Output often out-stripped quality. Very little labor poetry would meet the standards of literary criticism then or now.[9] If one subtracts reprints of popular literary icons—Burns, Morris, Swinburne, Whitman, and Whittier were favorites—much of the rest is amateurish verse. But style, meter, and construction were secondary concerns to most labor poets. Since the message was central, not its delivery system, most writers employed free verse. By genre, most KOL poetry is lyric or narrative. KOL poetry usually expresses the poet's personal reaction to the world and suggests an appropriate reaction for the reader. Their recommendations usually suggested one of four responses: resignation to one's fate, withdrawal to a safe haven, open defiance and direct action, or commitment to a purifying ideological cause.

Popular Press, Labor Press

One question remains: why poetry? Unlike song, the link to social protest traditions is less clear. Even if we make allowances for earlier labor poems and America's vibrant broadside tradition, both the content of the poems and the style of many KOL poets indicate that they drew on quite different inspirations. Nonetheless, poetry was integral to late nineteenth-century working-class life. Few labor newspapers excluded poetry from their pages. But this expectation came more from without the movement than from within. Whatever residual working-class verse

9. Kealey and Palmer called KOL poetry a form of "low culture." See Kealey and Palmer, *Dreaming of What Might Be*, 278–79.

traditions survived, the ubiquity of Gilded Age labor poetry owes more to the need for the labor press to compete with the popular press than to artistic expressiveness. Poetry was also a staple of urban newspapers, and an indicator of the bourgeois cultural power with which the KOL grappled.

Labor journals enjoyed a resurgence in the 1880s. By then, however, the popular press had evolved dramatically, and it reshaped the tastes of the reading public. Though not yet masquerading as models of objectivity and dispassionate reporting, Gilded Age newspapers were quite different from their more-modest antebellum progenitors. New technologies in communication, transportation, and management—such as telegraphs, improved printing presses, advances in wood pulp production, railroads, and compartmentalized bureaucratic structures—were used by newspaper entrepreneurs to develop a profitable medium for an increasingly urbanized population. As one historian put it, "In the span of two generations, the economic power of the modern city converted the newspaper, formerly a stodgy mercantile sheet or a struggling political journal, into another form of big business."[10] Moreover, newspapers were among the earliest American cultural products to cultivate a mass consumer base.

According to the U.S. Census, there were 971 daily papers and 1,141 weeklies in the United States in 1880.[11] Between 1880 and 1890—the decade in which the KOL grew, flourished, and declined—the number of newspapers nearly doubled, and KOL publications fell prey to their influences. The metropolitan press helped socialize new urbanites, and often served as the same sort of community-building agents as the numerous fraternal orders that met in urban America.[12] The same urban masses targeted by KOL organizers often formed their first opinions about the Order from accounts in city dailies.

Labor papers, though long an aspect of working-class life, reemerged in earnest during the 1880s. By one estimate, the labor press numbered about 400 weeklies, 17 monthlies, and 2 or 3 dailies in 1885—impressive growth, but weak competition for the powerful mass press.[13] The KOL realized this and required each local assembly to purchase its *Journal of United Labor*, partly to educate its members, and partly because Powderly felt the mainstream media treated him and the Knights unfairly.[14]

10. Gunther Barth, *City People: The Rise of Modern City Culture in Nineteenth-Century America* (New York: Oxford University Press, 1980), 59. See also Michael Schudson, *Discovering the News: A Social History of American Newspapers* (New York: Basic Books, 1978).

11. Statistics cited are from Barth, *City People*, 84.

12. Ibid., 59.

13. Foner, *History of the Labor Movement*, vol. 2, 29–31.

14. Powderly, *The Path I Trod*, 39, 69, 74, 95, 105, 172, 173, 214.

KOL locals published several hundred papers in the late 1880s, but labor papers were always a risky enterprise financially and legally, and many would-be labor editor-entrepreneurs like J. P. McDonnell, Charles Litchman, Joseph Buchanan, and John Swinton went out of business after a few years.[15]

Despite the valiant efforts of labor editors, most workers were untouched by their papers, while those who were read the mass press. And what did they read there? By the 1880s, the popular press had expanded beyond mere editorializing. Though one could pick up the *New York Herald* and find editorials critical of the KOL, one could also find sports, society pages, city features, human interest stories, and poetry. The KOL had disproportionate numbers of editors and printers within its ranks, and many of them naturally gravitated toward the Order's internal press. Leaders like Theodore Cuno, Joseph Buchanan, A. M. Dewey, and A. W. Wright learned their skills on mainstream newspapers, thus it is hardly surprising that they fashioned the Order's papers in their image. Their readers expected no less. Sometimes editors did so with a vengeance. Dewey assumed the editorship of the *JUL* in 1888, and almost immediately General Secretary John Hayes and Thomas O'Reilly complained of Dewey's work habits, writing style, and over-emphasis of general "news" and "scoops." After less than a year in his job, Dewey resigned under pressure, but his successor, Alexander W. Wright, fared little better. Hayes and O'Reilly complained bitterly of his editorial skills and decisions.[16]

15. For details concerning J. P. McDonnell, editor of the *Paterson Labor Standard*, see Gutman, *Work, Culture, and Society*, chap. 5.

Charles Litchman tried his hand at several short-lived papers when not the editor of the *Journal of United Labor*. These were published from his home in Marblehead, Massachusetts, and seldom survived more than a few issues. His career as a local journalist was plagued with as much controversy as was that with the *JUL*. At various times Litchman was accused of employing scab labor, siphoning funds for personal use, and turning over control of his business to his inexperienced 17-year-old son. Joseph R. Buchanan, active in both the Knights and in socialist and anarchist groups, founded Denver's *Labor Enquirer* in 1882 and was its editor until 1887, when he turned it over to Burnette Haskell and left for Chicago. While in Chicago Buchanan started that city's edition of the *Labor Enquirer*. Though he had been expelled from the KOL in 1886, Buchanan still thought of himself as a Knight, and his paper became one of the mouthpieces for dissidents in the Order. The Chicago *Labor Enquirer* ceased publication in 1888. The career of John Swinton is well known and is capsulized in Foner, *History of the American Labor Movement*, vol. 2.

16. Most of the correspondence between Thomas O'Reilly, John W. Hayes, and Terence V. Powderly in February and March 1889 concerned these matters. Correspondence is located in *PP*. See also O'Reilly to Powderly, October 3, 1890; November 5, 1890; November 7, 1891; May 10, 1892; all in *PP*. Also John Devlin to Powderly, July 29, 1893; Powderly to

In addition to the metropolitan dailies, the labor press also faced competition from the so-called "story papers" that flourished after the Civil War. Although their influence was most direct in KOL fiction (see Chapter 5), the papers also popularized poetry, especially that which was sentimental in tone and bourgeois in outlook. The inclusion of poetry and fiction in KOL papers clearly reflects story-paper influences. In fact, the Knights often reprinted poetry from those papers, and several members of the Order, including Mrs. Frances Sargent Osgood, T. DeWitt Talmadge, and John Erigena Barrett could be found in both story-paper and Knights' columns.

The sharing of poets and fiction writers alerts us to the fact that the relationship between the popular and labor presses was symbiotic on occasion. Urban dailies and story papers were owned by men of the middle class, but only part of their readership was bourgeois. Competition for circulation was keen in metropolitan markets (New York City had more than a dozen dailies) and few editors had the luxury of ignoring working-class tastes. Neither could they attack unions with the fervor with which the religious press could. Certain urban magazines and dailies, including *The North American Review*, the *Brooklyn Eagle*, the *Scranton Times*, and the *New York Sun*, enjoyed brief favor with the KOL, and even hostile papers often printed Powderly's editorials, letters, and rebuttals. All editors—friendly and hostile—found the labor movement good copy; ignoring it awaited the full bloom of consolidation.

All of this bode evil for struggling labor papers that lacked the financial base and technological resources of urban publishing houses. Most labor editors tried to create hybrid journals that mixed a laborist agenda with the expectations of Gilded Age readers. But the poem "One More Unfortunate" signals a problem with which post-1882 KOL culture had to wrestle. As cultural expressions moved out of the purely private realm it was difficult to check contaminants at the Outer Veil. By the mid-1880s, aspects of the hegemonic culture began to mix with the Order's organic expressions. For the most part, "One More Unfortunate" is Victorian and middle class in tone, while "Address to the Statue of Liberty" is pure working-class radicalism. Fusing the two strains proved difficult. As with all things, the KOL tried to be flexible enough to subsume its contradictions beneath the rhetoric of solidarity, and through common experience. As in many things, the attempt was perhaps more noble than successful.

A. W. Wright, December 4, 1892; A. W. Wright to Powderly, February 14, 1893 and February 24, 1893; in *PP.*

Brothers of the Cause

A favorite theme in KOL poetry was the Order itself. But since poetry belongs mainly to the KOL's public period, themes of fraternalism, mutualism, and manliness were not as explicit in poetry as they were in ritual and music. One of the few surviving pre-1880 KOL poems, "A Fallen Friend," shows the link between early verse and ritual fraternalism. It was read by KOL cofounder William Fennimore on March 16, 1871, at a memorial service for John Hobson. The poem uses *AK* imagery to eulogize Hobson. In the ninth verse Fennimore read:

> The hand that labored long has lost its grasp,
> And in repose is laid upon his breast,
> Yet memory holds the strong fraternal grasp
> That linked our hearts in labor or in rest.

Precisely what was meant by "fraternal grasp" was revealed two verses later:

> ADELPHON KRUPTOS, treasured in his heart,
> Was guarded well by silence, truth and trust;
> For never deigning with the gem to part,
> His praise to speak is only speaking just.[17]

Fennimore touched familiar themes of brotherhood and comradeship, and implied they were impossible to attain outside of Knights' mysteries. By capitalizing ADELPHON KRUPTOS, the poem elevated it as an ideal for the living. In death, Hobson is idealized as a comrade whose entire life was authenticated by his adherence to the *AK*. His death deprived the Order of a cherished comrade, but his life served as an object lesson in true Knighthood.

Not many Knights knew of Fennimore's poem, as it was not published. But the idea of brotherhood as a mysterious, quasi-religious experience dominated the early life of the Order. Ten years after Fennimore wrote, James Gold ended his own poem, "Labor's Cause," with:

> Talk not of soldier fame—heroes of battlefields
> Of those urged on by praise and fancied right;

17. Powderly, *The Path I Trod*, 96–97.

> But fight in labor's cause which home and comfort shields.
> You thus may die CROWNED by peers but OWNED a
> labor Knight.[18]

The high ideals of early Knighthood embodied in the Hobson eulogy
and in Gold's poem found their way into "Brotherhood," an 1882 effort
by R. J. Preston. In the very year the KOL became a public organization
Preston warned Knights of their duty:

> He is no Knight of Labor
>   Who sheathes his Knightly sword;
> And to an outside neighbor
>   Reveals his secret word.
> Divulging what has taken place
>   Within our sacred veils,
> I call him "traitor" to his face
>   Who thus our pledge assails.[19]

Brotherhood ideals were still alive in 1883, when Hugh Cameron sent
Powderly a poem, entitled "To the G.M.W. and Members of the G.A.,
K. of L.," that he hoped would defuse antifraternal feelings left over
from the 1882 Grand Assembly, in which Charles Litchman was removed as Grand Secretary and editor of the *JUL* for his mismanagement
of the Defence Fund.[20] Cameron wrote:

> Be earnest brothers in the work,
>   Drive prejudice away
> Don't spend your time in wrangling,
>   Nor give our cause away.
> Sit down on Litchman lightly,
>   Nor drive him from the fold;
> His brain and culture are worth more

18. *JUL*, August 15, 1881.
19. Ibid., June 15, 1882.
20. Litchman's misuse of the "Defence" Fund was directly responsible for his ouster as
General Secretary at the KOL's 1882 Grand Assembly. The 1880 Grand Assembly had
voted to apply 10 percent of the fund for "educational" purposes. Litchman treated that
allotment as the private domain of the *JUL*. He got into difficulty through deficit spending
based on inaccurate projections of the revenue the Defence Fund would generate. He
purchased presses and other equipment for the *JUL*, and spent over $4,600 at a time when
the actual Defence Fund allotment for education did not exceed $788. Robert Layton, who
replaced the beleaguered Litchman as General Secretary, charged Litchman with financial
malfeasance. Only Powderly's intervention saved Litchman from a lawsuit. For more on
Litchman, see Robert E. Weir, "When Friends Fall Out."

> Associated heart and hand,
> Be firm, be true, sincere;
> Of all the rest
> Right royal stand.[26]

Some of Aiken's imagery had hidden meaning for older Knights. The reference to crown and royalty harked back to older concepts of the "nobility" of toil, and there are oblique references to the S.O.M.A. principle. For real old-timers, the heart and hand evoked memories of the earliest KOL rituals that drew heavily on Masonic imagery. But the poem also opened wider; one could just as easily imply an appeal to solidarity as a reading of the *AK*.

As late as 1890, *AK* imagery still made its way into Knights' poetry. In "Knights of Labor Call," submitted by C. Drake, the Master Workman of LA 1519 (Victoria, Australia), one reads: "True Knights of Labor, every one, will bear the 'Lance and Shield.' " But the remainder of Drake's poem contains few veiled references; rather it is a compendium of labor's foes: employers, newspapers, self-help "fakirs," and "plutocrats and other rats."[27]

Drake's poem is indicative of a clear trend in KOL poetry away from older imagery and toward direct confrontation of contemporary concerns. As the Order matured, self-laudatory poems grew fewer in number, as did admonitions to respond to oppression through fraternalism, manliness, or moralism. In 1887, the Dubuque, Iowa, *Industrial Leader* reprinted "There Must Be Something Wrong," with its defiant passage:

> When earth produces rich and fair
>   The golden waving corn,
> When fragrant fruits perfume the air
>   And fleecy flocks are shorn,
> Whilst thousands move with aching head,
>   And sing the ceaseless song,
> We starve, we die, oh give us bread!
> There must be something wrong.[28]

This poem was not a KOL original, rather a reworking of a poem popular with New England mill operatives in the 1830s (Fig. 8).[29] *Industrial*

---

26. *JUL*, January 25, 1886.
27. *JKL*, November 13, 1890.
28. *Industrial Leader* (Dubuque, Iowa), June 25, 1887.
29. Philip S. Foner, *The Factory Girls: A Collection of the Writings on Life and Struggles in the New England Factories of the 1840s* (Urbana: University of Illinois Press, 1977), 91.

The Great Bartholdi Statue of Liberty Erected in New York Harbor to Enlighten the Nation Becomes Ashamed and Does Some Needed Work at Home.

In New York harbor they stuck me up;
"Enlighten the Nations," they said to me;
But behind my back I find a kid,
And his name is Monopo Lee.

Monopo Lee he would not work,
But robbed others of their share,
But I'll get down from my high perch,
And spank the rascal, So there!

My paddle is a dandy spanker,
It just exactly fills the bill;
I'll spank the mean thing till he's blue.
I will. So I will.

Fig. 8. After the KOL went public, its leaders recognized the need to replace ritual fraternalism with new forms of expression. "Let us have more poetry even though we have to make it ourselves," wrote Terence Powderly. Sometimes, however, poetry could strike a divisive note, as in this poem and cartoon by James Sovereign, editor of *Industrial Leader* and Powderly's successor as General Master Workman.

Leader editor James Sovereign likely plucked it from printed sources that he knew from his pre-KOL days working for various Iowa newspapers. In any event, Iowa Knights in 1887 found a contemporary ring to "There Must Be Something Wrong" that was missing from the KOL's self-congratulatory verse.

Despite the KOL's poetic preoccupation with itself, poets and readers—like those in Iowa—ventured out of the assembly hall and into the larger world of the laboring classes. Early KOL poems were like KOL songs in that their primary purpose was to reinforce the Order's internal values and concerns. When poems moved out of the assembly hall and into journals they became public property. Any thoughts the KOL might have had of keeping its journals private quickly vanished. Both the popular press and other labor organizations freely quoted from KOL publications, just as the Knights borrowed from other papers. As Knight poets confronted the larger social world, they faced the challenge of making their words speak to larger social realities in a language that did not require mastery of Knights' mysteries. This could be done by encoding symbols (as Stewart and Aiken did), or by following the example of Iowa Knights by addressing issues directly. For Knights whose mastery of KOL ritual was less detailed, KOL poems offered a more overt message: labor was oppressed. The grinding drudgery of toil and the tyrants who imposed it were contrasted with manly laborers whose noble minds transcended base greed. Knights were portrayed as patriotic, God-fearing, sincere, heroic, and faithful to their word. By contrast, enemies of the Order were greedy oppressors whose unmanly vanity, pride, and cruelty offended man, God, and nature. One needed little knowledge of the *AK* to understand this dualism.

Poison Pens

"There Must Be Something Wrong" is refreshing in its directness and suggestive of the themes labor poets took up in the 1880s. By then, fraternal ideals had given way to verse that tackled fundamental questions of finance, the nature of capitalism, the wisdom of political action, and the fight for an eight-hour work day. Poetry tended to underscore the gap between rhetoric and reality within the Knights, and it exacerbated tensions between national leaders and local concerns.

KOL poetry could be blunt, radical, and crude in its critique of existing social and economic conditions. Poets took seriously the Order's platform principle that called on the government "to establish a purely national circulating medium issued directly to the people, without the intervention of any banking corporations."[30] Like speculators, gamblers, and rum-sellers, bankers were banned from the Order. "The Banker and I Are Out," is typical of poetic attacks on bankers. The piece contrasts the lives of a poor laborer and his rag-clad wife and children with the ostentatious opulence of "Banker Jones":

> There's Banker Jones across the way,
>   who rolls in wealth and style.
> And yet he does no useful work,
>   but still he makes a pile;
> His wife can dress in silks and lace,
>   and make a splendid show,
> A coach and four to take her out,
>   wherever she may go.

Banker Jones is also castigated for loaning money to the government at 100 percent interest, foreclosing on the mortgages of war widows, and leading the battle against greenbacks after the Civil War. Yet, even an attack on banking could raise the specter of discord. Jewish Knights must have blanched at the poem's blatant anti-Semitism. Bankers were compared to Shakespeare's Shylock, and one verse proclaims:

> You ought to see them go to church
>   and sit in cushioned pews.
> And make believe they are Christians,
>   and yet they are aught but Jews.[31]

Rural Knights managed to attack banking without lapsing into anti-Semitism. "Facts For Farmers," appearing in the Dubuque, Iowa, *Industrial Leader*, begins on a wistful note:

> The farmer dares his mind to speak
>   He has no gift or place to speak,
> To no man living need he bow,
>   The man who walks behind the plow,

30. Preamble and Declaration of Principles, 1878, 1884. The 1878 Preamble and Declaration can be found in most issues of the *JUL* from 1880 through October 1884. The new Preamble and Declaration are found in the *Journal* from January 1885, on. They are also reprinted in the appendix to Ware, *The Labor Movement*.
31. *JUL*, June 10, 1885.

> Is his own master, what'er befall,
> And king or beggar, he leads us all.

The tone of the poem quickly changes and the reader learns that the opening image is a nostalgic remembrance of times before farmers bowed to masters with names like "interest" and "mortgage."[32]

The attack on financial institutions is emblematic of a larger debate within the Order over the nature of capitalism. Radicals found in poetry a vehicle through which to excoriate a system that they felt elevated profit over humanity. This was made explicit by Percy Braincourt, whose "The Sale of Labor" equates capitalism with slavery:

> The hammer rang on the still bright morn
>   Amidst the talk of gabbling throng.
> For labor here was all forlorn,
>   As the auctioneer sang his daily song—
>   Here's labor for sale,
>   Come list to the tale,
> Of labor lost and thrown away,
>   By men of wealth,
>   Gained by stealth,
> And now for a trifle sold to-day.

One by one pathetic figures make their way to the auction block: old men, youths, and even "a lady fair . . . sickly now from the factory's air."[33]

Braincourt was pessimistic about the possibility of educating capitalists, an opinion shared by a poet from Brooklyn's oath-bound Advance Labor Club (LA 1562). "Labor's War Cry, Advance!" opens:

> Brothers, arise! Proclaim the fact
>   That mankind shall be free!
> Let every word, and every act
>   Be one for Liberty.
> Too long we're fettered with the chain
>   By tyrants in our ranks.
> We bear no God-cursed mark of Cain,
>   Our name is yet—Advance!"

32. *Industrial Leader* (Dubuque, Iowa), August 27, 1887.
33. *JUL*, May 10, 1885.

The final verse calls the masses to rise:

> How long shall petty tyrants rule
>   In Labor's holy name?
> How long shall Justice play the fool
>   When "Mammon" is the game?
> 'Twas you my Brothers, 'Spread the Light'
>   'Tis you who will enhance
> The glories of the Wage-slave fight
>   Advance! Defy! Advance![34]

Politicians were also the object of poetic scorn, as well as internal tension. The third issue of the *JUL* printed a poem entitled "The Candidate" that scornfully lampooned office-seekers:

> He greets the woman with courtly grace,
> He kisses the baby's dirty face,
> He calls to the fence the farmer at work,
> He bores the merchant, he bores the clerk.

When a laborer's wife asks her husband why politicians didn't secure useful employment, he explains that most are, "Too stupid to preach, too proud to beg/Too blind to rob, and too lazy to dig."[35] "A Fable But Not a Fable" lumped "banks, rulers and monopolists" together, and denounced government as an exclusive fortress of crooked power-brokers.[36]

Political hypocrisy was condemned directly. A Baltimore Knight wrote:

> To-day honest labor submits to abuse,
> Its vote is adapted to corporate use.
> But election day passed, labor drops out of mind,
> And then they kick down the ladder
>   by which they have climbed.[37]

Such scorn was extended to fellow Knights if their actions were perceived as self-seeking. When Ontario's Alexander Wright ran as a Conservative against a popular member of Parliament who was not a KOL member, Ontario Knights turned out to trounce Wright at the polls. A

34. *The Boycotter*, March 20, 1886.
35. *JUL*, July 1880.
36. Ibid., December 1882.
37. Ibid., July 23, 1887.

satirical poem, "How Wright Was Left," was composed to complete his disgrace.[38]

A Dayton, Ohio, Knight even suggested dirty tricks as an antidote to political double-crossers. In "Politician's Prayer," the poet hoped for a pro-labor vote, but in case honest politics should prove ineffective, verses three and five suggest:

> Let slander, malice, force, and fraud
>   But this time fail;
> But if such tricks should be abroad,
> Expose our enemies', O Lord
>   Let ours prevail. . . .
>
> Give us by honest means, success
>   In this great fight;
> But if too strong the foemen press
> Let's save the state by crookedness
>   And call it right.[39]

If poets raised social consciousness over the deeds of bankers, capitalists, and politicians, they also opened wounds on subjects where rhetoric and practice clashed. Poetic attacks on banking, capitalism, and party politics were entirely consonant with the Order's stated principles. The Preamble to the KOL platform adopted in 1878 opened with a reference to the "alarming development and aggression of aggravated wealth." An 1884 revision attacked the "aggressiveness of great capitalists and corporations."[40] This shift allowed charges of greed, opportunism, and cruelty once confined to bankers, speculators, gamblers, and rum-sellers to be applied to all capitalists. Such charges could just as easily be directed at office-seekers like Wright, or cautious leaders like Powderly.

Radical Knights often found themselves up against leaders who shared their rhetoric but not their plans of attack. Powderly, for example, advocated an end to the wage system, but nonetheless sought accommodation with capital. Powderly was sincere in his call for economic alternatives like profit-sharing and cooperative production, but his innate conservatism led him to preach peaceful evolution through education as a means of attaining social change. Powderly found poetic allies in Iowa's Will Minnick (LA 1403, Oskaloosa), who penned "Would We

38. The poem "How Wright was Left" is reprinted in Kealey and Palmer, *Dreaming of What Might Be*, 223.

39. *Dayton Workman*, October 1, 1887.

40. Preamble and Declaration of Principles, 1878, 1884.

Strike?" and rejected lashing out at capital in anger, vengeance, or violence. Instead, Minnick counseled "logic, pen, and pencil . . . reason . . . education's word . . . wisdom [and] ballot box."[41]

Minnick's thoughts were echoed by "J.F." of Hickory Ridge, Pennsylvania, whose "Verses For the Toiler" evoked the sentiments of Uriah Stephens. Though acknowledging the reality of capitalist "rogues," J.F. blamed their existence on "ignorance," and encouraged Knights to educate employers. He also evoked the producerist imagery of Stephens: "Labor is noble in its place/And holy in its end/It honors all the human race/And makes us honest men." Like Powderly's, J.F.'s new dawn would be the result of education and mutual good will, not revolution: "The last great blow will not be given/By organized bands/Till honest toil and capital/Shall shake each other's hands."[42]

Ambivalence toward capitalism spilled over into attitudes about politics, where direction was less certain and debate more fierce. The 1878 Preamble never mentioned politics directly, though ten of its fifteen articles required legislative action for realization. This ambiguity led individual Knights to articulate what the General Assembly had not. Stephens tried to make the Order's position on politics more explicit. Addressing the third Grand Assembly in Chicago in 1879, he remarked,

> Sad experience assures us no relief can be expected from those elevated by the polluted channels of party politics to positions that should be held by patriotic and enlightened statesmen. . . . To this fact is owing, the existence of Knighthood. . . . No other organization in existence proposes to meet this great want [of oppressed humanity], or directs its efforts to this mighty work.[43]

Officially, then, the Knights of Labor was a nonpartisan organization. This position was underscored when the revised 1884 Preamble called on members to vote intelligently and elect "only such candidates as will pledge their support [to KOL principles] regardless of party," but added the codicil, "No [Knight] shall, however, be compelled to vote with the majority." This was softened further when the 1884 General Assembly insisted that the Order officially separate industrial questions from political ones, and proclaimed that "politics must be subordinated to industry."[44]

41. *JUL*, May 10, 1885.
42. Ibid., February 11, 1888.
43. 1878 and 1879 *Proceedings of the Knights of Labor Grand Assembly*, in *PP*.
44. Preamble and Declaration of Principles, 1878, 1884; Ware, *The Labor Movement*, 379.

While Powderly insisted that the Order was above politics, it could not escape the notice of any Knight that many of their leaders did as Alexander Wright and sullied themselves in the political muck that they and journal poets decried. Stephens resigned his post as Grand Master Workman in order to run for U.S. Congress on the Greenback Labor ticket. His replacement, Powderly, was the sitting mayor of Scranton, Pennsylvania. Other early leaders, including Charles Litchman and Joseph Buchanan, ran for political office. The penchant of each man for power politics and coalition-building belied claims of nonpartisan detachment.[45]

Radicals grew apprehensive at the political waffling of national leaders on economic and political matters. The poem "Labor's War Cry, Advance!" is one indication of their dissatisfaction. There can be little doubt that the poem was a backhanded swipe against KOL leaders who were deemed too conservative by the contentious radicals of Brooklyn's LA 1562. Its reference to "wage slavery" bespoke their attitudes toward capital, and the choice to submit the poem to *The Boycotter*, an independent radical journal, rather than the *JUL* or DA 49's *Daily Leader* signaled that LA 1562 envisioned a different sort of political solution to the problems of industrial capitalism than those embraced by cautious leaders.[46]

Similar rumblings come through in "Politician's Prayer," a poem that highlights two fundamental problems in the KOL's official stand on politics. The poem first recognized that political power was necessary to implement the KOL reform platform. It also acknowledged that playing by traditional ballot box rules had failed labor. What was to be done if neither education nor the ballot box could liberate labor? The Order split into camps over that question. A conservative faction, exemplified by Powderly, insisted that the Order avoid partisan battles, while politicized factions—like those in LA 1562—called for independent political action within or without existing legal channels. The politicized factions split into numerous subfactions that included anarchists, Lassallean and

45. Powderly was elected mayor of Scranton on the Greenback Labor ticket in 1878, 1880, and 1882. After his ouster as General Master Workman of the Knights of Labor he served in several Republican party patronage positions. Charles Litchman was active with the Greenback movement in his youth. In 1878, he was elected to the Massachusetts General Court on the Greenback Labor ticket, but turned to the Republican Party when he was defeated for reelection. He actively sought patronage jobs and finally secured one when he quit his post as General Secretary of the KOL to help Benjamin Harrison's 1888 presidential campaign. Joseph Buchanan made two unsuccessful bids for the U.S. Congress. Uriah Stephens was an active Republican before turning to ardent greenbackism. In 1878 he made a bid for Congress from Pennsylvania's Fifth District, but was defeated.

46. *The Boycotter*, March 20, 1886.

Marxist socialists, Single-Taxers, Bellamyite Nationalists, Farmers' Alliance followers, and supporters of local independent labor parties.[47]

In this atmosphere all that was needed to bring subsumed ideological debates to the fore was an issue on which to focus them. By 1886, two such issues surfaced: the eight-hour movement and the Haymarket bombing.

Few subjects captured the imagination of KOL poets like the eight-hour movement. A typical verse upholding its virtues comes from an 1884 *Journal of United Labor:*

> Long enough we've borne the cross,
>   We've raised the wage—they've pulled it down.
> To us has always come the loss,
> Strike for less hours—and wear the crown.[48]

Eight-hour sentiment reached the American heartland and was expressed by a poet from Glen Burn, Kansas:

> The hours you toil now more than EIGHT
> Don't as a rule, invigorate;
> Don't help the man, don't help the state,
> Don't manly virtues, elevate.[49]

One *JUL* used the poem—a popular Scottish poem, "Drew the Wrong Lever"—as a pretext for devoting much of the issue to a discussion of the eight-hour work day. Alexander Anderson's long narrative tells of a switchman whose fatigue caused him to divert two trains on to the same track, an error resulting in a crash with much loss of life. The poem's moral was direct: tragedies result "so long as twelve hours' strain/Rests like a load of lead on the brain."[50]

The sheer volume of poetry in the *JUL* extolling the eight-hour day added to the betrayal many Knights felt when the GEB refused to sanction the May 1, 1886, general strike in favor of it. Powderly tried to defend the Board's decision by saying that more "education" was needed. Dusting off a speech he made in 1884, Powderly charged that too many in the Order saw the eight-hour day as a panacea: "To talk of reducing the hours of labor without reducing the power of machinery to oppress

---

47. For more information on the success of the KOL in local elections, see Fink, *Workingmen's Democracy.*

48. *JUL,* April 15, 1884.

49. Ibid., February 25, 1885.

50. Ibid., October 10, 1884.

instead of benefit is a waste of energy."[51] But leaders like George Mc-Neill, Frank Foster, Joseph Buchanan, and Charles Sieb were infuriated by the GEB's inaction, as were KOL anarchists Dyer D. Lum and Albert Parsons, men who had been delegates to the 1880 Eight-Hour Convention. Thousands of rank-and-file Knights simply ignored the GEB directive.

The bomb thrown at Haymarket changed the nature of the debate. Two of the eight men accused of the May 4 bombing—Parsons and August Spies—were members of the Knights of Labor.[52] Much of the general public, fueled by denunciations from the popular press, associated the KOL with Haymarket. Powderly tried to distance the Order from the event by dismissing the affair as one led by socialists and anarchists.

After the indictments and trial in June 1886, the eight-hour question yielded to debates on whether or not to support the defense of the eight accused men. Since Powderly publicly equated Haymarket with anarchism, discussions of radicalism within the KOL surfaced for the entire membership to scrutinize. Some Knights took a bold stance against Powderly. An editorial in *The Knights of Labor* (Chicago) blasted Powderly and accused him of being "under the influence of men who would rather save the Democratic administration in Chicago" than concern themselves with justice. His failure to defend Parsons, an active Knight, struck the editorialist as particularly reprehensible.[53]

In January 1887, Powderly warned Elizabeth Rodgers, Master Workman of DA 24, that she must resist temptations to return the Chicago KOL to secrecy and avoid "partisan politics" in the assembly, a reference to the debate raging there over diverting funds for the defense of the Haymarket eight.[54] "Address to the Statue of Liberty" (see 145, above) was one of many poems composed amid the shock and rage following their convictions. Any hope that Powderly had of diffusing the Order's radical wing disappeared on November 11, 1887, when Parsons, Spies, George Engel, and Louis Fischer were hanged. William Clarke Marshall spoke for Denver Knights in his poem "Illinois":

> Illinois, thy gory deed
> Shall confront thee in thy need,
> When thy very heart shall bleed.

51. Powderly, *The Path I Trod*, 246, 253, 263.
52. August Spies's membership in the Knights is not well-known, though he acknowledged it. See his autobiography from Chicago's *JKL*, reprinted in Philip S. Foner, ed., *The Autobiographies of the Haymarket Martyrs* (New York: Monad Press, 1969), 71.
53. *Knights of Labor* (Chicago), December 30, 1886.
54. Powderly to Elizabeth Rodgers, January 16, 1887, in *PP.*

When 'neath flames thy city lay,
Was there one to say thee nay,
When for money thou didst pray?

Begged'st thou then from door to door—
And the lean hands of the poor
Freely sweep thine ashen floor.

Now, when women, children steep
In their tears thy dainty feet
Findst no mercy in thy keep.

Harlot! thou shall sue again,
Sue with tears or blood in vain,
When shall break yon cloud of flame.

Hear! While distant Peoples mourn,
Reck not thou the hovering storm,
Thou shall blight thy treach'rous form.

Freemen's hands capped thy brow,
Freemen's hands assail thee now,
Freemen's hands shall smite thee low.[55]

Scores of members grew disgusted with the conservatism of KOL leaders. In 1888, William H. Gleeson, a socialist Knight in Chicago, wrote a letter to Powderly to which he had attached Powderly's photograph. Gleeson wrote: "Enclosed please find photo of the grandest demagogue the world has ever seen. Powderly, when you look down in your heart you must be thoroughly disgusted with yourself. . . . Your attitude toward the labor movement may be likened to a 'Pauper's House.' "[56]

After Haymarket, Powderly no longer controlled the KOL's left wing. At a June 1886 Special Assembly called to address the problems of the Order's rapid growth, the New York City–based Home Club seized control of the KOL's central administration. The Home Club proved more adroit at fragmenting the Order than unifying it, and Knights of all political persuasions began jockeying for power. In the vacuum, the Order began to assume an identity that was the sum total of its constituent parts. The work of radical writers and poets appeared more frequently in KOL journals. Of 61 poems appearing in 1887 editions of Denver's *Labor Enquirer*, 10 were from Burnette Haskell, 9 were written by William Clarke Marshall, and 9 came from the Cheesewright brothers. Eight of

55. *Labor Enquirer* (Denver), November 19, 1887.
56. W. H. Gleason to Powderly, November 25, 1888, in *PP*.

the 52 poems appearing in 1886 copies of Chicago's *Knights of Labor* were penned by Christian socialist John Thompson.[57]

Even the stodgy *Journal of United Labor* changed its focus. Before 1886, the *JUL* favored classic poems from Tennyson, Scott, and Pope, or originals from long-time reformers like A. J. H. Duganne and John Mills. By 1887, the *JUL* printed poems from more vociferous poets like Gerald Massey, Phillips Thompson, Charlotte Perkins, Helen Hunt Jackson, and William Morris. By 1892, the *JUL* had changed so much that the socialist paper *The Weekly People* urged its readership to read it. Lucien Sanial, once head of the Knights' Cooperative Board, was a regular contributor to both papers. By 1893, the *JUL* ran poems like "Naked Truth," a ringing indictment by Chicago socialist George Howard Gibson of capitalist power networks:

> Battles for conquest, for booty, for slaves,
> Battles for 'business' still multiply graves,
> 'Each for himself' means the law of the strong,
> Robbers in power and pauperized throng.
> Business is brutal; it crushes what's noble,
> And fills up the world with temptation and trouble.
>
> Bad is the robber who pistols will draw,
> Worse are the men who 'frame mischief by law';
> Sheltered behind it they stand in the gates,
> Robbing at wholesale, by fixing the freights.
> And Armies, State armies, when called, must assist them
> In shooting the poor who unwisely resist them.

Others who felt Gibson's wrath included clergymen whose sermons defended "usury, rent, and wage-robbing."[58] Gibson's trenchant class language neither contains Powderly's optimism about the mutual interests of capital and labor nor implies that better-educated workers could dislodge entrenched power networks.

A final measure of the KOL's drift from Powderly conservatism is found in the popularity of William Morris's poetry. His "All For the Cause" was a staple for anarcho-socialist papers like *Solidarity*. By the 1890s readers of KOL journals also knew the poem.[59] Phillips Thompson included Morris's "The March of the Workers" in his songster, which

57. These numbers are based on my count from the complete runs of the *Labor Enquirer* for 1887 and the *Knights of Labor* for 1886.

58. *JKL*, May 18, 1893.

59. *Solidarity* (New York City), December 3, 1892. See also *JKL*, 1890–93.

was published on the Order's own presses.[60] As the Knights foundered after 1888, its radical wings began to compare the Order's leader to other role models, including Morris. In such a comparison, Powderly fared poorly.

There are striking parallels between William Morris and Terence Powderly. Each was profoundly affected by visions of medieval romanticism and Christian socialism in his youth; both initially approached the labor movement as something akin to a moral crusade. Both men possessed a semi-mystical belief in the nobility of labor, ridiculed politics yet served in public office, and were profoundly critical of their respective cultures. As E. P. Thompson argued, however, Morris successfully cast off most of his romantic baggage and immersed himself in the task of making "contact with the masses" in order to create "practical socialism." Morris's poems of the early 1880s questioned capitalism as much as Powderly and conservative KOL poets did, but Morris moved further to the left and embraced a political solution for labor with which Powderly never felt comfortable.[61]

The contrast between Powderly and Morris is emblematic of a larger tension within the Knights. Powderly and his followers were cautious individuals who constructed social visions for reform that combined a basic belief in the soundness of American political and economic institutions with the hope that a working-class social agenda could be grafted to middle-class drives for respectability. Others in the Order felt that fundamental changes should be made, and that autonomous working-class institutions were labor's only hope. The tension was never fully resolved. Even after discarding Powderly, the gutted KOL could not reach an accord on radicalism. The editorship of the *JKL* was promised to Lucien Sanial, but was not delivered. Neither was the KOL converted to the socialism of Daniel DeLeon. In 1895, both Sanial and DeLeon left the Knights.

Terry in the Soup

The debate over KOL policy invariably centered on its most visible figure, Terence V. Powderly. Historians have been equally quick to join with the chorus of Powderly critics, often without fully appreciating the

60. Thompson, *The Labor Reform Songster*, 20, 21.

61. E. P. Thompson, *William Morris: Romantic to Revolutionary* (New York: Pantheon Books, 1976).

intensity of KOL factionalism. The fates of DeLeon and Sanial—as well as the spectacular collapse of the Home Club—reminds us that KOL ideologues fared no better as leaders. Powderly's successors—James Sovereign, Henry Hicks, and John Hayes—proved far worse administrators and role models. For all his faults, Powderly remained leader of the Order for fifteen years by cultivating supporters to counterbalance his enemies. In fact, much of the North American working class held fast to values that these ideologues found appalling.

Few Knights viewed the world exclusively through the lens of class struggle. As Eric Hobsbawm notes, the social reality of class, class consciousness, and class struggle are distinct entities that may or may not exist simultaneously.[62] Most Knights shared the social reality of class, thinking that society was flawed, but not necessarily that change entailed class struggle. It is shortsighted to condemn Powderly without acknowledging his profound appeal to those workers whose views he embodied; local assemblies, cooperative stores, and even sons were named in his honor.[63]

Powderly, like many Knights, was a man of two eras. He came of age during the late Victorian period and recoiled from the bitter capital/labor strife from the 1870s on. Like many contemporaries, he donned a mantle of working-class respectability that was often indistinguishable from bourgeois Victorianism. He was not the arbiter of KOL taste and ideology, but he was the most visible symbol of views that were widespread in the Order. Many poets shared his commitment to slow reform. For every radical writer, the Order spawned a cautious one. In "The Factory Girl's Last Day," a sick girl rouses herself from her bed to her spinning frame. There she is savagely beaten by a cruel overseer and has to crawl home. When the factory bell rings the next morning, she bolts upright, announces "It's time," and dies.[64] This poem, though an indictment of factory discipline, is similar to scores of others found in the story papers. Its melodramatic narrative is more Victorian than working-class, and both its victims and villains are individuals, not systems. There is no ringing rejection of capitalism or class. What is condemned is the arbitrary misuse of power by a single factory overseer.

"The Factory Girl's Last Day" is similar to "One More Unfortunate."

62. Eric Hobsbawm, *Workers: Worlds of Labor* (New York: Pantheon Books, 1984), chaps. 1, 2.

63. The best-known attack on Powderly is that of Norman Ware, who called the General Master Workman "a windbag whose place was on the street rousing the rabble to concert pitch and providing emotional compensation for dull lives." See Ware, *The Labor Movement*, xvi.

64. *JUL*, August 25, 1885.

Few men in the Order admired Powderly more than Thomas O'Reilly. Despite the sentiments expressed in "Song of the Proletaire," O'Reilly was uncomfortable airing radical views in public. His poetic tragedy was couched in a classless formula and language familiar to nineteenth-century readers. O'Reilly shared Powderly's belief that the general public—workers and employers alike—would demand humanitarian reforms when informed of the reality of working-class poverty.

KOL poets who used religious imagery often appropriated Powderly's moralistic tone. Such poets expressed faith in the transformative possibilities of religion properly preached. B. C. Harris of Elizabeth, New Jersey, wrote "K. of L.—Kingdom of Love," a six-verse poem sprinkled with eight obscure footnoted Scripture references. In the midst of the Great Upheaval, Harris urged Knights forward to the coming Christian dawn:

> March on! Ye slaves, till the morning
>   Paint the brown mountain with gold,
> Till the light of love of the new time
>   Shall conquer the hate of the old.

Harris promised readers that Mammon's throne would crumble, and that Christ would restore the stolen "jewels of labor."[65]

Very few Knights identified with purely secular messages. In fact, the overly worldly appeared as models of foolishness, as in Deacon Stillwater's poem, "Mullins the Agnostic." Mullins doubted everything, including the existence of God. When confronted with anything he could not verify empirically Mullins retorted, "How do you know?" Hubris struck Mullins when he questioned a warning that a train was scheduled to cross the bridge on which he was walking. His haughty rejection of common sense were his last words: "Humph, how do you know?/I helped gather him up in a pail/The engine scattered him so."[66]

The later poetry of George McNeill typically reflects the way Knights mixed religion, labor militancy, and the desire for respectability. In the 1880s McNeill, the one-time disciple of Ira Steward, tempered his former hard-nosed pragmatism with a principled Christianity. "The Risen Laborer" is directed to capitalists and asks them whether they "would crush down" the laborer "or have him uplifted by Christ." McNeill wrote:

> O men of wealth and power, the pleading poor
> Cry not in vain to God's Almighty power!

65. *Knights of Labor* (Lynn, Mass.), March 13, 1886.
66. *JUL*, February 18, 1888.

> Throw off your burden of excessive wealth,
> Or it will bear you down to lowest gulf.
> Fulfill your duty to men of toil,
> And Peace and Plenty shall with Love abound.

McNeill pleaded with capitalists to restore the laborer to the "image of his God" and cease their heartless pursuit of Mammon so that "The gulfs of greed no longer shall divide/For all will labor for the common weal."[67]

McNeill's poem is at once cautious, defiant, naive, and firmly embedded in the mainstream of Gilded Age discourse on labor and religion. Veiled threats against capital round out his poem, but rebellion is justified in the name of Christ, not class. Implicit within the poem is a belief that struggle will not be necessary. McNeill's poem is directed at men of wealth whose reason and Christian values should lead to repentance, not rebellion.

Still, Powderly was such a visible figure that it was easy for those less thoughtful than George McNeill to equate principles with personality. Many poets and editors commented directly on the Master Workman and his ideas as if each idea was official policy. Michigan's Joseph Labadie blasted Powderly's 1886 General Assembly address for "uncertain and indefinite generalities" that bred "disorder" within the Knights. Labadie continued, "Mr. Powderly may win the applause of capitalism by such generalities, but the individual workmen are not working for capitalistic applause for Mr. Powderly." Labadie thought Powderly honest and upright, but "a worthless executive officer . . . [who] neglects every definite, direct action."[68]

But many KOL poets rejected Labadie's view. Shortly after Powderly's G.A. address that inflamed Labadie, the fifty-four-verse "K. of L., A Poem of Sir Powderly" appeared in *John Swinton's Paper*. In it Powderly appears as a medieval knight-errant leading the KOL on a holy crusade to bring the working and employing classes together. In his quest, Powderly is tasked by scabs, Pinkertons, and skeptics, who charge that "between the boss and workingmen/No good will can be found." Powderly preaches arbitration, education, and solidarity at every turn, but cautions all to be patient:

> But not till men in life's system move
> As stars do around the sun,

67. McNeill, *Unfrequented Paths*, 31–35.
68. *Advance and Labor Leaf*, December 29, 1886.

> Shall the rule of Might have taken flight
> And the race of Right be won.
>
> By the law of Unity alone
> Can Labor cope with Might;
> 'United we stand, divided we fall,'
> Has ever been, and will be, to all
> The legend of faith in Right.

Near the end of the poem, a worker asks Powderly if he will ever see the day "When the boss and the toiling workingmen/Will paddle in harmony." Powderly replies:

> 'Be still! be still!' said Sir Powderly
> 'Ye know not whereof you speak;
> For the promise has still been uppermost
> To get what now we seek.'
>
> 'Do not ask me where lies the promise!
> I answer; IN LIFE'S DEMAND;
> Claims echoed through all the centuries,
> On ocean and on land.'[69]

Powderly was frequently lionized in poetry, much of it as treacly as "Sir Powderly." Typical is Harriet Spaulding's 1890 ode:

> Have you seen him as up through the valley
> He comes in the strength of his power,
> While thousands press forward to rally
> Around him, the man of the hour?
> Though no helmet his brow is adorning
> As his cavalry sweeps o'er the plains,
> There is manhood outraged in his scorning,
> And the blood of a king in his veins.[70]

Hero worship like this appalled Knights who shared Labadie's views. William Clarke Marshall was infuriated by Powderly's compromises with Jay Gould, his refusal to support striking Chicago stockyard workers, and his role in ousting Tom Barry from the GEB. Marshall summed

---

69. *John Swinton's Paper*, January 16, 1887.
70. *JKL*, September 18, 1890.

up his frustration in his poem "Pooh! Powderly," one that also ridiculed the chivalric imagery with which Powderly was frequently praised:

> This is the language of the 'Times' of Chicago
>   Applied to you Terence, when down in New York
> You tried to teach Jay Gould, the wary old Hebrew,
>   The pride of his nation, that mutton was pork.
>
> And when you drew swords, what was yours but a tin one,
>   And he in steel mail from his head to his foot?
> You were wise not to linger to get a blow from him,
>   But you could not escape the sharp toe of his boot.
> Pooh! Powderly.

Marshall accused Powderly of leaving Martin Irons, a leader in the Southwest railway strikes, "in the lurch" by ordering, "Back to your tasks men! I speak for the Church."

The remainder of the poem uses metaphors of anti-Semitism and hog butchering to excoriate the General Master Workman. Marshall called Powderly the "Baron of Bologna" for betraying Tom Barry, and a fool for believing Philip Armour, "the Jew of Manhattan." In a final burst of venom before dismissing Powderly as a "barrel of pork," Marshall proclaimed:

> You are reaping in fields where you never sowed seed,
>   You moisten your bread in the sweat of the poor,
> But disaster and infamy wait on your steps,
>   For the blood of our Martyrs has splattered your door.
> Pooh! Powderly.[71]

Marshall's stinging verses were echoed by Denver's Burnette Haskell, who prefaced his "The Song of the Flag" with a poem declaring Powderly a traitor to the labor movement:

> Scarlet the wrongs, and scarlet the shames;
>   Scarlet the blood that sets men free;
> Scarlet the shame that soils their names,
>   Judas, Arnold, Monk, and THEE.[72]

71. *Labor Enquirer* (Denver), November 26, 1887.
72. Ibid., January 22, 1887.

Marshall and Haskell also lampooned topics dear to Powderly's heart, including religion. A Chicago Knight took up that theme in "The Church Walking With the World." The poem personifies the Church, and opens with it declaring itself above material enticements. But despite the pious pronouncments, the Church proved to be no Christ to Satan's temptations. Soon the world convinced the Church of the allure of "velvets and silks . . . and diamonds," and of gleaming edifices filled with carpets, carved furniture, "cushioned pews" and pompous ceremonies. Likewise, the Church agreed that too much attention was given to the poor, who were promptly "turned from her door in scorn."[73]

The charge of accommodationism was leveled directly at Powderly by other KOL poets. Rumors that Powderly was contemplating a run for public office led to outbursts of cynicism. As sentiment against Powderly gathered, he tried to make light of his declining popularity. In an 1890 poem of his own to John Hayes, Powderly wrote:

> They boasted and they shouted,
>   Of how they would be free,
> They were toasted and then roasted,
>   And went on a tarring spree.
> They were citizens of standing,
>   And to no man would they stoop,
> But they 'lected tother [sic] fellow,
>   And left Terry in the soup.[74]

As the fortunes of both Powderly and the KOL waned, a Newark, New Jersey, poet captured the moment. "Schomberg" sold an original poem, "Some Squibs on the Situation," for 5 cents a copy. The long poem chronicles the trade-by-trade flight of craftsmen from the KOL and ridicules Powderly's faith in religion and capitalism:

> But what must Powderly, assuredly do.
> As well as trust in God, say you?
>   Keep his powder dry.
>
> For Capital he's an awful squatter,
> And has squat so long will fight the hotter.

73. *Knights of Labor* (Chicago), October 9, 1886.
74. Powderly to Hayes, April 24, 1890, in *PP.*

> But with bone and sinew that can't be dodged,
> The Loafer—he's at once dislodged.[75]

    Powderly represented a strain of Gilded Age labor that pursued accommodation by walking a perilous path between working-class respectability and Victorianism. But clashes between labor and capital only focused more attention on class gaps. Poems about Powderly and religion illustrate this. Powderly was either a chivalric hero or a "barrel of pork," and religion was either labor's hope or an alluring opiate. In the 1890s, factions formed around extreme positions, and vied for supporters among a dwindling pool of members. Poetry highlighted the gap between capital and labor, and between bourgeois and working-class values, but it also added to the confusion over options.

Comrades or Domestics? Women and Poetry

Few issues revealed the dangers of Victorian contamination inside the KOL as clearly as gender relations. Consider first a poem entitled "Woman's Sphere" as it appeared in the *JUL* on June 25, 1887:

> They talk about a woman's sphere
>   As though it had a limit:
> There's not a place in earth or heaven,
> There's not a task of mankind given,
> There's not a blessing or a woe,
> There's not a whisper yes or no,
> There's not a life, or death, or birth,
> That has a feather's weight of worth
>   Without a woman in it.[76]

Yet the same journal, several months earlier, printed the sentimental "A Little Wife of the K. of L.":

> The dear little wife at home, John,
> With ever so much to do.

75. Undated printed card by "Schomberg" probably dates from late 1893 or early 1894 because of its reference to Powderly being "dislodged." The poem is located in a miscellaneous file in the *PP*.

76. *JUL*, June 25, 1887.

Stitches to set and babies to pet
And so many thoughts of you.
The beautiful household fairy,
Filling your heart with light,
Whatever you meet to-day John,
Go cheerily home to-night.[77]

KOL poetry by and about women illustrates that the Order was ambivalent and factionalized on the question of women comrades. As Susan Levine notes, nineteenth-century labor simultaneously toyed with
an "egalitarian principle" that allowed women "to carve a sphere of action outside the limits of contemporary womanhood," and an older Victorian ideal of "hearth and home" that accepted the "popular language
of domesticity with its sentimental and romantic definition of women's
spheres."[78]

The KOL at least tried to organize women, an effort that few other
nineteenth-century labor organizations could boast.[79] As women came
into the Order, male Knights had to rethink long-held assumptions concerning a woman's proper sphere. As we have seen, male Knights with
a fondness for ritual were uncertain of women's ability to become assembly-room "sisters." Like most Gilded Age men of all classes, many
Knights clung to Victorian notions of separate spheres. So, too, did
many women.

Leonora Barry, the Knights' General Investigator of Women's Work,
complained to Powderly that women were unreceptive to her efforts at
organization. Yet several of her columns in the *JUL* did little to help
women see themselves in a new light. Commenting on a report concerning women ironworkers, Barry wrote, "Every woman who went to work
in the iron industry threw a man out of employment . . . [probably]
compelling some other woman to leave her home and with one or two
of her little ones seek employment to support the home that the man
should have supported." She also thought an iron works was "not con-
ducive to culture or refinement in women, nor are its duties such as to
insure good physical conditions."[80] Barry reiterated this theme when
she resigned from the KOL in 1890. After organizing scores of women's

77. Ibid., January 15, 1887.
78. Levine, *Labor's True Woman*, 132.
79. Despite its many shortcomings in the area of advancing women, the KOL's efforts
appear more noble when contrasted with those of socialists or the AFL. See Mary Jo Buhle,
Women and American Socialism, 1870–1920 (Urbana: University of Illinois Press, 1983); Foner,
Women and the American Labor Movement.
80. *JUL*, July 5, 1888.

locals, giving more than five hundred lectures on behalf of the Order, and spending nine years as a wage-earner, Barry advised Powderly that she thought a woman's proper place was in the home.[81]

The Knights nevertheless provided limited opportunities for women who broke with tradition. From 1882 to 1890, the Order organized about sixty thousand women. Though they never constituted as much as 10 percent of the total membership, their voice was greater than their numbers. Poetry provided a point of contact between older ideals of womanhood and new possibilities. Female poets were prominent in KOL journals, and though not all were members of the Order—reprints of story paper poets like Emma Southworth, Alice Carey, and Lydia Sigourney were popular—there was an attempt to allow women to address the Order in their own voices. A sampling of local Knight (and KOL-affiliated) journals reveals that the number of poems written by women frequently surpassed 10 percent of the total:

Journal	Year	Total Poems	Poems by Women	Percent
The Critic	1889	68	11	16.2
Haverhill Laborer	1885	38	2	5.3
	1886	143	12	8.4
Knights of Labor	1886	52	8	15.4
The Labor Leader	1887	42	6	14.3
	1888	30	3	10.00
Labor Enquirer	1884	10	1	10.00
	1885	11	2	18.2
	1886	38	10	26.3
	1887	61	9	14.8

The *Journal of United Labor* also printed a large number of poems by women. (Percentages are impossible to determine since the bulk of *JUL* poems gave no author.) Of the attributed poems for 1887, ten different female poets were listed; in 1888, five more. As late as 1893, a year in which the *JUL* printed only forty-seven poems, eight of the poets (eleven poems) were women.

Oddly enough, some of the KOL's best-known and most outspoken women leaders were its most cautious poets. Frances Willard made sure the Order did not suffer from a shortage of poems as she incorrectly

81. See Mrs. Barry's reports to the 1889 and 1890 General Assemblies, *Proceedings of the Knights of Labor General Assembly*, in PP.

thought it did in the matter of songs. Yet her contributions to the *JUL* seldom broached suffrage or temperance, her primary concerns. Typical of her efforts was her 1887 poem, "A Good Great Name," reflections on the 155th anniversary of George Washington's birth.[82]

Another cautious poet was Mary Lease, the "Kansas Prophet." A poem inscribed to Leonora Barry praised the beauties of Ireland rather than taking up Barry's work, and featured verse such as: "Oh, Erin! my mother Erin! / I may never revisit thy shore? / But exiled far in a stranger land / I will love thee for evermore."[83] To be certain, Mary Lease wrote of an issue that concerned many in the KOL, an organization heavily represented by Irish-Americans. But Lease was a member of Columbia Assembly 3306 of Wichita, Kansas, and represented a group of rural Knights more interested in grain prices and temperance than sentimental longings for the auld sod. Lease became Master Workman of her KOL assembly, and was also active in the Women's Christian Temperance Union (WCTU) and the Farmers' Alliance. In her orations one finds little poetic wistfulness. In a speech delivered before the WCTU, she insisted that there was "no difference between the brain of an intelligent woman and the brain of an intelligent man" and defended the "zeal and enthusiasm" of women reformers. Lease also launched well-publicized attacks on the liquor trade, Wall Street, and Kansas senator John J. Ingalls, whom she took to task for his agricultural policies and misogynist opposition to votes for women.[84]

But if Willard and Lease were reluctant to make their poetry coincide with their politics, lesser-known women were not. Between 1882 and 1884, Leonora Barry assisted in organizing many of New York City's female carpet weavers into KOL locals. Annie Sheridan sent her "Song of the Carpet Weavers" to the *JUL* in January 1885. Her long poem smolders with class resentment:

> How many ladies proud and fair,
> Will tread o'er our carpets woven with care?
> With never a thought for the poor working girl,
> Whose youth is blighted with weary toil.
>
> Ladies by fortune and fashion spoiled
> But not our superiors, nay, the world
> Holds not the one who is above
> The working girl toiling for duty and love.

82. *JUL*, August 5, 1887.
83. Ibid., April 7, 1888.
84. For a typical speech from Mary Lease, see *JKL*, April 2, 1891.

Sheridan saw her plight as much in class as gender terms and praised:

> Men who can feel for a sister's grief,
> Aid and encourage, not like the thief,
> The robber who revels upon the spoil
> Of the laborer's unrequited toil.[85]

Sheridan's poem was written within weeks of the outbreak of the 1885 New York carpet weavers' strike led by John Morrison. The fate of that strike is a microcosm of the Order's factionalism and its schizophrenic attitude about women. The strike was originally won, but on terms unacceptable to the KOL's GEB, which was troubled by the independence of Morrison and the women strikers. When the GEB insisted on a closed-shop agreement, mill owners balked, and a new strike ensued that the GEB then refused to sanction. The matter was not settled until 1887. The closed shop came at the expense of a lower wage rate than Morrison negotiated in 1885, and many women were angry at being forced to join newly created National Trade Assembly 126. Soon male Knights complained that women were revealing signs and rituals to outsiders, and did not take their vows seriously.[86]

Despite the KOL's heavy-handed treatment of New York City carpet weavers, many women continued to see the Order as a forum for class expression. An Ontario "sister" contributed "Only the Working Class," which told readers that women made good Knights. She clearly envisioned women as part of the struggle to liberate the working class:

> It is not any woman's part
> We often hear folks say,
> And it will mar our womanhood
> To mingle in the fray.
> I fear I will never understand,
> Or realize it quite,
> How a woman's fame can suffer
> In struggling for the right.[87]

Many women shared her vision, especially Elizabeth Rodgers of Chicago, who by 1886 was Master Workman of powerful DA 24. By the time

85. *JUL*, August 5, 1885.

86. For more on this strike, see Levine, *Labor's True Woman*. For more on the conflict between men and women over ritual see Chapter 1 above.

87. *JUL*, April 25, 1886.

Rodgers served as delegate to the 1886 General Assembly, she had already been active in the Chicago labor movement for more than a decade, having organized women's trade unions in Chicago before the KOL arrived. A hard-nosed unionist, Rodgers told *The Labor Leaf* that she had "a great deal of experience in strikes."[88] Under her leadership DA 24 charted a different course from that which Powderly approved. In 1887, she led women Knights into active involvement with the United Labor Party, whose positions Powderly had repudiated; welcomed radicals like William Gleason and Charles Sieb into KOL ranks; and defended the Haymarket anarchists. Powderly tried to use Richard Griffiths, the Order's General Worthy Foreman, to control affairs in Chicago, but the aged Griffiths was no match for the strong-willed Rodgers.[89]

In addition to her work in politics and the labor movement, Elizabeth Rodgers bore twelve children, nine of whom survived to adulthood. With such a busy life, she had little time left to dabble in poetry. Nonetheless, she was a role model for other women who wanted to compete with men on their own terms. A poet who agreed with Rodgers was Clara Dixon Davidson, whose poem "We Struggle Up Together" ends:

> We struggle up together,—
> O' reach out helpful hands,
> In love to one another!
> Strengthen fraternal bands![90]

Though drawing on older Knights' imagery of fraternalism, Davidson insisted that the struggle could not be won without the participation of women.

For some women, their involvement in the labor movement meant there would be no return to sex roles-as-usual. One poet warned, "Oh! the mean won't be so mean/When the women vote," while Margaret

88. *Advance and Labor Leaf*, December 29, 1886.

89. *Knights of Labor* (Chicago), February 12, 1887; Powderly to Elizabeth Rodgers, January 16, 1887; Powderly to Leonora Barry, February 17, 1889; Richard Griffiths to Powderly, August 5, 1890; in *PP.*

Elizabeth Rodgers is sometimes confused with Elizabeth Morgan. Both were born in the United Kingdom, married Welshmen, emigrated to America, ended up in Chicago, and were active in socialist politics. Morgan was the founder of the socialist Ladies' Federal Labor Union. Elizabeth Rodgers was born in Ireland in 1847 and married a Welsh iron molder before coming to America. She was a remarkable woman. She took over as District Master Workman of DA 24 when her husband died in 1886. At his death she had an infant son. (She attended the 1886 General Assembly less than two weeks after his birth.)

90. *Labor Enquirer* (Denver), March 13, 1886.

Holmes savaged contemporary mores in "Les Miserables." Her poem ends:

> For what are we thankful? For prisons and pain:
>   For our babes, murd'ring sleep with their famishing cries;
> For the wind, the sleet, the hail and the rain,
>   Beating out the dull life from the heart and the brain;
> For the grave we at last in Potters' Field gain,
>   For the stone with its deeply cut lies.

Throughout the poem Holmes attacks a social system where "The labor was ours, not the spoil."[91]

But outspoken women like Rodgers and Holmes troubled patriarchal Knights. Passing resolutions for women's suffrage and equal pay for equal work was one thing, but confronting aggressive women was another. Neither the clamp-down on the carpet weavers nor publication of "A Dear Little Wife of the K of L" was an isolated incident. The battle that raged on the personal and poetic level is best illustrated by the fate of the Order's most important woman organizer, Leonora Barry.

Barry was neither a political firebrand, nor a cultural radical. Born in Ireland, she came to the United States at the age of two, took a teaching job at sixteen, and left it four years later when she married. Barry bore three children in seven years of marriage, but was forced to toil in an Amsterdam, New York, knitting mill when she was widowed in 1881. She joined the KOL in 1883, and quickly rose in its ranks. In 1886, she was appointed to the newly created post of General Investigator of Women's Work.[92]

From the beginning, Barry found her position difficult and her role vague. At times she was sent to intervene in matters relating only to women, at others she functioned as a combination general investigator, organizer, and lecturer. In 1887, Barry was sent on an extensive tour of local assemblies. Although her reports were not optimistic concerning the organization of women in the KOL, she won raves for her speaking ability and soon tried to redefine her role as that of lecturer and educator.

That sort of independence put Barry at loggerheads with Secretary-Treasurer John Hayes, who plotted to get rid of her. Powderly advised Barry to devote her efforts to investigation so as "to deprive your enemies of the opportunity which they will have at the next GA to say that

---

91. *JKL*, March 10, 1892; *Labor Leader*, March 26, 1887.
92. For a synopsis of Leonora Barry's career to 1888, see *Irish World*, April 7, 1888.

you took to the lecturer's platform instead of the field of investigation."
He also warned her that there was sentiment on the GEB for abolishing
the Women's Department, and that its expenses were "being carefully
scanned."[93]

But, by late 1888, Powderly also had turned against Barry. He used
the convenient tactic of claiming that she had revealed secrets and wrote
Tom O'Reilly:

> Mrs. B. is entirely too loose to place any confidence in. She should
> not have lisped a word about the change in the secret work; all
> the enemies will be on the lookout for the changes from now until
> they give them to the world. I shall talk to her next week in a way
> that will not be mistaken.[94]

In a carefully worded letter to Barry couched as gentle advice, Powderly
accused her of neglecting her duties and sowing discord in the Order.
He copied the letter, forwarded it to Hayes, and told him to gain Barry's
"confidence."[95]

Barry unwittingly played into Hayes's hands, and he manipulated her
into supporting the dismantling of the Women's Department. Hayes
then wrote a contemptuous letter to Powderly complaining of Barry's
"tale of woe during [which] . . . a big tear was dropped on the table . . .
because the women's department was a failure." He warned Powderly
that she was coming to see the GMW, so he should be prepared "to see
her *cry*." A few weeks later Hayes wrote, "I would suggest if there is an
opportunity for the abolishment of her department to do it and let her
go into the lecturer's field. That will only give the Order one more year
of *her!!*"[96]

Leonora Barry spent most of 1889 lecturing in the South. Clearly un-
happy in her role, she asked the GA to relieve her of her position as
head of the Women's Department and suggested that it be abolished.

---

93. Powderly to Leonora Barry, June 25, 1888, in *PP.*
94. Powderly to Thomas O'Reilly, December 11, 1889, in *PP.*
95. Powderly to Leonora Barry, December 27, 1888; Powderly to Hayes, December 27,
1888, in *PP.*
    The charge that Barry could not keep secrets draws, of course, on sexist stereotypes of
women's propensity for gossip, and was an old KOL weapon against women as well.
Uriah Stephens used the stereotype to successfully exclude women from the Order during
his time in office. There are numerous examples of women being dropped from the KOL
for revealing minute parts of the *AK.* In any event, the charge against Mrs. Barry in 1888
was especially specious given that most of the Order's ritual practices had been published
in the popular press.
96. Hayes to Powderly, September 24, 1889; October 26, 1889, in *PP.*

The GA accepted her first proposal, but rejected the second. Barry was recommissioned as a General Lecturer. Hayes was wrong in thinking that Barry merely coveted the lecturer's podium, for she did not serve out her term. In April 1890, Leonora Barry married O. R. Lake of St. Louis, resigned her position, and announced that women belonged in the home. With her remarriage, Leonora Barry-Lake ceased her involvement with the KOL.

But why would John Hayes systematically plot to rid the Order of one of its brightest and most capable women? Personal spite was a factor, but so were more sinister motives: sexism and financial malfeasance. Though married, Hayes had a reputation for being a womanizer. He was alleged to be having an affair with a secretary at KOL headquarters, while another woman there, Maggie Eiler, complained to a closed session of the GEB of sexual harassment and other abuse from Hayes.[97]

It is difficult to know how much weight to give some of the charges against Hayes, since Powderly was seeking scandals to use against Hayes for an upcoming showdown. But this much is clear: from 1890 to 1893, Hayes played a central role in eliminating all of the women working at KOL headquarters with the exception of alleged favorites. Women were dismissed one by one, including long-time employees like Mary O'Reilly. Hayes even fired Mary Stephens, the daughter of founder Uriah Stephens. At each step, Hayes justified his actions by appealing to the Order's declining numbers and sagging finances, a specious argument given that he periodically hired new help, including his brother, and Annie Traphagen, reputed to be another object of affection. He also pretended to mend his fences with Eiler, but used her to gain access to file letters documenting Hayes's administration of several KOL funds that subsequently disappeared. In July 1893, he fired her.[98]

John Hayes simply did not tolerate anyone questioning his will, least of all women. Part of his brief against Leonora Barry was that "we do not have sufficient control over her."[99] His lack of compassion was evident in his patronizing ridicule of Barry's crying. Hayes not only disliked Barry personally, he was troubled by her independence. Hayes may well have been a misogynist who cared little for women beyond their ability to assuage his ego and sexual appetite. Although his behavior was execrable, his attitudes were reflective of those Knights who preferred women

97. A. W. Wright to Powderly, December 5, 1892, February 19, 1893; Thomas O'Reilly to Powderly, December 2, 1892, December 7, 1892, in *PP.*

98. Wright to Powderly, February 14, 1893; O'Reilly to Powderly, May 15, 1893, July 29, 1893, in *PP.* Letters concerning Hayes's financial dealings were among those he apparently purloined from Eiler's files.

99. Hayes to Powderly, September 24, 1889, in *PP.*

more demure, and less powerful. Such men existed, though the KOL remained committed rhetorically to sexual equality.

Doubtless, such Knights were more comfortable with sentiments expressed by Victorian poet Ella Wheeler Wilcox. She spoke a language of reform without asserting herself too openly. Her poem "Reform" held the dubious distinction of being the *JKL's* most published poem. Hayes was so delighted with it that he ordered it reprinted nine times in 1892 and 1893, even though Tom O'Reilly objected. Her poem expressed such bland sentiments as:

> The time has come when men with hearts and brains
> Must rise and take the misdirected reins
> Of government, too long left in the hands
> Of tricksters and of thieves. He who stands
> And sees the mighty vehicle of State
> Hauled through the mire of some ignoble fate,
> And makes not such a bold protest as he can
> Is no American.[100]

For some Knights, women made good spiritual allies, but were best suited to be Victorian wallflowers. How else to explain the publication of Mary Gleason's "Woman's Warfare," an examination of why women shouldn't join the army: "Nay! for women are too frail/In the midst of battle's terrors/Tender hearts like theirs would fail." But Gleason's mawkish poem had wider implications. She went on to say that a woman's fight was "within the home" with weapons of "needles, scissors, duster, broom/Carving knife . . . long handled spoon." When that battle faltered, "Scripture texts wield thou with power."[101]

Many male Knights continued to view women as their social inferiors from infancy to old age. A filler item appeared in an 1882 *JUL* under the title "The New Arithmetic" and asked the rhetorical question, "Six times seven girls are how many girls, and what on earth are they good for?"[102] Likewise, an 1887 *JUL* printed Samuel Minturn Peck's "The Naughty Little Girl," a model for all that is excessive and awful about Victorian sentimentality:

> She is cunning, she is tricky
> I am greatly grieved to tell,

---

100. *JKL*, June 30, 1892.

Wisconsin-based Ella Wheeler Wilcox was a poet of some popularity among Victorian middle-class readers. Much of her work was highly sentimental. For examples of her other works, see Ella Wheeler Wilcox, *Poems of Passion* (Chicago: W. P. Conkey, 1883).

101. *JUL*, August 13, 1887. The poem was originally published in *Good Housekeeping*.

102. *JUL*, June 15, 1882.

> And her hands are always sticky
> With the chocolate caramel;
> Her dolly's battered features
> Tell of many a frantic hurl;
> She's the terror of her teachers—
> That naughty little girl.[103]

That such saccharine verses should appear at all in a labor journal is remarkable; that it appeared in the *JUL* one month after "A Little Wife of the K. of L." and less than six months after Leonora Barry was made General Investigator of Women's Work for the KOL, is revealing.

But we should not exaggerate sexism within the KOL any more than we should ignore it. Women Knights blazed new trails in the 1880s, even though Victorian snares made their journey perilous. Very few male Knights were as misogynist, Machiavellian, or cruel as John Hayes; most were ambivalent. Such Knights had a hard time deciding whether or not women belonged in the workplace and assembly hall. Were women to be comrades or domestics? Should a woman defy social limits, or be content to serve as a "dear little wife?" Women themselves stumbled over the questions. When Leonora Barry announced that women belonged in the home, her motives were perhaps disingenuous, but her reasoning raised few eyebrows. Still, the KOL was a path-breaking organization for women like Elizabeth Rodgers, Mary Lease, and dozens of female poets, just as it was a profound influence for young women like Mother Jones and Leonora O'Reilly, whose initiation into the labor movement came courtesy of the KOL. Even Leonora Barry-Lake regained her public voice. Within a year, she was on the temperance trail and remained an activist for that cause until throat cancer silenced her in 1929. Not surprisingly, she wrote a few poems for the cause.

Rote Learning or Public Education?

A few early fraternal forays aside, KOL poetry belongs to the organization's post-1882 public period. Poetry, along with the creation of journals, was part of the effort to "educate" members. The literary qualities of each were designed to supplement the orally transmitted practices of ritual and song, and to subsume private religious beliefs in the wider context of KOL policy.

103. Ibid., February 15, 1887.

The problem with "public" education—unlike the rote systems of early Knighthood—was that Victorian culture unfolded in a hegemonic marketplace of ideas in which highly selective forms, values, and relations were deemed desirable. The challenge was to find a way to put forth a laborist agenda within such a society. As KOL publishers made their sometimes curious, often inconsistent, editorial decisions, they did so in what was, ironically, a more ambiguous context than the symbol-ladden world of ritual. At least ritual had a fixed form, just as songs had set lyrics and religion had established doctrines. Much of the poetry in this chapter highlights issues over which Knights disgreed rather than rallied.

KOL leaders naively felt they could control the flow of information, modify cultural influences, and shape rank-and-file tastes through education and propaganda. They were mistaken. It was easy enough to agree, for example, that financial institutions were corrupt, and KOL poets duly noted this. It proved harder, however, to resist condemning them through the language of popular Victorian anti-Semitism. Likewise, it was one thing to accede to an abstract platform plank upholding gender equality, it was quite another to accept women as comrades inside local assemblies or on the GEB.

The education dilemma was part of a larger, more fundamental one that confronted the KOL as it moved from a private to a public Order: how much of existing society could Knights embrace? All Knights agreed that change was needed, but did this entail reform or revolution? And what did either path mean in practice? Of the two impulses, the reformist spirit was dominant. For every Daniel DeLeon the Knights produced, it spawned numerous Terence Powderlys. Most North American workers agreed with Powderly that positive social change was needed, not social revolution.

But a revolutionary agenda is easier to articulate than a reformist one. By attracting reform-minded individuals to its banner, the KOL opened itself for inevitable clashes over the nature of reform. Social critiques spanned a wide spectrum of beliefs. Many Knights held panacean hopes for very small changes; some thought little more than a reduction in the hours of labor, the creation of an investigative bureau of labor statistics, or the political education of workers would usher in a golden age. Others, including Powderly, articulated a much wider reform package that ranged from temperance to land reform. A few dreamed of revolution.

Reformers and revolutionaries alike required a vehicle for disseminating their ideals. For the KOL, the labor press was a logical place to turn. Ritual, religion, and music reinforced values within local assemblies, but to spread ideas across communities, districts, and nations required more. Public rallies, speeches, parades, and picnics were one way to do this, but newspapers offered unique advantages. Journals were easy to disseminate and they circulated widely. A single newspaper like New York's *Daily Leader* touched Knights in New York City, Brooklyn, New Jersey, and Long Island, and communicated information that would have required more than a half-dozen separate rallies. In addition, newspapers allowed for ongoing reflection by the reader, while rallies were more likely to elicit emotional, yet transitory, responses on the part of participants. The KOL founded scores of journals to educate its rank and file, and reformers and revolutionaries vied to control them.

But all KOL editors realized that the reading public was not holding its collective breath in anticipation of their journals. In order to compete, labor editors combined the most successful features of metropolitan and story papers with those that addressed the needs of working men and women. Invariably, some KOL papers looked more like popular presses than the small radical presses of nineteenth-century socialists and anarchists; few survived more than two years.

Journal articles and poems put forth reform issues boldly, but in such a haphazard way as to allow individual Knights to pick and choose their own values package. Just as members felt comfortable writing to journals expressing dissatisfaction with the Order's stand on secrecy or temperance, so too they felt free to express, in letter and verse, contrary opinions on issues like politics and gender. Thus could "Address to the Statue of Liberty" and "A Poem of Sir Powderly," which both speak for the Order, and "A Little Wife of the K. of L." and "Woman's Sphere" appear in the same journal. Poetry and other journal content confirms that there was not one KOL agenda, but many.

As a final point of departure, let us consider George E. McNeill. McNeill, born in Amesbury, Massachusetts, in 1837, rooted his labor reform pedigree in deeper soil than Powderly. By the time he joined the KOL around 1883, he was already a veteran of union and eight-hour movements. Once in the Knights, McNeill served as treasurer of DA 30, the largest in the Order by 1886. After 1886 he co-edited with Frank K. Foster Boston's *Labor Leader*, a paper affiliated with the KOL until they split with the organization over its policy on trade unions. From 1883 to 1887, however, McNeill sang Knighthood's praises louder than most, and before drifting away, he tried hard to convince the Order to abandon its suicidal position against trade unions.

In 1903, McNeill published *Unfrequented Paths: Songs of Nature, Labor, and Men.* They were poems rather than songs, the bulk of which had been written years before. McNeill's poetry reveals a personal odyssey in, through, and out of the KOL. Some of the earliest poems echo Uriah Stephens, as in "Knighthood":

> To-night we meet within mystic halls
>> Of these our brothers, whose emblazoned shields
> Glow forth in golden splendor on our walls,
>> Greeting with joy the sword our Order wields,
> Fraternal greetings give we back again
>> To Damon and to Pythias, Knights of old,
> Who counted friendship better than all gain
>> Of worldly praise or ill-begotten gold.
> Like them we succor, give, uplift the low,
>> Hold out the helping hand to all who need,
> And buckle on the armor 'gainst the foe
>> Whose impious hands are stained with blood and greed.[104]

Several took a more defiant tone. In "The Poor Man's Burden," McNeill skewered the profit motive:

> Pile on the poor man's burden—
> Drive out the beastly breed;
> Go bind his sons in exile
> To serve your pride and greed;
> To wait in heavy harness
> Upon you rich and grand;
> The common working peoples,
> The serfs of every land.

Yet for all of his defiance, McNeill assumed a very Powderly-like faith in Christian social change. A later verse warns "monopolistic rings" that they soon "Freedom's God shall hear," and He will try them "in the balance . . . [and] deal out justice true."[105]

For all of his trade union posturing, McNeill never made the leap toward class-based radicalism; he went on to found the Massachusetts Mutual Insurance Company. Like so many KOL poets, McNeill identified problems—crushing poverty, long hours, hunger, substandard housing—but echoed Powderly's belief that the answer to labor's woes was to Christianize, not revolutionize, society.[106] "The Risen Laborer"

---

104. McNeill, *Unfrequented Paths*, 111–12.

105. Ibid., 36–38.

106. Ibid. See the following poems: "The Risen Laborer," 31–35; "The Poor Man's Burden," 36–38; "Awake, Awake, Ye Sons of Toil," 39–40; "I Have Been Robbed," 45–46.

compares labor's cross to that of Christ and assures workers that soon they would be restored to "the image of . . . God," while "Awake, Awake Ye Sons of Toil" offered the following hope: "From sunken mine, from shop and mill/The weary toilers hail the morn/And childhood cheers with royal will/The Christmas Day when Peace was born." Even a poem with such a suggestive title as "I Have Been Robbed" ends a long catalogue of social injustice with supplicatory prayers on labor's part and the promise of "Peace on earth, good-will to man."[107]

McNeill and Powderly are typical of mainstream nineteenth-century labor leaders. A public person was one thrust into a kaleidoscope of possibilities in which radical politics, bourgeois reformism, Knighthood, trade unionism, fraternalism, feminism, and Victorian sentimentalism were among the options to choose. Most of McNeill's poems were not about labor at all—only seven of forty address that theme directly—but about "nature . . . and men." His nature poems are overdone metaphysical odes, with the remainder being eulogistic bits of fluff dedicated to his personal heroes, all of whom were male. All of the competing impulses of solidarity, segmentation, and sentimentality are present in McNeill's work, and they stand nicely as metaphors for the KOL poetic corpus.

Public education of members was perhaps necessary for the public organization that the KOL decided to become. If their goal was to communicate consistent principles and values, however, it must be concluded that the rote learning of early Knighthood was more successful. The public KOL never managed to resolve public debates over policy and ideology, or cultural battles over what outside practices should pass through its opened Outer Veil. I will examine more of this clash as I turn to fiction, material culture, and leisure.

107. Ibid.

5 Victoria's Sons and Daughters?

The Knights of Labor in Fiction

In 1889, the *Journal of United Labor* unveiled a plan to increase its circulation by 25,000 and attract new workers to the Order. Faced with a declining membership precipitated by savage attacks from employers and other labor organizations, the 1889 KOL was badly in need of a boost. But the campaign announced by the *JUL* was unorthodox, to say the least. Rather than appealing to working-class solidarity, educating laborers on the benefits of joining the KOL, or proclaiming any new initiatives, the editors trumpeted the forthcoming serialization of a "thrilling" novel, W. H. Little's serialized novel "Lever and Throttle." As an added inducement, the editors offered a gold watch to the Knight who solicited the most new subscriptions[1] (Fig. 9).

The *JUL* ran Little's novel and appended letters from locals that claimed miraculous rejuvenation. One correspondent claimed his local shrank to five members until he ordered twenty-five copies of the *JUL* and distributed them. Soon, extra copies were needed, and in a matter of weeks, membership in the newly thriving assembly more than quadrupled.[2] If the letters are genuine—and the lack of signatures or postmarks on some make them suspect—Little's story worked miracles inside the KOL. To revive sagging KOL fortunes, "Lever and Throttle" must have been a powerful novel indeed.

But what does the modern reader find? Little's story was set in backwoods New York in 1872, a time in which the KOL was a secret fraternal order confined to Philadelphia. The story revolves around railroad swin-

1. *JUL*, March 14, 1889; April 4, 1889.
2. Ibid., April 11, 1889.

SPECIAL PREMIUMS.

To any member who will send us one yearly or two half-yearly subscribers we will forward a handsome enameled gold-front badge; and for three yearly or six half-yearly subscribers a round or square emblematic watch charm.

Round Watch Charm.   Gold-front or Enameled Badge.   Square Watch Charm.

Jno. W. Hayes.

General Secretary-Treasurer.

EACH KNIGHT WANTS ONE!
ONE MILLION KNIGHTS IN THE UNITED STATES!
SOMETHING NEW WILL ALWAYS SELL!

CHAMPION.

This cut represents a 3 oz. Champion, O. F. Dueber Case, with a raised Gold ornamentation of the emblem of the **KNIGHTS OF LABOR.** We call your attention to the exquisite workmanship and to the fact that each emblem **is Solid Gold.** The low prices will speak for themselves.

Champion Dueber Silver Stem Winder, with raised ornamentation, 3 oz. $6.75, 4 oz. $7.75.

The same as above in Dueber Silverine, $3.85.

These are made in open face only.

The same emblem without ornamentation, but handsomely engraved on back of case:

3 oz. Champion Silver Stem Wind, $5.05.
4 "   "   "   "   "   6.05.
Silverine,   "   "   2.15.

Avail yourself of the opportunity and be the first one to have one.

SILVERINE.

Fig. 9. In 1889 the *Journal of United Labor* began a campaign to increase circulation. As an inducement, the editors offered "special premiums" for new subscriptions and a gold watch to the Knight who solicited the most new subscriptions.

dles and strikes that loosely parallel the Credit Mobilier. The major characters include Montreville Pierstone, a brave engineer; Arnold Gripman, a double-crosser; Arnold's father, Rufus, a dishonest lawyer; Shannon Coolcrafty, an unscrupulous railroad entrepreneur; and a mysterious "Spaniard" named Canute Seminaba residing in Contentment Castle with daughters Cayula and Syiska.

Pierstone is the novel's hero, and the love interest of Syiska Seminaba. He was once a Cornell classmate of Arnold Gripman, a man he still considered his friend even though his father ruined Pierstone's family, an act that forced Montreville to become a railroad worker instead of finishing his education. The two men remained friends even after the local railroad passed into the hands of Coolcrafty and Rufus Gripman, who fired Pierstone for union organizing. Arnold proved to be a villain who feigned friendship with Pierstone in order to gain access to Contentment Castle, where he plotted with Cayula Seminaba, a vain woman angered by her sister's romance with a common laborer like Pierstone.

Predictable plot turns involving strikes, scabs, and agent provocateurs unfold until hubris struck down all the blackguards in one fell swoop. During a strike, Rufus Gripman replaced experienced engineers with scabs. A train carrying the Seminaba family barreled into the station and exploded when the incompetent replacement forgot to water the boilers. Cayula is killed in the conflagration, and Arnold horribly scalded. Shortly thereafter, the strike was won, Pierstone's family regained its property, and the thievery of Coolcrafty and Gripman was exposed.[3]

Putting aside the melodramatic and formulaic structure of the story, "Lever and Throttle" is a puzzling choice for leaders seeking to inject new life into the Knights. The story is neither about the KOL nor does it promote KOL principles. The story indicts fraud, injustice, and theft, but not wealth and privilege. The aristocratic Canute Seminaba is the mirror opposite of the pompous Rufus Gripman and Shannon Coolcrafty. Moreover, for a working-class hero, Montreville Pierstone has a curiously aristocratic name that contrasts with the more lowly Arnold Gripman; rightly so, as Pierstone's laborer status is due to compulsion, not choice. The novel ends with Montreville and Syiska planning their marriage, a windfall that will release him from manual labor. At base, "Lever and Throttle" resembles a Horatio Alger story more than a proletarian novel.

How do we explain the inclusion of "Lever and Throttle" into the *JUL?* The genteel pretensions of KOL leaders will not answer as an explanation. Even Powderly was bothered by the direction KOL fiction was tak-

3. Ibid., March 14–July 4, 1889.

ing. Shortly after "Lever" finished its run he complained to John Hayes:
"I see that 'The Toilers of Babylon' is advertised for next week's *Journal*
and will have to go in now so I need to read the infernal thing through.
I went about 50 pages last night . . . and I cannot see any merit in it. It
is a nicely written love story and that is all."[4] And even if one could lay
the blame for such stories on editors and leaders, it would not explain
why they had an audience.

Like poetry, fiction came of age after 1882, during the KOL's public
period. As the Order opened outward, it confronted a cultural system
controlled by the very elites who threatened workers financially and socially. The Knights sought to transform American society and culture;
but by lowering the Order's veils, the way was opened for outside influences to shape rank-and-file tastes. This was especially the case for fiction since its roots were even more shallow than those of poetry. Thus
fiction offered fewer oppositional challenges to hegemonic culture than
ritual, religion, or music.[5]

We have seen how KOL poetry contained bourgeois sentiments—
especially in gender constructions—and how Victorian sexism co-ex-
isted with rhetorical stands on equality within the Order. But we also
see that the relationship between Knights' and hegemonic culture was
dialectical, which was also the case with KOL fiction. It is too pat to say
that the Knights yielded to bourgeois values when one finds KOL heroes
and heroines in Victorian fiction produced outside the Order. For a
time—roughly 1884 to late 1887—the Knights influenced bourgeois editors to the degree that the press was mildly favorable to the KOL. But it
is equally difficult to credit the KOL with transforming tastes or opinions. In the aftermath of the Great Upheaval, most of these same editors
found the KOL too radical. Soon they raised their pens against the Order, and noble Knights disappeared from the story-papers' list of stock
characters. A foray into KOL fiction involves suggestive "what might-
have-beens," but ultimately Powderly's fears came true; the Knights of
Labor found itself saddled with a cultural product that was neither educational nor inspirational.

Ten Cents a Knight

A disarmingly simple observation is in order: purveyors of popular culture who do not give their audience at least part of what it wants, usually

    4. Terence V. Powderly to John W. Hayes, August 21, 1889, in *PP.*
    5. I have borrowed the terms hegemonic, alternative, and oppositional from Raymond
Williams. See Raymond Williams, "Base and Superstructure in Marxist Cultural Theory,"
New Left Review (November–December 1973), 3–16.

end up without any audience at all.[6] This remark encapsulates a sentiment felt keenly by KOL editors. The Order's decision to become a public organization committed it to a frontal assault on hegemonic Victorian society that took place on cultural, as well as economic and political, turf. This put KOL culture in an ambiguous relationship with the currents of the Gilded Age cultural mainstream because the Order as a whole never reached consensus as to whether society ought to be mildly reformed, dramatically transformed, or totally reborn.

These competing tensions are obvious in KOL writings. A typical issue of the *JUL* might include temperance pleas, calls for protective labor legislation, angry advocacy of overthrowing constituted society, household hints, sophomoric riddles, and poetry and fiction suffused with Victorianism. When the KOL lifted its veils, its ideas had to compete with alternative views. Gradually, hegemonic culture seeped into the Order, where it sometimes clashed, and other times melded, with the KOL's organic expressions. As Powderly alluded in his attack on "Toilers of Babylon," the ultimate danger was that KOL culture would become Victorian.

The KOL wrote fiction for the same reason it produced poetry: it was part of the Gilded Age cultural landscape. As noted in Chapter 4, both literacy and the publication industry were in a take-off stage after the Civil War. KOL editors included fiction in their journals to sate the hunger of a voracious working-class readership. But once again, the models were outside the Order; in this case, dime novels and story-papers, both of which discovered the Knights before the KOL tried to co-opt their styles.[7]

Dime novels proliferated after the Civil War. Though some featured labor heroes, most writers cast workers as troublesome strikers, loathsome foreigners, or dangerous anarchists. As one scholar of dime novels notes, the view of labor "did not reflect reality; [it] reflected the fears and prejudices of a middle class confronted by a militant working class."[8] Such fears come through clearly in images of labor leaders, the

---

6. For more on the relationship between working-class and bourgeois culture, see Fink, *Workingmen's Democracy*, esp. chap. 1. Fink dubs working-class appropriation of values traditionally associated with the middle-class "popular gentility." The drive for respectability tempered much Gilded Age radicalism. Another historian who makes effective use of "popular gentility" is Edwin Gabler. See Gabler, *The American Telegrapher: A Social History, 1860–1900* (New Brunswick, N.J.: Rutgers University Press, 1988), 100–105, 125–30.

7. Michael Denning, *Mechanic Accents: Dime Novels and Working-Class Culture in America* (London: Verso, 1987); Fay M. Blake, *The Strike in the American Novel* (Metuchen, N.J.: Scarecrow Press, 1977).

8. Ruth S. Geller, "The American Labor Novel, 1871–1884" (Ph.D. diss., State University of New York, Buffalo, 1980), 2.

vast majority of whom are presented as "walking delegates," a derisive Gilded Age term for demagogic self-seekers who masquerade as working-class champions in order to line their own pockets.[9] Some novels were even more damning. Two of the most virulent antilabor novels were Thomas Bailey Aldrich's The Stillwater Tragedy (1880), and John Hay's The Breadwinners (1884). Aldrich revolves his plot around the dastardly deeds of two murderous immigrant strike leaders; Hay introduces an organizer whose crimes include rape and homicide. Hay detested the labor movement. He counted Jay Cooke and Jay Gould among his inner circle of friends, and married a woman whose father's railroad was struck in 1877.[10]

Bourgeois piety undergirded most dime novels, especially in the Social Darwinian guise popularized by Henry Ward Beecher. Novels like Martin Foran's The Other Side (1886), Abigail Roe's Free, Yet Forging Their Own Chains (1893), and Charles Sheldon's The Crucifixion of Phillip Strong (1894) typified novels of this genre; each even incorporated long sermons and Scripture quotes into their texts.[11] Did workers read such slander? No, they did not. The only antilabor novel to sell well was Hay's The Breadwinners and that was due largely to Hay's political reputation rather than his literary skill. It was the style of dime novels that made them popular, not their content. Most novels ignored workers altogether. The most common plot device involves a pluck-and-luck hero who overcomes long odds, and whose occupation is incidental. Especially successful were Lew Wallace's Ben Hur and Emma Southworth's Self-Raised. Antilabor writings did not go unchallenged however. The Knights of Labor launched a successful boycott that cut into the sales of several of Alan Pinkerton's fanciful works after he called the KOL an "amalgamation of the Molly Maguires and the Paris Commune."[12]

Gilded Age novelists pandered to popular tastes and found lucrative outlets for their fiction in the so-called "story-papers" that proliferated after the Civil War. Weekly papers like Chimney Corner, The Family Story Paper, The Fireside Companion, The New York Ledger, and The New York Weekly offered a diet of stock characters, time-worn plots, melodrama, romance, Victorian morality, and vicarious thrills. Readers faithfully followed the exploits of heroes like Buffalo Bill, Ragged Dick, Nick Carter, the Hindoo Detective, and Scalp King. By 1884, Knights of Labor occa-

---

9. Blake, The Strike in the American Novel, 22–52.
10. Geller, "American Labor Novel"; Blake, The Strike in the American Novel.
11. Blake, The Strike in the American Novel, 22–52.
12. Ibid., 38. Pinkerton's works were technically nonfiction writing, though anyone who has perused his writings realizes that the liberties he takes with historical truth make them de facto works of fiction.

sionally showed up in the pantheon of story-paper characters, and by the mid-1880s, story-papers and KOL journals often featured the same writers.

KOL editors could hardly have ignored the enormous popularity of story-papers. By 1880, Robert Banner's *New York Ledger* had a circulation of over 400,000, though Banner faced competition from four other New York-based papers. Increasing numbers of laborers read such papers. In fact, one scholar claims that workers made up the bulk of story-paper readership by the late 1870s.[13] Even rural readers had light fiction journals; *Farm and Fireside* enjoyed broad appeal into the 1880s.

Given the large number of working-class readers, it made financial sense for story-papers to embrace the KOL once it began to grow in size and power. The *New York Weekly* ran Powderly's picture, endorsed the Order, and launched several stories in which Knights appeared as heroes. In 1886, the paper bragged:

> The *New York Weekly*, nearly two years ago was the first to recognize the importance of the great labor question—the first to foresee the rapid growth of the organization which at this time has its local assemblies in every manufacturing center, working slowly, cautiously, and legitimately under the direction of its able, unswerving, and dispassionate chief [Powderly] with one object in view—to force from niggardly capitalists a fair day's wage for a fair day's work.[14]

Not to be outdone, the *New York Ledger* and the *Family Story Paper* promptly ran KOL stories and endorsements of their own; the latter even ran regular columns of KOL news.

By the mid-1880s, fiction was also a staple of KOL journals. From July through December of 1887, the *JUL* ran twenty-three works of short and

13. Denning, *Mechanic Accents*. Denning argues that the readership of dime novels and story-papers was primarily working class. His evidence is mostly anecdotal, however. Though the large circulation of story-papers and the vast number of dime novels sold suggest a vast working-class readership, the content of both reflects deference to a targeted middle-class clientele. Denning claims that fiction writers adapted their content to attract working-class audiences. I find that argument more convincing. Working-class readers need not have been in a majority to force editorial changes given the highly competitive nature of Gilded Age publishing. I adhere to a mutual feedback theory for Gilded Age fiction, and I am struck by the strong persistence of middle-class values in these works. I also share with Mary Noel the belief that the middle-class core values presented in the works are adaptable to virtually any plot device or context. See Mary Noel, *Villains Galore: The Heyday of the Popular Story Weekly* (New York: Macmillan, 1954).

14. *New York Weekly*, May 15, 1886; November 24, 1884.

long fiction; in 1888, it ran forty-two pieces. Prior to 1886, KOL fiction was rare, and most of it usually consisted of a short object-lesson followed by a serious editorial. The stated reason for the shift was to make the *JUL* a "welcome visitor at the fireside as well as the workshop."[15] But the paper's slavish adoption of story-paper style and conventions suggests that reader preference had more to do with the change in content than the predilections of KOL editors. By the late-1880s, editors needed either to attract readers or shut down the presses. Thus the KOL dedicated itself to the task of diverting dimes from pulp novels and story-papers into the Order's own coffers.

Orphan Sisters: The KOL and Popular Fiction

Victorian heroes and plots were cut mostly from the same cloth, but story details were more varied. When Gilded Age fiction writers used the KOL as a story backdrop, what did they see? Did their take on the Order differ substantially from the way KOL writers saw themselves? Before commenting further on the meaning of the KOL's own fiction, a look at images that appeared outside of KOL journals, which pre-date the KOL's own fictive efforts, is in order. Depictions of the Knights varied according to the publication, the year it appeared, and the individual writer's skill and knowledge of the Order. To illustrate this, I turn to three stories. The first was penned by a pulp writer with little understanding of the Order, the second by a writer who joined the Knights. To this I append later images from a skillful writer, Theodore Dreiser.

The first story-paper to feature KOL characters was the *Family Story Paper*. Editor Norman Munro tested the labor waters previously through such sensational offerings as "Jennie the Bookfolder" and "The Ragpicker's Daughter," stereotypical damsel-in-distress melodramas. In June 1884, Munro gave the go-ahead for Charlotte May Kingsley's "The Orphan Sisters: Daughters of the Knights of Labor."

Kingsley's authorship guaranteed a wide readership as she was one of the Gilded Age's most cherished pulp fiction writers (so much so that her name was credited to stories long after she died). Although Kingsley understood the story-paper genre, her stock-in-trade was formula ro-

---

15. This data comes from my own count. Long, serialized stories were counted as single units of fiction, and were thus given equal statistical weight with short stories. It was not possible for me to count column inches because the *JUL* is available only in microfilm form. Such a task would have little merit in any event, as the *JUL* changed its size and format numerous times between 1880 and 1893; *JUL*, July 9, 1887.

mance and melodrama, not labor. In all likelihood, her knowledge of the KOL was confined to gleanings from newspapers. Not that it mattered very much; beyond inclusion in the title, the Knights play very little role in Kingsley's potboiler of romance, murder, and intrigue.

The "Orphan Sisters" are Flossie and Lillian Marchmont, young women reduced to poverty when their father died and his factory fell into the hands of Magnus Hartwell and Manuel Grasp, who promptly put the Marchmonts out of their home. Their father's spectral image informs the young women that a forged will is the cause of their dismay, and the attempt to find his true last testament is the story's subtext. Romance is provided by Mark Talford, a handsome Knight and the beloved of Lillian; and Vane Charteris, an honest lawyer in love with Flossie. The other major characters are Magnus Hartwell's daughter, Olga, who loves Talford; Judith Bunch, the keeper of a bandit's roost; and Poppie Sarsfield, a street waif forced into petty theft by Bunch.

The KOL appear early in the novel to pick up the cost of Mrs. Marchmont's burial, and to save Lillian's job when Grasp tries to fire her. The KOL then quickly disappears into the background and the melodrama unfolds. Mrs. Kingsley spared nothing in her efforts to build suspense. A complex story unfolds in which Flossie is kidnapped just as she finds her father's real will, and Lillian is stabbed and dumped into the river by a disguised Olga. Her deed is witnessed by the evil Judith Bunch, who forms a pact with Olga and sells her a "Nubian drug" guaranteed to make a "love slave" of Mark Talford. As Flossie languishes in captivity, Hartwell admits to her that he plotted her father's death and he intends to protect himself by marrying her!

At this point in the story the incredible yields to the improbable. Wounded, but not dead, Lillian, is rescued by a fisherman who takes her to the Talford home to recover. Olga feigns concern long enough to enter the home and administer her potion to Mark, who then tells a group of startled Knights that he intends to marry Olga. The Knights retreat in bewilderment. Across the marsh from the Talford residence a failed rescue attempt, a forced marriage, the heroic efforts of Poppie, a gun battle, and figures lost in the fog form the basis of the action.

In good story-paper fashion, everything is rectified at dazzling speed. In a haze of confusion, Flossie actually marries Charteris, not Hartwell (who was mistakenly killed by a drunken guard who thought he was Charteris trying to escape), and the quick-thinking Charteris dons the dead man's clothes in time for the "forced" marriage. Flossie, Charteris, and Poppie rush to Talford's house in time to administer the drug's antidote, and prevent Mark's wedding to Olga. If that were not enough, they are followed by Judith Bunch's son, who recognizes Olga as a woman who married, and then abandoned him while pregnant with their child, Poppie! Olga confesses her crimes, the inheritance is restored, Lillian and Mark marry, and Poppie is adopted by Flossie and Vane.[16]

To follow the labyrinthine details of "Orphan Sisters" requires a more careful reading of the story than it deserves. It is fair, however, to ask where the Knights of Labor in Kingsley's story come in. Their early appearance aside, there are brief mentions of "secret meetings," several casual references, and a character who pronounces, "The day for capital to rule the world has passed . . . the poor have rights as well as the rich, and by union we assert them." Beyond this, one searches in vain for references to the KOL.

"Orphan Sisters" is hardly a piece of labor propaganda. Mark Talford is an oddly impotent hero; the true man of action is lawyer Vane Charteris. Talford could have been a cowboy or a shopkeeper for all the more his KOL affiliation mattered to the narrative. There is no overt challenge to existing capital/labor relations; in fact, there is no discussion of it. There was very little in Mrs. Kingsley's story that would upset middle-class readers, and even less to cheer those from the laboring classes.

Much of this can be overlooked since Kingsley was not a Knight. Did it make a difference if the novelist was an insider? If John Erigena Barrett's "A Knight of Labor, the Master Workman's Vow" is any indication, story-paper demands reigned supreme. Barrett's serialized novel, though demonstrating an insider's knowledge of the Knights, was every bit as formulaic and safe as Kingsley's story. It appeared in the *New York Weekly* from December 1, 1884, through February 16, 1885.

"A Knight of Labor" is set in Throckton, a steel town whose mills are owned by Alfred Brandon, whose feckless son Basil is in love with Ruth Watkins, the daughter of Reese Watkins, the Master Workman of a KOL local. Other key characters include KOL activist Tom Wilbur, who also pines for Ruth Watkins; arsonist/anarchist Jack Dabble; and Zeb Grinnell, a thug posing as a hotel bellhop. As in "The Orphan Sisters" much of the action of Barrett's story takes place in a bandit's roost, and key events are witnessed by a street orphan—in this case, newsboy Sam Lambert.

The novel opens with the flight of Basil and Ruth to New York to elope. Sam overhears their plan and reports it to Reese Watkins who exclaims, "By the eternal, if Basil Brandon has disgraced her, he shall die!" Unfortunately, that outburst is overheard by Jack Dabble. The elopement goes awry when Zeb Grinnell breaks into Basil's room to rob

16. *Family Story Paper* (New York), June 9–September 22, 1884.

him, clubs him, and throws his body out the window. Grinnell collects the corpse from the street below, and abandons it at a hospital far from the scene of the crime.

Back in Throckton, the Knights of Labor meet to discuss the expulsion of Jack Dabble. Tom Wilbur denounces him as "an extremist of the most pronounced pattern . . . as much at variance with the principles of the Order as is possible to be. He is an ardent admirer of the theories of Herr Most." A few days later, Dabble sets the KOL hall afire after knocking the peeping Sam Lambert (Fig. 10) unconscious. Sam is rescued by Reese just as the building collapses.

Dabble's ultimate revenge is afforded by the discovery of a mangled body identified as that of Basil Brandon. Dabble informs Alfred Brandon of Watkins's threat, and Reese is soon arrested, charged with murder, and imprisoned. As his fellow Knights meet to vote on Reese's expulsion, he makes a surprise visit. He explains to the startled assemblage:

"YOU WILL KILL ME BEFORE YOU TOUCH THE LAD."

Fig. 10. Scenes from John Erigena Barrett's novel, *A Knight of Labor, the Master Workman's Vow,* serialized in the *New York Weekly.* Pulp fiction of this sort probably did little to aid the KOL in its efforts to transform American society.

> I have pledged my honor to a man who is bound to all of us by
> the golden link of brotherhood, that within the hour I will return
> to my cell. . . . Knowing that you were in session tonight I longed
> to tell you that I am innocent of the great crime of which I am
> accused. I was vain enough to think that if I told you this, there
> would not be a man in this assembly who would doubt my word.

The Knights unanimously pledge their support, and Reese returns to jail
in time to find it too has been set afire by Jack Dabble. In an especially
ludicrous scene, Watkins and Tom Wilbur help the warden guard pris-
oners until assistance arrives.

Ruth Watkins is unaware of her father's fate. Assuming herself jilted,
she tries to find work in the city rather than return home dishonored.
She passes from one peril to the next, including a narrow escape from a
den of thieves run by Grinnell's mother, before she is located by Sam
Lambert, who convinces her to return to Throckton. In a classic Victorian scene, Ruth visits her imprisoned father, begs his forgiveness, and
insists on her purity, only to have him proclaim her "dead" and order
her from his sight.

Once again, we are treated to a *deus ex machina* ending. Ruth's honor
is restored by Basil himself. He recovered from near mortal injuries; the
body identified from the clothing and pocket watch was, in fact, that of
Zeb Grinnell, who was mangled by a freight train he had unsuccessfully
tried to hop. Ruth and Basil were duly married, Reese Watkins released,
Jack Dabble's crimes exposed, and Sam Lambert rewarded with a job in
the steel mills.

How does Barrett's story compare with Kingsley's? First, we have a
romanticized view of the working class. All workers speak impeccably
correct English, and their content is suffused with Victorian morality
even when challenging class hierarchy. When Tom Wilbur hears of
Ruth's flight to New York with Basil, he proclaims, "Let there be full
justice, and let us teach those ruffianly aristocrats who are not content
with squeezing out our life-blood on low wages, but also want to invade
the sanctity of our home and sacrifice the purity of our daughters, that
there is a God in Israel, and that they are not beyond his law." Later,
Reese refuses to consider his daughter's pleas; the very thought of scandal is too threatening to his worldview.

Nonetheless, Barrett's Knights are honest, forthright, and manly.
When Reese is grilled by lawyer Adam Pincher, he loudly protests unfair
insinuations, and dresses down the judge who tries to silence him.
When Pincher announces he will prove Watkins threatened Basil's life,
Reese shouts out, "I have sworn that . . . in the presence of this court

and the father of my daughter's betrayer. You needn't call [anyone] . . . to prove that I'm a man!" Throughout the trial, the forthright Reese Watkins is contrasted with the shifty lawyer Adam Pincher, who tries to twist words but cannot prevail in the face of men who mean what they say.[17]

Barrett also presents the Knights as an alternative between unrestrained capitalism on the one hand, and anarchism on the other. Before the story opened in November 1884, the *New York Weekly* ran Powderly's picture and several articles on him that praised him for his temperance and his attacks on anarchism.[18] Knights are portrayed as holders of true republican virtue, honest men whose toil creates all wealth, and who resent special privilege because it is unjust. They are also more moral than their bourgeois detractors, and serve as role models. At the story's end, a chastened Alfred Brandon rescinds wage cuts that precipitated a strike, and invites the Knights of Labor to co-manage the mills.

The novel's gender images proceed from Victorian patriarchal constructions in which women were viewed as male property. Ruth's "sin" was not sexual, rather it lay in her disobedience to her father. There are no positive female characters in the story; women are either helpless victims awaiting rescue like Ruth, or weeping, ineffectual ornaments like her mother. The one independent woman is "Mother" Grinnell, and she is represented as an agent of Satan.

The novel's pervasive sexism is overwhelmed by its naivete. Problems are resolved in face-to-face encounters more reminiscent of colonial proprietorship than Gilded Age industrial capitalist patterns. Alfred Brandon's transformation had few real-life manifestations. Men like Jay Gould responded to counterpressure, not moral revelation. Politics and ideology had no place in Barrett's novel either. The only theorist is the anarchist Dabble. Barrett would have us believe that moral reasoning leads inexorably to republican notions of justice and equal opportunity. Bound by Victorian fetters, Barrett saw corrupt individuals, not flawed systems. In the end, Barrett presented the details of the KOL, but not the implications of the Order's principles and goals. The latter proved too threatening for story-papers. In sum, Barrett's story closely resembles offerings by outsiders like Kingsley or Laura Jean Libbey.[19]

17. *New York Weekly*, December 1, 1884–February 16, 1885.
18. *New York Weekly*, November 24, 1884; reprinted May 15, 1886.
19. Libbey wrote "Ionie, the Pride of the Mill: Daughter of a Knight of Labor" for the *New York Ledger*. It was one of the last story-paper offerings featuring the KOL. After the Great Upheaval, most bourgeois-controlled papers found insurgent labor too threatening. *New York Ledger*, December 3, 1887–? (issues of the *Ledger* from January 28–October 20, 1888, are missing).

For a realistic fictional portrayal of the battle between the Knights and capital, one must look outside of the story-papers. One hard-hitting look came from Theodore Dreiser in *Sister Carrie*. The novel was not published until 1900, but its setting is 1889 through 1897. The Knights of Labor appear in a New York City street car strike in which one of Dreiser's protagonists, George Hurstwood, participates as a scab driver. The one-time Chicago banker is on the lam because of embezzlement and a bigamous marriage to Carrie. Hurstwood has been reduced to poverty and is one step from his ultimate fate as a skid row drunkard.

The strike that Dreiser highlights is one that likely convulsed New York and Brooklyn in 1895, a time when the KOL was greatly reduced in strength. In addition to issues involving wages and hours, workers struck to protest the "tripper" system in which operators were paid by the run, not the day. It was common practice to keep numerous operators sitting idly in train sheds—in effect, putting the men on call all day, but only paying them for several hours. The strike involving over six thousand trainmen from several unions eventually failed, and KOL 75 dissolved in its wake.

Dreiser's look at Gilded Age capital/labor relations contains little romanticism. Gone are the misguided proprietors awaiting enlightenment; the capitalists who own the trolley system are depicted as brutal and callous individuals willing to do anything to break the strike, even luring dupes like Hurstwood into employment through promises of protection and high pay. Hurstwood soon found that he had to lodge in the train sheds because to venture out would imperil him.

Likewise, the Knights he encounters are angry, not well-mannered, well-spoken, or chivalrous. Hurstwood's trolley was pelted with rocks, missiles, and slanderous insults. After four days of such treatment, Hurstwood confronts the Knights directly when track obstructions force him to stop his car. Strikers approach Hurstwood and ask him to quit work; when he pleads poverty, they stone him, pull him from the trolley, beat him, and shoot him in the shoulder. (Hurstwood quits, and slips away in defeat.)

At this point, strikes and the KOL disappear from Dreiser's novel. But his is a quite different view from that of Kingsley or Barrett. Rather than speak politely, Dreiser's Knights call opponents "scab," "thief," "coward," and "sucker." Instead of purging themselves of Jack Dabbles, angry Knights pull up tracks and set trains and buildings on fire. And far from the middle-class fantasies in which good ultimately triumphs, Dreiser sees "labor's little war" as a lost struggle.[20]

20. Theodore Dreiser, *Sister Carrie* (Cambridge, Mass.: Riverside Press, 1959); The Knights of Labor appear in chapters 40 and 41.

Although Dreiser wrote while the KOL was in decline, and years after the events he described, his is a more accurate portrayal of Gilded Age reality. Dreiser was a masterful literary figure, but his imagery has more to do with the medium than the skill of the writer. Dreiser lacked the sentimentality of Victorian dime novelists or story-paper writers, and avoided their conventions by placing himself outside those systems, a choice for which he paid dearly. *Sister Carrie* was pulled from publication because of its scandalous sexual arrangements, its frank discussions of social reality, and its failure to resolve difficult issues within the parameters of bourgeois convention. It was not until 1910 that Doubleday reissued the novel.[21]

Workers devoured dime novels and story-papers, and each medium made concessions to attract working-class readers, but there were lines that would not be crossed. Bourgeois culture was hegemonic, and its values normative, so much so that story-paper workers espoused them. Working-class heroes had two functions, to save other workers from anarchists and socialists, and to rescue middle-class backsliders from themselves. If anarchists threatened middle-class hegemony from one pole, pompous aristocrats, idlers, dandies, and cheats lurked behind the opposite. Heroism came from restoring the balance.[22] Suspending one's moral judgement, as Dreiser did, placed one beyond the pale, and relegated the novelist's work to obscurity. As we shall soon see, far too many KOL novelists opted for the safe road rather than the one studded with peril.

Home-Grown Short Stories

We would expect popular fiction neither to promote the KOL's agenda nor to reflect the Order's critique of Victorian society. It is a measure of KOL's success that the Victorian press bothered to trifle with it, and the very idea of KOL heroes must have been a stretch for some middle-class minds. But surely one would expect better from organic fiction. As Little's "Lever and Throttle" suggests, however, that expectation is quite often misplaced. The Order's own short fiction affords a deeper analysis of the ways in which the KOL often sent unclear messages about mainstream culture.

21. For more on the controversy, see George Simpson's introduction to *Sister Carrie*.

22. In this assessment I part with Michael Denning who sees more working-class shaping of popular fiction than I. See note 13 above.

KOL journals published scores of stories, usually containing a moral, that varied in length from a few paragraphs to a full page. The bulk of them tended to reinforce Barrett's optimistic belief that the bourgeoisie could be enlightened. Revelation often comes through a deserved come-uppance. "Mary's Quinces," for example, lampoons bourgeois preten-sion. In this tale of rural jealousy, the social climber Mrs. Biggard is brought to earth by the humble Mary Hay. Biggard enjoyed bragging of her church contributions until it is revealed that some of these came from the sale of fruit stolen from Mary's trees. Mary's simple virtue is rewarded when she marries the village's most eligible bachelor, the lo-cal preacher.[23]

Mary's marriage affords her a comfortable middle-class life. By con-trast, a middle-class idler rediscovers his nobility by renouncing comfort in "A Romance of Labor." The protagonist is Steve Gaskell, a restless working-class lad who longs to become a lawyer and flee his humble roots. He squanders an inheritance, but nonetheless marries the wealthy, domineering Elizabeth Braithwaite and enters his father-in-law's business firm. Lingering discontent boils over when he encounters a worker from his late father's shop. On impulse, Steve goes to the works, where he "looked upon the craftsmen with their bare, brawny arms and blackened hands, and felt his heart glow with admiration." Gaskell chucks his job, leaves home, and apprentices himself in the loco-motive shop. After two years of honest toil, he finally finds peace. Eliza-beth visits to find that "swarthy, bare-armed [and] clothed in leather, he never looked so handsome in [her] eyes." Reconciled, the two live hap-pily ever after.[24]

Steve Gaskell's return to working-class simplicity is rare in KOL fic-tion. More commonly, middle-class characters learn their lessons and resolve to live a truly Christian life in which they will use their fortunes well. Typical of such stories is "Paul Garwin's Christmas Eve," an obvi-ous reworking of Dickens's A Christmas Carol. Businessman George Gar-win learns humility from his fifteen-year-old son, Paul. On the night before Christmas young Paul befriends a poor family—complete with a Tiny Tim-like sickly child—headed by an overworked, underpaid em-ployee of his father. Paul uses money given to him by his father to help the Warsons have a joyous holiday. When George Garwin learns of his son's goodness he is chastened and resolves to treat his employees with more charity.[25]

23. JUL, November 5, 1887.
24. Ibid., June 1881.
25. Ibid., November 1881; December 1881.

Morality extended to personal behavior as well. In "A Story With a Moral," a rich philanderer commissions a street vendor to send flowers to his mistress. When the seller loses the address, he dutifully locates the gentleman's address, assumes that the flowers are for his wife, and delivers the bouquet to her. The mistake has a salutary effect as the next day the man and his wife walk arm-in-arm past the flower stand. As they pass by, the reformed philanderer hands the vendor money, winks, and says, "Johnny bring her as big a bouquet every week and save one big scarlet rose for me."[26]

Belief in the ability to change hearts and minds was so strong that some conversions make Barrett's bourgeois characters seem hard-boiled in contrast. In "The Shopkeeper and the Cooperator," grocer Johnson encounters an ex-customer named Jim. Johnson wants to know why Jim no longer buys goods in his store, and is informed that Jim only buys cooperative goods. After a heated exchange and an impassioned speech on the virtues of cooperation, Johnson is convinced. He thanks Jim for having shown him "how to work for all humanity," and promptly turns his shop into a cooperative enterprise.[27]

The above stories blur class lines so thoroughly that one wonders what unreflective readers concluded from them. This opened the possibility that fiction could unwittingly reinforce bourgeois values. Story-paper offerings often resolved problems through windfall fortune. The same happens in "The Model Millionaire" in which a character's kindness to a rich man posing as a beggar brings him the money needed to get married.[28] Dreams of quick fortune hardly reinforced the stated ideology of "by the sweat of thy face thou shalt eat bread" found in the Order's Preamble. Likewise, gender constructions found in KOL fiction owe more to Victorian influences than to the platform's pledge to work for equality.

Typical of such offerings is "One July Afternoon," a reprint that tellingly first appeared in *Farm and Fireside*. The simple plot involves a callous husband, Will Harris, who has neglected his hard-working, faithful wife, Molly. While in town buying supplies, Will berates Molly for wanting to buy calico for a new dress. Later, he overhears some men speaking of his cruelty and remarking on how beautiful Molly once was. In a repentant moment, Will buys the calico. When Molly dons her new

---

26. Ibid., May 1881.

27. Ibid., May 25, 1885. For another story concerning the merits of cooperatives, see "Every Man His Own Landlord" in the *JUL* from May 25–June 25, 1886.

28. *JUL*, July 30, 1887. This story was reprinted from *The London World*, a paper that shared many similarities with American story-papers.

dress, her radiance and the stagnant marriage are magically transformed.[29]

"One July Afternoon" is merely a rural version of "A Story With a
Moral." It could be dismissed as fluff were not its Victorian domesticity
so often reinforced in KOL journals. Just as Leonora Barry struggled to
define the place of women in the KOL bureaucracy, so too female readers must have been confused to read Barry's columns in one issue, and
household hints in another. Take for instance, a *JUL* column entitled
"Advice to the Engaged" that appeared the year after the Order voted
to allow women to join. Men were told not to squander money in bars,
and to cultivate good manners. By contrast, engaged women were told
to give up dreams of finery and dancing, to cultivate morals in the home,
and to abandon the idea that marriage would be liberating: "If you contemplate taking a husband in order to gain greater freedom, don't be
surprised if he should profit by your example." There was even a veiled
admonition they should be prepared to perform sexually: "If you have
an idea that a cook book and an allowance can make a happy home,
you should get yourself to a nunnery with all convenient speed."[30] Such
sentiments evoke the widely held Victorian notion that men were sexual
animals consumed by passions women lacked, and that it was a woman's job to temper men with morality.

Time did little to temper Victorian stereotypes. By the end of the
1880s, KOL papers like Baltimore's *The Critic* routinely offered women
advice on how to walk gracefully, how to prepare for weddings, and
how to copy the latest fashions cheaply. *The Critic* even printed fluff like
"The Kiss a Girl Likes," in which men were informed that women did
not like rough kisses, or breath reeking of tobacco and alcohol.[31] If one
combines information like this with the sentimental poetry one finds in
KOL journals, it becomes easier to understand the gender schizophrenia
within the Order.

Another issue that raises the question of Victorian penetration into
the Knights is temperance. It is true that founder Uriah Stephens was a
teetotaler, and that the organization forbade liquor tradesmen from its
ranks, but the 1880s saw moral suasion beget dogmatism. Powderly even
announced, "No person can be a member of the Order whose wife sells
liquor. He *must* either obtain a divorce from his wife or from this organization."[32] At the 1882 Grand Assembly, Powderly announced, "No

29. *JUL*, August 13, 1887.
30. Ibid., May 19, 1882.
31. *The Critic*, May 23, 1889.
32. Powderly, *Thirty Years of Labor*, 306.

workingman ever drank a glass of rum who did not rob his wife and children of the price of it, and in doing so committed a double crime— murder and theft."[33]

Under Powderly's leadership, fiction became a tool in his personal crusade against liquor. "Hard Times, Trade Unions and Whiskey" tells of a worker who pleads he cannot afford the 50-cent dues of his union, yet promptly expends that amount in five minutes at a bar.[34] Even more explicit is "A Grecian Legend," in which a boy inserts a plant inside a bird skeleton, then into a lion's bones, and finally, into a donkey jaw- bone. As the plant grows, it intertwines with the bones until they are one unit. The boy plants the assemblage in the ground, and from it a vine grows from which grapes are eventually harvested, pressed, and turned into wine. The story's moral? "When men drink it, they first sing like birds; next, after a little more, they become vigorous and gallant like lions; but when they drank still more, they began to behave like asses."[35]

Powderly usually followed temperance items with an editorial. The praise he received from inside and outside the Order only encouraged him. By 1887, Powderly was fanatic about the subject and unleased a torrent that was too much for some Knights:

> Ten years ago I was hissed because I advised men to let strong drink alone. They threatened to rotten egg me. I have continued to advise men to be temperate, and though I have had no experi- ence that would qualify men to render an opinion on the efficacy of a rotten egg as an ally of the rum drinker, yet I would prefer to have my exterior decorated from summit to base with the rankest kind of rotten eggs rather than allow one drop of liquid villainy to pass my lips, or have the end of my nose illumined by the blossom that follows a planting of the seeds of hatred, envy, mal- ice, and damnation, all of which are represented in a solitary glass of gin.[36]

Powderly told John Hayes how pleased he was with himself,[37] but Knights like Joseph Buchanan, himself a temperance advocate, grew tired of such moralizing and concluded too much time was wasted in trying to please Victorian moralists instead of doing battle against them.

33. Powderly, *Thirty Years of Labor*, 307; *JUL*, May 15, 1883; *JUL*, May 1883; June 1883; July 1883; June 15, 1884.
34. *JUL*, November 1880.
35. Ibid., October 1880.
36. Powderly, *Thirty Years of Labor*, 315.
37. Powderly to John Hayes, June 22, 1887, in *PP*.

In an editorial for the *New York Daily Leader* that Buchanan reprinted in Chicago's *Labor Enquirer*, New York's L. J. Palda agreed. Palda skewered Powderly for thinking that temperance alone would give the Knights the money and power to defeat organized capital. He turned to the economic argument put forth in Powderly editorials and short stories like "Hard Times" that money saved from drink could fund unions. Palda sarcastically noted that the same argument could be made about giving up tea, coffee, canned fruits, or beefsteak, and continued:

> The Chinese live very cheap on rice. Let us live on corn for a few years and be saved from the oppression and tyranny of monopolies. . . . Do you, my esteemed sir [Powderly], really believe . . . [that] under our present industrial system—the wage system— everything will be saved by workingmen will come to the benefit of workingmen?

He accused Powderly of living in the "world for which all labor reformers are longing, seeking [and] struggling, [but not] the actual world, with all its oppressions, tyrannies, follies, wrongs, and vices." He even took Powderly to task for threatening the livelihood of thousands of brewery workers.[38]

Palda and Buchanan represented Knights who thought the Order was making too many concessions to middle-class values. They are typical of "kickers" inside the KOL who hoped to force the organization into a more confrontational stance vis-à-vis Gilded Age society. Though not as numerous as the accomodationists, some "kickers" put their protests into fictional form. The naive belief that arbitration could mediate all disputes was lampooned in "Scene in a Criminal Court," and a veiled assault on secrecy fanatics was taken to task in "O.M.S.S. [Old Maid's Secret Society]."[39] Perhaps the best short story from the pen of a kicker was Lizzie Swank's "Society's Child."

Swank was the maiden and pen name of Lizzie Holmes, wife of anarchist William Holmes, and a fiery figure in her own right. Swank put the pathos of story-paper fiction into a journalistic voice to give her story a documentary feel. The piece follows the plight of Mary Conner, a poor girl forced to take up the dressmaker's trade at age ten. When she was thirteen, her proprietress moved to Chicago. Mary followed, but her meager salary was inadequate for the big city, even though she shared a room and subsisted on a daily meal of crackers and oatmeal. Eventually,

38. *Labor Enquirer* (Chicago), August 13, 1887.
39. *JUL*, February 5, 1887; July 30, 1887.

the scrappy Mary worked her way up the wage scale and could afford a few luxuries.

At the point where most Gilded Age stories waxed rhapsodic about diligence and pluck, Swank was just beginning. Mary fell ill and her employer dismissed her in the midst of a depression. After exhausting her savings, Mary went into domestic service, where she encountered bourgeois snobbery, overwork, and harsh treatment. When one employer tried to cheat her out of wages, she stole pillow cases in retaliation. May was caught, however, and sent to jail. While imprisoned, she met a professional shoplifter who showed her the ropes.

There is no neat ending for Mary Conner. She became a professional thief and is jailed three more times before she landed in Joliet penitentiary. But Mary was unrepentant and resigned to an existence that would be "flush" on some occasions, and "penniless" on others.[40] There were no fortuitous marriages, secret inheritances, or Victorian hearths looming in Mary's future.

Knights of Labor short fiction, at best, sent mixed messages to its readership. At worst, it mirrored middle-class value systems it ought to have confronted. An acceptance of the mutuality of capital/labor interests, an undercurrent of genteel pretensions, and a nod to Victorian morality undergirds much KOL short fiction. To be certain, much of this tapped into a deep spring of working-class respectability that valued temperance, polite speech, and personal morality on working-class terms, but it meshed too neatly with bourgeois story-paper morality for the two to not reinforce one another. Rare indeed were the hints of defiance and struggle that Dreiser documented, or the bitter despair captured by Lizzie Swank. KOL short fiction abounds with middle-class dreams come true like that in "Mary's Quinces," but mostly avoids the tragic implications of "Society's Child."

From Sealskin to Shoddy: Serialized Fiction

Short stories can mislead through morals that may reflect transitory concerns. In addition, much must be left unsaid in a short piece. Before concluding that KOL fiction conformed too closely to hegemonic values and styles, a look at longer works where one would most expect to find

40. *Labor Enquirer* (Chicago), March 26, 1887. For more on the career of Lizzie Holmes (AKA "Lizzie Swank"), see Paul Avrich, *The Haymarket Tragedy* (Princeton: Princeton University Press, 1984).

explicit descriptions of KOL ideals, ideology, and practices is in order. Was W. H. Little's "Lever and Throttle" typical of KOL fictional offerings? If full-length KOL stories conformed to the same desultory patterns as its short fiction, it must be said that the KOL contained factions whose vision of society was tainted by bourgeois Victorian sentiment. In truth, a case can be made for such an interpretation. Full-length fiction also offers more evidence of the gaps between official KOL policy and actual practice.

Two KOL novels are reprinted in Mary C. Grimes's *The Knights in Fiction.*[41] The first, *Larry Locke, Man of Iron,* is a bit of a problem, however, because its author, Frederick Whittaker, was not a Knight but a professional writer whose work often appeared in story-papers.

Larry Locke never appeared in a KOL journal; it was serialized in *Beadle's Weekly* from October 27, 1883 through January 12, 1884. Its pluck-and-luck story of a diminutive Hercules who overcomes adversity, dishonesty, and deceit has about as much to do with the KOL as Kingsley's "The Orphan Sisters." The character of Locke is not, as one commentator suggests, a "hero of mutualism and solidarity" so much as a compilation of three familiar folk motifs: the trickster, the clever person, and the strong hero.[42] Furthermore, behind Larry's rough exterior and coarse manners lies a middle-class values system based on party politics, property ownership, temperance, thrift, and patriarchal family relationships. Neither this nor Whittaker's other "Knights of Labor" novel, *Job Manly's Rise in Life,* is really about the KOL. Like many middle-class writers, Haymarket proved too much for his sensibilities; he stopped using labor protagonists and switched to cowboys.

More useful is the second novel, *Breaking the Chains: A Story of the Present Industrial Struggle.* Written by T. Fulton Gantt, it was serialized in a

41. Mary C. Grimes, *The Knights in Fiction: Two Labor Novels of the 1880s* (Urbana: University of Illinois, 1886). "Larry Locke, Man of Iron" appears on 137–326. Another interesting offering from Frederick Whittaker, author of "Larry Locke," is "A Knight of Labor, Job Manly's Rise in Life: The Story of a Young Man From the Country," which was serialized in *Beadle's Weekly* from April 12–June 28, 1884. Neither Grimes, nor David Montgomery, who penned the introduction to the Grimes work, attach much importance to Whittaker's lack of KOL credentials. This is, in my estimation, an oversight on their part.

42. Denning, *Mechanic Accents,* 179. Motifs found in folk literature, ballads, myths, fabliaux, and legends have been compiled in several indices, the most famous being that of Stith Thompson, whose six-volume *Motif-Index of Folk Literature* (Bloomington: Indiana University Press, 1955) is one of folklore's standard reference works. Thompson assigned numbers to various motifs and subnumbers to variants. Among the Thompson motifs relating to Larry Locke as trickster are: Trickster as culture hero, #A521; Trickster feigning death, #K1867.1; Trickster outwits rival (a king), #J1593. Clever retorts make up a subcategory in the Clever Persons motif. See #J1250–J1449; #X940; #F552.2; #H345.1; #F451.38.

Salem, Oregon, labor paper, *The Lance*, in 1887. Gantt worked as a clerk, telegrapher, blacksmith, and machinist before joining his father's North Platte, Nebraska, law firm in 1867. In 1878, he moved to Washington, D.C., where he joined a KOL local and worked as a government clerk. In 1888, he returned to North Platte and joined KOL Local 3343, although he had resumed his law career and should have been ineligible to join the Order.[43]

As an insider, Gantt was more successful than Whittaker in showing the inner workings of the Knights of Labor. His characters, though stiff and formulaic, were more realistic than the semi-mythic Larry Locke. The hero *of Breaking the Chains* is Harry Wallace, a highly cultured KOL plumber with a passion for opera and theater who is also in love with Maud Simpson, the daughter of a deceased KOL plasterer. Maud is inquisitive, intelligent, and a bold advocate of women's suffrage and the labor movement. The villains include Captain Barnum, a landlord, speculator, and opium addict; Peleg Grinder, the rabidly anti-union publisher of *The Atavist*; and General Bluster, a hot-air politician who patronizes working men to win their votes.

The plot is tedious and predictable. Harry and Maud find love against a backdrop of labor strife, land swindles, political double-crosses, and an attempted seduction by Barnum. Aid is given by a kindly lawyer, Abner Strong; by Gertie, Barnum's twelve-year-old niece whom he has mistreated; and by the Knights of Labor. In the end, all the villains get their just deserts: Barnum marries a cold-hearted heiress who dies from an opium overdose administered by the family's drug-dealing Chinese housekeeper, Grinder is broken by a KOL boycott, and Bluster is exposed as corrupt.

More interesting are Gantt's subplots involving the KOL. The novel opens with a Knight explaining the KOL's history, which involves long discourses on arbitration, boycotts, cooperation, education, and secrecy. Gantt also takes us inside both a local and a district assembly. The local was a lively mixed assembly where Knights discussed the burning issues of the day. On Sundays, the hall became a public debate chamber open to all except, "rum sellers, gamblers, and like objectionable characters." Gantt gives full accounts of the functions of the district assembly, its executive board, and several committees.

Though romanticized, Gantt's Knights have more personality than the interchangeable characters of story-paper fiction. Men and women take command of their lives rather than waiting for fate to intervene. Harry and Maud attend the theater, go to debates, and devour political and

---

43. Grimes, *The Knights in Fiction;* see Introduction for information on T. Fulton Gantt.

literary works. They hold their own in discourse with alleged social superiors. Maud reduces General Bluster to his namesake in an exchange over political economy, and overwhelms him with quotes from Thomas Carlyle, Christ, Benjamin Franklin, Henry George, the KOL platform, Frederic Lassalle, Thomas Malthus, David Ricardo, Herbert Spencer, and Adam Smith. When Bluster sputters that her views are socialistic, Maud counters with a lecture on true socialism.

After his verbal pummeling, Bluster retreats to a bar to "liquor up" with Grinder and rail against the "socialist heresy" that made his humiliation possible: the public school system. Bluster concedes that Maud was better read than he, and that he would be forced to support bills establishing an eight-hour work day and a bureau of labor statistics in order to keep his job. (He quickly assures Grinder that such measures could be easily circumvented.) Both men soon discover that they are no match for the KOL.

Maud embodies the ideals of KOL solidarity and it is she who most often articulates them. She warns Bluster against "savage individualism," and proclaims: "The command of Christ to 'love they neighbor as thyself' has, by the aid of theologians, become a mere abstraction, but the battle cry of the Knights of Labor is concretion itself—a solidarity, an irresistible combination to conquer and obliterate all forms of oppression." In a reflective moment with Harry she muses, "The Knights have learned that they are powerless to accomplish anything individually, and so labor for their whole class. It is the correct idea—solidarity." Even the KOL's enemies are chastened. After a boycott nearly ruins Grinder he admits, "As long as labor was unorganized it was possible to teach the sophistry that the interests of master and servant were identical. Now, however, we have succeeded in driving them into a solidarity that will force a division of the profits." Reluctantly, Grinder allows the KOL to organize his press as a pro-labor paper.

Breaking the Chains was a powerful propaganda piece for the Knights, and it contained one of the stronger female characters of Gilded Age fiction. There were, however, paradoxes. Images of working-class life are too respectable to be believable; all Knights are cultured, family-centered, honest, religious, thrifty, educated, and articulate. Their response to every evil deed is cool, logical, and measured. The villains, by contrast, are so corrupt that they are stupid. Barnum is a drug-addicted, agnostic masher; Grinder is a pig-headed alcoholic; and Bluster a loose-lipped drunken spendthrift. Missing from Gantt's novel are workers with less-than-perfect English, the degraded poor, angry workers, or those unconvinced by KOL appeals to solidarity. Missing also are calculating capitalists with well-reasoned plans to counter labor. Gantt's caricatures tinge the book in utopian sentimentality. Some also succumb to Victorian sentimentality. The central love story differs little from story-paper romances, and the Scripture-quoting Gertie bears an uncanny resemblance to Little Eva in *Uncle Tom's Cabin*.[44]

There is also the paradox of lawyer Abner Strong, likely a depiction of Gantt himself. Absent in Gantt's list of "objectionable characters" were attorneys, an oversight in direct conflict with KOL official directives. Other stories—"The Orphan Sisters" and "A Daughter of the Knights of Labor"—featured heroic lawyers, but their authors were not Knights. Gantt was doubtless making a plea to reconsider the rule that, if enforced, would push him from the Order.

The ban was as troublesome in practice as it was on the pages of KOL fiction. Despite the prohibition, Gantt was not the only lawyer Knight. In 1886, James Sovereign, the man destined to replace Powderly as General Master Workman, was nearly expelled from the Order over a controversy in Iowa. Sovereign organized a Clinton local that admitted a lawyer. When Powderly heard of this he told Sovereign to "return your commission and organizer's supplies. . . . If you have anything to say why your commission should not be revoked let me hear from you as soon as possible."[45]

Sovereign claimed to know nothing of the event, though he did offer the opinion that lawyer Arnold Walliker deserved to be a Knight for his "record on our side that dated back to his boyhood days." A subsequent investigation revealed that Clinton Knights initiated Walliker without Sovereign's knowledge.[46] Within days, Powderly heard from Walliker himself who argued, "[My] efforts in the cause of labor has almost driven me from my profession and my real living and support is derived from my labor as assistant boom keeper to the Germania Building Association." He gallantly offered to step down "if you think our cause can be better promoted with me out than in." The matter was quietly dropped when Powderly was informed that Walliker was acclaimed by five hundred local Knights who supported his candidacy for mayor of Clinton.[47]

44. "Breaking the Chains, A Story of the Present Industrial Struggle" is found in Grimes, *The Knights in Fiction*, 29–133. All quotes from "Breaking the Chains" are from Grimes as cited above. In addition to Gantt's story, another serial that takes the reader inside KOL assemblies is "The Nights of Laber [sic]," a periodic column that appeared in *John Swinton's Paper* in 1885–86. See esp. February 22, 1885; March 22, 1885; April 4, 1885; March 14, 1886.

45. Powderly to James R. Sovereign, February 17, 1886, in *PP*.

46. Sovereign to Powderly, March 2, 1886, in *PP*.

47. Arnold Walliker to Powderly, March 11, 1886, in *PP*; W. J. Wright to Powderly, April 19, 1886, in *PP*.

In 1887, the cases of Walliker and Gantt were joined by that of George Walthew in Michigan. Walthew began his career as a painter, and became recording secretary for a KOL local. He maintained his KOL ties even after he was admitted to the bar. In 1885, he ran for the state legislature on the Independent Labor Party ticket. Although Walthew lost, he turned his legal skills to the cause of labor and defended many Knights. By 1887, Michigan Knights were so enamored of Walthew that *The Advance and Labor Leaf* ran a feature on him.[48]

Breaking the Chains highlights the gap between rhetoric and practice in the KOL. It is also sanguine regarding the possibility of reforming individual capitalists and the establishments they command. In that regard, the novel parallels the reformist spirit of the Powderly wing of the Knights, the declining influence of radicalism after Haymarket, and the subsequent purges within the KOL.

Gantt's novel reflects a lawyer's sensibility toward reform that was not shared by the novelist who penned "The Autobiography of Ferret Snap," a work serialized in the *JUL* two years earlier.[49] Readers of this series were treated to bitter denunciations of the banking, credit, and stock systems, as well as the men who controlled them. Ferret Snap is corrupt, and a "decided enemy to hard work." He begins his nefarious rise by running flim-flam schemes on unsuspecting farmers before moving into a brokerage firm specializing in off-the-books speculation in gambling houses, loan sharking, and race horses. Snap's big break comes on a railroad swindle that ruins his benefactor, the descriptions of which parallel Andrew Carnegie's Keystone Telegraph scheme.[50]

No deed is too dastardly for Snap. He contracts a loveless marriage to a bank president's daughter, floats worthless bonds, uses non-existent assets to speculate on Western lands, and courts working-class votes in order to get elected to the state legislature, where he promptly represents banking interests. Soon, Snap is "rolling in wealth, the idol of brokers; the oracle of financiers, the controller of the stock market; the envy of all that miserable race which lives on property and labor."

Snap's downfall is administered by "big-pawed farmers and . . . hardworking mechanics and laborers" whose attack on the credit system and support for free silver causes his paper empire to crumble. But unlike the characters in Gantt's novel, Ferret Snap is not redeemed. At his bank retirement dinner he is given $80,000 worth of silver plate, and Snap immediately dreams of new swindles that windfall might finance.[51]

48. *The Advance and Labor Leaf* (Detroit), February 26, 1887.

49. *JUL*, August 25–November 10, 1885.

50. For more on Andrew Carnegie's stock dealings, see Harold C. Livesay, *Andrew Carnegie and the Rise of Big Business* (Boston: Little, Brown, & Co., 1975), chap. 5.

51. *JUL*, August 25–November 10, 1885.

One can easily criticize the story's resolution. There is no mention of political activity or mass demonstrations, merely essay-writing campaigns and calls for free silver. Real-life Gilded Age financiers were seldom undone by such paltry opposition. When a major mogul fell from grace—as Jay Cooke did in 1873—he was usually pushed by other bondholders, not "big-pawed farmers and . . . hard-working mechanics." The Ferret Snap series, like so many other KOL writings, paints the problems in lurid colors but fumbles for a solution. Still, "The Autobiography of Ferret Snap" contains an understanding of the systemic corruption of the Gilded Age political economy that goes beyond the evil individuals blamed in *Breaking the Chains*. Gone is the naive hope in moral regeneration; Snap is irredeemable and, by extension, so are his cohorts.

But "Ferret Snap" also points to the inadequacy of rhetorical battle plans in the midst of a concrete war. The inadequacy of words and noble sentiment is reflected in the fall-out from the Boston *Labor Leader's* "Ella Inness: A Romance of the Big Lockout, How a Knight Won the Prize." Unlike most KOL stories, "Ella Inness" was written in the midst of real events, the Worcester County mill strikes of 1887. When the serial began, strikers were fired by speeches and optimism that proved to be misplaced. The story's setting is Lakefield, "One of those villages which during the last quarter of a century have been undergoing the change from an agricultural to a partly manufacturing community," a town divided between "individual[istic]" farmers and "Socialist" factory operatives.

Ella Inness is a pretty farm girl with two suitors, a well-to-do farmer's son, and Ernest Rogers, the Master Workman of a KOL shoemakers' local. Contrary to her father's wishes, Ella prefers the silent Rogers. Rogers saves Ella from a mad dog, and their love blossoms until events at the Batchelburt Shoe Mill intervene. James Batchelburt—the name of a real-life proprietor struck by Worcester County lasters—was proud of "being a self-made man" and "the autocratic dictator" of his mill. He hated the KOL and "his mind was made up to take the first pretext of crushing the order."

That pretext was to fire Ernest Rogers simply for being a Knight. When Batchelburt rebuffs an arbitration committee, the Knights strike the mill. Lakefield seethes with unrest as shopkeepers, professionals, and farmers condemn the KOL, and preachers rail against it from the pulpit. Ella's enraged father forbids her to see Rogers.

Ella defies her father. In one clandestine meeting, she and Ernest discuss the hypocrisy of local churches. When she learns that Batchelburt prayed for the KOL's demise, Ella cries out, "What a parody it is on true Christianity that those who profess the faith of the Carpenter's Son should attempt to array the church against the efforts of the poor people." In a response mirroring real-life debate Rogers replies, "No wonder that too many . . . mechanics . . . as Rev. Joseph Cook said, 'hate the very shadow of the steeple on the dust of the village street. . . .' [W]hen the pew needs a golden key to unlock it, the pulpit too often pays respect to the man with the golden ring and fine apparel."

While the star-crossed lovers share theological musings, the Batchelburt factory burns. Ernest is charged with arson, but refuses to offer an alibi lest he betray Ella (who has swooned and is near death). Of course, Ella recovers and clears Ernest's name. The story ends on an ambivalent note, however. Although the KOL is absolved of blame and the factory is rebuilt, both "employer and employee had suffered severely" with Batchelburt nearly broke and Knights weakened from members who left to seek employment elsewhere. The only "prize" is Ernest's and Ella's marriage.[52]

The novel's spirited defense of KOL religious critiques aside, the ending is ominous. In the actual strikes that convulsed Worcester County shoe firms, the KOL and the Lasters Protective Union joined forces, and Powderly addressed huge rallies to replenish the strike fund. District Assembly 30 threw its support behind them, and *Labor Leader* editor Frank Foster filled columns in their defense. Efforts were undermined by the KOL's General Executive Board, which, faced by declining revenues and membership, withheld strike funds. As public point man, Powderly was scapegoated when the strike failed. To make matters worse, some Knights scabbed on the LPU during a Brockton strike a few months later, simply because the factory owner was once a Knight.[53]

Both Frank Foster and Massachusetts lasters quit the KOL in late 1887; both subsequently joined the AFL. By early 1888, the KOL's correspondent for the *Labor Leader* reported that KOL locals were weak throughout Worcester County.[54] The Order never recovered there, and Foster's paper never ran another story with KOL heroes. By September 1887, his paper featured the adventures of "Alan Quartermain," a dashing explorer who found romance in the midst of Africa's Zulu uprisings. "Ella Inness" marks the decline of the KOL's leadership in promoting labor solidarity. Craft workers like Foster left the Order, and neither non-KOL labor papers nor the popular press showed much inclination to praise the Knights.

Nonetheless, the apex of KOL fiction came in 1888, with the publication of W. H. Little's "Sealskin and Shoddy," the *JUL's* most popular

52. *Labor Leader* (Boston), March 19–April 30, 1887.
53. Ware, *The Labor Movement*, 205–7.
54. *Labor Leader* (Boston), January 7, 1888.

story of all time. It was certainly the best-promoted; front-page advertisements trumpeted its arrival and a free gold watch was offered to anyone who sold one hundred paid *JUL* subscriptions. *Journal* editors claimed that over 300,000 people eventually read it, a number that exceeded KOL membership by nearly one-third.[55]

The heroine of "Sealskin and Shoddy" is Mt. Holyoke graduate and society belle Mamie Symington, the daughter of the majority stockholder in a Cincinnati clothing factory, and the courting object of Herbert Standish, the plant superintendent. Mamie's comfortable existence is shaken by her encounter with Lizzie Knowlton, an orphaned factory hand. Lizzie falls ill on the job and has her pay docked by Standish, who attributes her sickness to union meetings, dances, and late-night dates. Out of curiosity, and wearing a sealskin coat, Mamie shadows Lizzie to the office of Dr. Hinston, where she learns that Lizzie has consumption but few friends and no money. Mamie enters into a secret scheme to aid the unfortunate shopgirl.

She dons a shoddy coat and assumes the name "Mary Stillson," a ruse known only to Dr. Hinston, his son Hal, and Mamie's aunt. As Stillson she acquires a second-hand sewing machine and Lizzie teaches her how to sew. She then assumes a third identity as "Betty Broadbird," and enters the seedy world of sweatshops and piece work where she is cheated and maltreated.

Mamie's enlightenment severs her relationship with Standish. When Mamie announces her desire to run the clothing factory on a cooperative basis with the KOL, Standish is scandalized and upbraids her on the foolishness of women's rights. He proceeds to brag of how he increased factory profits by slashing wages, speeding production, and using shoddy materials. When Mamie unveils a plan she and Hal Hinston developed to increase both wages and profits, Standish explodes, "You figure and talk like a labor agitator. It is a business man's duty to take advantage of supply and demand in labor as much as in materials." He curtly dismisses her plan as "socialistic nonsense."

Mamie gets a first-hand lesson in labor supply and demand when, as Betty Broadbird, she has to bribe a foreman to secure factory work. Predictably, she ends up in the Symington Company, only to learn she has replaced Becky Francher, a woman fired for rebuffing a foreman's advances. Betty finds the emaciated Becky in a dark hovel huddled be-

---

55. *JUL*, July 19, 1888–November 1, 1888. According to Norman Ware, the Knights of Labor had 221,618 members in good standing as of July 1, 1888. By 1889 that number had dipped only slightly to 220,607, but there was no indication of how many of these were paid members. The 1889 membership figures are probably padded.

side the starved corpse of her mother. Becky is rushed to the hospital, and her bills are paid by a mutual assistance club organized by Betty/ Mamie.

Despite a coroner's inquest denouncing the Symington Company for callousness in Mrs. Francher's death, all who give testimony, including Betty Broadbird, are fired. She and Hal immediately organize a protective association, but Standish ignores it and threatens to fire any employee who joins. Upon her release from the hospital, the despondent Becky Francher throws herself from a bridge, and Betty releases her suicide note to the press. But Standish remains unflappable, even after Mamie charges that "love of wealth has made you forget your love for God's creatures."

The KOL organizes a strike that closes the Symington factory. Mamie publicly pledges $500 to the strike fund, and company vice president William Watson demands that Standish silence her. Since all of Mamie's money comes from company accounts controlled by her father, who is abroad, Standish pens a deceptive letter that leads to a freeze on Mamie's funds. Standish and Watson also hire the Cut-and-Run Detective Agency to break the strike. Agents provocateurs promptly stage an attack on Jennie Robertson, a woman who crossed picket lines, and make it look like the KOL is responsible.

But the worm turns. "Betty" convinces a rival factory owner to settle with the Knights, and they mutually offer a reward for information on Robertson's attackers. The strike fund is replenished when Hal Hinston donates a salary advance, and Mamie contacts her father to set matters straight. The final act is played when Watson and Standish attempt a leveraged buy-out of Symington's stock. Unbeknownst to them, he transferred one-third ownership to Mamie. As a major stockholder, Mamie asserts her right to address the annual meeting. When she outlines her profit-sharing plan, reveals the amount that Standish squandered on detectives, and exposes the horrors witnessed while living her triple life, shareholders agree to implement her plan.

By story's end, all is well. The women return to work and find that the troublesome foremen have been replaced by none other than Lizzie Knowlton and Jennie Robertson. Standish resigns and a new board is organized upon which sit several Knights and a new convert to profit-sharing, William Watson's daughter. The community is magically transformed, with workers crowding into the KOL library in their off-hours. Of course, Mamie and Hal are married. To add a little spice, Dr. Hinston marries Mamie's aunt.[56]

56. All quotations are taken from the *JUL*, July 19, 1888–November 1, 1888.

Victorian romance and implausible resolutions aside, "Sealskin and Shoddy" was one of the best labor novels to appear in the *JUL*.[57] Although Little retained a Powderly-like faith in the mutuality of capital/labor interests, he did not gloss over the abuses done to labor by capital. Many KOL concerns surface in the novel, including arbitration, education, equal rights for women, mutual assistance, and temperance. And whereas most Gilded Age fiction puts women into precarious situations from which they are rescued at the last moment, "Sealskin and Shoddy" has a harder edge. While Mamie saves Lizzie Knowlton, it was too late for Becky Francher or her mother.

Though hardly a feminist tract, Little's novel is remarkable for its strong female lead, one more in keeping with the Order's official stance on women. Other novels, including *Breaking the Chains*, developed heroines, but few were as independent as Mamie Symington. In most Gilded Age fiction, women are moral bulwarks, but dependent on men for logic, planning, and administrative detail. In "Sealskin," Mamie is the intellectual and organizational equal of any man. It is she who refines the profit-sharing scheme, and she who pores over the company books to assure its feasibility. As a Mount Holyoke graduate, she is representative of the third generation of college-educated women, some of whom rejected the middle-class reforms of missionary work and temperance for the thornier problems of urban, industrial society.

Today, "Scalskin and Shoddy" seems sentimental and heavy-handed, but by late nineteenth-century standards it was remarkable. It is true that Little's work is more suggestive than explicit on questions of poverty and exploitation, and his style is pedestrian and conventional. But whatever its limits, the story had a combative spirit to it, and it certainly presaged possibilities for future KOL fiction. Unfortunately, that potential was never explored. To highlight the road not taken, one need look no further than the story that followed "Sealskin" in the *JUL*, Alice Woodbridge's "The Last Chance: A Story of the Labor Movement To-Day."

Woodbridge was a story-paper writer and that was obvious in her *JUL* piece. "The Last Chance" follows the fortunes of Master Workman Hugh Gresham, his beloved Lilius Stanton, and Frank Churchill, a fel-

---

57. Historian Ann Schofield is critical of "Sealskin and Shoddy" and feels it perpetuates Victorian views of weak and dependent women. Although I agree that Mamie Symington is hardly a feminist, in my judgment, Professor Schofield is too hard on the novel. When judged by the standards of most Gilded Age popular fiction, Little's heroine is quite remarkable. For the details of Schofield's argument, see her "From 'Sealskin and Shoddy' to 'The Pig-Headed Girl': Patriarchal Fables for Workers," in *"To Toil the Livelong Day": America's Women at Work*, ed. Carol Groneman and Mary Beth Norton (Ithaca: Cornell University Press, 1987).

low Knight who also adores Lil. The story opens with a KOL strike that fails when impatient workers break solidarity and reject the advice of KOL leaders. Gresham is blacklisted and becomes a transient in search of employment, leaving broken-hearted Lil behind, and Churchill secretly happy for the opportunity to court her.

Woodbridge's narrative telescopes ahead one year. Lil now resides in Churchill's house as a companion to his elderly mother. Mill conditions have grown steadily worse, but the jaded Churchill refuses to reorganize a KOL local. For unexplained reasons, workers acclaim Lilius Master Workman and she leads five hundred strikers out of the mill. After a bitter eight-week strike, the workers "win" the same conditions that Gresham negotiated one year earlier. Still, there was hope; workers flocked to the KOL reading room, enjoyed paid vacations, and were protected by a sick fund.

One of the first to benefit from the sick fund was Lilius. The strain of leading the strike and the lack of a "lover's word" from Hugh took their toll; she soon became an invalid. As Churchill tries to nurse her back to health, he offers a marriage proposal to which Lil agrees on the condition that no word arrives from Hugh before Christmas. Lil continues to decline, and Churchill finally sends a desperate telegram to Hugh Gresham, which does not catch up with the peripatetic Gresham until Christmas eve. Lilius, rather than break her word to Churchill or give up her love for Gresham, wills herself to die that very night. Her fate is unknown to Gresham, who rushes home in the midst of a raging blizzard. On Christmas day his frozen corpse is discovered at the local station: "In his hand was clasped tightly a ring of golden hair, and on his pale lips was a smile of peace."[58]

How utterly unlike Mamie Symington is Lilius Stanton. And how unlike the brave Knights described by Whittaker are the foolish men in Woodbridge's story. Woodbridge's story mirrors the KOL's deep troubles. In November 1888, the *JUL* claimed a weekly readership of 23,000, a far cry from the 300,000 who allegedly read "Sealskin and Shoddy."[59] Faced with deep erosion of support, KOL leaders sought to attract members and cut costs. Subscription schemes attached to new serials was one measure, deep cuts in the *JUL* budget was another. The success of "Sealskin and Shoddy" suggested that fiction might be a tool for revival, despite the disappointment over its follow-up. To that end, KOL editors poured on the pulp, not realizing that reading tastes were changing and that story-papers also were beginning to fade in popularity.

58. *JUL*, November 1, 1888–November 22, 1888.
59. Ibid., November 15, 1888.

"The Last Chance" is symbolic of the accommodations KOL leaders were willing to make to hegemonic popular culture. In 1889, the *JUL* did what must have seemed the most logical thing of all: it turned again to W. H. Little. This time, however, there was no magic in his pen; his offering was the desultory "Lever and Throttle." The *JUL* followed with "Toilers of Babylon," a story that even Powderly found trite. But though he complained, Powderly was acutely aware of the need to do something. In a letter to *JUL* compositor Tom O'Reilly, Powderly joked that the next *Journal* entry ought to be entitled "Jack the Ripper, or Guts to Clean in London":

> The title itself will recommend the story to the majority of our readers, and its fans attract new ones. . . . We will endeavor to show in this story that a woman cannot prance around the streets with her bowels hanging over her arm and the drapery of her stomach wrapped about the foundations of a gas lamp. . . . All this will give tone to the *Journal* and increase the sale of butcher knives so that our cutlery assemblies will experience a boon.[60]

Powderly's crude joke underscored a serious point: the *JUL* needed to find something—anything—to attract more readers. It never did. By 1890, the KOL's paid membership was under 100,000 and *Journal* readership much lower. Again, new schemes were launched. In July 1891, a new story, "Through Clouds to Sunshine," was presaged by promises of prizes and hopes of attracting 50,000 new readers. As a symbol of shifting fortunes, the gold watches dangled as premiums were inscribed with a hunting scene rather than the KOL's Great Seal.[61] Had the re-named *Journal of the Knights of Labor* achieved half of its goal, KOL membership would have surged by one-third. It did not happen. An 1893 membership roll of under 75,000 members proved that popular fiction could not rescue the Knights.

No Middle Ground

Fiction, even more than poetry, highlighted the gap between official positions and actual behavior inside the KOL, but for the same reason:

60. Powderly to Thomas O'Reilly, 20 September 1888, in *PP.*
61. *JUL,* "Through Clouds to Sunshine" was announced on July 16, 1891, and commenced on July 23, 1891.

the demands of public culture forced writers to make compromises with hegemonic culture. Just as KOL poets like George McNeill sometimes crossed the thin line between working-class respectability and bourgeois sentimentality, so too did fiction writers like John Barrett.

But to conclude that the KOL surrendered to middle-class values is simply incorrect. As Michael Denning argues, Gilded Age fiction was "contested terrain" in which "mechanic accents" could find voice.[62] Both the working classes and bourgeoisie made compromises. In the mid-1880s, story-papers across the land elevated Knights of Labor to heroic status and fashioned stories around them. But limits can be seen in the conformity of such characters to middle-class standards of refinement, speech, morality, and decorum.

These same dialectical tensions are found in the fiction that Knights themselves produced. Sometimes, fiction reinforced KOL values. By focusing on exploitation and corruption, fiction (like poetry) showed that—in the words of a KOL poem—"there must be something wrong."[63] KOL fiction was textured against a backdrop of long hours, lying politicians, sweated labor, unbridled greed, and unsafe working conditions. It was also remarkably consistent about organized religion. In keeping with the official line, Gilded Age churches are shown as villainous, and hypocritical ministers are contrasted with saintly, honest, and virtuous Knights who uphold the teachings of the Carpenter's Son, not the hollow tenets of "Churchianity."

The KOL showed little such consistency in other matters, however, and both poetry and fiction proved deficient educational tools. As traditional ritual bonds loosened in the 1880s, the Knights relied more heavily on public discourse to disseminate ideas. But speeches, rallies, and newspapers lacked the insularity of ritual, thus monologues yielded to dialogues. The tenets of "Knighthood" became debatable, not practices to memorize or master. The KOL frequently flayed hegemonic culture, but it also borrowed some of its forms and values. New members joined the Order after 1882, and found ideology in flux. It is little wonder that practice often failed to match rhetoric.

Fiction provides another frame through which we view the lack of unity in post-1882 KOL culture. All Knights agreed that existing power arrangements were flawed; but beyond that lay little consensus. Some critiques were radical, some cautious, and quite a few others were romantic. In the case of fiction writer W. H. Little, all three impulses converged in a single individual. In 1888, "Sealskin and Shoddy" points

---

62. Denning, *Mechanic Accents*, 3.
63. *Industrial Leader*, June 25, 1887.

toward a transformed economy based on profit-sharing and a society in which men and women are equals. Yet six months later, "Lever and Throttle" resurrected story-paper conventions of aristocratic virtue, passive unionism, and female helplessness. Montreville Pierstone is a reverse Hal Hinston. Pierstone only labors until he can return to middle-class comfort; Hinston is born into luxury and gives it up in order to fight for labor's cause. And Syiska Seminaba is certainly no Mamie Symington.

Little's competing impulses mirror those of the Order as a whole. Were lawyers a category to be banned from the Order, or individuals to be judged by their actions? Was temperance the working man's salvation or a false messiah? Should the Order work to abolish the wage system or recognize that the interests of capital and labor were mutual? The Order's fiction left these questions unresolved.

Once again, gender proved perplexing. Just as KOL poets could not decide if women were comrades or domestics, so too fiction writers waffled between the models of Mamie Symington and Lilius Stanton. Where did women belong? On the battle lines with Maud Simpson or ensconced in their Victorian homes like Syiska Seminaba? KOL writers usually avoided the pathetic stereotypes of the fawning, fainting females favored by story-papers, but not always their implications. Peril lurked for women who ventured forth too boldly, as in the case of frail Lilius Stanton. And what else can one make of the "advice" columns found in KOL journals?

Genteel influences loomed at the edges of the KOL with at least as much presence as radical visions. Much KOL fiction is cast in the story-paper mold. Writers like John Barrett and Alice Woodbridge seemed comfortable in both worlds; others, like Lizzie (Swank) Holmes saw little in bourgeois society that was useful or good. Most writers tried to walk a middle path. This meant that class ambivalence was omnipresent in KOL novels and class conflict was often expressed in individual, not structural, terms. In an attempt to combine the most noble aspects of bourgeois and working-class culture, such writers preferred characters like Maud Simpson and Harry Wallace, who valued education, manners, refinement, temperance, and thrift equally with hard work, honesty, justice, and solidarity.

In a more tolerant society, writers such as T. Fulton Gantt might have helped the Knights fashion a middle-ground culture between the extremes of bourgeois hegemony and anarchism. But the Order neither had time to adjust nor did it dwell in a tolerant society. The KOL did not surrender to Victorian culture; the shapers of Victorian culture destroyed the Knights. A mere four years separate the KOL's first year as a public organization from the Great Upheaval. As the KOL sought new identity, it simultaneously battled power elites dedicated to smashing the Order. As it made tentative forays into the cultural arena, it found enemies controlling prevailing cultural institutions. From their position of power, elites chipped away at the Knights. Writers like Frederick Whittaker abandoned the Knights for safe subjects like cowboys, while Powderly complained that his own writers made too many compromises with the mainstream. When Powderly was relieved of his duties in 1893, KOL fiction looked more like "The Toilers of Babylon" than "Sealskin and Shoddy." One year later, the *JUL* went the way of Frederick Whittaker and serialized "A Cowboy's Love Story." Not that it mattered much; there were few Knights left to read it.

6 Symbols of Solidarity/ Images of Conflict

Material Culture and the Knights of Labor

At the Knights of Labor's 1880 convention, Terence Powderly was besieged by supplicants clamoring for "some sort of badge" to signify Knighthood. He tried to avoid them, as the 1880 KOL was still a secret organization containing strict ritualists who felt he had already tinkered too much with time-honored practices. Nonetheless, one year later, the Grand Assembly approved an official badge.[1] Conventions in 1883 and 1884 spent passion over the proper color of cigar labels. Powderly's suggestion that any union label was valid was rejected by both conventions. At the 1891 General Assembly, Powderly was confronted by Knights who wished to develop a KOL uniform. Again, Powderly was reluctant, but he relented when he could "see no harm in it."[2]

In each instance, rank-and-file pressure forced convention delegates to adopt measures that leadership found unwise or trivial. It is tempting to dismiss such matters as convention sideshows or light-hearted departures from the serious business of passing resolutions, debating politics, and authorizing job actions. But to do so is to ignore a vital aspect of KOL culture. Just as the Order drafted hundreds of resolutions and position papers, so too did it produce scores of badges, banners, and material objects. For many Knights, their identity was as much shaped by a dime-sized lapel pin as by the weighty pronouncements of convention delegates. This chapter turns its attention to what anthropologist James Deetz calls "small things forgotten . . . the simple details of past exis-

1. *Proceedings of the Knights of Labor Grand Assembly*, 1880, 1881. Located in the *PP.*
2. *Proceedings of the Knights of Labor Grand/General Assembly*, 1883, 1884, in *PP*; "Remarks of the General Master Workman" from the *Proceedings of the Knights of Labor General Assembly*, 1891, in *PP.*

tence which escape historical mention, and . . . simple artifacts . . . not deemed important in art-historical terms."[3]

An analysis of material objects reveals much about the ordinary men and women who passed through the KOL. Many were moved profoundly by "small details" and "simple artifacts." Even Powderly recognized this. When speaking of the triangle enclosed in a circle design that became one of the Order's most visible symbols, Powderly noted that

> the circle which binds together the ends of the lines of the triangle indicates that the bond of unity by which the membership is bound together should be without end; placed on the outside of the triangle it also indicates that all of the business of the assembly should be transacted among members and for humanity. This circle can be broken from the inside very easily, but from the outside never.[4]

Such metaphorical language was common in secret ritual, but the study of material culture properly belongs to the KOL's public period. Few symbols existed prior to 1882, and material culture expanded during the 1880s, even as membership contracted. Meanings attached to material objects demonstrate continuity to earlier values, and highlight the rich symbolism that imbued KOL culture with meanings that went much deeper than surface appearances.

Anthropologists, folklorists, and historians have long recognized that language is symbolic and that meanings attached to words often transcend the literal. But since words remain the historian's domain, much of the spade work in material culture has been done by anthropologists, archaeologists, and folklorists.[5] American labor historians have yet to exploit fully the interpretive possibilities of material culture. Yet American labor produced, as a recent exhibit at the Smithsonian's Museum of

3. James Deetz, *In Small Things Forgotten: The Archeology of Early American Life* (Garden City, N.Y.: Anchor Books, 1977), 16.

4. Powderly, *The Path I Trod*, 439.

5. Deetz, *In Small Things Forgotten*; Clifford Geertz, *The Interpretation of Cultures* (New York: Basic Books, 1973), 5, 7, 9, 14, 17; see also chaps. 1, 2; Henry Glassie, *Pattern in the Material and Folk Culture of the Eastern United States* (Philadelphia: University of Pennsylvania Press, 1968), 2, 8; Richard Dorson, ed., *Folklore and Folklife: An Introduction* (Chicago: University of Chicago Press, 1972), 41; Ian M. G. Quimby, ed., *Material Culture and the Study of American Life* (New York: W. W. Norton, 1978); see esp. essays by James V. Kavanaugh, "The Artifact in American Culture: The Development of an Undergraduate Program in American Studies," 65–74; Brooke Hindle, "How Much Is a Piece of the True Cross Worth?" 5–20.

American History reveals, a rich array of material objects including badges, emblems, banners, uniforms, and ephemera.[6]

Many assembly rooms were as replete with KOL emblems as a medieval church was with the trappings of Christianity. At one time it was possible to decorate one's person and house with KOL symbols. Pictures of Uriah Stephens, Terence Powderly, and other leaders graced the walls of nineteenth-century working-class homes, and thousands of men and women marched proudly behind handmade banners in parades and demonstrations. It was possible for Knights to fasten their cuffs with KOL cufflinks, adorn their shirts with KOL buttons, check the time on KOL watches, and drink water from KOL glasses (Fig. 11). Knighthood was simultaneously psychological, mystic, ideological, and pragmatic. It had a material aspect as well. Appreciation of material objects brings us one step closer to a "thick description" of KOL culture.[7]

Since images were often the vehicle for how Knights defined themselves and through which others defined them, it is important to look at both internal and external production. KOL material culture existed in the same dialectical relationship to the outside world as its other cultural products, and objects could induce conflict. Objects that venerated the organization promoted pride and solidarity. Knights could don KOL collar stays and watch fobs that proclaimed Knighthood's universalism. Mutuality, unity, brotherhood, and identity were there for the viewing.

---

6. The exhibit to which I refer is "Symbols and Images of American Labor," developed by Harry Rubenstein of the Smithsonian Institution's Museum of American History and housed in the same. For the most part, British historians have been quicker to deal with labor iconography. See John Gorman, *Images of Labour* (London: Scorpion Publishing, 1985); idem, *Banner Bright: An Illustrated History of the British Trade Union Movement* (London: Allen Lane, 1973). Both of Gorman's books still enjoy distribution. By contrast, the only similar collection in the United States is M. B. Schnapper, *American Labor: A Bicentennial History* (Washington, D.C.: Public Affairs Press, 1975). Schnapper's book has been out of print for nearly a decade. One can further see the contrast in the number of labor museums that dot the British countryside, whereas museums in the United States tend to be dedicated to single events, such as Paterson's "Bread and Roses" strike (Haledon, N.J.), or evoke larger themes. The museum complex at the Lowell National Historical Park glorifies industrialization as much as it does the men and women who worked there.

Another American example is Philip S. Foner and Reinhard Schultz, eds., *The Other America: Art and the Labor Movement in the United States* (West Nyack, N.Y.: Journeyman Press, 1985). The book was originally printed in Germany, where the exhibit opened. An English translation did not appear until two years after the German edition. Though few labor historians are as well-known as Foner, this book was relegated to a small press, and the final product is a sloppy affair badly in need of both proofreading and editing. It is available almost exclusively through small speciality mail order houses. Perhaps the best analytical use of material images is Kornbluh, *Rebel Voices*. Kornbluh's use of graphics and cartoons is superb.

7. Geertz, *Interpretation of Cultures*, 45.

Fig. 11. After 1882, KOL symbols could be found everywhere, celebrating the special to the banal. Here is a KOL drinking glass. Courtesy, Smithsonian Institution.

As John Gorman notes, labor imagery evolved as a natural offshoot of religious images, craft guild icons, heraldic escutcheons, and Masonic regalia.[8] Like those earlier symbols, KOL emblems helped members formulate identity and ideology.

8. Gorman, *Images of Labour*, 14.

But such visions did not go unchallenged, even within labor's own ranks. Ironically for an organization with universalist pretensions, material culture became the focal point for the Order's dispute with trade unions. From the mid-1880s on, Knights and trade unionists waged a veritable "label war" in which symbols originally designed to promote producer pride and class-based consumerism became visible reminders of the rifts in labor's ranks. The rancor that was generated in the disputes and that focused on images was the delight of enemies of labor, and the bourgeois press responded with cartoons and editorials that exacerbated tensions.

Thus there is a third level of analysis for KOL material culture: its relationship to hegemonic Gilded Age culture. We have noted the ability of the Victorian press to promote or abuse the Knights in words. So too were newspaper graphics powerful shapers of public opinion. The expense involved in reproducing good graphics put KOL journals at a disadvantage. As a result, most Gilded Age cartoons and engravings involving the KOL were less than flattering. The KOL responded with belated but often brilliant counterimages, yet in the end it lost both the label and the graphic wars. By the time uniformed Knights showed up in the 1890s, much of the Order's material culture had been robbed of power, symbolic or otherwise.

Before continuing, a codicil is in order. My take on material culture is inspired by folklorists, but involves a more inclusive interpretation. Folklorists do not customarily consider commercially produced graphics, cartoons, or trademarks as folk objects. And though it is true that many KOL material goods are linked to older labor designs and methods, it would be a stretch on my part to call them folk art. My use of the term "material culture" is more in keeping with uses developed at various Winterthur conferences.[9] Some would argue that the term "artifact" is more appropriate, but my concern is less with category than with purpose. I will employ a functionalist approach that underplays taxonomy in favor of meaning.[10]

Badges of Distinction

KOL ritual predated its material culture. It was, after all, difficult to devise symbols for an Order whose name could not be used outside of

9. Henry Glassie lays out the folklorist's view of material culture in chap. 12 of Dorson, *Folklore and Folklife*, as well as his own superb *Pattern in Material and Folk Culture*. Winterthur's views are well-represented in 1975 conference papers published in Quimby, *Material Culture*.

10. The functionalist approach I adopt is briefly described by Dorson in *Folklore and Folklife*, 25, 253, 266.

assembly. By 1878, not even the Order's motto—"An injury to one is the concern of all"—was universal. Uriah Stephens's official stationary was stamped "Peace and Prosperity to the Faithful."[11] The first official seal bore the motto "Within the Limitations of the Law." When Powderly took over as Grand Master Workman, few official symbols of any sort existed.

But a purely psychic Order was not destined to last. Victorian scholar Stewart Culin, who one folklorist calls an "expert in material culture in a materialist age," was one of the first Americans to study everyday objects.[12] In pioneering works on the Chinese, Native Americans, and European peasants, Culin came to appreciate how so-called "primitive" art was present in the "decorative" art of his day. Americans were so enamored with ornamentation that they came to expect it in "houses, dress, implements and utensils."[13] Knights certainly encountered lots of it in their assembly halls. Interior decoration varied according to the tastes, politics, and financial status of the local, but all assemblies contained such objects as a globe for the Outer Veil, a lance for the Inner Veil, an altar, and a copy of the local charter to hang upon the wall.

By the mid-1880s, some locals were extensively ornamental. One assembly contained an ornately carved marble altar supported by Corinthian columns, while Leadville, Colorado, Knights decorated their halls with American flags and banners. Slogans hung behind each officer. For example, "Industrial and Moral Worth, Not Wealth, the True Standard of National Greatness" was superimposed at the base of the National Capitol and hovered over the Master Workman, while the Unknown Knight sat beneath "Educate, Legislate, and Arbitrate."[14]

KOL officers also adorned their bodies. The Master Workman wore an insignia featuring a three-foot reeded column with a coral base and a capital of leaves and fruits. It represented cooperation based on labor and directed by intelligence. The General Master Workman had a few

11. Uriah S. Stephens to Terence V. Powderly, March 15, 1878, in *PP.*

12. Simon J. Bronner, ed., *Folklife Studies from the Gilded Age* (Ann Arbor: University of Michigan Press, 1987), 151.

13. Ibid., p. 157.

14. The altar is found in the photo archives of the *Powderly Papers* housed at Catholic University in Washington, D.C. It may well come from Powderly's own Scranton LA 222, though it is equally likely that it was a special ceremonial altar used for events such as GAs. The photo is not dated, but it is certainly later than 1882 since its surface is rectangular and original altars were triangular. For information on the inside of Leadville, Colorado, LA 3928, see *JUL*, March 26, 1887.

The Venerable Sage used the motto "Honesty, Industry, and Sobriety," a slogan coined by the Order of United American Mechanics, a nativist fraternal lodge that thrived in northern and southern cities after 1840.

additional symbols by the 1880s. These included an eight-sided seal containing a triangle inside a pentagon enclosed by a circle. Inside the triangle was a fasces, the bundle of rods representing unbreakable interests bound together, and a blade, the traditional Roman symbol of authority. Some official documents sported a column—the folkloric symbol of strength, constancy, and fortitude—topped by a bust representing human intellect and wisdom.[15] In print, the symbol added a scroll and the motto "Hear Both Sides, Then Judge," indicating the GMW's impartiality.

The Worthy Foreman's emblem was a representation of coral—often used in good luck amulets—while the Worthy Inspector, who examined all who entered the Sanctuary, used the common Masonic sign of the watchful eye. Even lesser officers had formal symbolic regalia. The Almoner's open hand stood for assistance, the Financial Secretary's coin for "labor done," the Worthy Treasurer's safe for strength and the Statistician's book and lightning bolt for enlightenment and power.[16] Few Knight symbols were original; folkloric and Masonic imagery was adapted for KOL use.

By the mid-1880s, many symbols were simplified, with badges and ribbons replacing elaborate insignias. By 1886, Powderly wore a silk ribbon knotted into a series of bows, with crossed American flags pinned in the center (Fig. 12). The bow was affixed to his clothing by a pin that said "Gen. Master Workman," and from the entire assemblage dangled two gold tassels and two smaller ribbons. Other officers wore less elaborate ribbons, all attached to their clothing by pins that stated their office. At the GA, all representatives wore ribbons stamped "Delegate."[17] While far less elaborate, simplification led to proliferation (Fig. 13).

Likewise the move from deep symbolism to wider but less ritualistic usage validates another of Culin's observations. In an exhibit developed for the 1893 Columbian World's Exposition, Culin noted that ceremonial objects are often transformed into games and performances for the masses who might or might not understand their original meanings.[18] This interplay between symbolic understanding and mere use of symbols can be seen in uses made of the Great Seal of Knighthood (Fig. 14).

The Great Seal began life endowed with quasi-religious meanings to

15. Powderly, *The Path I Trod*, 435–36. Noted that the ornamental altar mentioned above contains motifs from the Master Workman's insignia, including coral, grape leaves, reeds, and leaves.

16. Ibid.

17. The ribbons are included in the manuscript collection of the *PP* at Catholic University. The archives include a box of miscellaneous memorabilia.

18. Bronner, *Folklife Studies*, 251–77.

Figs. 12 & 13.   Knights wore special ribbons while attending the General Assembly. Here are a delegate's ribbon and Terence Powderly's special "Gen. Master Workman" ribbon from the 1886 General Assembly in Richmond. Powderly Papers, The Catholic University of America.

which only longtime devotees were privy. Reading from inside out, the seal showed a triangle touching points of the Western hemisphere enclosed in a circle in which "A.K. the 9th" appears. A pentagon surrounded the circle and was enveloped by a radiating circle bearing the words "Prytaneum North America January 1st 1878." A hexagon engulfed the radiating circle, and a second circle with Solon's words, "That is the most perfect government in which an injury to one is the concern of all," held the hexagon. The configuration formed a circular body for a five-pointed star.

The lines of the equilateral triangle signified humanity, man's relationship to the Creator, and the three "elements which are essential to man's existence and happiness, land, labor, and love." It was also emblematic of "production, exchange, and consumption." The hemisphere represented the KOL's North American birthplace, and the inscription

Fig. 14. The Great Seal of Knighthood. Although the various elements of the seal have rich symbolic meaning, not all Knights understood the symbolism, and many local assemblies used a simplified seal.

denoted that the first GA of January 1878 was the ninth year that the *AK* was in effect. Prytaneum is a Latin noun referring to a state dining hall, but used by the Knights as place toward which "all eyes are directed and around [which] . . . all hopes cling and grow." The unifying circle was an "unbroken Circle of Universal Brotherhood."

The segments of the pentagon allude to the five principles of Universal Brotherhood: justice, wisdom, truth, industry, and economy. Knights added the novel interpretation that man should toil but five days per week. A circle with exterior "rays of light that are given out by the lamp of experience" enclosed the pentagon. This imagery drew upon the "spread the light" motif so favored in educational and organizing drives. It was also symbolic of how the Knights grew; local assemblies formed district assemblies that "illumine[d] our pathway toward the General Assembly." The figure was finally encircled by the motto and completed by the five radiating points of the star. Those points represented the "five races of men," and the "five grand divisions of the earth."[19]

But few Knights understood all of the symbolism. Many local assemblies used a simplified version of the Great Seal, a triangle enclosed by a circle. Outside of the triangle appeared letters highlighting the familiar S.O.M.A. pledge, while inside was the local assembly's number. These symbols were often crudely drawn on letters sent to Stephens and Powderly. Bureaucraticization expanded the Order's reliance on symbols, even as the purpose behind them changed from mysticism to identification with the KOL's public goals. Soon, the wearing of KOL regalia became a visible statement of opposition to constituted authority. By 1880, it was possible for locals to buy standardized supplies from the Grand Secretary's office. At first, only official documents, office supplies, assembly regalia, and copies of the *AK* were available. But by 1886, the list had grown to include gold KOL pins, badges, buttons, labels, "ladies' lace pins," collar buttons, books, and portraits of Powderly, Stephens, and the general officers. By the decade's end, it was possible to buy two different badges, seven varieties of buttons, seven batches of labels, two styles of lace pins, and three types of scarf pins. In addition, the *JUL* ran numerous advertisements for KOL insignia goods available through independent merchants.[20]

Knights held several paper documents that proclaimed their Knighthood, and the more positions one attained, the more certificates one collected. The KOL was hardly unique in granting these, but few nineteenth-century labor organizations stacked symbol upon symbol with such fervor. Some documents were quite ordinary in appearance. The working card consisted of little more than the number of one's assembly, a signature blank, and check-off spaces for dues and assessments on the back. Organizers' commissions contained numerous decorative seals, while traveling cards were even more elaborate. All of the documents conferred a sense of achievement and belonging; some were quite useful. Membership and traveling cards helped Knights find work in un-

19. Powderly, *The Path I Trod*, 438–42.
20. Lists of supplies available from the General Secretary are listed in nearly every issue of the *JUL*. There are also lists of supplies found in the *PP*.

known towns, and provided leaders with mechanisms to regulate entry into shops organized by the KOL.

The KOL also used material symbols to keep the Order foremost in the minds of members. The most visible symbol of all was Terence V. Powderly. His portrait appeared in the first issue of the *JUL* and frequently thereafter. His picture could be found everywhere from the mainstream press to working-class homes. The General Secretary-Treasurer offered large unframed photographs of the GMW for two dollars. Powderly's visage also appeared on lecture announcements and special events posters (Fig. 15). Whenever it was juxtaposed with pictures of other members of the Order, Powderly's photo was certain to loom larger. One of the most popular of these assemblages was a color lithograph produced by Kurz and Allison in 1886. In it, Powderly's profile dwarfs the images of the thirty-two labor leaders whose faces frame his (see Fig. 3).[21]

Powderly's portrait was also offered as a premium for paid *JUL* subscriptions. Invariably, some came to see Powderly's "star" qualities as self-deification. He protested:

> The use of my picture on flour barrels, soaps, cigars and even whiskey barrels has been carried out to such an extreme that I cannot recall a tenth of the cases brought to my notice. I am asked why I allow this thing to be done. The answer is I cannot help it. It is not in a spirit of egoism I say this, but I am a public man, and as such must pay the penalty by being caricatured by everyone who takes it into his head to do such a thing.[22]

Nonetheless, Powderly did much to encourage his sacralization. Powderly's face could even be found on bookmarks, which were avidly promoted, not dismissed in the spirit of modesty. In 1888, the *JUL* announced that the GMW's picture "woven in silk" and suitable for use as a "badge or a bookmark" was available for 50 cents each. Powderly's personal effects contain dozens of these (Fig. 16). This item was manufactured by Hynes and May of Paterson, New Jersey, a company specializing in bookmarks and woven pictures. Powderly is shown in left profile, below an eagle perched on a globe grasping an American flag in each talon. The eagle's beak holds a banner proclaiming "Knowledge is Power." Beneath Powderly's portrait, his signature is superimposed

21. A copy of this poster is owned by the Smithsonian Institution.
22. *John Swinton's Paper*, February 6, 1887.

LECTURE!

Will be given by

Sunday Evening, April 7,

New National Theatre.

T. V. POWDERLY,

AT 8 O'CLOCK,

Under the Auspices of

PLATE PRINTERS' ASSEMBLY,

KNIGHTS OF LABOR.

Other Speakers of the Evening: Hon. John M. Farquhar
and Mrs. Lenora M. Barry.

TICKETS, To any part of the House, 50 CENTS.

To be had of G. Y. Joyce, 1705 Penna. Ave. N. W.; W. G. Duckett, cor. 22d St. and
Penna. Ave. N. W.; Whiteside & Walton, cor. 20th St. and Penna. Ave. N. W.;
R. L. Magruder, 19th St. and Penna. Ave. N. W.; W. H. Reichenbach,
909 Penna. Ave. N. W.; L McCall, cor. 9th and H Sts. N. E.;
E. R. Morcoe. 421 12th St. N. W.; Fishman's Sons, 430 7th
St. N. W.; Sullivan's. cor. 1st and H Sts. N. E.

GRAY & CLARKSON, Prs.

Fig. 15. In the hands of KOL leaders, Terence Powderly's face became a familiar symbol in the minds of members and nonmembers alike. Here a poster announces a Powderly lecture in Washington, D.C. Such lectures often drew huge crowds.

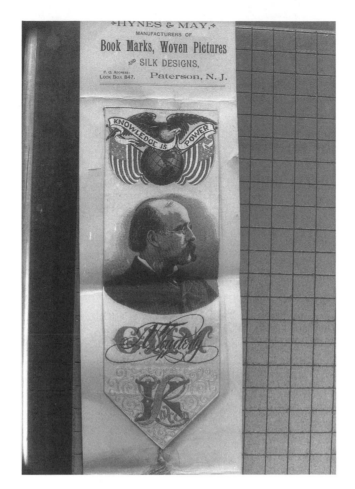

Fig. 16. Bookmark with Powderly's image woven in silk, available for 50 cents each. Powderly Papers, The Catholic University of America.

over a Gothic-scripted "GMW," with the point of the ribbon featuring an interlaced "K of L" and a trailing gold tassel.[23]

But it was the rank and file who were most responsible for the expansion of KOL material culture. In 1880, Colorado Knights wore black scarves to funerals of fallen comrades; soon, others were doing the same. In that same year, Indiana Knights demanded to know where they could get badges and pins like other locals had, a summons that baffled the GEB as no authorized versions existed.[24] In 1881, leadership relented

23. These can be viewed only at Catholic University and have not yet been microfilmed.
24. Joseph Murray to Powderly, February 26, 1889, in *PP*; *JUL*, July 15, 1880.

and appointed a committee to design a badge. The one-inch diameter final product was completed in early 1882. It contained a triangle enclosed by a circle with "K of L" emblazoned across the middle. Anger erupted when the many orders were delayed due to a manufacturing flaw.[25]

By 1884, the adoption of an official trademark and of the Great Seal necessitated design changes. The *JUL* offered solid-gold badges, "about the size of a penny," for three dollars each. The triangle was now enclosed in a square within the circular badge, and the letters "K of L" appeared at the top, and "SOMA" at the bottom. A larger version, mounted to a scroll with gold links, was available to any member who wanted to part with nine dollars.[26]

Both legitimate and unscrupulous commercial manufacturers sought to jump on the KOL bandwagon. In March 1886, the *JUL* warned members against merchants hawking "spurious" badges, telling them that the only official badge was sold by the General Secretary-Treasurer's office and manufactured by E. T. Bartholomew of Boston.[27] The injunction had little impact, however. The *Labor Leaf* complained that several Detroit Knights bought Bartholomew badges only to find agents selling comparable badges for half the price. Canadian brothers across the Detroit River wore a more attractive badge that was likewise touted as "official."[28]

The 1886 GEB was too swamped with work to resolve the badge dilemma. By late 1886, KOL regalia was open to any manufacturer who wanted to try his hand. Powderly received a letter from Charles F. Irons of Providence, Rhode Island, suggesting that the KOL needed an official badge and that his company could provide it. Whether Irons manufactured KOL badges is not known, but a Providence competitor did. C. C. Darling and Company offered fourteen different pins and charms for the discriminating Knight.[29] By 1890, the *JKL* offered several different badges.[30] To date, more than three dozen designs have surfaced (Fig. 17).

25. 1880 *Proceedings of the Knights of Labor; JUL*, October 15, 1881; November 15, 1881; February 15, 1882; May 15, 1882.

26. *JUL*, February 14, 1884.

27. Ibid., March 25, 1886; *Labor Leaf*, June 23, 1886. Note: Bartholomew was a member of KOL Local 4257.

28. *Labor Leaf*, September 8, 1886.

29. Charles F. Irons to Powderly, November 23, 1886, in *PP*. The catalogue of C. C. Darling and Company is located in the library of the Museum of Our National Heritage, Lexington, Mass.

30. *JKL*, January 23, 1890.

Fig. 17. Knights of Labor pins and charms from C. C. Darling catalog. Courtesy, Museum of Our National Heritage.

Knights had a variety of other items available that featured emblems of the Order. Probably the most popular were lapel buttons. Made of bronze, these buttons were very affordable, selling for 10 cents each or $7.50 for one hundred. About the size of a dime, KOL lapel buttons employed several bits of familiar imagery—pentagon, globe, and triangle—adding an arrow that penetrated the triangle from bottom to top. The exact meaning of this arrangement remains a mystery, but arrows traditionally denote spiritual service to God, a meaning in keeping with KOL ideology. The arrow is also the personal symbol of two Catholic saints (Ursula and Sebastian), perhaps an inducement for the Order's many Catholics.[31]

Members clearly relished material objects. In 1884, a Baltimore Knight bragged of an excursion he took on the Chesapeake Bay with fellow Knights. All of the brothers boldly donned blue ribbons stamped "K of L." In an obvious swipe at secrecy advocates, the writer praised Knights with the "manhood" to proclaim to both "the public . . . [and] employers . . . their connection with the K. of L."[32] Throughout the 1880s, em-

31. George Ferguson, *Signs and Symbols in Christian Art* (London: Oxford University Press, 1979).
32. *John Swinton's Paper*, August 3, 1884.

boldened Knights showed their allegiance through ever-increasing amounts of regalia. Some wore KOL insignia and joined the Order's newly formed Blue and Gray Association. Still others clamored for a KOL uniform that had no connections to military orders. Powderly's office was flooded by regalia cataloges, and he reluctantly yielded to their demands.[33]

One of the most visible symbols of any labor organization is its banners. By all accounts, the KOL made many, though few have yet surfaced.[34] H. G. Oesterle and Company of Philadelphia even offered banners by mail. Knights in St. Catharines, Ontario, marched three thousand strong behind banners proclaiming, "Labor Rise and Defend Your Dignity," "The Land For the People," and "Long Hours Must Go."[35] The Order produced so many banners that the GEB had to judge which ones would be sent to the 1889 Paris World's Fair to be displayed in the Exposition of Social Economy exhibit.[36] (The GEB finally sent fifteen banners, along with the 1878 Grand Assembly proceedings, bound volumes of the *JUL*, a crayon portrait of Uriah Stephens, and photographs of GEB members.)

Some KOL banners were quite elaborate. Toledo Knights of LA 3031, a German assembly, had a particularly ornate silk banner. One side featured a paint brush, hammer, and wheat surrounded by oak leaves, and the slogan *"Eintracht macht Stark*—Union Makes Strength." The reverse was a hand-woven American flag.[37] In fact, the KOL and its banners had international impact. Britain's Haggerstown No. 1 Branch of the National Union of General Workers featured a banner with five workers in front of a gas plant and saw mill. At the bottom of the banner is a variant of a familiar slogan: "An Injury to One is an Injury to All."[38]

33. *JKL*, November 12, 1891.

34. The problem of locating KOL banners is magnified by the fact that many museum curators are unfamiliar with KOL symbolism. The peculiar structure of the Order makes it likely that a lot of KOL-associated banners look like trade union banners; often local craft unions were organized as local assemblies. Assemblies were usually named, but monikers like "Friendship" or "Unity Assembly" do not betray a KOL connection. I assume that many banners mark their KOL affiliation with a symbol (most likely the triangle symbol of local assemblies), but this would be indecipherable to anyone unfamiliar with KOL imagery. A final problem is that many banners featured slogans rather than iconography and thus cannot be associated with any particular organization unless the observer finds official slogans with which he or she is familiar.

35. Kealey and Palmer, *Dreaming of What Might Be*.

36. *JUL*, February 28, 1889.

37. *JKL*, November 19, 1891.

38. Gorman, *Banners Bright*, 165. The slogan is also used on a poster of the Dockers' Union Export Branch in the 1890s. On a poster used by the Workers' Union around the time of World War I, one finds the slogan "He Who Would Be Free Must Strike the First

The sentiment expressed on the English banner echoes Knighthood's great dream of universal solidarity. In the heady days of late 1885 and early 1886, even the most grandiose fantasies seemed attainable. In 1886 William Tisdale published *The Knights' Book* linking the KOL to chivalrous heroes of the past. The Smithsonian Institution owns a glass mug produced about the same time. Into the mug is pressed the design of a worker, hammer in hand, shaking hands with a fully-armored knight (see Fig. 11). The symbolism could not be more clear: workers in the KOL embraced an organization that bound them beyond craft identity.

Material culture was so ingrained in the identity of both the Order and its members that it could become a focus of public battles. This was the case with KOL watches and watch charms. They were originally offered by the Dueber Watch-case Company of Newport, Kentucky, and sold through agents across the United States and Canada. In early 1886, however, a dispute with local Knights led the GEB to issue a boycott of Dueber goods.[39] The boycott was eventually raised, but the relationship between Dueber and the KOL remained stormy, and boycotts were reinstated throughout 1886 and 1887. The KOL simply shifted its patronage to other companies—like C. C. Darling and Company—and membership complied. By 1890, most of the Order's watches and charms were supplied by the Solidarity Watch Case Company of Brooklyn, with whom the KOL enjoyed a brief profit-sharing scheme.

KOL watch design also highlights the Order's shifting fortunes. We have noted how watches were dangled metaphorically in front of *Journal* readers as premiums. By 1890, any member who sent in a yearly, or two half-yearly, subscriptions could choose a premium of a watch charm or an enameled badge. But that was the last year a KOL watch appeared. In 1891, John Hayes announced another contest to increase *Journal* readership. Once again, gold watches were offered as inducements, but these bore no KOL insignia; rather they featured a deer on one side, and a bird by a pond on the reverse.[40]

But nostalgia for KOL material culture lingered well past the Order's useful life span. General Assemblies were opened when the GMW rapped a gavel of fine mahogany and encircled with brass on which the dates and places of past GAs had been inscribed. In 1887, Powderly was gifted with a carved chair made by a KOL cooperative chair company in

---

Blow," a rallying cry for anarchists in the United States, but also popular among Knights in Chicago and Denver in the late 1880s, and common to laborers in the Jacksonian years.

39. *JUL*, January 10, 1886.

40. This contest ran throughout 1891 and most issues of the *JKL* contain announcements.

Toledo, Ohio. Many years later, an elderly Powderly posed with old friends John Devlin and Alexander Wright for a photo that appeared in the *United Mine Workers Journal* (Fig. 18). In the shot, Powderly proudly grasps his GMW chair while clutching the gavel, as Wright and Devlin

Fig. 18.   An elderly Terence Powderly posing with friends John Devlin and Alexander Wright in front of chair given to Powderly by a Knights of Labor cooperative chair company in Toledo, Ohio. Note the gavel in Powderly's right hand. Powderly Papers, The Catholic University of America.

stand stiffly at either flank.[41] The symbols with which Powderly and company posed evoked better times and grander designs, remnants that bespoke the shattered promise of the Order.

Look for the Union Label

Material culture sustained group identity among the Knights of Labor, and it helped focus opposition to the Gilded Age status quo. But the same symbols of internal solidarity could prove divisive when they wandered beyond the assembly room's Outer Veil. In the larger society, Knights encountered workers who rejected visions of solidarity stamped with a KOL worldview. Nowhere was this more evident than in the Order's battles with resurgent trade unions. The split was, at its core, an ideological dispute between the broad producerist values of the KOL, and the narrower craft identities of trade unions. These visions clashed repeatedly in the 1880s and 1890s, with material culture often intensifying the debate. The most visible symbols in the battle were humble little stickers attached to goods that identified their makers. From 1884 on, the Knights and various trade unions waged veritable "label wars" that shattered labor unity to the delight of its enemies.

Scholars disagree over causes of the split. One sees it as the inevitable result of confusion arising from the KOL's rapid growth, while another blames antitrade ideologues within the Order. Other studies suggest trade union culpability. If the KOL was inconsistent, so too was AFL policy. Samuel Gompers at one moment supported dissident factions on state and local levels, only to condemn similar movements elsewhere as "dual unions." Still another scholar chastises the Cigar Makers International Union (CMIU)—the body whose battles with the KOL was a defining moment for the AFL—for a racialist and masculinist exclusionism that harmed class solidarity and was inconsonant with KOL liberalism.[42]

41. The *United Mine Workers Journal* is located in the *PP*. It is undated, but most likely dates from 1913 as reference is made to Woodrow Wilson's intention to open the next session of Congress with the gavel in Powderly's hand. That may not be the KOL gavel I have described, as the *UMWJ* mentions that the one Powderly holds is one used by every President from Hayes to Taft to open Congress. This photo is also found on Reel 93 of the *PP* and is one of the few photos from the original collection that has been microfilmed.

42. An historian who blames problems with unions on KOL growth is Ware, *The Labor Movement in the United States*, chaps. 8, 9. One who accuses antitrade unionists within the KOL is Foner, *History of the Labor Movement*, vol. 2, chap. 9. Elizabeth and Kenneth Fones-Wolf note Gompers' shifting policies and his near-obsession with dual unionism in "Rank-

All of these interpretations have merit, and it is safe to say that trade unions and the Knights were grounded in different fundamental assumptions about work, class, and society.

One should also bear in mind that the KOL was born from the ashes of trade union failures that pushed craft workers into the Order during the 1870s and early 1880s. From the start, the bulk of KOL locals were craft assemblies, a situation that persisted even during the mid-1880s when radicals upheld mixed assemblies as higher expressions of class consciousness. Founder's LA 1 of Philadelphia consisted for a time entirely of garment cutters, and many of the Order's early leaders— including Uriah Stephens, Charles Litchman, James L. Wright, Richard Griffiths, Richard Trevellick, James Campbell, Robert Schilling, and Hugh Cavanaugh—were craftsmen who felt the KOL would be the salvation of the trades.[43] So weak was 1870s trade unionism that only Campbell's Window Glass Blowers boasted vitality, which the KOL acknowledged by chartering it as LA 300, even though membership was spread across the country and abroad. As late as 1881, the Order was comfortable enough with the trades to send delegates to the founding of the Federation of Trade and Labor Unions (FOTLU), the body that preceded the AFL. Further, KOL journals printed the FOTLU constitution and Knights served as representatives for its entire life span.[44]

Matters grew more complicated as the KOL expanded into large industrial centers in the 1880s. The 1882 chartering of New York City DA 49 brought scores of anarchists, Fourierists, and Lassallean socialists into the KOL, groups distrustful of the value of trade unionism and committed to cooperative production and the destruction of the wage system.[45] Most KOL leaders, Powderly included, embraced the idea of cooperative enterprise, not simply better conditions on the shopfloor. All of this was in accord with the official policy; the Preamble called for "an end" to the wage system and for the establishment of "co-operative institutions,"

---

and-File Rebellions and AFL Interference in the Affairs of National Unions: The Gompers Era," *Labor History* 35, no. 2 (Spring 1994): 237–59. An historian who is critical of the CMIU's internal policies is Eileen Boris. See her " 'A Man's dwelling Is His Castle': Tenement House Cigarmaking and the Judicial Imperative," in Baron, *Work Engendered*, 114–41.

43. Uriah Stephens and James Wright were garment cutters. Charles Litchman, Hugh Cavanaugh, and Richard Griffiths were shoemakers. Richard Trevellick was a ship carpenter, and Robert Schilling a cooper.

44. *JUL*, November-December 1881. (This was a combined issue due to a mistake on Litchman's part which delayed the November issue. He was roundly criticized for this, especially by Robert Layton, the man who replaced him as Grand Secretary.

45. For more details on antitrade unionism, the Home Club, the composition of factions, and internal disruption inside the Knights of Labor, see Weir, "Tilting at Windmills."

while Powderly proclaimed "that the . . . competitive system is rotten to the core." Even in his declining years Powderly called cooperation "the lever of labor's emancipation."[46]

As a national organization, the KOL established only one cooperative enterprise, the Cannelburg Coal Company in Indiana, which it bought in 1884, mismanaged, leased in 1886, and sold at a loss in 1887. This has made some observers critical of the KOL's commitment to cooperation.[47] It is true that the KOL tapped into preexisting working-class romanticism for cooperation and sported rhetoric more grandiose than its actual efforts. Nonetheless, local Knights proved more adroit than national leaders and founded hundreds of local cooperatives.[48] Those efforts intensified after 1884 when John Samuel became head of the Co-Operative Board. Samuel was a decentralist who encouraged locals to experiment rather than await direction from the top. They responded. In 1883, only nineteen locals reported cooperative ventures, but one year later 132 reported, about 1 out of every 10 locals. Two years later there were over two hundred KOL cooperatives.[49]

Most of these ventures were humble, undercapitalized, and short-lived. Distributive efforts such as groceries and tobacco stands far outnumbered productive coops. Typical was a small cooperative store established in Northampton, Massachusetts, where local Knights purchased newspapers, cigars, and sundries at low prices but which lasted just over a year. Efforts like this were widespread. Southern Knights undertook dozens of ventures ranging from insurance schemes to retail stores to KOL factories. One of the most ambitious schemes took place in Birmingham, Alabama, where Knights bought land and laid out plots for the new town of "Powderly." By February 1888, there were twenty-six completed homes, plans for twenty-five more, a cooperative cigar factory, and a general store. The experiment fell apart in late 1888, when the GEB failed to capitalize the project, but Knights remained optimistic.[50]

46. Powderly, *Thirty Years of Labor*, 223, 225; Powderly, *The Path I Trod*, 269; see also the Preamble to the Knights of Labor platform located in most *JUL*s and in the appendix to Ware, *The Labor Movement in the United States*.

47. For one example of criticism of the Knights of Labor's cooperative efforts, see Grob, *Workers and Utopia*, 45–46.

48. For more on the cooperative movement, see Edward Bemis, ed., *Co-operation* (New York: Johnson Reprint Corporation, 1973). The original study was published in 1888. See also John Curl, *History of Work Cooperation in America* (Berkeley: Homeward Press, 1980); Selig Perlman, *History of Trade Unionism in the United States* (New York: Augustus M. Kelley, 1950); Ware, *The Labor Movement in the United States*.

49. Grob, *Workers and Utopia*, 45; Perlman, *History of Trade Unionism*, 126.

50. *Daily Hampshire Gazette* (Northampton, Mass.), September 23, 1886; McLaurin, *Knights of Labor in the South*, 113–30.

Some Knights tried their hand at manufacturing. In the 1880s, Knights could be found operating ice plants, making boots, ginning cotton, baking biscuits, rolling cigars, etching watch cases, and cutting leather goods.[51] Few of these enterprises proved any more successful than distributive concerns and thus passed quickly from the scene. What all this activity meant, however, is that the KOL contained numerous individuals whose goal for the political economy entailed revolutionary revisions. At precisely the moment in which Knights were experimenting with cooperation, craftsmen were moving toward "pure and simple" unionism. Although it is facile to label this "job consciousness," one can say that the propensity to view working-class life through a lens of wages, hours, and conditions placed craftsmen at serious visionary odds with many Knights. By the mid-1880s, some of them regarded trade unions as parochial and reactionary.

As the KOL developed its labels, it did so in the hope of linking the Order's larger reform efforts to consumer buying patterns. Labels identified goods made by Knights or allied trades, and by the 1880s workers were accustomed to looking for a union label before making purchases. Some even hoped that consumer solidarity would force capitalists to adopt cooperative practices. Sometimes it worked. Bernard Langer, a Rochester Knight, advised that the coopers' label was so effective that employers insisted their workers join the Knights as "they cannot make sale of their barrels without the stamp, or label, attached." It was quite a big step to acquire a modest slip of green paper five inches long and one and one-half inches wide stating, "This stamp is placed on all cooperage made by Union men only. It is for the protection of their Trade, Home, Industry, and Consumers, from unclean and filthy packages."

Soon sanctioned labels appeared in the *JUL*, and the General Secretary's office offered KOL labels for 10 cents per hundred that could be affixed to goods. Trades routinely petitioned the KOL's GEB to accept their label. By 1888, there were specific labels for watch cases, collars, cigars, hats, boots, cans, trunks, gloves, files, and shirts, as well as a generic KOL label. Most designs featured an identifying mark or lettering that made them instantly recognizable as a KOL product. For example, the coopers' label was a barrel with a circle and triangle and the letters "K of L," while the trunkmakers featured a large trunk with two small valises hovering over it at an angle so that the entire design formed a triangle in which "K of L" was printed[52] (Fig. 19).

51. The most complete survey of KOL cooperative efforts to date is the 1888 study by Bemis, *Co-operation.* See also Ware, *The Labor Movement in the United States,* chap. 14; Powderly, *The Path I Trod,* chap. 23.

52. *JUL,* January 15, 1883. Most issues of the *JUL* contain reproductions of labels which the Order officially supported.

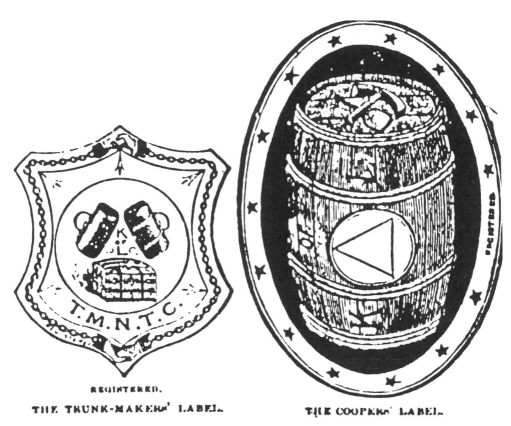

REGISTERED.

THE TRUNK-MAKERS' LABEL.   THE COOPERS' LABEL.

Fig. 19.   KOL cooperatives, such as trunkmakers and coopers, were permitted to incorporate the KOL trademark into their union labels. Sanctioned labels appeared in the *Journal of United Labor* so that workers could look for a union label when making purchases.

Journals exhorted members to check labels when buying goods. The *Haverhill Laborer* boldly declared, "We do not ask capital to use this stamp; capital comes to us and asks permission to use it, as the customers of capital are demanding it."[53] The claim was not far from the mark, retailers and manufacturers indeed courted the KOL. Colored trade cards (Fig. 20) were given out as premiums by clothiers, haberdashers, and tobacconists trying to solicit KOL trade. Most featured workers engaged in noble toil with Powderly's portrait hanging above them. On a card offered by H. S. Brokaw, a man and woman work side by side in a clothing manufactory above the slogan "By Industry We Thrive." Brokaw's concessions to the Knights are obvious; his establishment sold

53. *Haverhill Laborer*, February 27, 1886.

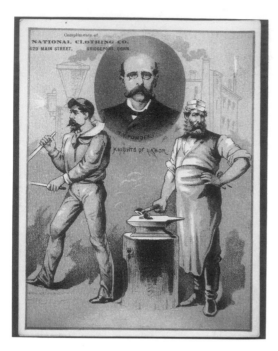

Fig. 20.   Knights of Labor trade cards. Merchants gave out such cards as premiums to solicit KOL trade. Courtesy, Smithsonian Institution.

tobacco products, fruit, and confections, not clothing. Similarly, the National Clothing Company of Bridgeport, Connecticut, issued cards on which Powderly oversaw the work of KOL foundry workers.[54] The D. Buchner & Company tobacco firm of New York City even offered "Master Mechanic" smoking and chewing tobacco, with Powderly's picture prominently displayed on the label. Even the Duryea Starch Company, a company with whom the KOL frequently clashed, took out ads in KOL journals.

The Knights' greatest enthusiasm was reserved for cooperative goods. Ads appeared in KOL journals for retailers who sold KOL goods, but large spaces—often with explanatory text—appeared for goods like King of Labor Washing Compound, or Globe Tobacco. The former ad was a KOL cooperative and the latter a Detroit firm that employed only Knights of Labor and that practiced profit-sharing until 1892. Many KOL cooperatives opted for the name "Solidarity," such as the Solidarity Watch-Case Company of Brooklyn and the Solidarity Co-operative Garment Workers of Rochester, New York. Perhaps the best inducement for solidarity came from a Chicago tailoring company that offered suits, overcoats, and pants by mail order. Proudly displayed was a pair of scissors astride the KOL triangle. Above the label was printed the slogan "Practice What You Preach!"[55] Labels and endorsements really mattered, and the KOL hoped its own would build solidarity.

Yet these same labels came to embody the Order's struggle against trade unionism, the roots of which lay in the 1881 FOTLU founding conference. Delegate Robert Layton, soon to become the Knights' Grand Secretary, argued that FOTLU should exclude skilled workers. When delegates rejected Layton's proposal, several small jurisdictional skirmishes broke out between trades and the Knights.[56] Especially rankled by Layton's suggestion was the Cigar Makers' International Union. Soon, the KOL's white and CMIU's blue trademarks vied for supremacy.

The label conflagrations of 1886 began as brushfires. The initial spark occurred in 1880, when a renegade branch of German socialists in New York City left the CMIU, formed the United Cigar Makers of North

54. The trade cards to which I allude are the property of the Smithsonian Institution and were included in the "Images of American Labor" exhibit.

55. When the Globe Tobacco Company abandoned profit sharing, the KOL launched a boycott against it. See *JKL*, April 14, 1892, and subsequent issues.

56. One such dispute took place in Washington, D.C., where KOL and trade union carpenters battled over jurisdictions. See Kenneth and Elizabeth Fones-Wolf, "Knights Versus the Trade Unionists: The Case of the Washington, D.C. Carpenters, 1881–1886," *Labor History* 22 (Spring 1981): 192–212.

America, and elected Samuel Schimkowitz their president. Since both groups belonged to KOL Local 144, peaceful coexistence was impossible. In 1882, DA 49 was formed. Its powerful anarcho-socialist, antitrade unionist leadership cadre sided with the Schimkowitz faction. But Schimkowitz was outmaneuvered by Adolph Strasser and Samuel Gompers, who suspended him. Predictably, DA 49 found in favor of Schimkowitz, but both groups continued to claim KOL affiliation. The United Cigar Makers reorganized in late 1882 as the Cigarmakers' Progressive Union of North America (CMPU), and entered the KOL as the newly formed Progressive Labor Club, LA 2814. The CMPU, remnants of LA 144, and the Gompers/Strasser-led CMIU, of LA 2458's "Defiance Assembly," battled openly, with DA 49 favoring the CMPU.[57]

By early 1886, the DA 49-led Home Club controlled the Knights, and Powderly could not oppose its crusade against the CMIU. Historians have been skeptical of Powderly's claim to have taken "no part in the fight against the cigar makers," but there is little reason to doubt his claim that he thought the decision to expel the CMIU was neither "lawful or warranted." Powderly contemplated resigning before the 1886 General Assembly when he saw that the Order was heading for a confrontation with national trade unions, and that he was under the Home Club's control. He decided to continue in his post and cooperate with the Home Club, and in vain hope of influencing the Order's trade union policy from the inside.[58]

57. Ware, The Labor Movement in the United States, chap. 11; Stuart B. Kaufman, ed., The Samuel Gompers Papers, vol.1: The Making of a Union Leader, 1850–1886 (Urbana: University of Illinois Press, 1986), 365–427 [hereafter cited as Gompers Papers]; Dennis East, "Union Labels and Boycotts: Cooperation of the Knights of Labor and the Cigarmakers International Union, 1885–1886," Labor History 16 (Spring 1975): 266–71.

58. Powderly, The Path I Trod, 142. Powderly's intention to resign over the Order's trade union policy is made clear in letters to Robert Layton and Charles Litchman during late 1885 and early 1886, and a secret circular issued May 23, 1886 (see PP). In 1887 he complained to Hayes that the decisions made at Richmond in 1886 were wrong. See Powderly to Hayes, April 29, 1887, in PP. For once Powderly's threats to resign were sincere. Though he often used such threats as a ploy to get what he wanted, Powderly was genuinely frustrated. He certainly realized by mid-1886 that the Home Club, not he, controlled KOL policy. Powderly made the fateful decision to play power politics in the Order and cooperate with the Home Club in hopes of overthrowing it. He was only partly successful in this gambit; the Home Club reorganized in 1887 and gradually faded in importance, but not before doing irrevocable damage to the KOL's relationship with trade unions. Further, the Home Club reorganization of 1887 also threw out a few such as James Quinn, who Powderly considered more pliable. Though Powderly spoke of reversing the 1886 decisions at the 1887 General Assembly he did not press the issue. Socialist factions in DA 49 were still very powerful in the Home Club; to reverse course could have toppled Powderly in 1887. By 1888 the enmity between the Knights and trade unions was so great that compromise, though often discussed, was unlikely. The personal dispute between Powderly and Sam-

Passions ran high throughout 1886. In February, the CMIU condemned the use of the KOL label on cigars, and Adolph Strasser noted "complaints from New York City, that the K. of L. label is issued to tenement house manufacturers, and to manufacturers paying from $1.00 to $2.00 less per thousand than is the scale adopted by the International Union."[59] He neglected to mention that most of those workers were women ineligible for CMIU membership. When DA 49 showed little interest in attacking working women, Strasser accused it of interfering in CMIU strikes, an action he called a "bold and unscrupulous attack upon recognized trades' union principles." He demanded that Powderly take action lest he "merit the condemnation [of] every national trades' union in the nation."[60]

In April, a *JUL* article added to the confusion by announcing that the GEB had adopted a new label for cigars. Like its CMIU rival, it was blue, and was supposed to supplant the white one.[61] That same month, however, employees of Sutro and Newmark were issued a white label when the KOL organized the plant. A few cigar makers protested that membership in LA 2458 was forced on them by their employer.[62] The CMIU responded by leveling a boycott of all KOL cigars.

Unionists and Knights alike learned to scan cigar labels for their content rather than merely their color, while their leaders whipped them into frenzies. In May 1886, Detroit cigar makers gathered to hear Gompers speak on "Scabs, Knights of Labor, and Trades Unions." Both the KOL and DA 49 were denounced. Gompers accused the Knights of initiating strike breakers into their assemblies. He described the KOL's new label to the audience: "[It is] blue and in the shape of a seal, and I want you to crush it when you see it. . . . [The] Knights of Labor first had a white label, and when they noticed the success of the International label they changed the color the correspond with the latter."[63]

The popular press delighted in reporting the KOL/trades battles. A

uel Gompers escalated the debate; though KOL and trade union locals often did cooperate, they did so largely independently of their national leadership.

59. Adolph Strasser to Powderly, February 25, 1886, in *Gompers Papers*.

60. Strasser to Powderly, March 16, 1886, in *Gompers Papers*.

61. *JUL*, April 25, 1886.

62. Employees of Sutro & Newmark to Powderly, April 19, 1886, in *Gompers Papers*.

63. *Detroit Free Press*, May 24, 1886; reprinted in *Gompers Papers*.

There is some truth in Gompers' assertion that the KOL changed their label due to the success of the CMIU blue label. At least one manufacturer, the important Lichenstein Brothers of New York City, complained to Frederick Turner that the CMIU boycott of nonblue cigars was hurting business and that many retailers were refusing white label cigars. Lichenstein Co. to Frederick Turner, May 10, 1886, in *PP*. For more on the dispute between Powderly and Gompers, see Foner, *History of the Labor Movement*, vol. 2, chap. 9.

cartoon in *Harper's Weekly* represents the two as ridiculous jousting knights squaring off in front of a pavilion labeled "arbitration" while a figure with a money bag for a head smiles approvingly from the judge's seat.[64] *Puck* was even harsher, as its cartoon features two horse-drawn wagons rushing down the "Road of Lawlessness and Disorder." Menacing figures from each wagon wield large clubs; the trade unions are marked "No Dictation," while that of the KOL says "Home Club." The horses of the Knights' wagons wear collars bearing the slogans "Political Intrigue" and "Boycott." This curse-on-both-houses scene unfolds as the train of the Brotherhood of Locomotive Engineers (BLE) runs smoothly down a track of "Law and Order," powered by the locomotive "Progress." Apparently the editors of *Puck* found the antistrike/antiboycott policies of the BLE more to their liking.[65]

The trades and the Knights continued to club one another rhetorically. Each side accused the other of scabbing and undercutting wages. Numerous compromises were proposed, and a conference among several trade unionists and the KOL's GEB was held in September 1886. Little came of it except more rancor. More typical than half-hearted peace overtures was a forty-eight-page circular issued by the KOL's Executive Board, and a CMIU-sponsored parade. The circular accused the CMIU of betraying the Progressive Cigar Makers and New York City's Central Labor Union, called Samuel Gompers a drunkard, and cataloged a series of insults hurled at the KOL. In July, the CMIU responded with a rally, picnic, and parade on DA 49's home turf. Nearly six thousand CMIU paraders marched in New York City behind blue satin facsimiles of the CMIU label, and slogans like "Buy Blue Label Cigars."[66]

The KOL's October GA expelled all cigar makers affiliated with the CMIU. Periodic attempts were made to heal the breach but little except bluster was accomplished. Long after Powderly's ouster in 1893, labor journals recounted rumors of concord between the Knights and the unions. In the end, the label battles helped unify trades about to consolidate under the aegis of the AFL, but fragmented the Knights. As the KOL attempted to redefine Knighthood in the 1880s and replace older ritualistic models with newer ones based on solidarity, the label wars were harsh reminders of how far from that goal the Order remained. Individual workers faced a fundamental choice between bread-and-butter unionism and visionary Knighthood.

64. *Harper's Weekly*, June 12, 1886.

65. *Puck*, August 25, 1886.

66. Knights of Labor, "The Order and the Cigarmakers," reprinted in Kaufman, *Gompers Papers*, 409–11; *U.S. Tobacco Journal*, July 24, 1886, in *Gompers Papers*.

Some workers sought middle ground. The *Haverhill Laborer* addressed a letter to Gompers in which it held out a stunted olive branch: "You must remember this, Sam, that your fight should not be against the entire Order, but solely with those who are false to their first principles of labor organization, and are acting in either malice or ignorance in thus prostituting the label of the K. of L."[67] Haverhill was part of Massachusetts DA 30, an area where the trades debate raged with white-hot intensity since as late as 1893; 93 of its 170 assemblies were trades locals. Leaders like George McNeill, Frank Foster, Harry Skeffington, and A. A. Carlton pushed the district into unilaterally declaring that the KOL's boycott of CMIU cigars applied only to New York City. (Denver Knights took a similar position.) They blamed the entire controversy on a "secret combination" (that is, the Home Club) in the Knights.[68]

Middle positions proved untenable, and soon trade unionists left the KOL. By 1888, McNeill, Foster, Skeffington, and Carlton were out of the Order, and Frank Foster's labor papers attacked the KOL on a regular basis. Ironically, Skeffington's engraving, "Founders of the Knights of Labor," was once offered as a premium for subscribers to *John Swinton's Paper*.[69] Massachusetts was not the only place where fierce debate over trade unionism occurred. *The Labor Leaf* dutifully reported the news of CMIU's expulsion from the KOL and the call for a boycott against them. But reporters in the Detroit area found opinion split over the expulsion of the cigar makers. Merrit Shindler, a cigar maker, reluctantly noted, "I do not want to leave the Knights, but I will support the Cigarmakers' Union as against the K. of L." John Leys, a tailor and Master Workman of LA 901, was blunt: "I think the order is unconstitutional, and shall certainly advise 901 to refuse to obey the order."[70] Chicago sentiment was even more direct. Joseph Buchanan's *Chicago Labor Enquirer* summed up the CMIU action under the headline "It Is Unlawful," and reprinted Joseph Labadie's blast against the GEB as it first appeared in *The Labor Leaf*.[71]

With the Home Club faction in disarray, Powderly tried to set matters right at the 1887 General Assembly, where delegates agreed that actions taken against the CMIU the previous year were unwise and unconstitutional. But it was too late for the Knights to undo the damage. Though the KOL rescinded the CMIU expulsion order, peace overtures between

67. *Haverhill Laborer*, May 15, 1886.
68. *The Laborer* (Boston) June 5, 1886; July 2, 1887; July 23, 1887.
69. *John Swinton's Paper*, June 5, 1887, and other issues during the year include advertisements for the Skeffington poster.
70. *The Advance and Labor Leaf*, February 19, 1887.
71. *Labor Enquirer* (Chicago), March 5, 1887.

the Order and trade unions involved more posturing than sincerity. An 1890 *JKL* editorial reminded Knights of their "duty" to give "preference" to their own labels, and many probably did.[72] But, as fewer and fewer Knights existed, the pressure on manufacturers and retailers to bother with KOL labels evaporated. In 1892, the Globe Tobacco Company ended its profit-sharing program with its KOL employees. The Knights responded with a boycott, but since it had fewer than one hundred thousand members nation wide, and the Order had exhausted its reserve of cross-organizational solidarity, the Globe survived nicely without the KOL's patronage. By then KOL labels had lost their status as symbols of solidarity, and were well on their way to becoming "small things forgotten."

Graphic Descriptions

As the KOL and trade unions battled to inconclusive results, the popular press skewered both groups in editorials and graphics. As the *Harper's* and *Puck* cartoons show, more was at stake than simply the territorial squabbles between competing labor organizations. Up for grabs was nothing less than public opinion concerning labor's right to bargain collectively. The brief popularity enjoyed by the KOL on editorial pages and in popular fiction proved even more fleeting among Gilded Age graphic artists and photographers. Very few press images of the KOL were flattering. Material culture focused rifts within the labor movement, and they calcified negative opinions from without.

Graphics were used as a weapon against the KOL. Pictorial images— cartoons, drawings, lithographs, photographs, and woodcuts—became increasingly popular in the late nineteenth century. Publications like *Frank Leslie's*, *Harper's*, and *Puck* promoted themselves as "illustrated" newspapers, and images like the cartoon attacks of Thomas Nast against the Tweed Ring, or Matthew Brady's horrific Civil War photos had tremendous impact on public opinion. Illustrated papers shaped the pictorial content of urban papers even more than story-papers changed writing styles.

No Gilded Age labor paper could hope to compete graphically with the urban press as illustration was a relatively new and exceedingly costly art form. In 1873, *The New York Daily Graphic* became the first newspaper to use illustrations regularly, but graphics were not widespread

---

72. *JKL*, March 6, 1890.

until the 1880s. It was not until 1889 that Joseph Pulitzer integrated graphics into his papers.[73] Illustrations were not easily transposed onto newsprint. The *Daily Graphic* used a zinc etching process that was time-consuming and expensive. Even the half-tone process, pioneered in the 1880s, was beyond the budgets of most small papers. Charles Litchman, the first editor of the *JUL*, lost his post as Grand Secretary for spending too much money on the *Journal*. The Order was chronically short of money, and the humble *JUL* remained a small in-house publication with grandiose pretensions. Its illustrations never advanced much beyond experimentation with Gothic lettering on the nameplate, and an occasional woodcut. Woodcuts were often fuzzy, indicating the use of inadequate technology.

The symbiosis between the labor and popular press in their fictive and poetic content was lacking in graphic content, and positive images of the KOL were far fewer. It was a minor victory when newspaper graphics delivered mixed or ambiguous messages. One such example was an 1882 satirical illustration published in *Puck* that depicts a KOL picnic, and the central event, a greased pole climb. A worker fails to surmount a pole coated with "Monopoly Grease," while Jay Gould, William Vanderbilt, Russell Sage, Cyrus Field, and shipbuilder John Roach sip champagne. Field is doubled over with laughter, while Gould and Vanderbilt stare with amusement at a distraught woman with two ragged children on her back urging the worker to continue his futile quest. Undoubtedly, *Puck* is attacking monopoly and greed, but its image of the Knights is hardly flattering. Strike banners fly and angry fists are shaken, but the overall sense is one of hopelessness and wasted energy. Furthermore, the climbing worker vainly strains to reach a summit of "Higher Wages," "Bread," and "Ham," but the pole is topped by two other objects of his desire, "Tobacco" and "Wine" (Fig. 21). The latter pursuit was particularly insulting to an organization officially committed to temperance.[74]

Frank Leslie's Illustrated Newspaper did not really bother with the Knights until 1886, though an 1882 print shows them marching in the September workers' demonstration thought by many to be America's first Labor Day celebration. (The Knights are identified through their banners.)[75] For the most part, the paper viewed labor agitation as the work of wild-eyed, bomb-throwing anarchists, or the result of unruly mobs in need of the policeman's club.[76] As it ushered in 1886, the paper

73. For more on graphic production and the urban press, see Schudson, *Discovering the News.*
74. *Puck,* June 21, 1882.
75. *Frank Leslie's Illustrated Newspaper,* September 16, 1882.
76. Ibid., February 7, 1885; February 14, 1885.

Fig. 21. *Puck*'s depiction of a KOL picnic. The inability of the worker to climb the pole is an indictment not only of monopolies in American society but of the Knights as well.

included "Labor Strikes" in a retrospective of 1885's misfortunes, which paraded before Uncle Sam and the infant "1886." In the procession, strikers appear in step with "Hard Times, Mormonism, Business Failures," free silver agitation, and the deaths of Ulysses S. Grant and George B. McClellan. Uncle Sam implores the youthful 1886, "Hope you can do better than that."[77]

The Southwest Railway strikes of 1885 and 1886 briefly forced *Frank Leslie's* to reevaluate the Knights. Like other papers, mild sympathy for the KOL surfaced when it was trendy. In March 1886, illustrations of the second Gould strike appeared. At first, accompanying editorials avoided the KOL by name and enjoined a generic "labor organization" to avoid "the insensate violence and wanton destruction that have marked the strikes of earlier days." The paper confessed "some degree of sympathy" for the strikers, but mostly counseled against violence and for a speedy resolution of the dispute.[78]

When optimistic hopes were not realized, the paper's sympathies began to shift. In April, a drawing appeared of angry strikers hurling rocks and shaking fists at U.S. marshals guarding a freight train in East St. Louis, Illinois. The editors praised Terence Powderly for his "firmness, dignity, practical good sense, and honesty," and ran a short biography of him and a brief synopsis of KOL history.[79] The next issue, however, ran a front-page illustration of deputy sheriffs clearing the East St. Louis yards, and an editorial condemnation of KOL strikers who "greatly injured their cause by their resorts to violence." Martin Irons was blamed for leading an "irresponsible body of men" into violence, and for destroying positive public opinion regarding the KOL.[80]

The very next week, *Frank Leslie's* again turned on the Knights, when the content of letters exchanged between Powderly and Gould came to their attention. A novel reading of those notes led editors to conclude that the Knights had broken a no-strike pledge, and that Irons headed a wildcat action called to protest the firing of an employee for whom the "Gould system was in no way responsible." The paper accused Pow-

77. Ibid., January 2, 1886.

78. Ibid., March 20, 1886.

79. Ibid., April 10, 1886.

80. For an attack on Martin Irons, see *Frank Leslie's Illustrated Newspaper*, April 17, 1886. To be fair, the same editorial also attacked Jay Gould.

Martin Irons was the District Master Workman of DA 101 based in Sedalia, Missouri. From there Irons organized many locals along the Missouri Pacific line. Irons was widely hailed as a hero in the successful 1885 strike against Jay Gould, and just as widely blamed for the defeat in 1886. A Congressional committee also blamed Irons of precipitating the second strike, and Powderly and the GEB of the Knights ignobly allowed Irons to become the scapegoat. Irons was blacklisted, and died in poverty in 1900.

derly of changing the issues and saw "only one chance for arbitration
. . . let the Knights of Labor who are out of employment by their own
act apply to the industrious men who are now at work on Mr. Gould's
lines, and ask them if they . . . will give up their positions to their predecessors."[81] There was little Powderly could do but repeat his call for arbitration, a call neither Gould nor Missouri Pacific general manager H. M.
Hoxie were wont to answer. By May 1886, the Southwest strike was
lost.[82]

Powderly's constant calls for arbitration attracted notice, though not
the sort he craved. In one cartoon, the figure of Puck stands on a box
labeled "Common Sense," while capital and labor stand atop ladders on
opposite sides of a clock marked "Business" and argue over the positions of the hands (dollar signs replace numbers on the clock's face).
Puck holds the clock pendulum, marked "Arbitration," in his hands and
tries vainly to attract the attention of the disinterested combatants.[83] In
a subsequent drawing, giant figures of "Capital" and "Labor" appear in
a room in which that same clock hangs on one wall and a sign announcing "Rusted High Horses For Sale CHEAP" on the other. The "high
horses" are labeled "Monopoly" and "Socialism." Capital holds a large
club marked "Monopoly," while Labor wields a large hammer bearing
the tag "Strikes." Both figures have relaxed their grips, however, as they
intently bend over a diminutive Terence Powderly clutching a proposal
for a bill to establish arbitration." On one level, *Puck* seems to endorse
arbitration, but on another, its advocates appear as mosquitos among
giant beasts.[84]

The Great Upheaval challenged the popular press in ways in which
fear eventually outweighed fascination. A May 1886 lithograph showed
Powderly and P. M. Arthur of the BLE desperately trying to pull a worker
up a steep bank above a pool labeled "Bloodshed and Disorder." They
hold his right arm, while "Socialist" and "Anarchist" firmly clasp his
left leg, "Boycott" urges them on, and the snake of "Demagogism"
writhes at the pool's edge. In response to third-party successes in November, *Frank Leslie's* depicted Uncle Sam counseling a worker clutching
ballots and election results. Behind the worker raved a wild anarchist
with dagger in hand and dynamite at his feet. His arm around the

81. *Frank Leslie's Illustrated Newspaper*, April 24, 1886.

82. One of the best accounts of the Southwestern troubles remains that of Ware, *The
Labor Movement in the United States*, 140–54. See also Stromquist, *A Generation of Boomers*;
Michael Cassity, "Modernization and Social Crisis: The Knights of Labor and a Midwest
Community, 1885–1886," *Labor History* (June 1979): 41–61.

83. *Puck*, March 17, 1886; reprinted in Schnapper, *American Labor*, 177.

84. *Puck*, April 7, 1886.

worker, Uncle Sam tells him, "You did splendidly . . . for a first attempt, but for your own good and that of your country, get rid of that dangerous companion of yours as soon as possible."[85] The point of both cartoons was obvious: American workers were poised on the brink between respectable, lawful activity and violent anarchism.

Frank Leslie's also provided what is probably the single most enduring material image of the KOL. In October 1886, the paper ran a front-page lithograph of Frank M. Ferrell of DA 49 introducing Powderly to the 1886 General Assembly while an apprehensive Governor of Virginia looks on (see Fig. 4). Ferrell, DA 49's black delegate and Socialist Labor Party comrade, attracted great attention in solidly Jim Crow Richmond, especially when his DA 49 comrades arrived in the city with tents to protest of the city's refusal to lodge Ferrell in the same hotel as white delegates. James Quinn, DA 49 Master Workman, pressured Powderly to have Ferrell introduce Governor Fitzhugh Lee. In an artful compromise, Ferrell introduced Powderly, who introduced the Governor. In strongly worded speeches, both Ferrell and Powderly upheld the KOL's commitment to racial brotherhood (though Powderly later softened a GA resolution that would have unequivocally denounced racism for fear of further antagonizing white southern Knights).[86]

Frank Leslie's noted that some members felt KOL actions were "an insult to the people of Richmond," but that most delegates acted "without a surrender of principle," and "with discretion." A measure of nervousness ended the editorial, however.

> Hitherto, while contending strongly for their rights, the colored people have not been . . . disposed to be intrusive in intercourse with whites. They are not inclined to go where they are not welcome, and they are, we believe, sensible enough to see that their own cause can best be promoted by avoiding obstacles which time is sure to remove.

The ambivalence extended to Powderly who was credited with stimulating KOL growth despite "a series of mistakes, failures, and disasters on the part of the Order," like the Southwest strikes and the Haymarket

85. *Puck*, May 12, 1886; *Frank Leslie's Illustrated Newspaper*, November 13, 1886.

86. *Frank Leslie's Illustrated Newspaper*, November 13, 1886. Powderly softened the resolution offered by James Quinn calling for the KOL to recognize "the civil and political equality of all men and women in this broad field of labor [with] no distinction on account of color" by amending it to add the words, "but it has no purpose to interfere with or disrupt the social relations which may exist between different races in any part of the country." See Foner, *American Socialism and Black Americans*, 62–69.

riots. Further illustrations showed black and white Knights were engaged in serious discussion inside the convention hall, and side bars showed African Americans in normal discourse with whites.[87]

The brief reconsideration of racial equality and the Knights soon faded and *Frank Leslie's* showed its true position. Both before and after illustrations of the KOL General Assembly, the paper portrayed African Americans in a degrading and stereotypical manner. Typical of its graphics is a series of 1889 "Camp Meeting Sketches" showing blacks in animallike caricatures from whose thick lips emanates a semiliterate patois.[88] Subsequent references to the KOL were few and far between, and never flattering.

From late 1886 on, the KOL was fair game for satirists and pundits. *Puck* presented Powderly in a lampoon of a confused orchestra. Powderly tries to play his "Harp of Harmony" while reformers, assorted anarchists, "walking delegates" and AFL leaders create cacophony by playing different tunes.[89] *Puck* also ridiculed the Order for courting the Catholic Church, and accused it of hypocrisy. In a cartoon combining these themes, a crowd of angry Knights stands outside a tavern from whose window hangs the slogan "An Injury to One is the Concern of All." The Knights are busy stoning a worker as a Catholic bishop and his entourage walk down the street dispensing blessings (see Fig. 7).[90]

By October 1887, *Puck* saw the working class in a no-win situation faced with the choice of being devoured by the ravenous wolf of "Starvation," or remaining chained to a statue labeled "Union Tyranny." To reinforce the point, the November issue ran a cartoon of "Puck's Thanksgiving Dinner to the Destitute and Disappointed Politicians and Labor Agitators" (Fig. 22). Ragged figures—including Henry George, Benjamin Butler, James Blaine, and Terence Powderly—hungrily await the carving of "Old Consolation," a tough bird they will smother with "Caustic Sauce."[91]

After 1887, the KOL seldom appeared in the illustrated newspapers except for incidental captions linking them with bigger labor disturbances such as the 1888 Pennsylvania anthracite strikes or the 1892 Homestead troubles. Shortly after the collapse of the Pullman strike, *Puck* recorded one of the last graphic images of the KOL. The female figure of "Law and Order" stands above an abyss marked "Dumping

87. *Frank Leslie's Illustrated Newspaper*, October 16, 1886.
88. Ibid., August 10, 1889.
89. *Puck*, December 22, 1886.
90. *Puck*, April 13, 1887; March 23, 1887; reprinted in Schnapper, *American Labor*.
91. *Puck*, October 1887; November 1887.

Fig. 22. "Puck's Thanksgiving Dinner to the Destitute and Disappointed Politicians and Labor Agitators." In *Puck*'s view, the working class was stuck between starvation and the tyranny of labor unions. Courtesy, Neilson Library, Smith College.

Ground for Kings of Misrule." Her right hand has already released Eugene Debs who is plummeting into the canyon, and she has a firm grasp on J. P. Atlgeld in her left. They will soon join four other erstwhile kings in the pit: Jacob Coxey, Homestead leader Hugh O'Donnell, Martin Irons, and Terence Powderly.[92]

Self-Portraits

How did Knights respond to images like these? For the most part they avoided them and attempted to plant alternative, more positive pictures

92. Ibid., July 1894.

in the minds of members. Only on rare occasions did KOL self-portraits respond directly to graphic insults. The *JUL* was a rather stodgy paper. As the mouthpiece for the entire organization it was, necessarily, broad, even generic, in its editorial policy. The paper's central mission was to educate the rank and file, familiarize it with KOL policy, and foster identification with the Order. This meant that organizational goals took precedence over local concerns.

The *JUL* created images that accomplished those limited goals quite well. Weekly printings of approved labels and trademarks guided KOL consumers, just as periodic engravings of official badge designs protected them from unscrupulous purveyors of KOL gear. By far the most common of all *JUL* images were those of leaders. The premier issue of May 15, 1880, featured an engraving of Grand Master Workman Powderly. Subsequent issues featured Uriah Stephens, Charles Litchman, Gilbert Rockwood, Robert Layton, Richard Griffiths, Daniel McLaughlin, and Frederick Turner. Each picture was accompanied by a short biography, the teleological intent of which was to show how each had found true hope in the KOL after toiling in vain for defunct labor organizations.[93] These served to give a swelling rank-and-file visual identification with the Order and object lessons in the merits of broad-based Knighthood. Perhaps an unstated function was to promote centralization efforts championed by Powderly.

What better way to promote this than to reify images of the Grand Master Workman? Thus two images dominated: Uriah Stephens and Terence Powderly. One could buy life-size pictures of Stephens for a dollar. Soon Stephens's portrait appeared on the official list of supplies available through the General Secretary's office and was sold well into the 1890s. In fact, the administration of James Sovereign promoted it quite heavily in 1894. Though it is natural that Stephens be honored during celebrations of the Order's twenty-fifth anniversary, Sovereign found an evocation of the founder a useful way to distance himself from his predecessor, Terence Powderly. Stephens's picture looms large on page one

93. *JUL*, May 1880; June 1880; August 1881; February 1883; April 1883; May 1883; June 1883; July 1883.
    Of these figures, Gilbert Rockwood is probably the least known. He served as Assistant Grand Secretary under both Charles Litchman and Robert Layton, and was a close friend of Powderly's. In the mid-1880s Rockwood suffered a nervous breakdown and was out of the labor movement for a while. He resurfaced at decade's end and moved from Pittsburgh to Washington, D.C., where he renewed his KOL activity. Rockwood remained a Powderly stalwart and tried to martial support for him in Washington during the chaotic days of 1892–93 when John Hayes plotted to rid the Order of its longtime Master Workman. Daniel McLaughlin was a western organizer who brought the KOL to the coal fields of Illinois. He was a member of LA 376, Braidwood, Illinois.

of the *JKL*, while those of Powderly and Sovereign were placed on page three, with Sovereign's picture drawn slightly larger than Powderly's.[94]

In the 1880s, however, Powderly was never treated so shabbily. Far more Knights had Powderly's picture hanging in their homes than Stephens's. Powderly's image was so ubiquitous that it would have been the rare Knight who could not instantly visualize the General Master Workman. The General Secretary's office sold photographs of Powderly for two dollars each, while Knights elsewhere offered his image as premiums. Though Stephens loomed larger than Powderly in 1894, this was not the case in 1887, when the Toledo editors of *The Industrial News* offered a larger-than-life engraving of Powderly.[95]

Aside from the occasional engraving of a banner or building, the only other graphics in the *JUL* were those found in advertisements. A small, curious exception appeared a few times beginning in April 1888, when a diminutive black cat topped the "Quaint Quirks" column and was labeled "Our Office Cat." Black cats symbolized sabotage, and were a favorite symbol among anarchists and syndicalists. Its brief appearance and quick exit from the *JUL* likely reflects the shifting fortunes of internal factionalism within the KOL. (Early 1888 was the last gasp of Home Club conspirators who would have been sympathetic to sabotage imagery.)

To find local concerns and more explicit graphics, one must leave the *JUL* and look at local and allied newspapers. Not even the Southwest strike led the *JUL* to respond with strong visual images. The best labor graphics of that event were found in *The Irish World and American Industrial Liberator*, edited by Powderly's friends Patrick and Mary Ford. The Fords commissioned lifelike sketches of the strike and added captions such as "Unprovoked massacre of innocent citizens by Jay Gould's deputy sheriffs."[96]

Many New York City Knights associated with DA 64 were printers. Their concerns were often better expressed by *The Boycotter*, the journal of International Typographical Union (ITU) Number 6. In 1884, "Big 6" began a boycott of Whitelaw Reid's *New York Tribune*, an action supported by both DA 64 (some of whose members held joint ITU membership), and the KOL's General Executive Board.[97] *The Boycotter* used illustrations to excoriate enemies. Scab editors were represented as rats

94. *JKL*, November 22, 1894.

95. *Toledo Industrial News*, June 11, 1887, microfilm edition, Ohio Historical Society.

96. *The Irish World and American Industrial Liberator*, April 24, 1886.

97. The era of good feelings between the Knights and ITU No. 6 ended in 1886 when DA 49 called a boycott against the *New York Sun*, a union paper. The ITU objected to this and eventually made its way into the American Federation of Labor. See Ware, *The Labor Movement in the United States*, 236–42.

being clubbed by the ITU, while tired old "protective cat" James Blaine sat idly by. In another image, the biggest rat of all, Whitelaw Reid, is trapped by the aggressive "Boycat." Blaine's head, on a cat's body, lies beneath his younger rival and the "Plumed Knight's" lance lies broken.[98]

Greater experimentation took place in local and district papers. Joseph Buchanan's *Labor Enquirer* (Chicago) paved the way for KOL political cartooning in its 1887 call for a separate labor party. A worker representing the "True People's Party" was placed between a Republican with his hand out and chained to the ball of "gang weight," and a Democrat dressed in a suit tailored on one side and ragged on the other.[99] Powderly's successor, James R. Sovereign, was also a creative lithographer. In an elaborate print reproduced in *The Industrial News*, the "Goddess of Liberty" appears girdled with a KOL belt, crowned by the Order's badge, and wielding the sword of "Education," with which she severs the bandages of "Party Rule" from a man's face. Enemies of the Order, including the "Subsidized Press," "Watered Stocks," and "Usury" clamor up a dead tree encircled by ribbons marked "Monopoly," "Cornered Markets," and "Mortgages" (Fig. 23).[100]

Other locals responded with well-executed graphics. Philadelphia Knights were shown at the head of a boycott battering ram manned by trade unionists about to breach the doors of the castle of "Patronage." Wilkes-Barre Knights celebrated the "political death" of defeated congressman John Lynch by showing the strong arm of "Organized Labor" in front of the U.S. Capitol grasping a knife marked "Labor Vote" with Lynch's name carved in the blade. Knights from Baltimore ridiculed workers who failed to use their votes intelligently by showing two Irishmen eating their lunch engaged in the following conversation:

McPheely—Pat, which ticket be's ye votin' this time?

Pat—Divil a bit do I know. Has the boss sed anythink to you, yit?[101]

98. *The Boycotter*, October 4, 1884; November 15, 1884.

99. *Labor Enquirer* (Chicago), March 26, 1887.

100. *Toledo Industrial News,* June 11, 1887; for Statue of Liberty graphic and poem see *PP.*

101. *The Labor Herald and Tocsin,* April 7, 1888; *The World* (Wilkes-Barre) November 11, 1888; *The Critic* (Baltimore), October 19, 1888. I am uncertain as to the exact title of the Wilkes-Barre paper as the article I cite is located in the *PP* and the banner head has been partially cut. Newspaper guides have not been helpful in identifying the exact title.

DEDICATED TO ORGANIZED LABOR BY THE "NEWS."

Fig. 23. The Goddess of Liberty, girdled with a KOL belt, wields the sword of education to free people from the bondage of party rule, cornered markets, and monopolies through education. From *The Industrial News* of Toledo, June 1887. Courtesy, Ohio Historical Society.

Brooklyn Knight James B. Connell (LA 2275) used a woodcut to express his proposal to institute the single tax. He sent Powderly a graphic that he intended to use for his run for supervisor of the 18th Ward.[102]

The Knights' central organ did not print a substantial number of graphics until after 1889. By then, the renamed *Journal of the Knights of Labor* addressed a smaller audience, but was bolder in content, style, and editorial policy. The same paper that featured A. W. Wright's bitter anticlerical ravings also printed pictorial diatribes against enemies of the KOL. In 1890, the *JKL* reprinted a cartoon on ballot reform that had originally appeared in *The Irish World*. "She's A Popular Lass Now" represented the issue as a shy woman being courted by a respectable-looking man labeled "General Public" as politicians looked on in admiration and envy.[103]

By 1892, the *JKL* even responded to political cartoons in other papers. When a *Puck* illustration lampooned the People's Party at a time when the KOL was indistinguishable from it in many areas of the country, the *Journal* responded with an antimonopolist/anti-Semitic cartoon of its own dedicated to *Puck*. A monopolist was shown with a net full of fish ("Dividends, Interest, Usury, Rent, Wage Reductions") dangling from a pole marked "Bond and Financial System." Under his arm is a banner identifying him as an agent for the "Monopolist Democratic/Republican Party." On the pier, with empty nets, stand a worker, a farmer, and a small businessman, while a "Tariff Humbug" sits perched on a fence identifying various monopolies. The party agent floats in "American Fish Pond," his boat anchored in England and pulled toward shore by a "Gold Basis" rope in the hands of "Rothschild." The caption reads, "All For Him—The Jew."[104]

The harshest graphic of all appeared in an 1892 *JKL*. In a cartoon "respectfully dedicated" to the governor of Pennsylvania, a black, grotesque monster stands atop two fallen workers. The monster represents "King Coal," a "despot whose tyranny is felt at every fireside" (Fig. 24). Appearing at a time in which Powderly's own DA was suffering from the dual attacks of coal owner combines and jurisdictional haggling between the United Mine Workers and KOL National Trade District 135, the cartoon made a powerful statement, but one which the KOL was no longer capable of backing with significant action.[105]

102. James B. Connell to Powderly, October 11, 1890, in *PP.*
103. *JKL*, May 8, 1890.
104. Ibid., January 13, 1892.
105. Ibid., June 6, 1892. For jurisdictional battles between the Knights of Labor and the United Mine Workers, see Ware, *The Labor Movement in the United States*, 209–21.

Fig. 24. This graphic from the *Journal of the Knights of Labor* depicts the monster King Coal standing on the bodies of vanquished workers. "Respectfully dedicated to the Governor of Pennsylvania," this image was a bitter reminder of the KOL's problems with coal magnates and labor in Pennsylvania.

These graphics aside, it should not escape notice that labor's own images were few in number and often crude in execution. Neither did they reach large numbers. By 1892, an entire year's readership of the *JKL* had trouble reaching as many readers as the single issue of *Puck* for which a countering cartoon had been devised. Aside from modest success in enhancing identification with leaders, KOL graphics were no match for the images of the Order's enemies.

Looking Backward

By the time Powderly, Devlin, and Wright posed for their picture with chair and gavel, the KOL and its images were fading memories for most Americans. The picture was taken some time between November 1912 and March 1913. By then the Order was within five years of its official funeral, though it had been near death for well over a decade. The three graying reformers probably swapped stories and shared memories at the photo session. Though some of their youthful optimism might have seemed a trifle embarrassing in hindsight, their discomfort was tempered by nostalgic longings for a day in which hundreds of thousands of men and women thumbed through the *AK*, donned KOL badges, and marched behind banners that linked them psychically and materially to Knighthood's rituals and principles.

Images like the Great Seal once created, in Powderly's words, a "bond of unity by which the membership [was] bound together."[106] This was important, as the KOL was often amorphous in structure, and divided along ideological lines. As common ritual behavior declined, Knights wore badges, watch fobs, and buttons with pride, and shared moments of solidarity with passing "brothers" and "sisters" sporting the same. What is today an antiquarian relic had profound meaning in its own day. By 1886, few American organizations could boast of symbols that brought the instant recognition of Powderly's picture, the KOL triangle, or the Great Seal.

Knighthood was an idea as well as a set of organizational arrangements. Objects played an important role in the process by which abstractions were bonded to institutions. A single Knight glancing at a watch embossed with KOL imagery might simultaneously reflect on the Order's usefulness and its vision. Objects imbued with meaning had the ability to penetrate group psyche as well. Those Knights parading be-

106. Powderly, *The Path I Trod*, 439.

hind a banner shared cause, experience, and vision that at least tempo-rarily transcended individual agendas. For some this created a sense of belonging that, once forged, was difficult to abandon. How else are we to explain the elder Powderly's attachment to objects linked to an organi-zation that unceremoniously dumped him two decades earlier?

But the same objects underscore problems associated with lifting the veils of ritual and secrecy. It was one thing to uphold symbols of solidar-ity, universalism, and Christian charity; it was quite another to construct a society that practiced those ideals. A Knight might gaze upon a cigar label sporting the KOL triangle and think of working-class unity, while a trade unionist might fear erosion of craft privilege. Similarly the dreams of economic transformation represented by a cooperatively-made watch was a dangerous threat to hegemony for a manufacturer. In the end, the very materialism of KOL material culture robbed it of efficacy. Visible symbols draw attention, but not always the right kind. Objects can mean one thing for the initiate, while those in the dark draw different conclusions. Too many KOL symbols of solidarity ended up as symbols of conflict. When the very cigar a man smoked was wrapped in discord, dreams of working-class unity went up in smoke. By the 1890s, KOL universalism had given way to craft parochialism.[107]

There is a difference between being known and being notorious, and in the 1880s, the KOL crossed that line. Lifting its veils and displaying ideological and material wares ensnared the Order in a complex political and cultural web that required more than high-sounding principles to disentangle. As the KOL struggled to articulate its rhetoric and build institutions—like cooperatives—it made enemies of craftsmen who came to despise the very symbols of Knighthood. Standing by to poison public perceptions of all working-class movements was the capitalist-controlled popular press. In their most charitable moments, graphic artists por-trayed workers as well-intentioned but prone to excitability and excess. Far more often they were displayed as buffoons or dangerous anarchists. Middle-class readers learned to fear unions, not embrace them out of Christian charity.

It is appropriate that Powderly, Devlin, and Wright posed for a nostal-gic photograph, as KOL material culture often gazed backward. Al-though most objects appeared in the public period, they evoked the days of secrecy. The imagery of the Great Seal is more reminiscent of *AK* mysticism than of pragmatic GA resolutions, just as badges and uni-forms are more in keeping with ritual behavior than with political action.

107. The very symbols of craft unionists bespoke their exclusivity. This idea was devel-oped by Harry J. Rubenstein, "Symbols and Images of American Labor" (Paper delivered at Lowell Industrial Conference, October 1988).

But even among Knights, material culture often failed to forge the "bond of unity" of which Powderly spoke. Like much KOL culture, it took on a more local cast by the late 1880s. Individual assemblies bought different badges, unfurled unique banners, and developed graphic art whose images were more parochial than catholic. By 1895, some Knights were cynical of the power of objects. Brooklyn's E. Stillman Doubleday attacked "emblem adoration" through the ages. For him, all symbols masked reality and discouraged critical reflection. One year after the KOL peddled Uriah Stephens's portrait to a dwindling membership Doubleday wrote, "Pictures are most sought and prized after the subject is dead."[108] It was not hard to read between the lines.

Stillman's embittered remarks were those of a man whose organization was crumbling around him. A decade earlier, few Knights would have agreed with him. Emblem adulation is natural among those for whom the objects embody identity, hope, and a sense of belonging. Few healthy organizations fail to clothe themselves in symbolic garb. It is only when those organizations lose their vitality that the symbols mask reality. At that point, many quickly become "small things forgotten," mere artifacts of a bygone era. Fade to the photographic anachronism: Powderly and cronies wistfully posed with the trappings of an abandoned dream.

108. *JKL*, November 7, 1895.

7 Knights of Labor, Knights of Leisure

In April 1889, Ralph Beaumont traveled to Philadelphia to deliver a series of lectures on KOL reform efforts. As the Order's paid Capitol Hill lobbyist, Beaumont was well known and well respected. Brothers from LA 1 took it upon themselves to show Beaumont a good time while he was in their midst. But if Beaumont expected tributes to the KOL founders who first sanctified LA 1, he was soon disappointed. Instead, he was taken to Curio Hall to see "gum-chewers." Beaumont reported that twenty-four brightly clad women masticated "a sort of gum of an elastic nature, which enabled them to hold one position of it with their teeth while they stretched the other out the full length of their arms, and then gradually lapped it back into their mouths with their tongues."

Having witnessed this remarkable performance, Knights whisked Beaumont off to a twenty-five-minute "variety show" for which he paid a 10-cent admission. Later, they took him to view the wonders of a local dime museum. By the end of his stay, Beaumont was 30 cents poorer, but perhaps wiser. It did not escape his notice that there were some fifteen hundred workers crowded into the variety theater but none of his three lectures attracted more than one hundred. In disgust he jested, "I have made up my mind that I will change my occupation as Lecturer to gum-chewing."[1]

This amusing little anecdote contains several lessons. First, how people play can be just as revealing as their work or the ideas they profess to hold. Ralph Beaumont came to Philadelphia with one agenda, but the Knights he encountered had lighter things on their minds. What did leisure mean to frolicking Knights? Although KOL leisure activities were frequently riddled with deeper political and ideological meanings, they were not uniformly so. Leaders did not have an easy time controlling or shaping rank-and-file diversions. Further, the patterns of play do not fit neatly into any analytical category. One finds equal doses of politics and

1. Ralph Beaumont to Terence Powderly, May 2, 1889, in *PP*.

escapism, of pure fun and defiant opposition, and of working-class identity and what Marx called "false consciousness."[2]

The Beaumont episode holds another lesson as well, one about the
KOL's place in the changing nature of late nineteenth-century American
culture. As we have seen, the KOL's move from a private to a public
organization put it on a collision course with hegemonic Victorian cultural elites. But Gilded Age society was more complex than merely a
struggle between working-class and bourgeois cultural systems. As the
two battled, a third force entered the fray: mass, commercial culture.
The final two decades of the nineteenth century were an interesting time
in American cultural history. By then, both middle and working classes
had well-articulated cultural practices, and both groups resisted efforts
to control, diminish, or supplant their respective expressions. Some of
the fiercest ideological battles of the era took place over cultural issues,
and there was, as yet, no such thing as an American monoculture.

Nonetheless, the purveyors of homosocial, homogeneous, commercial leisure were in the ascendancy. They were a new breed, one that
cared little about ideology as long as patrons deposited their dimes at
the box office. Most middle-class observers were just as disgusted by
gum-chewing spectacles as Ralph Beaumont. But commercial leisure
proved irresistible. Through the late 1800s, articulated ideology was increasingly divorced from leisure. Through time, working-class culture
lost a lot of its bite and much of its creativity. This occurred as laborers
began to spend less time in their local assemblies and more time in dime
museums, amusement parks, and baseball stadiums. Increasingly, they
found one-time bourgeois enemies in the adjacent seats as the middle-

---

2. For more on the debate on the social significance of leisure, see Fred Blum, *Toward a
Democratic Work Process* (New York: Harper & Row, 1953); J. Dumazedier, *The Sociology of
Leisure* (Amsterdam: Elsevier, 1974); Norbert Elias, *The Civilizing Process*, vol. 1: The History
of Manners (Oxford: Basil Blackwell, 1978); Norbert Elias and Eric Dunning, *Quest for Ex-
citement: Sports and Leisure in the Civilizing Process* (Oxford: Basil Blackwell, 1986); Michel
Foucault, *Madness and Civilization* (London: Tavistock, 1967); Foucault, *Discipline and Pun-
ishment* (Harmondsworth: Penguin Books, 1977); Antonio Gramsci, *Selections from Prison
Notebooks* (London: Lawrence and Wishart, 1971); Alan Ingham and Stephen Hardy,
"Sport, Structuration, Subjugation, and Hegemony," *Theory, Culture & Society* 2 (1984):
85–103; Emmanuel Le Roy Ladurie, *Carnival in Romans* (New York: George Braziller, 1979);
Stanley Parker, *The Future of Work and Leisure* (New York: Praeger, 1971); David Reisman
and Warner Bloomberg, "Work and Leisure: Fusion or Polarity?" in *Man, Work, and Society*
ed. Sigmund Nosow and William Form (New York: Basic Books, 1962), 417–36; Anne S.
Sassoon, *Approaches to Gramsci* (London: Writers and Readers Publishing Cooperative,
1982); Max Weber, *The Protestant Ethic and the Spirit of Capitalism* (New York: Charles Scrib-
ners' Sons, 1985). A very useful, if oblique, summary to the debate on leisure is Chris
Rojek, *Capitalism & Leisure Theory* (London: Tavistock Publications, 1985).

class world of opera, orchestra, and theater gave way to the circus, nick-elodeon, and vaudeville hall.

The cultural battles continued, though the context shifted. Since com-mercial entrepreneurs cared most about the bottom line, they were con-tent to allow the middle and working classes to fight over the standards of their product. By century's end, both the bourgeoisie and workers had come to accept the inevitability of mass culture, but each struggled mightily to place its own imprimatur on the new form. Neither got ev-erything it longed for.

All Work and No Play: The Ideology of Leisure Time

Long before mass culture rose, working-class culture existed as a set of practices distinct from those of social and political elites. They were, by both accident and design, alternative forms that elites could and often did interpret as threats to their own hegemony.[3] So long as this was the case, it was difficult to separate the workplace from the playing field. The KOL was hardly the first labor organization to fuse a labor agenda with leisure; trade unions and socialist groups held entertainments ev-ery bit as rich as the Knights. Further, the parades, picnics, dances, and sporting events used by the KOL were long a staple of working-class culture, and were probably as close to a mass cultural expression as what existed prior to the emergence of commercial leisure.

The KOL's cultural uniqueness derives from an organizational iden-tity that demanded it cross ideological, ethnic, racial, occupational, geo-graphic, and gender boundaries to a greater degree than the other labor groups. Like earlier groups, the Knights did not separate work from leisure. Perhaps unlike some of them, the KOL was less content to rele-gate its expressions to a segregated subculture. As in all things, the Or-der sought to infuse itself into all levels of society, a practice that fre-quently made it an amalgam of organic, co-opted, and borrowed traits. Francis Couvares's term, "plebeian" culture, seems a good one.[4] In the

---

3. I once again draw upon the work of Raymond Williams. For more on dominant, alternative, and oppositional cultures, see Williams, "Base and Superstructure," 3–16.

4. The concept of plebeian culture is elaborated in Francis G. Couvares, *The Remaking of Pittsburgh: Class and Culture in an Industrializing City 1877–1919* (Albany: State University of New York, 1984).

hands of the KOL, leisure was often the nexus where the dominant culture fused with working-class alternatives.

Knights of Labor did not see leisure as "other." As Knights toiled, they dreamed of more free time; as they played, they thought of issues relating to the workplace. A picnic could be simultaneously a release from work pressures, an occasion for bodily expressiveness, a solidarity-building event, an open-air school where workers were indoctrinated, and a cathartic moment where anger was vented. It could also be a place where naive dreams of capital/labor cooperation were verbalized, or a local pol seeking votes could pump the flesh. For an individual Knight, leisure might involve well-articulated ideology, for another it might not go much deeper than the popular "eight hours for what we will" slogan in vogue in the 1870s and 1880s.

But thanks to the pioneering work of E. P. Thompson, social historians now assume that working-class leisure usually meant something.[5] Leisure patterns reveal the agency of laborers and demonstrate the eclecticism of working-class life. Coal miners in remote sections of western Maryland devoured newspapers, joined fraternal and temperance orders, wagered on cock fights, danced during ethnic holidays, planted liberty poles on the Fourth of July, and manned baseball teams. But some were well-spoken and well-educated. Andrew Roy, a KOL organizer, bragged of having read Allison's history of Europe, Bancroft's history of the United States, and reams of works by his favorite literary figures: William Cullen Bryant, John Bunyan, Robert Burns, Henry Wadsworth Longfellow, John Milton, and William Shakespeare. Roy, a Scottish immigrant, also enjoyed evenings at the Burns Club, especially the festival honoring the poet's birthday in which he consumed haggis, sang songs, listened to speeches, and danced quadrilles, schottisches, polkas, waltzes, and country dances.[6]

Andrew Roy's experience is typical. Knights in Denver created a cultural network that embraced reading rooms, baseball teams, family theater, social clubs, dances, and parades. In Pittsburgh, the KOL threw itself into a battle to lower the price of baseball tickets; in Cincinnati, it sponsored dances, picnics, and trade fairs.[7] Bryan Palmer reminds us that what may seem "trivial and commonplace in the cultural arena may

5. Thompson, *The Making of the English Working Class*.
6. Harvey, *Best-Dressed Miner*, chap. 8.
7. Buchanan, *Story of a Labor Agitator;* also *The Labor Enquirer* (Denver), September 23, 1883–November 15, 1887; Thomas Neasham to Terence Powderly, July 4, 1886, in *PP,* Brundage, "The Producing Classes and the Saloon;" 29–52; Couvares, *The Remaking of Pittsburgh,* 123–24; Steven J. Ross, *Workers on the Edge: Work, Leisure, and Politics in Industrializing Cincinnati, 1788–1890* (New York: Columbia, 1985), xix.

be . . . an important source of creativity and inspiration [in] the process of resistance." This was certainly true in Ontario, where the KOL used sporting events and picnics to draw crowds for the speeches and rallies that followed, appropriated Uriah Stephens's birthday to agitate for an official Labor Day, and sponsored parades in backwater hamlets to build its rural base.[8] As one historian notes, "The Knights became more than a union. . . . Its leaders became neighborhood heroes."[9] And why not? KOL drill teams, drum corps, glee clubs, and sports teams seasoned working-class life, and left an unpleasant taste in the mouths of would-be oppressors. Brooklyn's ultrasecretive LA 1562, organized "Spread the Light" clubs early in 1881 to provide free public lectures on a variety of subjects relating to labor. Soon, these clubs transformed themselves into the educational wing of the Order that demanded an eight-hour work day, an act that fused cultural and political agendas in a single act of rebellion.[10]

The Knights' defense of the eight-hour day borrowed bourgeois rhetoric, but twisted its logic, doubtless adding to the discomfort of many respectable Victorians. Blending economics and morality, G. H. McCallum, Master Workman of San Francisco LA 1573, argued that the long work day eroded the nation's wealth and its morality. Tired workers were less productive, and thus unable to realize the promise of increased efficiency brought by mechanization. Further, workers were so physically and emotionally exhausted that they sought replenishment in the tavern. In the home, it was unrealistic to expect these workingmen to educate their children to be "freemen and then expect they will be content to live as slaves." Children were especially at risk, since long workdays gave parents too little time to shape their morals or supervise their activities: "They form their own habits, choose their own associates, and with their feet stray off the path of virtue and honor. You reflect that had you a little leisure to watch over them it would have been different."[11]

Others were more direct and saw the withholding of leisure as a form of capitalist exploitation. An 1884 demonstration at New York City's Union Square saw thirty thousand workers rally in support of "labor's trinity: eight hours' work, eight hours' rest, and eight hours' recreation." Among the speakers that day was KOL Executive Board member John McClellan, who exhorted the crowd to abolish wage slavery,

8. Bryan D. Palmer, *A Culture in Conflict: Skilled Workers and Industrial Capitalism in Hamilton, Ontario, 1860–1917* (Montreal: McGill University Press, 1979), 38; Kealey and Palmer, *Dreaming of What Might Be*; Buhle, "The Knights of Labor in Rhode Island," 33–73.

9. Buhle, "The Knights of Labor in Rhode Island," 57,59.

10. *JUL*, June 1881.

11. Ibid., September–October 1881.

praised banners that read "Down With the Capitalist Method of Production," and gladly affixed his name to a resolution calling on the New York legislature to pass an eight-hour bill.[12]

Most, however, left inflammatory statements to the Order's fire-eaters, and made more prosaic appeals for more free time. An 1886 *Labor Leaf* editorial noted:

> recreation plays a part in the economy of nature which has been too much disregarded. A change of work is said to be as good as a rest. So it may be for a time, but the recreation needed is what will build up and strengthen both physical and mental natures instead of further taxing them. A blacksmith after a hard day's work would be still more exhausted by rowing a race, while judicious exercise would rest his tired muscles and prepare him to take advantage of a refreshing sleep. . . . Work, rest, and recreation must be combined to produce the best results. All work and sleep will not do any better than all play and sleep. A moderate amount of labor . . . is necessary to physical health. But recreation is equally necessary to enable sleep to recuperate the tired body.[13]

What is interesting about these examples and dozens more like them is the insistence that recreation and leisure had a function. The hours of toil were a matter of social justice. In this regard the demand for a shorter work day was linked to the bigger struggle to reclaim labor's noble birthright. But leisure also determined the development of individuals, the nation's economy, and the moral fiber of society. In this sense, demands for "eight hours for what we will" were linked to notions of true patriotism as expressed in songs and poetry. In this logic, a nation of over-worked and under-educated workers imperiled the Republic. The KOL neither privatized nor trivialized leisure. In fact, Knights took their battles over the issue into the nation's parks, streets, buildings, and public spaces.

Greased Pigs and Propaganda

The bulk of KOL leisure activities belongs to its public period. Though certain leisure activities were ostensibly private, once the KOL aban-

12. *John Swinton's Paper*, April 26, 1884.
13. *Labor Leaf*, February 24, 1886.

doned secrecy, it did little to escape public notice, and members themselves used the public press to publicize KOL events. Notwithstanding, the Knights designed certain leisure activities for members and friends only, particularly picnics, founding celebrations, dances, and entertainments.

Long a staple of working-class life, picnics were the most common internal leisure form used by the KOL. Labor picnics were a diversion from the rigors of the workplace and were boisterous affairs featuring escapist games and heavy drinking.[14] The KOL inherited picnic traditions, but transformed them into political expressions by blending pastime and politics, greased pigs, and propaganda. Though restricted to Knights, their families, and invited allies, the exuberance and size of gatherings held in public spaces drew press coverage, not all of it desirable. As we have seen, even *Puck* humorists found KOL picnics worthy of comment.

Aside from rituals outlined in the *AK*, picnics were the most common experience shared by all Knights. There were few assemblies that did not report having held a picnic at some point. They were an important part of the KOL calendar, and the Order broke with precedent by scheduling them throughout the year rather than waiting for traditional dates like the Fourth of July. In fact, at a time in which few states had an "official" Labor Day, local workers often used a picnic to declare one of their own choosing. Frostburg, Maryland, Knights held a picnic on Sunday, September 3, 1881, a date chosen by a committee of miners. Picnics were so important that the opening of the GA was rescheduled so that KOL officers could attend the festivities.[15]

Not all Knights waited for the weekend. Baltimore Knights held a picnic attended by over twenty-five hundred people on Wednesday, August 1, 1883. This extraordinary midweek event lured many laborers from their work posts, including black workers. The *Baltimore American* noted that "there were a number of colored people present, one colored man being on the Committee of Arrangements." The paper found more at which to marvel. The picnic was accompanied by speeches from Powderly and Henry George, both of whom marched to the podium behind the Wilson Post Band. In addition, "the dancing pavilion was filled the entire evening, and back of it a game of baseball was played."[16]

14. See Roy Rosenzweig, *Eight Hours for What We Will: Workers and Leisure in an Industrial City, 1870–1920* (Cambridge: Cambridge University Press, 1983), chaps. 3, 6.
15. Printed card received by Powderly, August 15, 1881, in *PP*; Frederick Turner to Powderly, August 18, 1881 in *PP*.
16. *Baltimore American*, August 2, 1883, in *PP*.

Two days later, Powderly found himself in Philadelphia at another picnic. Typically, this one had a dual purpose: celebrating the birthday of Uriah Stephens and raising funds for the striking Brotherhood of Telegraphers. After an afternoon of dancing, picnickers assembled to hear Powderly and other speakers mix eulogies to Stephens with attacks on Jay Gould. After the speeches, more dancing ensued.[17] KOL picnics were seldom restful. A picnic held in Brazil, Indiana (on a Tuesday) advertised two bands and an address by Powderly to be preceded by mass singing of "Hold the Fort, Ye Knights of Labor." It also featured a two-hundred-yard footrace, a shooting match, a football game, a dance, a greased pole climb, and a greased pig chase.[18]

The expressive nature of KOL picnics bothered Powderly, who worried that political content was being lost. Powderly announced that he no longer wished to speak at picnics "for there is not attention paid to what I say. Men and women go there for fun and lager not for wind; besides when I am speaking on so serious a subject as this labor question is I would like to have a more attentive audience than I can find at a picnic." He scorned the popular entertainments that were the staple of these events and found it "mortifying" to travel "hundreds of miles to speak at a pic-nic [when] not over half a dozen will pay any attention" and even they break away "to watch a boy climb a greased pole, or to chase a greased pig." More troubling was the tendency of the audience to "adjourn to the nearest beer stand, leaving the speaker to 'chaw the air' if they don't invite him along, and as I don't drink I have to wait for my audience to come back."[19]

A few locals responded to Powderly's concerns. Rock Island, Illinois, Knights bragged of their picnic in honor of Stephens's birthday, one at which "no beer stands were allowed on the grounds." They sent along clippings from the *Moline Daily Republican* that commented on the exemplary propriety of the assembled three thousand.[20] For the most part, however, few shared Powderly's reservations, and locals ignored the concerns of central leadership. Colorado Knights threw a picnic and dance in which the "refreshment stands were presided over by brisk young men and bright-eyed ladies, and they were frequently called upon by thirsty and hungry dancers."[21] By 1884, many of the trappings Powderly found offensive were a standard feature of KOL culture; it was

17. *The Times* (Philadelphia), August 4, 1883, in *PP*.
18. Handbill for event of July 12, 1883, in *PP*.
19. *JUL*, July 1883.
20. Ibid., September 1883.
21. *The Labor Enquirer* (Denver), August 4, 1883; hereafter citations refer to the Denver edition unless otherwise noted.

not until 1887 that the KOL forbade alcohol at all of its picnics.[22] Nor could Powderly make good his threat not to speak at picnics. On May 24, 1884, he complained to Frederick Turner, "I must talk at a damned picnic this afternoon. Oh for a ton of dynamite." At the bottom of the letter was a crude drawing of Powderly atop a soapbox with a few listeners, while behind him a much larger crowd watches a greased pole climb in progress by the refreshment stand.[23]

In 1884, Colorado Knights held another picnic at which no alcohol was sold—possibly because of Joseph Buchanan's new-found zeal for temperance—but popular entertainment again reigned supreme. Planning committee members labored to create an atmosphere in which the "hard-worked mechanic and laborer [might] for the time forget the weary and discouraging struggle for existence." Thus the Knights and their guests tripped "the light fantastic to the sweet strains of the First Brigade Orchestral band," watched foot races, and participated in sack races. The day's big hit, however, was a game of "football":

> Two of these spheres, loaded with pure Colorado air, were tossed into the crowd early in the day, and for six or seven hours there was not a moment's intermission in the vigorous kicking which old men, young men and boys administered to the bags of wind. They kicked the balls over the trees, into the refreshment stands, into the dancing pavilion, into each others' noses and faces, and Lord only knows where. Noses were skinned, shins were barked, and hats were mashed, but still the fun went on, and there was never a cross word used.[24]

In a similar vein, reports from a Montreal picnic held in September 1886 mention brass bands, boat excursions, dancing, and a variety of games ranging from pole vaulting to a "fat woman's race," but fails to note a single speech.[25]

Picnics drew large crowds despite Powderly's lack of enthusiasm for them. Powderly refused J. R. Mansion's invitation to attend a picnic in Troy, New York, and sarcastically replied,

> I have quite given up replying to invitations to attend picnics. When I go anywhere it is my desire that what I say will be remem-

22. *Irish World*, April 23, 1887.

23. Powderly to Frederick Turner, May 24, 1884, in *PP.*

24. *Labor Enquirer*, August 2, 1884. The game being described is a form of either soccer or rugby, not American-style football.

25. *John Swinton's Paper*, September 12, 1886.

bered. Such a result never follows a picnic. It is only to draw a crowd that my name is used at picnics. What I say amounts to nothing. People go to a picnic to be amused and not to be talked to. When I go . . . I expect to endure the tortures of the damned by being talked to, pawed all over, walked on and buzzed to death. Loafing around a picnic, being invited to take a soft drink, a plate of ice cream or some other cholera morbus inspiring ingredient is the most distasteful thing I can imagine. Would not a suit of my old clothes, stuffed with straw and labeled 'Powderly' be just as good at a picnic as I would be?[26]

But Powderly was wrong; most Knights were better at mixing amusement, fun, and politics with political agitation and organizing than their Master Workman. Over fifteen hundred Knights closed down the mines of Shire Oaks, Pennsylvania, to play football, dance, and run races. But they also listened to speeches and dedicated a new KOL assembly hall.[27] Baltimore's DA 79 built alliances with the city's trade unions through picnics and baseball games, while Haverhill, Massachusetts, Knights sold over three thousand tickets for a picnic and plowed the proceeds into educational and cooperative projects. An 1885 picnic in Philadelphia attracted over nine thousand revelers who also heard speeches on the labor question. Northampton, Massachusetts, Knights used their picnic to raise money for assembly hall furniture to match their altar, while those in Topeka, Kansas, used the funds to assist needy members. Bowie, Texas, Knights held a joint picnic with local Grange societies, Good Templars, and Farmers' Alliances. It was attended by over two thousand and the assembled organizations used the occasion to reaffirm their solidarity. Huge crowds were the norm: three thousand in Galion, Ohio; eight thousand in Aurora, Illinois; ten thousand in Troy, New York; and six thousand in Montreal, Quebec. St. Paul, Minnesota, Knights held a monstrous picnic attended by more than twenty thousand that raised $10,000 for the construction of a KOL assembly hall.[28]

The Minnesota event typified the manner in which KOL picnics could take on defiant tones. *The Knights of Labor* (Chicago) noted that "nearly all" of St. Paul's industries and businesses shut down for the day, while Knights and trade unionists overtaxed the city's transportation system in their trek towards Lake Calhoun. Unlike the mass game of football in

26. Powderly to J. R. Mansion, July 7, 1887, in *PP.*
27. *National Labor Tribune*, May 28, 1887.
28. *John Swinton's Paper*, August 3, 1884; September 7, 1884; July 12, 1885; June 13, 1886; June 30, 1886; July 18, 1886; August 22, 1886; September 12, 1886.

Colorado, "the great feature of the day was the open air mass meeting within the park." Benjamin W. Goodhue, the KOL's state lecturer for Illinois, lambasted monopolies, extolled the nobility of toil, outlined KOL demands, and urged the audience to make judicious use of the ballot to turn out the "worst set of lickspittle that ever tried to run a government [Congress]." He was followed by Governor Hubbard of Minnesota, and by Ignatius Donnelly of the Minnesota Farmers' Alliance and author of the popular dystopian novel *Caesar's Column*. Only then did the huge throng retire to such merriment as three-legged races, hammer throws, tugs of war, wheelbarrow races, and dances.[29]

What was true of metropolitan areas like St. Paul and small mining towns like Shire Oaks was true elsewhere. Chicago's DA 24 held a picnic in June 1887, which featured baseball and football, along with sillier events such as a tub race, a greased pig chase, a fifty-yard fat men's race, and a quarter-mile race between local radicals William Gleeson and George Schilling. Neither man would let such an opportunity to harangue a crowd pass; both later gave speeches. Game prizes reinforced worker solidarity and included KOL badges, KOL cuff buttons, six white shirts made by a Chicago cooperative clothing company, sixty pounds of cooperative soap, a hand-tailored suit from a KOL manufacturer, and a dozen KOL brooms. The gentleman winning the evening's "Prize Waltz" was given a cane, and his partner a KOL rug.[30]

Throughout the 1880s, the KOL used picnics to reaffirm Knighthood's principles, show the Order's solidarity with other organizations, raise money for various causes, lecture crowds on labor matters, defy local elites, and have fun. Bethel, Michigan, Knights listened to speeches on the principles of Knighthood, the need to fly the flag, and the virtues of cooperation, while those in Mansfield, Ohio, held a Fourth of July picnic with the Grand Army of the Republic and the Grange.[31] Cumberland, Maryland, Knights organized a picnic for over five thousand at a time in which the Order's membership there was under five hundred, an event that revitalized the moribund Cumberland lodge.[32] Even the fractious Knights of New York City came together for a picnic. In 1887, DA 49 held a "fraternal" picnic with the city's Central Labor Union. *John Swinton's Paper* wryly noted that bitter enemies joined hands, including several recently purged leaders and their successors.[33]

29. *Knights of Labor* (Chicago), August 14, 1886.
30. *Labor Enquirer* (Chicago), May 28, 1887.
31. *The Industrial News* (Toledo), June 11, 1887.
32. *John Swinton's Paper*, July 10, 1887; Harvey, *Best Dressed Miners*, 254–56.
33. *John Swinton's Paper*, July 31, 1887.

By 1892, the KOL was willing to concede that greased pigs and propaganda could go together. In an article entitled "Politics and Picnics" the *JKL* gave accounts of "tariff-reform" and "third-party picnics" held in Missouri and Texas. The *JKL* noted that all that was needed for success was "timely notice, good water, and abundant shade. The cause does the rest."[34] Alas, the *JKL* belatedly embraced another organization's efforts to do what the KOL itself once tried to do. The central leadership of the Knights lagged behind local assemblies in understanding the value of combining propaganda and play. Leaders, especially Powderly, proved reluctant to sully themselves with working-class culture and responded with contempt toward rank-and-file preferences. They would have been wiser to climb a few greased poles.

Dances, Debates, Drama, and Delights

Two years after the KOL announced the efficacy of picnics, the KOL celebrated its twenty-fifth anniversary. By then, spirits were dampened by decline, and palpable desperation belied public excitement and optimism. But in its heyday, KOL founding ceremonies and anniversaries abounded, and Knights gathered to commemorate special events like birthdays of prominent leaders and the dedication of new meeting halls. In contrast with the solemnity of 1894, Knights from Hamilton, Ontario, honored Uriah Stephens's birthday in 1883 with a demonstration, parade, speeches, and games.[35]

Stephens's birthday was frequently the occasion for activities combining celebration, leisure, and agitation. Powderly spoke at Philadelphia picnics on that day in both 1883 and 1884. In his 1884 remarks he called it "labor's holy day" and suggested that Congress recognize it as Labor Day.[36] In 1890, Powderly returned to Philadelphia and led two thousand marchers to Mt. Peace Cemetery, where he laid a floral design of the Great Seal of Knighthood on Stephens's grave. Local assemblies sent flowers, and cofounders John Hilsea and Henry Sinexon were on hand to accompany Mrs. Stephens and her son to the grave.[37]

But local assemblies did not always await Stephens's birthday to celebrate; each developed their own clusters of commemorations and enter-

34. *JKL*, September 22, 1892.
35. Circular of Hamilton, Ontario, demonstration located in *PP.*
36. *JUL*, January 1884.
37. *JKL*, May 15, 1890; June 5, 1890.

tainments. A favorite local event was the founding party that celebrated new assemblies and the birthdays of old ones. New York LA 2985—a women's assembly—commemorated its founding with music and the recitation of an original poem. A DA 49 correspondent noted that "our sisters had not forgotten to provide an excellent collation: sandwiches, cakes, ice cream, tea, and coffee were all abundant."[38] Alton, Illinois, LA 2913 capped its anniversary with speeches, a picnic, and a dance, while Garfield Pioneer LA 1684 chose a "musical and literary entertainment."[39]

Knights seized on a variety of reasons to make merry. Those in Houston, Texas, held a picnic and dance to impart the principles of Knighthood to new members, while brothers in Boston toasted George McNeill on his fiftieth birthday. Many of McNeill's DA 30 allies were there, including Frank K. Foster and Rev. Jesse H. Jones, and telegrams were received from colleagues like John Swinton, Mrs. Uriah Stephens, and the six remaining KOL cofounders. After the usual complement of testimonial speeches and the presentation of a gold Dueber watch, participants were treated to an original poem from C. Fannie Allyn, and a banquet.[40]

The opening of a new meeting hall was a favorite time for Knights to rejoice, and few locals failed to inform the *JUL* of such an event. Knights in Hot Springs, Arkansas (LA 2419) bragged of a new reading room; Gilberton, Pennsylvania, LA 3615 held a "grand bazaar and industrial exhibition of useful articles [of] novel and artistic workmanship" to fund its new building.[41] Gardner, Massachusetts, LA 4540 opened its new hall with a fair and dance, and the sale of KOL cooperative goods provided a windfall that financed a reading room.[42] Knights from Rutland, Vermont, held a "grand jollification" in 1891 to commemorate the fifth anniversary of LA 5160. A recitation from Kittie Crowley, Master Workman of LA 2113, was sandwiched between songs and speeches. The 450 guests danced until midnight.[43] In December 1891, Philadelphia Knights gathered to toast the KOL's twenty-second anniversary. Powderly was

38. *JUL*, December 25, 1884.
39. Ibid., August 25,1885; November 25, 1885.
40. *John Swinton's Paper*, September 5,1886; *The Laborer*, August 7, 1886. McNeill received telegrams from past District Master Workman Albert Carlton and from old friend Hugh Cavanaugh. Noticeably absent from McNeill's celebration was a telegram from Powderly. The two were already at odds over the Order's trade union policy and would soon clash over Powderly's reluctance to endorse George C. McNeill, *The Labor Movement: The Problem of Today* (New York: Augustus M. Kelley, 1887).
41. *JUL*, March 25, 1885; May 10, 1886.
42. Ibid., June 11, 1887.
43. *JKL*, February 12, 1891.

surrounded by friends like the Rev. James Huntington, John Devlin, and John O'Keefe. Tom O'Reilly graced the assemblage with his renowned baritone solos.[44]

Most KOL local assemblies were short-lived, with the bulk of them having been formed in 1886. For those with longer lives, there was a period of maturation between the heady days of their founding and the turmoil of the 1890s. During their mature phase, locals attempted to reach deep into working-class life and create counterhegemonies. Clubs, societies, and debate circles were often central, the most famous being Victor Drury's "Spread the Light" clubs, the anarcho-communist study groups that fostered the Home Club conspiracy.

Drury's group was more controversial than most, but few Knights paid attention to the Order's official nonpartisan political stance. Debate and lecture societies were a common form of leisure for nineteenth-century workers, and many Knights spent their free time attending them. Bridgeport, Connecticut, Knights sponsored a weekly "Labor Lyceum." Attendance often topped four thousand, and long after formal debate ended, participants lingered to prolong an evening of comaradery and sociability.[45]

For Knights political societies were hybrids between didactics and entertainment, because politics was a passion for working-class men and women. New York, Brooklyn, and Boston Knights were encouraged to attend meetings of the Sociologic Society in their cities, while those in Trenton, New Jersey, set up their own weekly debates.[46] Detroit Knights enjoyed evenings at the Dialectical Union where speakers and audience engaged in spirited discussions over such questions as whether anarchy was preferable to autocracy. *Labor Leaf* columnist Joseph Labadie was especially active in the Union and used his "Cranky Notions" column to advance its positions, even when they differed from official KOL policy. For example, Labadie did not shy from blasting the GEB's blanket condemnation of anarchism and wrote:

> I believe men have the right to their own opinions, and that they have no right to coerce or attempt to coerce others from holding opposite opinions. So far as I am concerned I propose to speak and write what I think best to speak and write. . . . My voice

44. Ibid., January 7, 1892. Noticeably absent were John Hayes and DA 1 stalwart James L. Wright, the two linchpins in the conspiracy that toppled Powderly two years later. So stacked was the event in Powderly's favor that Madge C. Eiler, a woman harassed by Hayes, gave a recitation.

45. *John Swinton's Paper*, December 13, 1885.

46. *JUL*, July 15, 1883.

and pen will not be deterred from doing active work in whatever
direction that seems to me right. He who upholds me in this right
is truly a friend; he who denies this right is a bitter enemy. . . . I
believe in discussion of any question that bears upon the good
or evil of mankind. It is a coward or a fool who shrinks from
such discussion.[47]

Labadie's remarks show how local KOL cultures nurtured their own
definitions of propriety. He was not the only Knight whose passions
were fired in his local and who reached different conclusions than the
Order's central leadership. In Denver, the interlocking KOL and Rocky
Mountain Social League structures functioned much the same way as
Detroit's Dialectical Union. There the affable Joseph R. Buchanan pat-
terned local institutions after William Morris's Socialist League. Buchan-
an's *Labor Enquirer* proclaimed "Who Would Be Free Must Strike the First
Blow" from its masthead, and featured more stories on Johann Most,
Morris, and the Avelings than on Powderly or GEB members. The Social
League was often cosponsored by KOL DA 89, and the two tackled is-
sues like the merits of anarchism, the demerits of the Home Club, and
Powderly's ineffectiveness as a leader.[48]

But more than politics stirred passions inside KOL locals. In fact, few
KOL debates ended without reminding the audience that Knighthood
meant more than politics. An 1886 *JUL* editorialist complained that there
were no American equivalents of English workingmen's clubs, but he
was wrong. Of the features and activities he noted of English clubs—
lecture rooms, libraries, bars, recreation rooms, athletic clubs, musical
societies, dances, and garden parties—only bars were not a feature of
strong KOL locals. Toledo, Ohio, Knights had their own marching band
and a drama club, while New York's DA 49 organized the city's church
choir and included them in their entertainments. Providence, Rhode Island, Knights helped operate a dining hall where a full-course dinner
cost 15 cents.[49]

KOL assemblies even extended their concerns to art, literature, and
drama. The work of the Pre-Raphaelite Brotherhood was much admired,
and both John Ruskin and William Morris often quoted. Like the Pre-

47. *Labor Leaf*, July 21, 1885; July 7, 1886.

48. *Labor Enquirer*, September 29, 1883; July 30, 1886; August 7, 1886; November 20,
1886; "Concerning the Visit of GMW Powderly to Denver," in *PP*; Buchanan, *Story of a
Labor Agitator; JUL*, May 17, 1886.

49. *John Swinton's Paper*, July 12, 1885; November 5, 1885; *Weekly People*, July 7, 1891; Paul
Buhle, Scott Molloy, and Gail Sansbury, *A History of Rhode Island Working People* (Providence: Regini Printing Co., 1983).

Raphaelites and other late Victorian painters, the *JUL* agreed that "the aim and end of art should be to moralize the people; to give birth to and fortify elevated sentiment in the human heart, to reveal the dignity and ameliorate the condition of mankind by guiding it toward the good; by inspiring a love for the just, the pure, and the beautiful, and to despise that which is false and ignoble." The *JUL* is similar to Ruskin's own musings on art and morality: "Nothing assists the working man so much as having the moral disposition developed rather than the intellectual, after his work; anything that touches his feelings is good, and puts new life into him, therefore I want modern pictures . . . of that class which would ennoble and refine."[50] Denver's *Labor Enquirer* responded with an article from William Morris in which he equated art with goodness, truth, and beauty, and commerce with greed, falsehood, and ugliness. Colorado Knights were familiar with those ideals. Thousands turned out for Oscar Wilde's 1882 lectures, and he was lionized in Leadville when he descended a silver mine to chat with miners.[51] St. Louis LA 481 included in its ranks a professional painter, C. W. Hoffman.[52] Even Powderly immersed himself in art after an 1881 encounter with James Mc-Neill Whistler in which the two mercurial egoists exchanged insults.[53]

Most Knights preferred drama to all other art forms. Pittsburgh Knights were given a private reading of a new five-act play, while those in Detroit joined a dramatic society sponsored by the International Working Peoples' Association.[54] Preferred plots often mirrored those of pulp fiction. One involved a widowed entrepreneur named Dahlgreen

50. *JUL*, October 25, 1884; Linda S. Ferber and William H. Gedts, *The New Path: Ruskin and the American Pre-Raphaelites* (Brooklyn: Brooklyn Museum, 1985); Jeremy Maas, *Victorian Painters* (New York: Harrison House, 1969). The English painters who attracted the most attention in America were Edward Burne-Jones, Albert Moore, Walter Crane, William Holman Hunt, Ford Maddox-Brown, Frederick Lord Leighton, John Ruskin, Dante Gabriel Rossetti, Alfred Stevens, John Millais, J. M. W. Turner, and James McNeill Whistler (an American expatriate working in England and France).

51. *Labor Enquirer*, November 15, 1884; Richard Ellman, *Oscar Wilde* (New York: Vintage Books, 1987).

52. *Labor Enquirer*, December 10, 1883. I was unable to locate Hoffman in any art catalogues. However, descriptions of his painting "Chair of Solomon" shares a pre-Raphaelite love of historical drama. The piece glorifies an apocryphal event in which King Soloman placed a chair to his right to honor the craftsmen who built the Temple.

53. Powderly, *The Path I Trod*, 194–97. Powderly insulted Whistler after he referred to workers as a "beastly lot." Powderly turned to Thomas O'Reilly and asked if Whistler painted houses or signs! Whistler unleashed a stream of invectives against Powderly, but was assuaged when Powderly commented favorably on one of the artist's canvases. Whistler even promised to visit Scranton, descend a mine, and paint men at work. Unlike Wilde, Whistler never made such a journey.

54. *National Labor Tribune*, January 23, 1886; *Labor Leaf*, November 18, 1885.

whose infant son was kidnapped by a jilted nurse. Twenty years later Dahlgreen promotes a marriage between his niece, Myrtle, and his plant superintendent. She, however, loves an out-of-work pattern maker named Simpson, fired for agitating for the eight-hour day. A strike ensues in which the superintendent plants a bomb to try to discredit the strikers. The plan fails when Myrtle startles him, he accidentally shoots her, and her falling body extinguishes the fuse. All ends well, however. Myrtle was only slightly wounded, Simpson's "mother" confesses she is the nurse who abducted the child, Simpson, twenty years ago, Dahlgreen puts the plant on the eight-hour day, and Simpson wins both an inheritance and Myrtle's hand.[55]

Denver Knights shared a predilection for Victorian melodrama. In "A Knight of Labor," mine proprietor Henry Maxwell steals miner Mark Spencer's wife, Cora, by enticing her with promises of travel. When the dastardly deed is discovered, rash miners plot to dynamite the mine, but Spencer foils them. The play ends in tragedy. Cora regrets her actions and reconciles with Mark, who hides her in a humble cottage. But Maxwell discovers her whereabouts. In a stormy encounter, Mark strikes Maxwell, who fires a pistol shot that misses Mark but kills Cora.[56]

As audience members, Knights were not afraid to flex their muscles to advance their cause. San Francisco Knights bragged of how they helped close McKee Rankin's theater. Rankin's shows were patronized heavily by Knights and unionists until he found himself on the wrong side of the second Gould strike. When Rankin refused to sponsor a benefit for the strikers, or release any of his players for an independent production, workers boycotted his theater, and Rankin was forced to close.[57]

Wiser managers cooperated with the Knights. Chicago playwright Lawrence Marston instructed his business manager to approach Powderly for permission to write a "K. of L. play [for] the advancement of the order." Marston envisioned a scene marked by a "great strike" that was settled by eloquent oration. Powderly was asked to send an old speech or compose a new one.[58] Powderly did not respond, but this did not deter playwrights from using the KOL as their foils. On July 28, 1890, "King of the Knights" opened in New York City's Harlem Theater. Publicity material stressed that the company was managed by "Messrs. Dixon and Mack, both well-known in labor circles in New York."[59]

55. *Labor Leaf*, August 4, 1886.
56. *Labor Enquirer*, December 26, 1885.
57. *National Labor Tribune*, September 25, 1886.
58. C. J. Ohrenstein to Powderly, September 2, 1886, in *PP.*
59. *JKL*, July 24, 1890.

Since theater was an elaborate affair requiring large expenditures of time and money, most Knights only experienced it vicariously as audience members. Some Knights, like those in Toledo, launched a few of their own productions and some assemblies had dramatic societies that performed for the amusement of the rank and file. Generally, however, assemblies found fairs and entertainments more manageable.

In 1885, Haverhill, Massachusetts, Knights held a pre-Christmas fair for interested citizenry. They secured the use of city hall for the occasion and transformed it into a KOL museum covered with banners such as "Labor Creates All Wealth," "Arbitration Instead of Strikes," "Eight Hours for a Day's Work," "No Distinction of Color or Sex," "The Watchwords of Success, S. O. and M.A.," and "An Injury to One is an Injury to All." In addition to a band concert and games like ring toss, visitors admired the needlecraft skills of women in the "fancy article pagoda," viewed handicrafts displayed by shoe lasters, reflected on the work of city artists, witnessed demonstrations of craft, and sampled refreshments. A similar event held in Trenton, New Jersey, netted an $8,000 profit.[60]

An even bigger event took place in Cincinnati under the sponsorship of LA 4457. C. Fannie Allyn of Boston, for whom all-female LA 4457 was named, held the event from March 21 to to March 28, 1886. It featured KOL cooperative goods, many of which were given away as raffle prizes. Members from all over the country attended or bought tickets. A Knight from Wyandotte, Kansas, won a KOL suit; a gentleman's watch went to a ticket-holder in Maysville, Kentucky; and a ladies' watch to one in Rushville, Indiana. Other prizes included a sewing machine, a patent rocker, a Japanese quilt, a KOL rug, a bed lounge, a basket, and a barrel of flour.[61]

Wheeling, West Virginia, Knights, cooperated with local trade unions for that city's 1887 industrial fair. Among the participants were Prosperity LA 1551 and the controversial Garfield Assembly, a cigar maker's local feuding with the CMIU. Harmony LA and the Brotherhood of Carpenters cooperated in a display of wood works, while a black hodcarriers local furnished "a quartet of talented vocalists."[62]

Socials, dances, and entertainments were even easier to organize. By the mid-1880s, these were nearly as frequent as picnics. An 1883 Denver social attracted more Knights than the hall could hold and nearly two hundred were turned away. The evening dragged on past midnight,

---

60. *The Laborer* (Haverhill), December 26, 1885; *The Boycotter*, February 6, 1886.
61. Handbill located in *PP*; see also *JUL*, May 10, 1886.
62. *National Labor Tribune*, February 19, 1887.

when the First Brigade Band struck up "Home on the Range" and the dancers retired from the floor.[63] The Denver affair mixed profit with pleasure, with the proceeds going into the LA coffers. By contrast, Haverhill Knights mixed politics with their pleasure in a dance held to support striking shoe lasters. The dancers were given "order" forms that were in the shape of a laster's tag, with the words "A reduction will be made on all inferior dancing and errors" stamped on each. The usual dances were mixed with specials such as "Our Walking Delegate" and "Prepare for the Lockout."[64]

Massachusetts DA 30 featured an especially rich leisure life. Webster Knights renovated the local opera house for their meeting hall and invited Leonora Barry, Thomas Barry, Frank Foster, and George McNeill to speak at their gala opening. Dedham LA 3455 held a dance organized by the women of the assembly in which all the ladies wore muslin caps and aprons. The dance turned a tidy profit even though an expensive Boston orchestra was hired. Marlboro LA 3221 gave a "grand concert," a "box party," a dance, and "coffee party" to support Worcester County strikers.[65]

Other locals had equally rich cultural expression. Washburn, Wisconsin, LA 9369 gave a ball to raise money for an organ, then formed a glee club. Dancers graced the floor in Rice's Point, Missouri, while songs and recitations rang out in the KOL hall at Town of Lake, Illinois.[66] New York's DA 64 gave an especially elaborate entertainment on March 18, 1888. A sixteen-page booklet was printed for the occasion that interspersed advertising with a history of DA 64, musings on political economy, a short story, two poems, and the program. The entertainment included four soloists, three story readers, a musical club, and an actor recreating "humorous selections."[67] In 1890, Toledo Knights held a jubilee—largely organized by Joan of Arc Assembly 10,062—that was capped by a long speech by GEB member John O'Keefe.[68]

Local assemblies across North America attested to the vibrancy and diversity of KOL culture and its genius in combining the political, the social, and the practical. Knights saw no contradiction in debating one moment and dancing the next, or in attending amateurish theater as

---

63. *Labor Enquirer*, September 15, 1883.

64. *The Laborer*, March 13, 1886.

65. *Labor Leader* (Boston), April 2, 1887; April 23, 1887; April 30, 1887; May 14, 1887; May 21, 1887; May 28, 1887; August 27, 1887.

66. *The Industrial News* (Toledo), June 11, 1887 (Microfilm of the Ohio Historical Society).

67. DA 64 entertainment program located in *PP*.

68. *JKL*, March 27, 1890.

long as its heart was in the right place. Like a picnic feast, local assembly culture was a smorgasbord of delights, debates, and high drama.

The Sporting Life

Whether it was Denver Knights engaging in a game of kickball or a pair of "picked nines" showcasing their baseball talents at a picnic, KOL members vigorously participated in the popular sports of the day. Sports, like picnics, were an interstice through which private leisure spilled into the public realm. Sports also linked emotional and physical release with politics and organizing.

As with other activities, local patterns and preferences held sway. Knights in mining regions preferred blood sports like cockfights, pigeon shoots and prize fights.[69] Urban Knights could be equally brutal— several baseball games ended in fisticuffs—but their games tended to be less bloody. Boxing, for example, was second only to baseball in working-class affections, but attracted little commentary in KOL newspapers. This is odd given that one of the period's great champions, John L. Sullivan, shared the Irish ancestry of many KOL rank and filers. The failure of KOL editors to comment on boxing is a measure of the sway that middle-class respectability held for the Order's more conservative leaders.

For the most part, though, working-class sports fans shared a love of rough play that disturbed Victorian moralists.[70] The Denver kickball marathon was a violent affair that bloodied and bruised many participants. And Knights on the local level enjoyed the rough-and-tumble world of boxing despite their leaders' opinions. A match involving two Knights in Lynn, Massachusetts, was raided by the police and the event elevated into class conflict. Police smashed a window in a "private athletic club" and arrested "two well known and respectable men with soft boxing gloves as big as pillows on their hands, which they immediately

---

69. Harvey, *Best-Dressed Miners*.

70. For more on the role of rough play in working-class sport, see Couvares, *The Remaking of Pittsburgh*; Elliot Gorn, *The Manly Art: Bare-Knuckle Prize Fighting in America* (Ithaca: Cornell University Press, 1986); Harvey Green, *Fit for America: Health, Fitness, Sport and American Society* (Baltimore: Johns Hopkins University Press, 1986); Donald J. Mrozek, *Sport and American Mentality 1880–1910* (Knoxville: University of Tennessee Press, 1983); Robert Weir, "Take Me Out to the Brawl Game: Sports and Workers in Gilded Age Massachusetts," in *Sports in Massachusetts: Historical Essays*, ed. Martin Kaufman and Ronald Story (Westfield: Institute of Massachusetts Studies, 1991).

ironed as you would murderers and brought them to city hall." Both fighters were charged with violating a city ordinance against prize fighting and were discharged. An outraged *Labor Leader* editorialist warned that the officers "responsible for this uncalled for raid on peaceful and law abiding citizens will have to pay handsomely for their actions."[71]

A love of rough play is also seen in the Knights' embrace of "polo," a rudimentary form of ice and roller hockey that enjoyed brief popularity in the 1880s.[72] New England enjoyed a thriving league and the Haverhill, Massachusetts, *Laborer* regularly reported on matches. The city boasted two teams, the Stars and the Globes, whose battles rivaled "the feud[s] of the Montagues and Capulets, of the Houses of York and Lancaster, [and] the Vendettas of the blue-grass region." One February match was witnessed by a standing-room only crowd. City rivalry aside, the large throng is hard to explain. The Stars-Globes match commenced at 9 P.M. on a Wednesday evening. What possessed laborers accustomed to ten-hour work days to stand by a frozen river on a cold night? Apparently the thrill of the event outweighed considerations of rest. There was plenty of vicarious violence to savor. A reporter noted that the play was "too rough . . . for those who prefer polo to the ring, and several exhibitions of temper were shown by individual players." Haverhill fans disagreed, and cheered loud enough to cause the "Chinese lanterns around the rink to vibrate and the ice on Little River to crack."

The game was less than four minutes old when a Stars player was thrown to the ice and a fight ensued. The *Laborer* account is peppered with allusions of exciting rushes on goal, of men falling to the rink, of free-flowing wagers, and of wild applause. Violence threatened spectators as well as players; a woman and her daughter were hurt by an errant ball, and one fan was assaulted by opposing partisans. Boston-area Knights witnessed equally violent polo matches. In one game, a player's arm was shattered and the "bone protruded into the flesh"; in another, a New Bedford player charged into the dressing room to assault a referee.[73]

Moralists were appalled by such scenes, but the KOL stood its ground. *The Laborer* blamed bourgeois opposition to working-class lei-

---

71. *Labor Leader*, February 19, 1887.

72. The details of nineteenth-century "polo" remain sketchy. Apparently, polo could be played on a frozen rink with ice skates, or in an indoor area using roller skates. A ball was used instead of a puck, and descriptions of rushes on the net sound more akin to field hockey than modern-day ice hockey. Ice hockey rules were codified in Canada in 1879, but were not widespread in the United States until the early twentieth century.

73. *The Laborer*, February 28, 1886; January 23, 1886. See also *Boston Globe*, February 2, 1886 and February 9, 1886.

sure for the rougher turn sport was taking, and accused critics of profit-ing from it. A Brockton correspondent noted that he paid 20 cents to the "lordly creatures" who owned the city's skating rink. However, ice skating was not on the evening's agenda, rather "that old-time popular diversion of slugging, tripping, and wrestling called polo." The use of the phrase "old-time" was deliberately ironic. The article was entitled "A By-Gone Amusement" and claimed that polo's popularity was due to clergy and press crusades against the heterosocial world of skating where they imagined all manner of vices took hold.[74]

Polo and boxing clearly represented counterhegemonic values. But what of Gilded Age baseball, the sport that was transformed into the "national pastime"? Few things aroused working-class passion like baseball, but what did the experience of playing and watching mean? It is customary to equate the rise of baseball with the triumph of commer-cial capitalism. Some historians have argued that the sport is exemplary of the emergent industrial order, a game marked by efficiency, special-ized expertise, competition, formal rules, record-keeping, and factory-like teamwork. Moralists like Albert Spalding are credited with taming baseball to the point where middle-class men and women felt comfort-able in flocking to the ballparks.[75] But does such an interpretation stand up in the face of Gilded Age reality? The answer is a resounding "no"; baseball was still a raw sport marked by cheating, drinking, heavy gam-bling, and occasional violence. When used by the KOL, it was also a weapon in the war against capital.

KOL baseball was a community event that combined enjoyment with mutualism and solidarity. When Providence Knights agitated for the es-tablishment of an official Labor Day, the demonstrations ended at Rocky Point Park where a KOL team from Providence defeated their brothers from Worcester 5 to 1.[76] Hamilton, Ontario, Knights used baseball matches to attract crowds to their rallies and speeches. Games were powerful inducements; matches often drew more than one thousand

74. *The Laborer*, February 13, 1886.
75. For more on those who see baseball as reinforcing capitalist hegemony, see Barth, *City People*; Steven Gelber, "Working at Playing: The Culture of the Workplace and the Rise of Baseball," *Journal of Social History* (Summer 1983): 3–22; Allen Guttmann, *From Ritual to Record: The Nature of Modern Sports* (New York: Columbia University Press, 1978); Peter Levine, *A. G. Spalding and the Rise of Baseball: The Promise of American Sport* (New York: Oxford University Press, 1985); Lee Lowenfish and Tony Lupien, *The Imperfect Diamond* (New York: Stein & Day, 1980); Mzorek, *Sport and American Mentality*; Steven A. Riess, *Touching Base: Professional Baseball and American Culture in the Progressive Era* (Westport, Conn.: Greenwood Press, 1980).
76. Buhle et al., *History of Rhode Island Working People*.

spectators.[77] The Order had its own cooperative team by 1884 and, as Bryan Palmer notes, baseball helped "illuminate class inequalities and generate fierce opposition to the fundamental wrongs of the social order."[78]

Baseball games generated solidarity. Denver Knights listened to their picnic speakers and then gathered to watch LA 3218 play a picked nine from DA 89.[79] Typographers associated with both ITU No. 6 and KOL DA 49 divided the craft for a pickup game, but came together to discuss mutual concerns after bets were settled.[80] Both the KOL printers of Detroit and the Knights of Windsor, Ontario, had their own baseball teams.[81] So did Haverhill Knights. On Monday July 25, 1886, the Haverhill Knights defeated the Lasters Union nine by a score of 11 to 8 in a game that featured thirteen errors, nineteen strikeouts, nine stolen bases, and seven wild pitches. If the KOL/Lasters game was less than a baseball classic, it nonetheless provided workers with a frenzied alternative to the dullness of the work routine. But the speeches that followed prove that far more than escapism was on the minds of the participants. The next year, Haverhill Knights used a baseball game to raise money for striking Worcester County mill workers.[82]

The KOL used baseball to reinforce its image as a champion of community and working-class life. KOL papers frequently provided better coverage of local nines and regional professional teams than the mainstream press. Haverhill's *Laborer* ran "Base Ball Gossip" columns throughout the summer months that gave scores, schedules, and news of a league consisting of Boston, Brockton, Portland, Haverhill, Lawrence, and Newburyport. The paper also reported games played between KOL locals and their challengers.[83] Likewise, a correspondent from Marlboro took great pride in the success of his local club, a team that regularly drubbed opponents by large scores. The Marlboros were good enough to entice National League champion Chicago to the city for an exhibition match. The powerful professionals of Chicago, anchored by superstars Mike "King" Kelly and Cap Anson, easily defeated

77. Palmer, *A Culture in Conflict.*

78. Ibid., 58. For others who interpret baseball as a counterhegemonic form, see Couvares, *The Remaking of Pittsburgh*, and Rosenzweig, *Eight Hours for What We Will.* For more on violence, cheating, gambling, and rough play in Gilded Age baseball, see Weir, "Take Me Out to the Brawl Game."

79. *Labor Enquirer*, October 2, 1886.

80. *The Boycotter*, August 14, 1886.

81. *Labor Leaf*, April 7, 1886; October 27, 1886.

82. *The Laborer*, July 3, 1886.

83. Ibid., June 5, 1886.

Marlboro by a 10 to 1 margin, but the *Laborer* devoted nearly one-third of the article recounting the drubbing by recapping the crowd's excitement when the score was tied 1 to 1 at the end of the first inning.[84]

The Knights participated fully in what contemporaries called the "base-ball craze." Baseball was embraced by a joyous public that zealously followed the home team and turned out in droves for bizarre events like baseball on horseback; matches between two-legged, one-armed men and one-legged, two-armed men; and games pitting two female nines, one consisting of brunettes, the other of redheads.[85] The Chicago *Knights of Labor* printed a letter from a fourteen-year-old to his father. The lad, sent from Pittsburgh to Columbus, Ohio, on vacation, recounts that he was sorry to have been on the train when there was a match in Pittsburgh, but was much relieved to get his father's telegram informing him "that the game went all right." He was disappointed to learn that Columbus no longer had a team: "I suppose that before the Columbus club was sold all these corn fields were diamonds. It certainly looks desolate now, cattle roaming and nothing but harvest hands trudging around." The letter ends with the son asking his father for permission to go to Cleveland where there was "a live club," and a warning not to let his younger brothers play with his "professional dead league [baseball]."[86] The letter was probably apocryphal, since it appeared under the headline "Base Ball Craze" in a December issue when no games were played, but its mere inclusion indicates keen interest in the subject. Few critics enjoyed baseball as much as Chicago, and the humorous undertones of the "letter" would have induced knowing nods.

The Dubuque, Iowa, *Industrial Leader* kept readers informed of happenings far from the city. Iowa Knights must have thoroughly enjoyed the game, for how else can one explain the outrage with which an *Industrial Leader* columnist recounted a game in which an umpire lost track of the count and allowed a batter to get a hit on the fourth strike? The travesty in question occurred in a game played in Toronto, Ontario, in a match against Syracuse, New York. The *Leader* printed all manner of trivia and gossip. In 1887, it informed readers of such tidbits as "league players have made about 250 home runs this season," "Anson says the

84. Ibid., June 19, 1886; July 10, 1886; October 16, 1886. Cap Anson did not play in the Marlboro exhibition, but the *Laborer* reporter was delighted to report that Marlboro's only run scored on an error by the hated Michael "King" Kelly error. Kelly was soon transformed into a New England hero when Spalding sold him to Boston. Aside from Sullivan, Kelly was New England's most popular sports star of the Gilded Age.

85. Irving A. Leitner, *Baseball: Diamond in the Rough* (New York: Criterion Books, 1972), chap. 10.

86. *Knights of Labor* (Chicago), December 18, 1886.

trouble with Conway of the Detroits is with his arm," and "knitted jerseys adopted by Chicago are becoming popular with Detroit and Washington this season." In case there was any doubt as to why the *Leader* ran so much baseball news, editor Bert Stewart informed readers that "for every man that takes an interest in any other branch of sport, there are a score if not 100, who take a decidedly lively interest in baseball."[87]

KOL papers in Baltimore, Boston, Milwaukee, and Philadelphia were equally dutiful in recording the latest baseball news and gossip. *The Labor Leader* gave tips on how to play better, and included humorous explanations of the game's jargon. The *Labor Herald* preferred more serious matters like the clash between the National League and the American Association, but both papers kept readers well informed. The anticipation of opening the 1889 baseball season made the front page of *The Critic*, which indignantly reported the theft of home plate from Baltimore's ballpark. When the team did not perform according to expectations, *The Critic* criticized both players and Manager Barney, who was accused of trying to save money by not purchasing good hitters. Despite disappointment with the team's 1889 fifth-place finish, *The Critic* was once again brimming with optimism for the 1890 season.[88]

By the 1880s, love of professional baseball was common ground for the laboring and middle classes. *Frank Leslie's Illustrated* captured many scenes relating to the baseball craze. The opening of the 1886 season saw New York upset Boston and a jubilant crowd carry the players off the field on their shoulders. An 1888 engraving shows an unruly crowd at the Polo Grounds. Tempers flared, fists and fingers waved, and violence seemed imminent. Outside young boys climbed telegraph poles to peer inside, while top-hatted bourgeois and paper boys alike huddled around holes in the outfield fence to catch a glimpse of the action. By 1889, an uneasy mix of classes seems to have taken hold. A crowd gathered outside the *New York World* office to eagerly await game results; bare-footed boys, young workers wearing paper hats, men with straw boaters and the occasional top hat all were caught up in the excitement.[89]

But the mix was indeed uneasy. The Knights' love of professional baseball led it into clashes with baseball entrepreneurs. When the American Association and the Atlantic Association contemplated raising ticket prices to 50 cents to match prices charged by the National League,

87. *Industrial Leader*, August 27, 1887; September 3, 1887.

88. *Labor Leaf*, June 23, 1888; *Labor Herald and Tocsin* (Philadelphia), December 17, 1887; *The Critic*, March 23, 1889; June 1, 1889; April 12, 1890. See also the *Daily Review* (Milwaukee), 1886–87.

89. *Frank Leslie's Illustrated Newspaper*, May 8, 1886; September 1, 1888; July 27, 1889.

Knights in affected cities protested vigorously. Philadelphia's *Labor Herald and Tocsin* called such actions "ill-advised" and warned it would "injure the game in at least four Association cities." It was correct; the American Association was in precarious shape and was kept afloat largely because its 25-cent admission price attracted laborers, as did its Sunday games and ballpark beer sales. As individual franchises raised prices between 1887 and 1891, attendance dropped and the league foundered, with only Boston and Baltimore remaining solvent. In 1892, the Association folded.[90]

Baltimore and Boston remained financially healthy partly due to local Knights who spearheaded boycotts that forced management to rescind ticket price increases. In 1889, *The Critic* announced that the Orioles' season would open with the old 25-cent price in effect and noted, "Baltimore is essentially a city which, accustomed to a fixed rate of admission, will rebel against an advance. This was proven last year by the refusal of the patrons of the game to attend and pay increased rates." Talk of raising the price again in 1890 prompted the remark, "The local situation may be described in one paragraph: The public wants good ball; [owners] Vonderhorst and Barney want to make money."[91] In Boston, fans dubbed the 25-cent ticket the "popular price," and even the *Boston Globe* warned owners not to tinker with it.[92]

Pittsburgh Knights were unsuccessful in their fight to lower ticket prices and allow Sunday baseball. Pittsburgh was a member of the National League, then under the financial and tactical control of the ruthless A. G. Spalding, who felt that a 50-cent ticket price, Sunday prohibitions, and the banishment of alcohol from National League parks would win middle-class patrons. (The KOL supported an alcohol ban.) Pittsburgh entered the National League in 1887, and team president William A. Nimick was a solid ally of Spalding. Though the glassworkers of LA 300 complained bitterly about 50-cent tickets and argued that such fees would only benefit weathly clubs like New York and Chicago, their protests fell on deaf ears. *The American Glass Review* predicted accurately that the "50 cent tariff prevents hundreds of honest hard working young men from seeing the national game," without realizing that this was precisely the intent. But Pittsburgh Knights had the last laugh. By 1889, Pittsburgh was losing money and the next year most of its team jumped to the renegade Players' League. Losses were severe, and even though

90. *Labor Herald and Tocsin*, December 17, 1887; *The People*, June 21, 1891; *The Critic*, August 2, 1890.
91. *The Critic*, March 23, 1889; April 12, 1890.
92. *Boston Globe*, October 11, 1891.

the Players' League disbanded before the 1891 season, Pittsburgh receipts remained sluggish into the mid-1890s. Faced with a huge deficit, the club dismissed Nimick as team president.[93]

The KOL played a supporting role in the period's biggest baseball controversy, the Players League revolt of 1890. In 1885, John Montgomery Ward, a star pitcher with Chicago, assumed the presidency of the newly formed National Brotherhood of Professional Baseball Players. After the Knights' 1885 strike victory over Jay Gould, Ward contemplated affiliating the Brotherhood with the KOL. Though the Brotherood did not join, Knights were sympathetic to its cause. When a strike almost occurred in 1888, the *Labor Herald* quickly chose sides. Responding to a St. Louis *Republican* remark that laborers making $2 for a ten-hour day would not support the Brotherhood's fight against a proposed salary cap, the *Herald* commented, "There is no doubt whatever, if a fight occurs, but what the members of labor unions . . . would go to the grounds where the Brotherhood men are in preference to the 'regular' game where the amateurs play who are owned by the magnates."[94]

This was no idle threat. Though a strike was averted in 1888, a classification plan that capped salaries at $2,500 per year was announced at the end of the 1889 season. Hastily, the Brotherhood formed the Players' League to begin play in the 1890 season. Despite Spalding's intensive propaganda efforts against the league and dreadful luck with weather, the new Players' League out-drew the National League cities where the two competed, 913,000 to 853,000. In Boston, stronghold of DA 30, the Players' League attendance was more than 25 percent higher (197,346 to 147,539), and the Nationals' gate receipts were scarcely half of its 1889 total (283,257). Interestingly, the Players' League (PL) operated on cooperative principles endorsed by the KOL: backers kept the first $10,000 in profits and split the remainder fifty-fifty. The PL folded after the 1891 season, but not from lack of solidarity from unions and Knights; it was done in by a lack of cash reserves, inadequate capitalization, poor management, and bad weather.[95]

Whether playing, rooting for local teams, or following professional

93. Levine, *A. G. Spalding;* William E. Benswanger, "Professional Baseball in Pittsburgh," *Western Pennsylvania Historical Magazine,* 30 (1947): 9–14; *American Glass Review,* November 6, 1887; March 10, 1888; May 5, 1888. I would like to thank Professor Francis Couvares of Amherst College for his help in guiding me to the Pittsburgh materials.

94. Lowenfish and Lupien, *Imperfect Diamond; Labor Herald and Tocsin,* November 10, 1889.

95. Lowenfish and Lupien, *Imperfect Diamond;* Levine, *A. G. Spalding; Boston Globe,* October 7, 1890. For attacks on the Brotherhood, including letters from Spalding, see *The Sporting News,* various issues, 1890–91.

clubs, the KOL embraced baseball both as leisure and as a vehicle for advancing the larger goals of Knighthood. There were limits, however. Women were noticeably absent from KOL baseball discussions as either participants or spectators. The Order did not use its clout to promote racial harmony; Toledo Knights were sadly silent on the 1884–87 campaign to remove black star Moses Fleetwood Walker from the city's team.[96] Nonetheless, the KOL was a part of the baseball craze that left cultural and political changes in its wake. By 1889, religious journals like *The Independent* demanded in vain that Sunday blue laws be enforced. By then, pickup games and professional matches were part of the American social landscape.[97] Baseball even assisted labor organizations with ethnic assimilation; the *Irish World* proudly hailed "Irish-American champions" like Mike Kelly and Cap Anson, and Powderly kept an autographed picture of Kelly among his personal effects.[98]

But the KOL's foray into the sports world paralleled its experiences with poetry and fiction; that is, it yielded to the mainstream as well as transformed it. If sports were useful in reinforcing solidarity, they were also arenas in which compromise was foisted upon the Order. Much of the rank and file of the Knights and of trade unions thought the KOL overly squeamish about boxing, and on the wrong side of the campaign to remove beer from ballparks. The Knights' fragile community networks could not survive the counterassault of organized capital. By the mid-1890s, little remained of the KOL or its counterhegemonic sports world. Polo declined, boxing was regulated, industrial teams supplanted local assembly squads, leagues were under the aegis of city recreation departments, the Players' League was defunct, and the National League firmly grasped by Spalding-like reformers. Surely this is the triumph of commerical capitalism in the field of leisure.

But it was at best a Pyrrhic victory. The KOL was an important part of a Gilded Age working-class cultural rebellion that transformed the nature of sports.[99] As Francis Couvares astutely observes, sports like baseball gained in popularity precisely because they "never became too respectable." Gambling, rowdyism, rough play, and violence were not the values of the Gilded Age elite, but they were characteristic of its sports.

96. Levine, *A. G. Spalding.*

97. *The Independent,* August 29, 1889.

98. *Irish World,* October 19, 1889; autographed picture of Mike Kelly is found in the original *Powderly Papers* (Catholic University, Washington, D.C.).

99. For more on sports, muscular Christianity, fears of "over-civilization," and the cult of strenuous life, see Gorn, *The Manly Art;* Lears, *No Place of Grace;* Mrozek, *Sports and American Mentality;* Steven Riess, *City Games: The Evolution of American Urban Society and the Rise of Sports* (Urbana: University of Illinois Press, 1989).

Entrepreneurs tried to tame these aspects, but could not push too hard if they wished to retain their profits. William Nimick found out that the middle class alone could not fill ballparks, just as mainstream newspapers discovered that reporting the raw and seamy side of sports sold newspapers. What elites feared most is what the KOL did best: creation of a self-contained, working-class subculture. Better to make accommodations of style, values, and organization. Gilded Age sport was tamed, but it remained a dangerous force.[100]

Marching to the Crusades: Parades and the Knights

Entertainments, dances, and assembly room activities were private events; picnics, fairs, and sports were only incidentally public. By contrast, KOL parades—second only to picnics in popularity—were boisterous public affairs. Initially secrecy-conscious Knights stepped gingerly into parade lines. Individual members paraded before the 1880s, but they did so under the aegis of other organizations. When the KOL's restrictive notions of fraternalism gave way to wider ideas of solidarity, Knights marched behind their own banners.

Parades were a residual form of working-class expression to which the KOL added renewed vigor. Demands for a shorter workday, protests against wage cuts, political rallies, and celebrations of labor's nobility often sent working-class marchers to the street.[101] Like earlier parades, KOL marches were multipurposed. Parades were fun, but neither the workplace nor wider reform objectives was far from the KOL's collective consciousness.

In June 1885, Baltimore Knights of DA 41 and invited trade union guests marched to the opera house led by the Wilson Post Band and followed by Oriole Assembly with its bright yellow banner that bore the Great Seal of Knighthood. They were followed by the Brotherhood of Carpenters, Monumental Assembly (shoemakers), KOL cigar makers, and numerous trade unions, with KOL canmakers and pianomakers bringing up the rear. In all, over six hundred marchers started toward

100. Couvares, *The Remaking of Pittsburgh,* 124; For more on accommodations made to working-class patrons in order to make sports more commercially viable, see Weir, ''Take Me Out to the Brawl Game.''

101. Susan Davis, *Parades and Power: Street Theatre in Nineteenth-Century Philadelphia* (Berkeley and Los Angeles: University of California Press, 1986), 1–22, 113–53.

the opera house while "along the route many inquiries were made by spectators as to what such an imposing turnout meant." By the time the opera house was reached, the parade was more than a mile long and numbered over two thousand. The evening's main speaker was Richard Trevellick and he reminded everyone that the marchers had axes to grind. Trevellick attacked the press, ruthless capitalists, the Maryland legislature, the U.S. Congress, land speculators, lawyers, and crooked politicians. He upheld Knights' goals of free public education, child labor laws, rights for working women, arbitration, and Universal Brotherhood.[102]

The Baltimore event was typical of the inclusiveness of KOL parades. Denison, Texas, Knights held a parade with eight hundred marchers and twenty-five floats, each honoring a trade organized by the KOL. Afterward, a barbecue was held for four thousand. Tarrant Assembly 4008, an all-black local, was singled out for commendation: "The colored brethern did themselves great credit, and the occasion will long be remembered as one of the most enjoyable of the season."[103] The poignancy of this should be savored; it would be hard to find similar moments of racial solidarity in the deep South among trade unions later affiliated with the AFL.

The KOL knocked down numerous social barriers through parades. An 1887 parade in Springfield, Ohio, saw thirty-five hundred marchers turn out, including more than four hundred women from Cincinnati's Hannah Powderly Assembly. Detroit Knights brought together all of its feuding political factions for an 1885 parade. Some three thousand men and women marched behind banners like "The Land for the People," "K. of L., Clear the Way," "Eight Hours for a Day's Work," and "Schools for Children, Work for Men." Held aloft was a large transparency emblazoned with portraits of Thomas Barry, Henry George, Richard Trevellick, and Terence Powderly. As the parade snaked its way down Gratoit Avenue it passed a huge portrait of Ferdinand Lassalle. Powderly was uncomfortable being associated wtih Henry George—whose theories he thought were unsound—or with the socialist Lassalle. John Hayes and Thomas McGuire were apoplectic over the inclusion of a division from the International Cigarmakers' Union; but Detroit's rank and file found common ground that their national leaders lacked the wisdom to seek.[104]

The Knights often chose holidays to hold their parades, with Washing-

102. *Baltimore Labor Free Press*, June 6, 1885, PP.
103. *John Swinton's Paper*, June 27, 1887.
104. Ibid.; *Labor Leaf*, October 7, 1885.

ton's Birthday and the Fourth of July being favorites.[105] An 1885 Denver parade for Washington's Birthday caused middle-class outrage as the day fell on Sunday. As businessmen, ministers, and journalists attacked the Order, the wily Joseph Buchanan turned the tables by appealing to patriotism. When February 22 came, more than five thousand marched despite a pelting snowstorm. Many of the forty-three banners carried in the parade expressed scorn toward the moralists. The fact that "there was no color line in the parade" also outraged Denver's elite, as did the large contingent of German socialists. In veiled mockery of their critics, the open-air meeting that followed the parade was solemnized by an opening prayer. Buchanan noted, "Within two weeks after the parade I had organized four new assemblies in Denver."[106]

Powderly championed the Fourth of July as a good day for parades. In 1887, he complained that the Fourth no longer commanded the patriotic passions he thought it deserved and he lamented the passing of past celebratory trappings such as Liberty Poles, readings from the Declaration of Independence, and speeches on the tyranny of kings. Powderly blamed the declining Fourth on his enemies on both flanks: "Two classes, representing diverse feelings and interests, would have the common people forget that we have a country or a flag. The monopolist and the anarchist care nothing for American liberty or institutions." He called upon all Knights to turn out on the Fourth of July to honor "the birth of a people's government."[107]

Powderly overstated the decline of the Fourth, but his clarion call met with enthusiastic response. A parade in Leadville, Colorado, saw hundreds of Knights march down the city's main street in fraternal bliss, many linked arm-in-arm.[108] Likewise, Iowa Knights turned out in force for Dubuque's grand parade, picnic, fireworks, and balloon ascension. Pittsburgh Knights paraded to Silver Lake Grove for its Fourth of July celebration, where a picnic and monument dedication was held. The fervor generated for the Fourth surpassed even Powderly's dreams. He was swamped with requests to speak at Fourth festivities and, on one

105. For more on the history of Washington's Birthday parades, see Davis, *Parades and Power*, 1–22.

106. Buchanan, *Story of a Labor Agitator*, 140–41; *Labor Enquirer*, February 28, 1885. See also Thomas Neasham to Powderly, July 4, 1886, in *PP*. Neasham was a conservative Republican who served as District Master Workman of DA 82. He disliked the radical politics of Buchanan and Burnette Haskell. The above letter accused Buchanan of trying to sabotage Denver's Fourth of July celebrations, but the day came off without a hitch.

107. *JUL*, May 14, 1887.

108. Picture of Leadville parade found in both original and microfilm editions of *PP*.

occasion, shared a platform with rival Thomas McGuire in St. Joseph, Missouri.[109]

The Fourth of July was not universally accepted by Knights; Joseph Buchanan was among those who thought its celebrations reinforced capitalism. For some, the revolutionary defiance of May Day was more appropriate than the knee-jerk patriotism of the Fourth. May Day was officially celebrated for the first time in 1886, and some Knights chose to confront American institutions rather than celebrate them, especially Chicago socialists, New Yorkers close to Victor Drury, and French and German immigrant radicals. May Day parades tended to be smaller than Fourth parades, and nowhere did Knights sponsor one. Instead, individuals marched with socialist, anarchist, and trade union groups with which they felt kinship. But many Knights were willing to do so, particularly when May Day was coupled with demonstrations for reforms like the eight-hour day. Despite Powderly's circular demanding that Knights stay away from the May 1, 1886, agitations, thousands in Detroit, New York, and Denver ignored their GMW. The events in Chicago that culminated in Haymarket counted many Knights among the demonstrators, including two of the men eventually hanged.

After Haymarket, most Knights were more circumspect when celebrating May Day. St. Louis Knights paraded in 1887, but only after resolving to carry only the American flag.[110] The same was true of Chicago's 1890 parade in which thirty thousand marched, the majority of whom hoisted the stars and stripes. One contingent of KOL carpenters featured a transparency of a tramp carried by a man "made up in the garb of a typical Italian street sweeper." The transparency bore the words "What I Was Before I Joined the K. of L." on its front. The reverse featured a "brawny workman, full of health and vigor," and a KOL emblem.[111]

The St. Louis and Chicago May Day parades were among the last in which the KOL maintained a separate identity. Despite a brief flirtation with DeLeonite socialists after Powderly's ouster, the remaining Knights found James Sovereign's radical agrarianism easier to stomach. By the 1890s most May Day celebrations were purely anarcho-socialist affairs.

109. *Industrial Leader*, July 2, 1887; 1888 Proceedings of District Assembly 3, in *PP*; undated handbill announcing the Powderly/McGuire lecture located in *PP*. The monument was dedicated to Thomas Armstrong, instrumental in building DA 3 in its early days. Armstrong also made several unsuccessful bids for the governorship of Pennsylvania in the 1870s and 1880s.

110. Notice of the upcoming May Day parade in St. Louis was listed in the *Saturday Telegram* (New Haven, Conn.), April 23, 1887.

111. *Chicago Herald*, n.d. (1890), in *PP*.

Though KOL rank and filers participated, it was as individuals, not Knights of Labor.[112]

For most Knights and trade unionists, Labor Day surpassed all others as a time for parades. When the Knights marched in their first Labor Day parade in 1882, there was no official holiday; in 1885, Oregon became the first state to recognize legislatively the first Monday in September as Labor Day. Historians have confused details of Labor Day's establishment and few have given the KOL its proper due.

Typical of such errors is that which gives New York City credit for holding the first Labor Day and ascribes it the brainchild of P. J. McGuire.[113] Actually, Providence, Rhode Island, laborers turned out on August 23, 1882 to agitate for Labor Day, nearly two weeks before New York City's demonstration. Over one thousand laborers paraded, and thousands more turned out for picnics, speeches, and a baseball game between two KOL squads. The Providence parade included two divisions of Knights of Labor, one of which was led by twelve drummers from the Zouave Corps Band of Worcester, Massachusetts. The day's speakers included P. J. McGuire, Robert Blissert of New York City's Central Labor Union (CLU), and DA 49's Victor Drury.[114]

Providence was a dress rehearsal for New York City's monster parade of September 5. Blissert, Drury, and McGuire were present in New York City, but were not major organizers. Confusion lies in the fact that P. J. McGuire was active in the city's CLU, the body that sponsored the event. The Knights of Labor Grand Assembly convened in New York City on the morning of the parade and recessed to participate and watch. But it was not P. J. McGuire who was in charge of arrangements, rather the machinist Matthew Maguire, the Secretary of the CLU and a member of New York City DA 49, bodies that interlocked. Matthew McGuire was an ally of Victor Drury and it is likely that Drury played a role in the planning of Labor Day. Drury's absence from the speakers' roster is easily explained; DA 49 operated in total secrecy and Drury preferred to stay out of the limelight and used others to front his ideas. (Drury's friend John Caville served on the Committee of Arrangements.) This much is clear: P. J. McGuire played little role beyond that of speaker.

The KOL contributed the very label "Labor Day." The term originated with GEB member Robert Price of Lonaconing, Maryland, who was inspired by the New York City parade and began to agitate for a Labor Day

112. *The People*, May 3, 1896.
113. For example, Foner, *History of the Labor Movement*, vol. 2, 96–101.
114. See Scott Molloy, "Rhode Island Hosted America's First Labor Day Parade," in Buhle et al., *History of Rhode Island Working People*, 15–20.

in the Welsh social clubs to which he belonged. After one of his speeches, a Scranton newspaper picked up the phrase and it gained in popularity.[115]

The KOL provided far more than the planning and naming of Labor Day. Among the more than ten thousand marchers in 1882 were many Knights. Brooklyn's Advance Labor Club marched behind a banner proclaiming "Correct Ideas Must Precede Successful Action" and carried a large reproduction of an *Irish World* cartoon of the awakening American Gulliver of Labor about to tear off the puny bonds applied by Lilliputian monopoly. Other KOL assemblies marching included Brooklyn's Protective Labor Association and the CMPU. Somebody carried a banner emblazoned with LA 1562's rallying cry, "Organize and Spread the Light." Powderly watched the parade with scores of trade union officials and KOL friends, including Robert Price.[116]

New York's 1883 Labor Day parade was even larger. More than twenty thousand marched, and this time Victor Drury came out from the shadows to mount the speakers' podium with Henry George, Louis Post, and *Irish World* editor, Patrick Ford. The first year that Labor Day was held on Monday was 1884, and parades took place in Buffalo, Cincinnati, Lynn, and Haverhill, as well as New York City. That year George K. Lloyd of DA 49 introduced a resolution asking the New York state legislature to make the first Monday in September Labor Day, a status it did not achieve until 1887. But by 1885, Knights across the country simply assumed that Labor Day was a holiday and did not wait for the official sanction of legislatures or employers. The *Haverhill Laborer* reported, "September 1st of last year [1884], the first National labor Holiday, was inaugurated by the Knights of Labor of America. The day was generally observed in all large manufacturing centres throughout the country." This matter-of-fact report belies the fact that Labor Day was not an official holiday in 1884, and Massachusetts did not recognize the day until 1887. Nonetheless, Haverhill's laborers turned out for a parade, picnic, baseball exhibition, and a band concert and dance whose opening tune was a march entitled "Knights of Labor."[117]

In 1886, both the Knights and Labor Day enjoyed a huge upsurge. Laborers all over North America seized September 6 as their own. As many as thirty thousand marched in New York, ten thousand in Brooklyn, and more than ten thousand in Newark, New Jersey, areas also

---

115. Powderly to Secretary of Labor James J. Davis, n.d., in *PP.*

116. *Irish World,* September 16, 1882.

117. Ibid., September 15, 1883; September 12, 1885; Foner, *History of the Labor Movement,* vol. 2, 96–98; Powderly to Davis, n.d., in *PP; The Laborer* (Haverhill), September 5, 1885.

infused with excitement over Henry George's bid for New York City mayor. Newark DA 51 alone issued 10,715 parade badges. Baltimore's eighteen thousand marchers made it the largest demonstration in the city's history, while the citizens of Albany, Buffalo, Denver, and Elizabeth, New Jersey, witnessed parades ranging from two thousand to five thousand marchers. Knights in Chicago donned matching clothing and identifying insignia for the day.

Members of DA 57 wore green and red caps, while KOL ore shovelers sported maroon badges, and eighteen hundred hod carriers carried red bandannas. KOL divisions marched behind a banner warning "Beware of Politicans." Detroit's DA 50 joined that city's ten thousand marchers and carried the banner of *The Labor Leaf*, the official journal of the district. Accounts singled out the patternmakers of the Terence V. Powderly Assembly for their "handsome banner and excellent drilling."[118]

Boston's Labor Day parade is typical of 1886 celebrations and bears closer examination. Ten thousand marchers paraded from Columbus Avenue to Fort Hill Square along the city's busiest commercial streets and past the Post Office and City Hall. At the head of the parade were mounted police, a band, and parade officials. The Tailors' Union of Boston (KOL) came next, followed by KOL hatmakers "heralded by one of the hugest drums that ever vibrated on the streets of Boston." They also carried an enormous hat as a symbol of their trade and marchers wore round hats which they doffed in unison. The bakers came next, each dressed in white with bunches of wheat pinned to their breasts and loaves of bread under their arms. The bricklayers bore a huge trowel while the tenders carried a large banner with a picture of Atlas. The first division was completed by woodworkers. Printers and typographers headed the second division, followed by CMIU members wearing badges fashioned from its famous blue label. A float illustrated the cigar-making process. Furniture finishers, painters, and decorators brought up the rear. Building tradesmen made up the entire of the third division and one of their props was a gigantic saw on which the slogan "Set on Eight Hours" had been painted. The fourth and final division was headed by the Sons of St. Cloud (ironworkers), followed by women cordwainers "looking as though they were ready for other ties besides those of the ropemakers," boot and shoemakers, and carriagemakers.[119]

118. *Irish World*, September 11, 1886; *The Boycotter*, September 4, 1886; *John Swinton's Paper*, September 12, 1886; *Knights of Labor* (Chicago), September 11, 1886; *National Labor Tribune*, September 11, 1886; *Labor Leaf*, September 8, 1886; *John Swinton's Paper*, September 19, 1886.
119. *The Laborer* (Haverhill), September 11, 1886.

Nonetheless, 1887 and 1888 were the last years in which Labor Day boasted of unity between working-class organizations. Boston's celebrations brought together men as ideologically diverse as the CMIU's George McGuire, typographer and Marxist Edward O'Donnell, and KOL District Master Workman Charles Chance. In Baltimore, an equally mixed group came together: Frank G. Boyd, the manager of the Chesapeake Telephone Company; AFL delegate Gottlieb Hohn; J. G. Schonfarber, the District Master Workman of DA 41 and editor of *The Critic;* Jeff Wade, who belonged to both the KOL and the AFL; and Joseph Edwards, a black Knight from LA 2397 and delegate to the 1886 General Assembly. So cooperative was the atmosphere that *The Freeman* complained of the "paucity of colored mechanics" in Labor Day parades around the country and urged its black leadership to rally behind the KOL: "Colored men should awake to [the] important fact that this great labor organization can aid the race in the South and make the white people there respect their social and political rights." In Boston, only "fifteen or twenty coal handlers" marched "with their white brothers" though the KOL "employed the colored Boston Brass Band." *The Freeman*'s complaint had some effect; in 1888 Pittsburgh's black hod carriers marched two hundred strong, all sporting bowler hats, white gloves, and canes.[120]

The KOL took an active role in establishing Labor Day as a vehicle for the working class to show its solidarity. Nonetheless, by 1889, labor's day to come together began to magnify its internal differences. By then, the Order's trade union policy had thoroughly filtered down to local assemblies and an ascendant AFL aggressively contested descendant KOL assemblies at every turn. Chicago's 1889 Labor Day came off without a hitch, but Knights elsewhere were not so lucky. In Baltimore an AFL boycott threat was averted only after DA 41 asked it to form a division. Even then, the Federation assembled at a different part of the city. The conflict in Boston was not so easily resolved. The city's CLU refused to march with the KOL unless cigarmakers' LA 80 was banned from the parade. When DA 30 upheld LA 80's appeal to take part in the festivities, the boycott was on.[121]

Boston presaged the future. By 1890 Labor Day parades were still popular affairs—thirty-five thousand attending in New York, fifteen thou-

120. *The Labor Leader* (Boston), September 3, 1887; August 8, 1888; *The Critic,* September 1, 1888; September 8, 1888; *The Freeman,* September 10, 1887; *National Labor Tribune,* September 29, 1888.
121. Richard Griffiths to Powderly, September 9, 1889, in *PP; The Critic,* July 13, 1889; September 7, 1889; September 14, 1889; *The Labor Leader* (Boston), August 17, 1889.

sand in Denver, nine thousand in Milwaukee, six thousand in Jersey City, and four thousand in San Francisco—but Boston, Chicago, Detroit, and New York saw separate parades. The KOL parades tended to attract more marchers than the trade unions, but that supremacy was short-lived, and reported numbers in the 1890s were often inflated by the KOL's cooperation with other groups. Parades in New York and Albany were bolstered by striking New York Central workers, while those in Topeka, Kansas, and Lincoln, Nebraska, included large numbers of Farmers' Alliance members.[122]

Sadly, Labor Day parades came to look like trademarks and labels: symbols of labor schisms, not solidarity. By 1891, separate parades were standard in Labor Day celebrations and KOL festivities were increasingly modest. The Knights could still turn out big crowds, but little unity could be found. In Brooklyn's 1891 parade the Brotherhood of Carpenters and Joiners refused to march with the KOL, and held their own parade. In Paterson, New Jersey, it was not the KOL that attracted attention but rather the Scotch Caledonian Club with its bagpipe band, plaid costumes, and raucous Highland games. Even the *JKL* had little to say about KOL participation in Labor Day beyond reporting a large rally held in Wilkes-Barre, Pennsylvania, at which Powderly addressed his own DA 16. By 1892 *The Critic* was reduced to pointing out that KOL Labor Day marchers were proof that the KOL was not dead.[123] But *The Critic*'s cry was all the demoralized KOL could muster. Leadership of Labor Day, like most other aspects of the labor movement, rapidly passed to other organizations and the KOL, once a mover and shaker, was reduced to the role of ancillary.

The Triumph of Commercial Culture?

On December 6, 1891, New York City's DA 49, historically the most ideological of all KOL districts, held a "Grand Entertainment and Lecture."

122. *JKL*, September 4, 1890; *National Labor Tribune*, September 6, 1890; *The Critic*, September 6, 1890. The KOL angered trade unionists in other matters relating to parades. Milwaukee unionists were angered when the city's Knights refused to march in an 1887 parade honoring Grover Cleveland. Though the more conservative unionists found the Knights' behavior disrespectful, the KOL argued that President Cleveland was an enemy of labor. Subsequent events—Pullman and Homestead to name two—belatedly proved the Knights correct. For more on the dispute in Milwaukee, see *The Daily Review*, October 3, 1887.

123. *JKL*, September 10, 1891; *The Critic*, September 5, 1891; September 10, 1892.

Alexander Wright, the editor of the *JKL*, gave a talk on land reform, but his speech was oddly out of place on a bill that featured jugglers, parlor exercises, recitations, and various musical performances. Some of the evening's fare was un-Knightly to say the least. Mathile Gebhardt entertained with "artistic" dances, while the duo Whitely and Reid offered "Dutch songs, dances, recitations, and funny sayings." The featured act was "The Great Brophy" demonstrating his "refined whistling specialty."[124]

During the 1880s the KOL assembled, by accident and design, a rich culture that embraced leisure as an escape from the drudgery of work, a challenge to constituted authority, and a reinforcement of Knighthood. Yet by 1891, leisure was clearly more escapist than oppositional. What went wrong? More is involved than merely the Knights' declining fortunes; if culture and Knighthood had continued in a symbiotic relationship the Order might have found a way to reverse its course. In the heady days of the mid-1880s, excitement was at fever pitch and leisure was used as an organizing tool, even when leaders vaguely understood its potency. As part of the "everyday stuff" of Knightly life, leisure was part of a larger context that embraced political action, reform principles, shopfloor action, and other cultural expressions.

But despite the vibrancy of its internal culture the working class was not a hermetically sealed folk subculture. Because workers participated in society and struggled to enjoy more of its pleasures, they often fell prey to external desires and fads. As members of plebeian culture, laborers mixed organic expressions with outside activities that caught their fancy. In the debate over the social significance of leisure, too few sociologists or historians have given escapism its due. Yet clearly people embrace leisure for a very simple reason: it is fun. KOL newspapers proudly touted their own entertainments, but they just as enthusiastically announced other things that Knights could do for amusement. Lynn, Massachusetts, Knights had their picnics and parades, but they also went to see plays like "East Lynne, the Elopement," "Maggie, the Midget," "Alone in London," and "Naramattah, an Indian Drama."[125] In a single week, Chicago's *The Knights of Labor* informed members that they could go to the Opera House to see "The Crowing Hen," to Mc-Viker's Theatre for "Mademoiselle Nitouche," to the Columbia for "Romeo and Juliet," to the Criterion for "Wages of Sin," to the Casino for "Little Lohengrin," to the People's Theatre for "The Cattle King," or to the Academy of Music for "Alone in London," the Victorian melo-

---

124. Handbill for the 1891 DA 49 entertainment is located in *PP.*
125. *Knights of Labor* (Lynn), October 24, 1885; March 3, 1886.

drama that thrilled audiences in Lynn. If melodrama, musical comedy, or Shakespeare did not appeal, racist and sexist tripe abounded: McNish Johnson and Slavin's Burnt Cork Brigades, the Chicago Minstrels in "Don Caesar de Crazy Patch," Chinese actor Ah Took portraying Washee-Washee in McKee Rankin's "The Dainties," and the comedy "The Woman-Hater."[126]

Rankin made his peace with the Knights and attracted KOL attention everywhere he went. In 1889, he and his wife played the Dayton, Ohio, Grand Opera House in the musical comedy "The Golden Giant." That same venue featured comedies like "Lord Chumley," "The Fat Men's Club," and "The Queen's Mate," and dramas such as "Spartacus." The city also offered high-brow entertainment in the form of the opera "The Bostonians," and low-brow diversions such as the Gorman Brothers' minstrel show. A night at the theater was expensive. At a time in which Knights complained of the prices of baseball tickets, not a ripple was stirred by the price structure of the Grand Opera House where the cheapest seats cost 35 cents and good seats a dollar.[127]

Local Knights gleefully anticipated local celebrations of popular culture. In 1887, Dubuque's *Industrial Leader* ran huge advertisements announcing the Sells Brothers Circus. Readers were told of the wonders they would enjoy: a "Real Roman Hippodrome, a five continent menagerie, an Indian Village and Museum, the Grand Firemen's Tournament, and Pawnee Bill's Historical Wild West Show." Pawnee Bill was ex-Chief of Army Scouts Major G. W. Lillie, and he planned to recreate the Battle of Little Big Horn. The following week the *Leader* lamented that the circus skipped Iowa because of an incident in Clinton in which four persons were wounded when real bullets were used in a cowboys-and-Indians cast feud. Dubuque Knights were saddened, but Baltimore Knights were luckier. In 1889, they saw Pawnee Bill's Wild West Show as part of Adam Forepaugh's circus.[128]

As Ralph Beaumont complained, by the late 1880s Knights were flocking to popular amusements in greater numbers and with more zeal than they filled their assembly halls. It was rank-and-file disinterest in his reform lectures that shocked him even more than the sight of female gum-chewers. Powderly was equally alarmed at the rate at which amusement was divorced from the KOL's larger objectives. When the Pilling's World Museum of Boston wrote to request a photograph from which a wax figure could be constructed, Powderly—no stranger to the

---

126. *Knights of Labor* (Chicago), October 2, 1886.
127. *Dayton Workman*, March 1, 1889; March 8, 1889; March 22, 1889; April 5, 1889.
128. *Industrial Leader*, July 6, 1887; July 23, 1887; April 5, 1889; *The Critic*, May 4, 1889.

art of self-deification—hurriedly stamped the letter "No Answer Required" and filed it.[129]

In the end, Beaumont and Powderly fought a losing battle to get the American working class out of the curiosity museums and into the lecture halls. This is illustrated in the Order's last great cultural struggle, the effort to assist in the planning of the 1893 World Columbian Exposition in Chicago. When plans for the fair first surfaced in 1889, Powderly demanded that labor have a major presence. The Knights had taken part in earlier world's fairs, but Powderly felt more was needed for Chicago:

> Labor must take a deep, indeed a selfish, interest in the event and be prepared to demonstrate to all who gather there that all of its claims are just and based on equity. In the machinery, which will arouse the wonder and admiration of the visitor, will be exhibited the reason why the workman asks that the hours of labor be reduced; he will be able to point to the handtool of a century ago and trace its evolution down through the years until it finds perfection in the marvelous wonder-working machine of to-day. . . . There should be erected somewhere on the Exposition grounds two dwellings; one the hovel of the laborer; the other the palace of the millionaire. The starving needlewoman, as she toils her weary hours, should be represented side by side with the one who takes advantage of her poverty. The uses which both make of their proceeds should in some way be illustrated.[130]

Industrial conferences were held, and labor displays planned, but the KOL was upset by the content of both. The GEB directed John Hayes to petition Congress to withhold the Exposition's $5,000,000 appropriation until they heard from a KOL committee, a request that was ignored.[131]

On one score, however, the KOL was successful: the Order joined trade unions and other groups in convincing Congress to open the fair on Sunday. Powderly attacked the "great violation of the Constitution . . . contemplated largely by Southern members [of Congress]." He lectured Congress of the Constitutional proviso forbidding the establishment of a state religion and called Sunday closing an insult to Jews, Muslims, Buddhists, free thinkers, and "heathens." He also reminded it of the 1876 Centennial Exposition where no tickets were sold but "high potentates and their friends had free access to the grounds" on Sunday

129. Clarence McElroy to Powderly, August 28, 1890.
130. *New York World*, September 2, 1889.
131. John W. Hayes to U.S. Senate and House of Representatives, July 14, 1892, in *PP.*

while "the poor people, hungry and thirsty for beauty, were excluded." Despite vicious counterattacks from clerics such as the Rev. Wilbur F. Crafts, who charged that the KOL and AFL were "composed of foreign immigrants" who cared little for America or the Sabbath, the fair stayed open on Sundays.[132]

More than 1.2 million of the fair's 21.4 million paying customers poured through the gates on Sunday.[133] But what did they see? Commentators and promoters alike agreed that the masses ignored the educationally uplifting free exhibits of the White City, including those devoted to labor and industry. They flocked instead to the commercial low-brow pleasures of the Midway Plaisance with its sideshows and pseudo-ethnic streets where "Little Egypt" danced, jugglers and sword swallowers thrilled viewers, and costumed performers impressed gawking multitudes with displays of exotica. Hundreds lined up to pay 50 cents for a ride on the huge wheel built by George Ferris even though they could have gotten the same panoramic view by climbing stairs to the torch of Daniel French's statue on the Court of Honor.[134] Knights were not shy in recording what caught their attention. Throughout the fair the *JKL* listed wonderments to be viewed, but seldom included items related to the labor question. A typical entry marveled at glass bricks, a $1,000 arm chair, an alabaster buffalo, a tree twenty-six feet in diameter, billiard balls valued at $80,000, a huge floral display representing the national capital, a chocolate tower worth $40,000, a thousand pots of Irish shamrocks, an eighty-two pound salmon, the first umbrella imported to America, and a tanned elephant hide weighing five hundred pounds.[135]

Such unabashed celebrations of popular culture seldom produce labor reform or revive waning movements. What happened to the KOL is indicative of what was happening to working-class culture across North America. Organic expression increasingly gave way to a commercialized, sanitized, and homogenized national culture that was quite different from that envisioned by working-class propagandists and elite moralists alike. Leisure was transformed from a largely participatory to a mostly passive, consumptive activity. In amusement parts, nickelodeons, dance halls, and movie palaces leisure became another product to be purchased in the national marketplace. Rather than send messages, leisure

132. *JKL*, February 9, 1893; March 23, 1893.
133. Ibid., November 16, 1893.
134. John F. Kasson, *Amusing the Million: Coney Island at the Turn of the Century* (New York: Hill and Wang, 1978), 17–28.
135. *JKL*, November 2, 1893.

became something to be consumed for the sheer joy of experiencing it. Any meaning beyond the desire of promoters to turn a profit was implicit, not explicit.[136]

It is important to remember that the ideology of commercial leisure is profit-driven, not value-laden. Leisure did not obliterate social values, and to survive it forged compromises between warring Victorian and plebian cultures. Working-class people left their mark. For example, the Midway Plaisance at the 1893 Columbian Exposition was not part of the Exposition's original design; its inclusion came as a result of popular demand. While the deserted White City garnered the accolades of moralists, clerics, and newspapers, it was the Midway that gathered patrons, and the purveyors of popular culture who collected their coins.[137] In a similar vein, Gilded Age baseball became the national pastime because the men who controlled it learned to temper Albert Spalding's moralism with healthy doses of working-class rowdyism. Patrons of leisure continued their debates, while commercial entrepreneurs made such content adjustments as were necessary to insure a healthy box office. Culture remained a class battleground as twentieth-century debates over gambling, dance halls, and media content attest. Before one postulates the destruction of working-class culture, one should envision what commercial leisure would look like had Victorian moralists carried the day.

Nonetheless, there are essential differences between the late nineteenth-century and early twentieth-century leisure. Working-class cultural resistance was robbed of its active nature, and took the form of consumption decisions rather than the formation of oppositional culture. In terms of control, attending a theater is not the same thing as writing, producing, and acting in one's own play. New York City laborers of the early twentieth century decided which of Coney Island's three amusement parks to attend; Knights of Labor in the 1880s sponsored their own picnics, baseball games, and entertainments. Twentieth-century workers cheered parades; nineteenth-century Knights marched in them.

Whatever leisure has become, there was a time when it was more than fun and diversion. For the KOL in the mid-1880s, leisure was part of a total packet of ideas and actions that threatened to assemble many of

136. For more on the triumph of commercial culture see Couvares, *The Remaking of Pittsburgh*; Rosenzweig, *Eight Hours for What We Will*; Kasson, *Amusing the Million*.

137. For a thorough treatment of the 1893 Columbian World Exposition, see R. Reid Badger, *The Great American Fair: The World's Columbian Exposition and American Culture* (Chicago: Nelson-Hall, 1979).

America's social and class divisions on a common playing field where bonds might be forged. Because of external oppression, financial insolvency, and internal conflict, the KOL only rhetorically bridged the gulfs and never realized the power within its grasp. It was not fully cognizant of the usefulness of leisure forms such as parades until it had no power left to wield. As leisure separated itself from the KOL, the Order was left with comedic incongruities such as poor Alexander Wright trying to lecture on land reform from the same stage upon which "The Great Brophy" whistled a different tune.

Conclusion

Do I contradict myself?
Very well then I contradict
myself
(I am large, I contain multitudes.)[1]
—Walt Whitman

By 1893, KOL culture was losing its distinctive identity, and was in the process of shaping and fusing with commercial culture. I have warned against calling this "surrender" or "defeat" and, in my final words, I wish to argue that we must view the Knights of Labor as a totality. The KOL ousted Terence Powderly as its national leader in 1893. But neither the emergence of commercial capitalism nor the removal of Powderly mark the end of the KOL; they are signposts for a new phase of KOL history.

That phase remains understudied. Powderly was succeeded by Iowa's James Sovereign, though the immediate power lay with New York DA 49. By 1893, however, control of that body lay with Daniel DeLeon, not anarchists, Lassalleans, or ritualists. DeLeon, like Theodore Cuno a decade earlier, wanted to make the KOL a Marxist organization. When he failed in 1895, DeLeon bolted the Order, and formed his own Socialist Trade and Labor Alliance. According to DeLeon's biographer, the KOL was reduced to seventeen thousand when Marxists quit the Order.[2]

Such a figure is assuredly too low. Details of the post-1893 Knights are sketchy; some would say irrelevant. But we know little about the late KOL for the same reason we know little about its early days: It was a secret organization that kept members and alliances veiled from public view. After DeLeon's departure, the organization returned to ritual se-

1. Walt Whitman's "Song of Myself" quoted from James E. Miller, Jr., ed., *Walt Whitman: Complete Poetry and Selected Prose* (Boston: Houghton Mifflin, 1959), 68.
2. L. Glen Seretan, *Daniel DeLeon: The Odyssey of an American Marxist* (Cambridge, Mass.: Harvard University Press, 1979), 150.

crecy. Sovereign served a few more terms as GMW and was succeeded by Henry Hicks, then John Hayes. All three men commanded an organization whose power base was shifting from urban, industrial centers into the countryside. For much of the 1890s, Knighthood was so intertwined with the Populist movement that the two were synonymous in many rural areas.

In all likelihood, the KOL remained a healthier organization into the twentieth century than is often assumed. A central office was maintained until 1917, and it is possible that there were more Knights than there were members of the well-studied IWW for many of the years between 1905 and 1917. The Knights held a convention as late as 1932, and had operating local assemblies until 1949. It is foolhardy to conclude that the KOL was a sleeping giant, but equally so to assign it a premature death.

For much of its history, the KOL was an odd, even contradictory, organization. Its members were cooperators in an age of competition, ritualists in an increasingly rationalized society, nonpartisans in a politicized era, and generalists among specialists. Furthermore, Knights upheld principles of universal solidarity, equality, "true Christianity" and "true patriotism," yet violated them when they bickered with trade unionists (and each other), treated women as Victorian wallflowers, launched xenophobic racial and ethnic attacks, and harbored agnostics, anticlerics, and anarchists in local assemblies. Yet therein lies the peculiar genius of the KOL. For a fleeting moment it stood as all things to all people, a spongy but all-encompassing Order in which "an injury to one [was] the concern of all."

More than a century has passed since the KOL was a viable organization. In that time we have grown skeptical of the KOL's goal of making the world anew. If such doubts are warranted, they are also reminders of how distant we are from the Gilded Age men and women who seriously entertained such utopian dreams. Knights faced the enormous task of trying to transform society's economic, political, social, and cultural institutions. In the end, the war was lost; the Gilded Age status quo was too powerful for the KOL to topple, and popular culture proved too attractive to supplant.

But one should resist the temptation to dismiss the Knights as devoid of practical content. Its ranks were polluted by bumblers, self-seekers, "labor fakirs," ineffective bureaucrats, bourgeois sentimentalists, starry-eyed dreamers, power-hungry plotters, and assorted "high kickers." But it also sported hard-headed pragmatists, shrewd politicians, effective lobbyists, class-conscious radicals, wily propagandists, nuts-and-bolts trade unionists, and creative tacticians. No one leader or group was synonymous with the Order; for good or ill, the KOL contained multitudes.

Little agreement existed as to what a Knight was, but members were not shy in articulating their own interpretations. Some critics took the Order to task for lacking class consciousness. Actually, most Knights held a expanded consciousness in which class was only one facet. This ambiguity has deterred many would-be chroniclers. Though the KOL was easily the nineteenth century's largest labor organization, no one has attempted a national survey of it since Norman Ware in 1929. Despite their cumbersome nature, the papers of Terence Powderly have been available for decades, and several of the KOL newspapers I found through routine interlibrary loan searches have seldom been cited. There are more books devoted to the Haymarket martyrs alone than to the KOL; the same is true of Gilded Age socialist and anarchist groups. Yet socialism and anarchism as independent movements—thousands were shielded by the KOL umbrella—were small when compared to the KOL, and they had less impact.

Historians have been quick to point out the contradictions in Social Darwinism, but have applied Darwin's "survival of the fittest" dictum to the Knights by arguing that because the KOL waned and the AFL waxed, the AFL was better suited to the realities of industrial America. But the decline of the KOL did not lead to greater unity or more efficient organization of workers; it reinforced working-class fragmentation. In 1929, Robert and Helen Lynd found an "old-timer [who remembered] the Knights of Labor as a 'grand organization' with a 'fine ritual.' " And why not? The Middletown the Lynds observed was drained of the excitement of Gilded Age worker culture. Gone was the Workingmen's Library and Reading Room, steelworkers' concerts, the cigar makers' baseball team, parade banners, KOL picnics, and the days in which town officials addressed KOL meetings. The Lynds noted, "Labor Day, a great day in the nineties, is today barely noticed." In several trenchant passages, they described a virtual rout of working class culture:

> The social function of the union has disappeared in this day of movies and the automobile, save for sparsely attended dances at Labor Hall. The strong molders' union . . . has to compel attendance at its meetings by making attendance compulsory under a penalty of a dollar fine. . . . public opinion is no longer with organized labor. . . . [The] Middletown press has little good to say of organized labor. The pulpit avoids such subjects, particularly in

the churches of the business classes, and when it speaks it is apt to do so in guarded, equivocal terms.[3]

Like Knights in the 1890s, Middletown's working-class culture faced stiff competition from consumer culture. Rather than dreaming of a transformed society, working-class families longed for automobiles, cosmetics, radios, refrigerators, silk hose, and telephones. Instead of trudging to a KOL or union hall, workers and their families were found at movie theaters, YMCA dances, and school athletic contests.

In 1929, there was little to cheer old-timers. The AFL organized more workers than the KOL, but its craft-centered exclusiveness stifled grandiose dreams. Mechanization threatened to reduce AFL craft unions to the anachronistic status of which Gompers once accused the Knights. Communist and socialist parties proved more adroit at forming splinter groups in the name of doctrinal purity than in marshaling support at the polls. The only labor organization with broad enough entry criteria to attract mass participation was the IWW. By 1929, it was a small underground movement, having been crushed by the same combined power of capital and state power that decimated the KOL.

Richard Oestreicher notes, "The Knights should be remembered not for the alleged lessons to be drawn from their extinction but for their capacity to bring workers of different backgrounds and experiences together at a critical moment in American history . . . no one else did much better than Powderly or the Knights over the next forty years."[4] It was the KOL—not anarchists, socialists, or trade unionists—that most captured labor's imagination in the 1880s. The Order's moment in the limelight was brief but brilliant, and its passing was disastrous for the immediate future of working-class movements.

To assess the importance of the KOL to Gilded Age men and women one must reverse the failure assumption and ask why the KOL was so successful. Oestreicher stresses the Order's ability to convince members to cross traditional social barriers. True enough; once the KOL was gone where could working women or people of color find solidarity? For all of the KOL's shortcomings, neither socialists nor the IWW came close to its achievements on this score, and few AFL craft unions bothered to try. But there was something beyond the social commitments of the

3. Robert and Helen Lynd, *Middletown: A Study in Modern American Culture* (New York: Harcourt, Brace, Jovanovich, 1929), 73–92.

4. Richard Oestreicher, "Terence Powderly, the Knights of Labor and Artisanal Republicanism," in Melvyn Dubofsky and Warren Van Tine, eds., *Labor Leaders in America* (Urbana: University of Illinois Press, 1987), 31, 59.

KOL that attracted men and women to it: its rich, flexible culture. Call it "movement culture," a "subculture of opposition," or "plebeian culture," workers from all walks of life found it possible to embrace an abstraction called "Knighthood." When the KOL worked best, it did not define that abstraction too rigidly.

How could so many workers rally to an organization so loosely defined? A syllogism is only as good as its major premise, and one of the most flawed runs thus: True working-class culture expresses class-consciousness; the KOL was not fully class-conscious; therefore, KOL culture was not working-class culture. Such logic is riddled with wrongheadedness. First, the Gilded Age working class was not monolithic. It makes more sense to speak of multiple working-class cultures and credit the Knights with trying to fuse them. Second, the KOL did not reject class consciousness; it merely found it inadequate as a sole unifying principle. The KOL understood that the majority of workers were unorganized and in need of "education." Leaders knew that the uneducated were not class conscious, but that they were susceptible to appeals for a more just, producer-centered society. Generalities reached more workers than dogma. It is no accident that the KOL's most divisive leaders were its most doctrinaire.

The KOL tried to accommodate the diverse multitudes that inhabited labor's house. In the heterogeneous world of Gilded Age workers, a poem, short story, or song can be just as indicative of opinion as a platform principle, political editorial, or fiery speech. The gaps between practice and rhetoric show that culture and ideology may or may not be linked. Plenty of Knights behaved the way they did because of ideology, while still others evolved ideology because of the culture to which they were drawn. For a few, there was no identifiable bridge between their words and their lives. It is hard to believe, for example, that John Hayes really identified with the working class he championed. His actions, schemes, and private behavior reveal a man who felt himself trapped in a class he did not admire, but which he hoped he could shrewdly use to advance himself. I suspect that Hayes read KOL fiction and identified with characters, like Montreville Pierstone, whose windfalls landed them in the lap of luxury.

There is much about KOL culture that is startling and puzzling. John Hayes represents a strain that is bourgeois, not merely a variant of working-class respectability. Many Knights—Joseph Buchanan and Leonora Barry spring to mind—were simultaneously political radicals and cultural conservatives. Others, like Powderly and his legions of followers, were fairly conservative in both respects, while Knights like Victor Drury and Albert Parsons were thoroughly radical. The majority of Gilded Age men and women likely approached ideology and culture as though it were an à la carte menu and chose among its offerings according to their needs and pleasures. Men like Home Club conspirators Thomas Mc-Guire and James Quinn allied themselves with Drury or Powderly as circumstances dictated, just as George McNeill defended socialism with one stroke of the pen and wrote bland religious poetry with the next. KOL culture was a Gilded Age amalgam of competing ideologies, value systems, and practices. Knights read treatises on the abolition of the wage system in the same paper in which they read *Lever and Throttle;* they sang moving radical songs and soppy Victorian parlor standards at the same meeting. To begin an understanding of the KOL and the world in which it thrived is to embrace ambiguity, contrasts, and surface contradictions.

Does this mean that the concept of a KOL culture lurking behind the veils dissolves into fragmented nothingness? I do not think so. Knights' culture was fluid, but it was not amorphous. It existed in the interstices between public and private realms, and between mass and working-class/folk culture. Above all, it was an evolving form that unfolded in five overlapping phases. In its earliest days, KOL culture was fraternal, secretive, ritualistic, exclusive, and oral. After 1882, it became more public, activist, universalist, political, and literary after passing through an intermediary phase (1878–84) marked by controversy and backlash. That third phase, dating roughly from 1882 through 1889, was the KOL's most vigorous and vital. As KOL culture declined as a universal expression after 1887, it grew more parochial and local cultures more creative. This phase (1887–95) ended as KOL cultures yielded their centers to mainstream popular culture. The final phase (1895–1917) saw an attempt to turn full circle and return to ritual secrecy.

Unifying all efforts was the very idea of Knighthood, that original dream of Universal Brotherhood held by Uriah Stephens. Such a grandiose vision required that the KOL thrust itself into every aspect of working-class life, and it did so with gusto. Stephens and his followers rejected Lassallean politics, Marxian unions, and craft exclusiveness as too narrow to contain their dreams. Stephens died in 1882. Had he lived a few more years, he would have been astonished by the array of KOL cultural activity. By 1886, it encompassed ritual, music, poetry, fiction, education, parades, picnics, dances, fairs, sports, entertainments, regalia, material objects, and religion—as well as politics and unionism. When one adds the various sublayers of Knights' culture and concern— arts and crafts, cooperative production, ethics campaigns, internal debate societies, KOL restaurants, temperance, several hundred newspapers, and even its own towns—the depth of KOL culture is astounding.

Vision was the Order's Achilles' heel. As more men and women joined the KOL, it was inevitable that they would disagree. In the earliest years of Knighthood, ritual fraternalism tended to dissolve individual differences. The Knights never found an adequate replacement for fraternalism, which eroded after 1882. The rhetorical attractions of solidarity were no match for the concrete, shared experiences, which is why clamors for ritual never subsided. As the Order grew, internal disagreements simmered, boiled, and exploded, leading to expulsions, desertions, and nasty revolts like that of the Home Club. Even then, the excitement of growth, the diversity of the rank and file, and success against capital allowed the Order to thrive and create a rich cultural and material base.

It was its success against capital that did in the Knights, not internal conflicts. It is impossible to exaggerate the euphoria the KOL's 1885 victory over Jay Gould generated. Coupled with lesser strike and boycott victories in 1885 and early 1886, hundreds of thousands—perhaps more than a million—of workers stormed the KOL veils and begged entry. But capital's resolve to crush the surging KOL deepened and closed ranks before the Knights could regroup and digest its new converts. In 1886, Gould offered no quarter in the second Southwest strike, a pattern repeated by Philip Armour later that year, by Worcester County shoe manufacturers in 1887, and William Vanderbilt in 1890. Demoralizing losses sapped the Order's ephemeral strength and left factions to bicker over who was to blame. With the expulsion of the CMIU in 1886, the KOL announced its final break with fraternalism and betrayed its commitment to solidarity. For the first time, the KOL declared an entire segment of the working class beyond the pale, a pattern foolishly repeated against its radical fringe in the days following Haymarket. Knighthood began to be more carefully defined and the act of definition became one of exclusion. In 1890, the *Journal of United Labor* symbolically changed its name to the *Journal of the Knights of Labor*.

But let us make no mistake, the KOL did not commit suicide; it was murdered. Had the Order confronted Gould, Armour, and Vanderbilt unified and fraternal, it still would have lost. The Knights could not possibly match the financial resources of its determined opposition, and it could not win the battle for hearts and minds when organized capital controlled Gilded Age purse strings, politics, presses, and pulpits. One need only return to what came next to realize the magnitude of capital's triumph. Transparent gains, fragmentation, and weakness followed in the wake of the KOL's demise as the tragedies at Homestead and Pullman attest. And what could be more pathetic than Alexander Berkman's attack on Henry Clay Frick, an enduring symbol of working-class anger reduced to acts of individual desperation? Organized labor regrouped from 1898 to 1902, but the power of sprawling trusts and capitalist conspiracies blunted its gains. When U.S. Steel crushed the Amalgamated Association of Iron, Steel, and Tin Workers in 1901, it would be thirty-six years before the steel industry was effectively organized, despite mass strikes in 1906, 1909, and 1919. In 1912, the magnetic and courageous Eugene Debs mustered 900,000 working-class votes for president; this came more than a quarter of a century after the bumbling Terence Powderly attracted roughly that many workers to the KOL, many of whom clamored for his election to Congress.

By the time the Lynds arrived in Middletown, even Debs was a fading memory. But not all workers were seduced by consumer goods. The KOL died, but it left a legacy. "Storm the Fort, Ye Knights of Labor" became "Hold the Fort" and was sung by the CIO in the 1930s. The CIO also organized women and people of color, and it vigorously thrust itself into worker culture as had the KOL. The CIO, of course, did not usher in a labor millennium. Today, the Knights' goal of making "industrial, moral worth, not wealth, the true standard of individual and national greatness" remains elusive. Still, broad vision continues to inspire champions for working-class justice. Perhaps Mary "Mother" Jones wrote the most appropriate epitaph for the KOL. She credited the Order with her own conversion to labor's cause and fondly recalled evenings listening to KOL speeches and Sundays spent on its outings.

> Those were the days of sacrifice for the cause of labor. Those were the days when we had no hall, when there were no high salaried officers, no feasting with the enemies of labor. Those were the days of the martyrs and the saints.[5]

5. Mary Jones, *The Autobiography of Mother Jones* (Chicago: Charles H. Kerr, 1980), 13–14. First edition published 1925.

Select Bibliography

Primary Sources

Knights of Labor Manuscripts and Published Materials

Adelphon Kruptos, Microfilm Edition, University of Massachusetts/Amherst.

Baker, Monssini. *The Songs of Monssini, or the Cry of Labor Defrauded*. Minneapolis: Thomas A. Clark, 1889.

Buchanan, Joseph R. *The Story of a Labor Agitator*. Freeport, N.Y.: Books for Libraries, 1971. Reprint of 1903 edition.

Carman, Harry et al., eds., *The Path I Trod: The Autobiography of Terence V. Powderly*, New York: AMS Press, 1968.

Cook, Ezra, *Knights of Labor Illustrated: Adelphon Kruptos—The Full, Illustrated Ritual Including the Unwritten Work and An Historical Sketch of the Order*. Chicago: Ezra Cook, 1886.

Grimes, Mary C., ed. *The Knights in Fiction: Two Labor Novels of the 1880s*. Urbana: University of Illinois Press, 1986.

Hayes, John W., Papers. Microfilm, University of Massachusetts/Amherst.

Knights of Labor. *Labor: Its Rights and Wrongs*. Washington: Knights of Labor, 1886.

McNeill, George C. *The Labor Movement: The Problem of To-Day*. New York: Augustus M. Kelley, 1887.

———. *Unfrequented Paths: Songs of Nature, Labor, and Men*. Boston: James H. West, 1903.

Powderly, Terence V., Papers. The Catholic University of America, Washington, D.C. Microfilm Edition, University of Massachusetts/Amherst.

———. *Thirty Years of Labor, 1859-1889*. New York: Augustus M. Kelley, 1967. Reprint of 1889.

Tallmadge, J. D. *Labor Songs Dedicated to the Knights of Labor*. Chicago: J. D. Tallmadge, 1886.

Thompson, Phillips. *The Labor Reform Songster*. Philadelphia: Knights of Labor, 1892.

Tisdale, W. L. *The Knights' Book*, Microfilm Edition, University of Massachusetts/Amherst.

Wright, Carroll. "An Historical Sketch of the Knights of Labor." *Quarterly Journal of Economics* (January 1887), 137–68.

Knights of Labor Journals, Newspapers (includes affiliated papers)

Advance and Labor Leaf. Detroit, 1884–89.

American Glass Review. Pittsburgh, 1887–88.

The Boston Knight, 1886.
The Boycotter. New York, 1886–87.
The Critic. Baltimore, 1883–93.
The Daily Review. Milwaukee, 1887–89.
Dayton Workman, 1885–86.
The Industrial Leader, Dubuque, Iowa, 1885–89.
The Industrial West. Atlantic, Iowa, 1882–87.
Irish World and American Industrial Liberator. New York, 1882–95.
John Swinton's Paper. New York, 1883–87.
Journal of the Knights of Labor. Philadelphia, Washington, 1889–1901.
Journal of United Labor. Haverhill, Mass., Philadelphia, 1880–89.
Knights of Labor. Chicago, 1886–89.
Knights of Labor. Lynn, Mass., 1885–86.
Labor Enquirer. Chicago, 1887–88.
Labor Enquirer. Denver, 1883–87.
Labor Herald and Tocsin. Philadelphia, 1887–88.
The Labor Leader. Boston, 1887–97.
The Laborer. Boston, 1886–87.
The Laborer. Haverhill, Mass., 1884–87.
National Labor Tribune. Pittsburgh, 1870–90.
The People. New York, 1891–96.
Solidarity. New York, 1892.
Toledo Industrial News, 1887–88.
Union Printer. New York, 1887.

Manuscripts and Primary Source Materials Not Specifically Related to the Knights of Labor

American Federation of Labor Records. Microfilm Edition, University of Massachusetts/Amherst.

Blewett, Mary H., ed. *We Will Rise in Our Might: Workingwomen's Voices from Nineteenth-Century New England*. Ithaca: Cornell University Press, 1991.

Bliss, W. D. P. *American Trade Unionism*. Boston: Church Social Union, 1896.

DeCaux, Len. *Labor Radical: From the Wobblies to the C.I.O*. Boston: Beacon Press, 1970.

Dreiser, Theodore. *Sister Carrie*. Cambridge: Riverside Press, 1959. Reprint of 1900 original.

Ely, Richard T. *The Labor Movement*. New York: Thomas Y. Crowell, 1886.

Garraty, John, ed. *Labor and Capital in the Gilded Age: Testimony Taken by the Senate Committee upon Relations Between Capital and Labor*. Boston: Little, Brown & Company, 1968.

Gladden, Washington. *Tools and Man: Property and Industry Under the Christian Church*. Boston: Houghton-Mifflin, 1893.

Huntington Family Papers. Amherst College, Amherst, Mass. Also at Porter-Phelps-Huntington Museum, Hadley, Mass.

Industrial Workers of the World. *The I.W.W. Songbook: Songs to Fan the Flames of Discontent*. Chicago: Charles Kerr, 1935, 1946.

Jones, Mary. *The Autobiography of Mother Jones*. Chicago: Charles H. Kerr, 1980. Reprint of 1925 edition.

Kaufman, Stuart, ed. *The Samuel Gompers Papers, Volume One: The Making of a Union Leader*. Urbana: University of Illinois Press, 1986.

Pentecost, Hugh. *Popular Lectures and Discussions Before the Brooklyn Ethical Association*. Boston: James West, 1890.

Strong, Josiah. *Our Country*. Cambridge: Harvard University Press, 1963.

Twain, Mark. *A Connecticut Yankee at King Arthur's Court*. Hammondsworth: Penguin, 1986.

———, and Charles Dudley Warren. *The Gilded Age*. Garden City: Doubleday, 1969.

Gilded Age Newspapers and Journals Not Specifically Relating to the Knights of Labor

Baltimore Sun, 1891.
Beadle's Weekly, 1882–84.
Chicago Tribune, 1886–88.
Christian Advocate. New York, 1880–95.
Christian Union. New York, 1884–90.
Family Story Paper. New York, 1882–86.
Frank Leslie's Illustrated Newspaper, 1880–94.
Harper's Weekly, 1880–95.
The Independent. New York, 1880–95.
Montgomery Advertiser. Montgomery, Ala., 1886.
The New York Age, 1886–87.
The New York Freeman, 1886–87.
The New York Globe, 1880–84.
New York Herald, 1882–86.
New York Ledger, 1880–95.
New York Times, 1884–90, 1916.
New York World, 1889.
Presbyterian Review. New York, 1880–89.
Puck, 1880–94.
The Sporting News, 1886–94.
Unitarian Review, Boston, 1880–95.
The Working Woman, New York, 1887.
The Working Woman's Journal, Philadelphia, 1887–90.

Secondary Sources

Relating Substantially to the Knights of Labor

Balch, Elizabeth. "Songs for Labor." *The Survey* (January 3, 1914), 408–28.

Bemis, Edward W. *Cooperation in the Middle States*. Baltimore: Johns Hopkins University Press, 1888.

———. *Cooperation in New England*. Baltimore: Johns Hopkins University Press, 1888.

Birdsall, William C. "The Problem of Structure in the Knights of Labor." *Industrial and Labor Relations Review* 6 (July 1953), 532–46.

Browne, Henry. "The Catholic Church and the Knights of Labor" (Ph.D. diss.,
    The Catholic University of America, 1949).
Brundage, David. "The Producing Classes and the Saloon: Denver in the 1880s."
    Labor History 26 (Winter 1985), 29–52.
———. *The Making of Western Labor Radicalism: Denver's Organized Workers, 1878–
    1905.* Urbana: University of Illinois Press, 1994.
Buhle, Paul. "The Knights of Labor in Rhode Island." *Radical History Review* 17
    (Spring 1978), 39–73.
Cassity, Michael J. "Modernization and Social Crisis: The Knights of Labor and
    a Midwest Community, 1885–1886." *Journal of American History* 66 (June
    1979), 41–61.
Fink, Leon. *Workingmen's Democracy: The Knights of Labor and American Politics.*
    Urbana: University of Illinois, 1983.
Fones-Wolf, Elizabeth and Kenneth. "Knights Versus Trade Unionists: The Case
    of the Washington, D.C., Carpenters, 1881–1886." *Labor History* 22 (Spring
    1981), 192-212.
Garlock, Jonathan. *Guide to Local Assemblies of the Knights of Labor.* Westport,
    Conn.: Greenwood Press, 1982.
Goldberg, Judith L. "Strikes, Organizing and Change: The Knights of Labor in
    Philadelphia, 1869–1890" (Ph.D. diss., New York University, 1985).
Kealey, George S., and Bryan D. Palmer. *Dreaming of What Might Be: The Knights
    of Labor in Ontario, 1880–1890.* Cambridge: Cambridge University Press,
    1982.
Kessler, Sidney. "The Organization of Negroes in the Knights of Labor." *Journal
    of Negro History* 37 (1952), 248–76.
Landon, Fred. "The Knights of Labor: Predecessors of the C.I.O." *Quarterly Re-
    view of Commerce* (Summer–Autumn, 1937), 133–139.
Levine, Susan B. *Labor's True Woman: Carpet Weavers, Industrialization, and Labor
    Reform in the Gilded Age.* Philadelphia: Temple University Press, 1984.
Mapes, Mary Lynne. " 'As You Have Been the World's Providers, So Now You
    Are to Be Its Saviors': A Study of Christianity and the Knights of Labor"
    (M.A. thesis, Michigan State University, 1991).
McLaurin, Melton. *The Knights of Labor in the South.* Westport, Conn.: Greenwood
    Press, 1977.
———. "The Racial Policies of the Knights of Labor and the Organization of
    Southern Black Workers." *Labor History* 17 (Fall 1976), 568–85.
Oestreicher, Richard. *Solidarity and Fragmentation: Working People and Conscious-
    ness in Detroit, 1875–1900.* Urbana: University of Illinois Press, 1986.
Palmer, Bryan. *A Culture in Conflict: Skilled Workers and Industrial Capitalism in
    Hamilton, Ontario, 1867–1917.* Montreal: McGill University Press, 1979.
Rachleff, Peter J. *Black Labor in the South: Richmond, Virginia, 1865–1890.* Philadel-
    phia: Temple University Press, 1984.
Schofield, Ann. "From 'Sealskin and Shoddy' to 'The Pig-Headed Girl': Patriar-
    chal Fables for Workers." In Carol Groneman and Mary Beth Norton,
    eds., *'To Toil the Livelong Day': America's Women of Work.* Ithaca: Cornell
    University Press, 1987.
Scontras, Charles. *Organized Labor and Politics in Maine, 1880–1890.* Orono: Uni-
    versity of Maine Press, 1966.
Stromquist, Shelton. *A Generation of Boomers: The Pattern of Railroad-Labor Conflict
    in Nineteenth-Century America.* Urbana: University of Illinois Press, 1987.

Voss, Kim. *The Making of American Exceptionalism: The Knights of Labor and Class Formation in the Nineteenth Century*. Ithaca: Cornell University Press, 1993.

Ware, Norman J. *The Labor Movement in the United States, 1860–1895: A Study in Democracy*. New York: D. Appleton, 1929.

Weir, Robert E. "Take Me Out to the Brawl Game: Sports and Workers in Gilded Age Massachusetts." In Ronald Story and Martin Kaufman, eds., *Sports in Massachusetts: Historical Essays*. Westfield: Institute for Massachusetts Studies, 1991.

———. "Tilting at Windmills: Powderly and the Home Club." *Labor History* 34 (Winter 1993), 84–113.

———. "When Friends Fall Out: Charles Litchman and the Knights of Labor." In Kenneth Fones-Wolf and Martin Kaufman, eds., *Labor in Massachusetts: Selected Essays*. Westfield: Institute of Massachusetts Studies, 1990.

Selected Other Secondary Sources

Abrahams, Roger, and George Foss. *Anglo-American Folksong Style*. Englewood Cliffs: Prentice-Hall, 1968.

Ahlstrom, Sydney E. *A Religious History of the American People*. Garden City: Image Books, 1975.

Avrich, Paul. *The Haymarket Tragedy*. Princeton: Princeton University Press, 1984.

Baltzell, E. Digby. *The Protestant Establishment: Aristocracy and Caste in America*. New York: Vintage Books, 1964.

Barth, Gunther. *City People: The Rise of Modern City Culture in Nineteenth-Century America*. Oxford: Oxford University Press, 1980.

Baron, Ava, ed. *Work Engendered: Toward a New History of American Labor*. Ithaca: Cornell University Press, 1991.

Bender, Thomas. *Community and Social Change in America*. New Brunswick: Rutgers University Press, 1978.

Benswanger, William E. "Professional Baseball in Pittsburgh." *Western Pennsylvania Historical Magazine* 30 (1947), 9–14.

Blake, Fay. *The Strike in the American Novel*. Metuchen: Scarecrow Press, 1977.

Brunvand, Jan H. *The Study of American Folklore*. New York: W. W. Norton, 1978.

Buhle, Mari Jo. *Women and American Socialism, 1870–1920*. Urbana: University of Illinois Press, 1983.

Buhle, Paul, and Scott Molly and Gail Sansbury. *A History of Rhode Island Working People*. Providence: Regini Printing Company, 1983.

Carnes, Mark C. *Secret Ritual and Manhood in Victorian America*. New Haven: Yale University Press, 1989.

Carter, Paul A. *The Spiritual Crisis of the Gilded Age*. DeKalb: Northern Illinois University Press, 1971.

Clawson, Mary Ann. *Constructing Brotherhood: Class, Gender, and Fraternalism*. Princeton: Princeton University Press, 1989.

Colloms, Brenda. *Victorian Visionaries*. London: Constable & Company, 1982.

Commons, John R., et al. *History of Labour in the United States*. New York: Augustus M. Kelley, 1966.

Couvares, Francis G. *The Remaking of Pittsburgh: Class and Culture in an Industrializing City 1877–1919*. Albany: State University of New York Press, 1984.

Cumbler, John T. *Working Class Community in Industrial America: Work, Leisure and*

Struggle in Two Industrial Cities, 1880–1930. Westport, Conn.: Greenwood Press, 1979.

Curl, John. *History of Work Cooperation in the United States.* Berkeley: Homeward Press, 1980.

Davis, Susan G. *Parades and Power: Street Theatre in Nineteenth Century Philadelphia.* Philadelphia: Temple University Press, 1986.

Deetz, James. *In Small Things Forgotten: The Archaeology of Early American Life.* Garden City: Anchor Books, 1977.

Demott, Bobby J. *Freemasonry and American Culture.* Lanham, Md.: University Press of America, 1986.

Denisoff, R. Serge. *Great Day Coming.* Baltimore, Penguin Books, 1971.

Denning, Michael. *Mechanic Accents: Dime Novels and Working-Class Culture in America.* London: Verso Books, 1987.

Dorson, Richard, ed. *Folklore and Folklife: An Introduction.* Chicago: University of Chicago Press, 197.

Dubofsky, Melvyn and Warren Van Tine, eds. *Labor Leaders in America.* Urbana: University of Illinois Press, 1987.

Dumazedier, J. *The Sociology of Leisure.* Amsterdam: Elsevier Press, 1974.

Dumneil, Lynn. *Freemasonry and American Culture.* Princeton: Princeton University Press, 1984.

Elias, Norbert. *The Civilizing Process, Volume One: The History of Manners.* Oxford: Basil Blackwell Publishers, 1978.

———, and Eric Dunning. *Quest for Excitement: Sports and Leisure in the Civilizing Process.* Oxford: Blackwell, 1986.

Everett, John R. *Religion in Economics.* New York: King's Crown, 1946.

Foner, Eric. *Politics and Ideology in the Age of the Civil War.* New York: Oxford University Press, 1980.

Foner, Philip S. *American Labor Songs of the 19th Century.* Urbana: University of Illinois Press, 1975.

———. *American Socialism and Black Americans: From the Age of Jackson to World War II.* Westport, Conn.: Greenwood Press, 1977.

———. *History of the Labor Movement in the United States, Volume II: From the Founding of the American Federation of Labor to the Emergence of American Imperialism.* New York: International Publishers, 1955.

———. *Women and the American Labor Movement: From the First Trade Unions to the Present.* New York: Free Press, 1979.

———, ed. *The Autobiographies of the Haymarket Martyrs.* New York: Monad Press, 1969.

———, and Reinhard Schultz, eds. *The Other America: Art and the Labor Movement in the United States.* West Nyack, N.Y.: Journeyman Press, 1985.

Fones-Wolf, Kenneth. *Trade Union Gospel: Christianity and Labor in Industrial Philadelphia 1865–1915.* Philadelphia: Temple University Press, 1989.

Foucault, Michel. *Discipline and Punishment.* Hammondsworth: Penguin Books, 1977.

———. *Madness and Civilization.* London: Tavistock Press, 1967.

Franco, Barbara. *Fraternally Yours: A Decade of Collecting.* Lexington, Mass.: Museum of Our National Heritage, 1986.

Fraser, John. *America and the Patterns of Chivalry.* Cambridge: Cambridge University Press, 1982.

Gabler, Edwin. *The American Telegrapher: A Social History, 1860–1900*. New Brunswick: Rutgers University Press, 1988.

Geertz, Clifford. *The Interpretation of Cultures*. New York: Basic Books, 1973.

Gelber, Steven. "Working at Playing: The Culture of the Workplace and the Rise of Baseball." *Journal of Social History* (Summer 1983), 3–22.

Girouard, Mark. *The Return to Camelot: Chivalry and the English Gentleman*. New Haven: Yale University Press, 1981.

Gist, Noel P. "Secret Societies: A Cultural Study of Fraternalism in the United States." *University of Missouri Studies* 15 (1940).

Glassberg, David. *American Historical Pageantry: The Uses of Tradition in the Early Twentieth Century*. Chapel Hill: University of North Carolina Press, 1990.

Goodwyn, Lawrence. *The Populist Moment: A Short History of the Agrarian Revolt in America*. New York: Oxford University Press, 1978.

Gordon, David, et al. *Segmented Work, Divided Workers: The Historical Transformation of Labor in the United States*. Cambridge: Cambridge University Press, 1982.

Gorman, John. *Banner Bright: An Illustrated History of the British Trade Union Movement*. London: Allen Lane Publishers, 1973.

———. *Images of Labour*. London: Scorpion Books, 1985.

Gorn, Elliot J. *The Manly Art: Bare-Knuckle Prize Fighting in America*. Ithaca: Cornell University Press, 1986.

Graham, Marcus, ed. *An Anthology of Revolutionary Poetry*. New York: The Active Press, 1929.

Gramsci, Antonio. *Selections from Prison Notebooks*. London: Lawrence & Wishart Publishers, 1971.

Green, Archie. *Only a Miner*. Urbana: University of Illinois Press, 1972.

———. *Wobblies, Pile Butts, and Other Heroes: Laborlore Explorations*. Urbana: University of Illinois Press, 1993.

Greenberg, Brian. *Worker and Community: Response to Industrialization in a Nineteenth Century City, Albany, New York, 1850–1920*. Albany: State University of New York Press, 1985.

Greenway, John. *American Folksongs of Protest*. Philadelphia: University of Pennsylvania Press, 1953.

Grob, Gerald N. *Workers and Utopia: A Study of Ideological Conflict in the American Labor Movement, 1865–1900*. Evanston: Northwestern University Press, 1961.

Gutman, Herbert. *Power & Culture: Essays on the American Working Class*. New York, Pantheon Books, 1987.

———. *Work, Culture & Society in Industrializing America*. New York: Alfred A. Knopf, 1966.

Guttmann, Allen. *From Ritual to Record: The Nature of Modern Sports*. New York: Columbia University Press, 1985.

Halker, Clark D. *For Democracy, Workers, and God: Labor Song-Poems and Labor Protest, 1865–95*. Urbana: University of Illinois Press, 1991.

Handy, Robert T., ed. *The Social Gospel in America*. New York: Oxford University Press, 1966.

Harris, William H. *The Harder We Run: Black Workers Since the Civil War*. New York: Oxford University Press, 1982.

Harvey, Katherine. *The Best-Dressed Miners: Life and Labor in the Maryland Coal Region, 1835–1910*. Ithaca: Cornell University Press, 1969.

Herron, George D. *The Christian Society*. New York: Johnson Reprint Corporation, 1969.

Hirsch, Susan B. *Roots of the American Working Class: The Industrialization of Craft in Newark, 1800–1860*. Philadelphia: University of Pennsylvania Press, 1978.

Hobsbawm, Eric J. *Workers: Worlds of Labor*. New York: Pantheon Books, 1984.

Hoxie, Robert F. *Trade Unionism in the United States*. New York: D. Appleton, 1936.

Ingham, Alan, and Stephen Hardy. "Sport, Structuration, Subjugation, and Hegemony." *Theory, Culture, and Society* 2 (1984), 85–103.

Ives, Edward P. *Joe Scott: The Woodsman-Songwriter*. Urbana: University of Illinois Press, 1978.

———. *Larry Gorman: The Man Who Made the Songs*. Bloomington: University of Indiana Press, 1964.

———. *Lawrence Doyle: The Farmer Poet of Prince Edward Island*. Orono: University of Maine Press, 1971.

Kasson, Jonathan. *Amusing the Million: Coney Island at the Turn of the Century*. New York: Hill & Wang, 1978.

Kornbluh, Joyce, ed. *Rebel Voices: An I.W.W. Anthology*. Ann Arbor: University of Michigan Press, 1968.

Korson, George. *Coal Dust on the Fiddle*. Philadelphia: University of Pennsylvania Press, 1943.

———. *Songs and Ballads of the Anthracite Miner*. New York: Grafton Press, 1927.

Lapides, Kenneth, ed. *Marx and Engels on the Trade Unions*. New York: International Publishers, 1987.

Laurie, Bruce. *Artisans into Workers: Labor in Nineteenth-Century America*. New York: The Noonday Press, 1989.

———. *Working People of Philadelphia, 1800–1850*. Philadelphia: Temple University Press, 1980.

———, and Mark Schmitz, "Manufacture and Productivity: The Making of an Industrial Base, Philadelphia, 1850–1880." In Theodore Hershberg, ed., *Philadelphia: Work, Space, and Group Experience in the 19th Century*. Oxford: Oxford University Press, 1980.

Lears, T. Jackson. *No Place of Grace: Antimodernism and the Transformation of American Culture, 1880–1920*. New York: Pantheon Books, 1981.

Leitner, Irving. *Baseball: Diamond in the Rough*. New York: Criterion Books, 1972.

Levine, Lawrence. *Black Culture and Black Consciousness: Afro-American Folk Thought from Slavery to Freedom*. New York: Oxford University Press, 1977.

———. *The Unpredictable Past: Explorations in American Cultural History*. New York: Oxford University Press, 1993.

Levine, Peter. *A. G. Spalding and the Rise of Baseball: The Promises of American Sport*. New York: Oxford University Press, 1985.

Lowenfish, Lee and Tony Lupien. *The Imperfect Diamond*. New York: Stein & Day, 1980.

Maas, Jeremy. *Victorian Painters*. New York: Harrison House Publishers, 1978.

Marty, Martin E. *The Righteous Empire: The Protestant Experience in America*. New York: Harper Torchbooks, 1970.

May, Henry F. *Protestant Churches and Industrial America*. New York: Harper Torchbooks, 1967.

Meier, August. *Negro Thoughts in America, 1880–1915: Radical Ideologies in the Age of Booker T. Washington*. Ann Arbor: University of Michigan Press, 1963.

Montgomery, David. *The Fall of the House of Labor: The Workplace, the State, and*

American Labor Activism, 1865–1925. Cambridge: Cambridge University Press, 1989.

Mzorek, Donald J. *Sport and American Mentality 1880–1910.* Knoxville: University of Tennessee Press, 1983.

Nelson, Bruce. *Beyond the Martyrs: A Social History of Chicago's Anarchists, 1870–1920.* New Brunswick: Rutgers University Press, 1988.

Noel, Mary. *Villains Galore: The Heyday of the Popular Story Weekly.* New York: Macmillan, 1954.

Parker, Stanley. *The Future of Work and Leisure.* New York: Praeger, 1971.

Preuss, Arthur. *A Dictionary of Secret and Other Societies.* St. Louis: B. Herder, 1924.

Quimby, Ian M., ed. *Material Culture and the Study of American Life.* New York: W. W. Norton, 1978.

Ransom, Roger, and Richard Sutch. *One Kind of Freedom: The Economic Consequences of Emancipation.* Cambridge: Cambridge University Press, 1977.

Reiss, Steven. *Touching Base: Professional Baseball and American Culture in the Progressive Era.* Westport, Conn.: Greenwood Press, 1980.

Rojek, Chris. *Capitalism and Leisure Theory.* London: Tavistock, 1985.

Rosenzweig, Roy. *Eight Hours for What We Will: Workers and Leisure in an Industrial City, 1870–1920.* Cambridge: Cambridge University Press, 1983.

Ross, Stephen J. *Workers on the Edge: Work, Leisure, and Politics in Industrializing Cincinnati, 1788–1890.* New York: Columbia University Press, 1985.

Salvatore, Nick. *Eugene Debs: Citizen and Socialist.* Urbana: University of Illinois, 1982.

Schnapper, M.B. *American Labor: A Bicentennial History.* Washington: Public Affairs Press, 1975.

Schudson, Michael. *Discovering the News: A Social History of American Newspapers.* New York: Basic Books, 1978.

Seeger, Pete, and Bob Reiser. *Carry It On!: A History in Song and Picture of the Working Men and Women of America.* New York: Fireside Books, 1985.

Seretan, L. Gene. *Daniel DeLeon: The Odyssey of an American Marxist.* Cambridge: Harvard University Press, 1979.

Sorge, Frederich. *Labor Movement in the United States: A History of the American Working Class from Colonial Times to the Present.* Philip Foner and Brewster Chamberlin, eds. Westport, Conn.: Greenwood Press, 1977.

Stevens, Albert. *The Cyclopedia of Fraternities.* New York: E. B. Treat, 1907.

Thelen, David. *Paths of Resistance: Tradition and Dignity in Industrializing Missouri.* New York: Oxford University Press, 1986.

Thompson, Edward P. *The Making of the English Working Class.* New York: Vintage Books, 1966.

———. *William Morris: Romantic to Revolutionary.* New York: Pantheon Books, 1976.

Thompson, Stith. *Motif-Index of Folk Literature.* Bloomington: University of Indiana Press, 1955.

Toelken, Barre. *The Dynamics of Folklore.* Boston: Houghton-Mifflin, 1979.

Truant, Cynthia. "Solidarity and Symbolism Among Journeymen Artisans: The Case of Compagonnage." *Comparative Studies in Society and History* 21 (April 1979), 214–26.

Turner, Victor, ed. *Celebration: Studies in Festivity and Ritual.* Washington, D.C.: Smithsonian Press, 1982.

Wallace, Anthony F. C. *St. Clair: A Nineteenth Century Coal Town's Experience with a Disaster-Prone Industry*. New York: Alfred A. Knopf, 1987.

Waller, Altina. *Feud: Hatfields, McCoys, and Social Change in Appalachia, 1860–1900*. Chapel Hill: University of North Carolina Press, 1988.

Whalen, William J. *Handbook of Secret Organizations*. Milwaukee: Bruce Publishing, 1966.

Wiebe, Robert. *The Search for Order, 1877–1920*. New York: Hill & Wang, 1967.

Wilentz, Sean. *Chants Democratic: New York City and the American Working Class, 1788–1850*. New York: Oxford University Press, 1984.

Williams, Loretta J. *Black Freemasonry and Middle-Class Realities*. Columbia: University of Missouri Press, 1980.

Williams, Raymond. "Base and Superstructure in Marxist Cultural Theory." *New Left Review* (November–December 1973), 3–16.

———. *Marxism and Literature*. Oxford: Oxford University Press, 1972.

Index